The Games People Play

The Games People Play

Theology, Religion, and Sport

Robert Ellis

WIPF & STOCK · Eugene, Oregon

THE GAMES PEOPLE PLAY
Theology, Religion, and Sport

Wipf & Stock
An Imprint of Wipf and Stock Publishers
199 W. 8th Ave., Suite 3
Eugene, OR 97401

www.wipfandstock.com

ISBN 13: 978-1-60899-890-6

Manufactured in the U.S.A.

In grateful memory of Mum
who took me to my first rugby match
with thanks to Dad
who made and held me on the box upon
which I stood at my first big football match
and with loving admiration for Sue
who has learned to like sport in loving me

Contents

Contents

Introduction

A Grandstand View at the Cotswold Olimpicks

On an unusually warm Friday evening in early June, my wife and I took our places on a grassy bank in the Gloucestershire countryside. Before us was a wonderful panorama of the Vale of Evesham and in the foreground a fenced-off area surrounded by half a dozen security guards. Seated in this natural amphitheater we were among several thousand spectators gathered for sporting entertainment. Behind us on the plateau of Dover's Hill we had just bought our supper from one of the food stalls, and there were to be displays of performing pipers, dancers, martial artists, dogs with their handlers, and single-stick fighters (not all at the same time, you understand).

To the casual onlooker what we were about to witness—including team obstacle races, a five-mile run, hammer-throwing and shot-putting, and, most remarkably of all, shin-kicking—seemed part village fair, part school sports, and part It's a Knock Out.[1] But Robert Dover's games have a fine pedigree, going back four hundred years to 1612. Dover, a local Catholic gentleman, appears to have had some kind of royal blessing on his attempt to preserve and foster the traditional English games which were under threat from Puritan sensibilities in many areas of England. James I sent Dover a suit of clothes as a mark of this blessing, and Dover wore this suit (or so we believe) complete with feathered cap to open the

---

1. Those too young to recall the whacky BBC TV game show which ran from the mid-1960s could consult the website dedicated to it: http://www.its-a-knockout.TV/.

games year by year—for they were an annual event. In the 1630s many of the great poets of the day celebrated his munificence by contributing to a volume of poetry in which these Cotswold Games were associated with the ancient Olympiad, and they became known as the "Cotswold Olimpicks."

The annual celebrations came to end when James I's successor Charles I was deposed and the Commonwealth established. The Puritan parliament suppressed the games, but Charles II then reinstituted them in or shortly after 1660 following the Restoration. In the 2010 games which we witnessed the local Catholic priest played the part of Robert Dover in the opening ceremony—though, somewhat ironically, a team from the local Baptist church won the team competition of the evening. What would their Puritan forbears have made of that?

Dover's games continued until the nineteenth century when they became more chaotic and finally fell victim to opposition from landowners wanting to enclose Dover's Hill as pasture, and from clergy who became censorious about what they saw as rowdy behavior. In the twentieth century the games were revived once more and are now an annual event again. The British bid to host the Olympic Games in 2012 included a reference to Dover's Games. The London Olympic Committee wrote that "An Olympic Games held in London in 2012 will mark a unique anniversary—it will be exactly 400 years from the moment that the first stirrings of Britain's Olympic beginnings can be identified."[2]

Why might any of this be interesting to those not within easy reach of Chipping Campden, or to those without curiosity concerning Olympic trivia? This book will seek to explore the relationship between Christianity and the all-pervasive cultural phenomenon of modern sport. In so doing we will be examining theories which suggest, among other things, that sport has become a kind of surrogate religion in the twenty-first century. We will also be attempting to outline a theology of sport—that is, suggesting how sport might fit into our understanding of God's way with the world and our attempt to live godly lives in the world.

The Cotswold Olimpicks clearly have interest to sports historians (and there are many of them). But they seem also to have particular significance for those concerned with theology, religion, and sport. The games began as a theological and political gesture; James I supported them because he believed they presented opportunities for conversion

2. *Robert Dover's Cotswold Olimpicks,* "About the Games."

(of Catholics!); they were suppressed on ostensibly theological grounds by Puritans, showing attitudes which have proved pervasively influential down to the present day; in the nineteenth-century, crowd trouble was one of the factors in their discontinuance. Robert Dover's Games, we shall see, present many of the issues about theology, religion, and sport in a kind of microcosm.

The first three chapters in this book are each relatively self-contained, though the total argument requires readers to work through the whole. The history of sport, in particular in relation to Christianity, is traced in the first chapter—noting the major changes of mood and policy as the phenomenon which we know as modern sport develops over many centuries. The second chapter considers sport as a feature of contemporary society by exploring it in relation to a number of themes: business, the media, consumerism, gender, race, and politics. In chapter 3 the focus switches to a discussion of both contemporary religious belief and practice, and sporting experience, and examines the interrelation between these phenomena.

The chapters in the second half of the book, chapters 4 through 6, belong together and build in various ways on the discussions of the earlier chapters. In them we attempt to outline a theology of sport. In chapter 4 the main focus is on a biblical theology of play; in chapter 5 we consider what motivates us to be involved with sports and why winning might matter to us; we also ponder the distortions of sport which sometimes arise from a disordered desire to win. In chapter 6 the concept of transcendence is given a key role in this developing theology of sport, and questions of sin and salvation are considered. A conclusion answers one or two remaining questions while leaving others for another time. Throughout the whole we make use of the responses received in empirical research among sports players and supporters which ground the reflections in particular ways.

I owe thanks to many people for their help with this project. At Wipf & Stock, Robin Parry has been encouraging from the moment (to use an appropriate sporting metaphor) the idea was first pitched to him, and Christian Amondson and Matt Wimer have been patient supporters through the writing and editing phase. My copy-editor Trisha Dale has attempted to tame my text for publishing.

Colleagues and students at Regent's Park College, Oxford, have allowed me to present various parts of this work to them and offered helpful comments. The college's Oxford Centre for Christianity and Culture invited me to take part in a lecture series on Christianity and sport in early 2011 for which I am grateful, and the contributions of other participants in that series was a valuable spur to my own thinking. Justin Barrett (now of Fuller Theological Seminary) offered invaluable advice on the empirical work I undertook. Pamela-Sue Anderson offered advice and reading on the issues of gender as I began to explore them in the book, and Nick Wood has shared some of his own thinking on play and given some useful bibliographical suggestions. Parts of my manuscript have been read by Paul Fiddes and Anthony Clarke, and their suggestions have been incisive and helpful. None of these colleagues and friends can bear any responsibilities for the book's many shortcomings which are mine alone, but it is a better book for their wise counsel.

Readers will soon recognize the immense debt I owe to academic colleagues and others who have explored aspects of sport, or religion, or both, before me. Stuart Weir, of Verité Sport, has given particularly valuable assistance in initial orientation to the literature and in discussing various ideas and lines of argument. In the wider academic sphere I have been helped by countless colleagues, most of whom I do not know, and some of whose work I have drawn on significantly in my writing. Naming them all at this point would be lengthy and risk omissions, but my gratitude is real.

For the research I undertook with sports fans and players I would like to give special thanks to all those who responded, but perhaps also give a special word of thanks to the generous supporters of the following clubs who responded to my surveys en masse: London Irish, Cardiff Blues, and Bristol rugby union; St Helen's rugby league; Cardiff City, Reading, and Everton football. Also thanks to the players of: Gosford All Blacks Rugby Football Club, Kidlington Cricket Club, Ranelagh Harriers athletics club, and footballers from the Berks, Bucks & Oxon League. Finally, my thanks also go to all my American respondents who returned the American versions of the surveys, especially staff and students at Georgetown College, Kentucky. If only all our teams could prosper!

1

Reaching for the Heavens

A (Very) Brief History of Religion and Sport

To those whose association with sport is mainly a matter of the grandstand or the TV, or indeed the sports center or swimming pool, it may come as a surprise to discover that the study of sport has become a major growth area in universities across the Western world. The sports pages of our newspapers give ample evidence of an interest in the physiological and even psychological aspects of sports performance, but in the academy scholars have been gainfully and increasingly employed on tracing the history of sports, in studying sport as a social phenomenon, and also considering sport's relation to religion—a relationship which properly and inevitably presents itself for scrutiny in any serious study of sport. Historically, taking a rather grand view and simplifying somewhat, we can say that the relationship between religion and sport (specifically, between Christianity and sport) has been characterized by three kinds of attitude. These attitudes have tended to predominate (or are very well illustrated) in particular historical phases and it permits the narrative which follows to be arranged into three distinct parts.

In ancient times sport appears to have been seen as a vehicle for communion with the divine and for regulating humanity's relationship with God or the gods. In such a world, sport was a sacred practice that enabled humans to reach for the heavens, so to speak, and many historians argue that the roots of modern sport are to be found in religious rituals of one sort or another. While few would seriously speak of religion and sport as being coterminous today, there are some contemporary attitudes to sport that might be seen as similar to aspects of these ancient characteristics.

By contrast, another response typical of some early Christian and post-Reformation attitudes has been to see sport as a dangerous diversion, a frivolous exercise, a distraction from the serious business of living. If not sinful in itself, then it is quite likely to lead its performers and spectators towards sin and needs to be treated with caution or even hostility. This attitude has often been manifested in official pronouncements from church authorities, though various pieces of evidence suggest that the situation "on the ground" has often been more hospitable. Those who opposed games and sport did so because, far from believing that it allowed people to reach through sport for the heavens, they feared that it might lead them instead to hell.

A third response, again evident in antiquity but also in Christian responses within the last two hundred years, has seen sport as a means of character-building and moral improvement, and as such a highly appropriate activity for Christian participation. According to a typical instance of such an attitude, sport may not have any intrinsic religious substance but it may be an instrument in developing godly habits or states of mind. Alongside approval for sports generally we frequently see its instrumental usefulness—for spiritual growth, as an attention-grabbing tool in evangelism or a wholesome pastime for the disadvantaged, or indeed for more commercial purposes: sport has been useful to all kinds of people, some of them Christian ideologues and practitioners. Sport might be the ladder upon which its players might climb to godliness.

As we consider the history of sport we will see these three broad types of response manifested chronologically. To some extent all three are still characteristic of our contemporaries' more ambivalent responses to sport, and all three will offer fruitful themes for our later theological reflections.

In chapter 4 we will define sport more carefully, but a word about what is meant by "sport" will be useful for us as we begin—if only to show that in this sphere, as in so many others, complex human activity defies neat definition. We need to distinguish "sport" from both "play" and "games," though the three terms may be said to nest inside one another. This will be significant when we consider the theology of sport, because we will also need to consider play and games in that context. "Play" is generally thought to be an unstructured activity, entire to itself and for its own sake. Some scholars thus speak of play as "autotelic"[1]—it has no end or purpose beyond itself. Play is throwing a Frisbee to a friend on the beach or trying to hit a can with pebbles, or it may be a child's make-believe game. In sporting terms though, a "game" may also involve playing Frisbee on the beach but now there are makeshift rules, changing and possibly unequal teams, common agreement on what might constitute a score. But this remains very local. There may or may not be an agreed finish time, though it is quite likely that it will be set by external requirements (dinner) or just fizzle out as people leave. Frisbee becomes "sport" when the rules that govern the game are universalized and bureaucratized. They are fixed away from the location of the game, and they remain the same on repeated playing of the game. Soccer on the beach will have many of the universalized rules (goals, equal teams, fouls, and free kicks) but probably not all: touch lines, off sides, referees, standardized measured goals with posts, and so on. These types of activity perhaps cannot be entirely and definitively separated from one another, there will be transitional instances such as that soccer game on the beach, which show how they bleed into one another. Generally, full rules (and, we might say, "true *sport*") are found on the playing field and the court. And we should also note that *wherever* and *whenever* this sport has manifested itself, other things have tended to be found too: in particular, commercial interests have never been far away. Someone will sell the spectators a drink, and there is a good chance that someone else will open a book to take bets. Those who lament the lost innocent days of sport are lamenting an illusion. In fact, even when sport was primarily a religious ritual it is likely that commercial considerations intruded.

The term "sport," then, refers precisely to a relatively modern phenomenon. What we now mean by "sport" in our everyday conversation,

1. Johan Huizinga speaks of play as "pointless" and suggests that in its purest sense play serves no other purpose beyond itself. It shares this characteristic with religious ritual. See his *Homo Ludens*, 2, 19. Allen Guttmann wants to argue that the suggestion that all ancient play is essentially cultic is a *denial* of its autotelic nature. See *From Ritual*, 19. We will consider in chapter 6 whether play, and indeed sport, should be considered necessarily autotelic. Guttmann, incidentally, also helpfully proposes that sport needs to be distinguished from contests as well as play and games—thus helping us distinguish rugby from scrabble, for instance (*From Ritual*, 5–7). We return to this at the beginning of chapter 4 where I will propose that contest needs to be part of the definition of sport.

"modern sport" in its universalized and bureaucratized forms, may generally be said to be less than two hundred years old—though a case could be made in a few instances to go back further. However, as we shall see, the sport of the ancient Greeks has many features in common with "modern sports," while many of the major public spectacles of the Romans perhaps had rather fewer such common features. By the Middle Ages, most of the activities that we might consider in a history of sport are not really sports at all in the sense in which I have defined them. I use the term "sport,"[2] then, with some elasticity in my historical narrative. The ancient proto-sports have some connection with our modern activities, but were also technically different in important ways. It would be tiresome to note this at each and every juncture but the reader ought to bear the differences in mind.

Sacred Sport?

Sport appears to have its ancient origins in religion and ritual. Nowhere is this more graphically evident than in an ancient and deadly Meso-American ball game that was very important for three thousand years until the invasion of the Conquistadors and had a number of permutations. It was played on a court rather than a field, and more than fifteen hundred of these courts have been discovered. Mayan records suggest a mythology relating to the sun and the moon played out in the ball game: the game is variously described now according to the narrator as a cross between football, lacrosse, basketball, and volleyball. It appears that any part of the body except the hands could be used to hit the ball, and in some variations what we might call rackets and bats were used. In some early versions it is likely that the ball had to be played with the hip. The goal was a ring only slightly larger than a basketball hoop, placed high on a wall at right angles to the center of the court. A five-foot-high wall in front of the main wall and under the hoop meant that a direct angle of approach was not possible—the ball had to be bounced off the wall into the goal. Each team had seven players.

Sometimes the game appears to have been played for entertainment alone, often on more or less improvised courts, but the ceremonial

2. From hereon I will generally drop the use of quotation marks when referring elastically to ancient practices which we may consider do not meet our modern definitions.

version of the game was a much more serious affair. It seems that the ball may have been a symbol for the sun and the court for the galaxy; or the game may have played out a grisly mythological tale relating to the founding of the world, and the transition from death to life. In any case, the game would end when the first goal was scored in the hoop twenty feet off the ground—though it was so difficult to score a goal that the game could last for days.[3] There is some debate about what happened next. In one location on the smaller wall under the hoop are carvings of the "award ceremony." Seven players of one team face seven players of the other team. In the center, underneath each goal, are the captains. One is holding the other's severed head.[4] It has usually been thought that the winning captain executed his losing counterpart at the end of the game, but more recently it has been suggested that the winner may have been given the special prize of an immediate trip to paradise. It was the former Liverpool Football Club manager, Bill Shankly, who said, "Some people believe football is a matter of life and death. I'm very disappointed with that attitude. I can assure you it is much, much more important than that."[5]

In this Central-American ritual, sport had cosmic significance, and was used to reflect and perhaps regulate the relationship of humanity with the cosmos in the broadest sense, or its gods more particularly. Something similar can be seen much more recently in the aboriginal ball games of Native Americans. The Cherokee people engaged in a game that is often seen as the precursor to modern lacrosse, on a huge pitch with a goal at either end. When we read the accounts of these games now what strikes us are not only the similarities with modern sports (they are often more like modern rationalized sports than many traditional Western games, for instance) but the way in which the game is surrounded by religious ritual and preparation.[6] The medicine men are present throughout the build-up and playing of the game, which could be extremely violent. The game is understood to be played in the presence of, and addressed

3. For a detailed description of the game and its variants see Schele and Miller, *Blood of Kings*, chapter VI.

4. For a description of this mural see Foster, *Ancient Maya*, 197.

5. See the beginning of chapter 5 for more on the context of this remark. It can be found online in *Mirror Football*, "Wit and Wisdom."

6. ". . . the most obvious difference between 'our' sports and 'theirs' is the constant presence of medicine men and their performance of elaborate ritual acts which are, from our perspective, extraneous to the game." Guttmann, *Whole New Ball Game*, 19.

to, the Great Spirit, and players undergo ascetic preparation and engage in ritual chants and dances. The ball seems to have been thought of as sacred—perhaps representing the sun or the moon—and so cannot be touched by hand. When the men play the women dance and sing while watching. It appears that, as in Central America,[7] women had their own versions of the game but that the ceremonial version was male only. The gender divide has a long sporting history. The Cherokee game was understood to be a means of assuring fertility for the tribe, its livestock, and land, as well as manipulating the weather. This sport is the vehicle by which humankind relates to greater powers. It is not so much true to say that this sport is *related to* religion as that it *is* religion.

The same might be said of other Native American games, such as the Apache relay races in which one team represented the sun and the animals, the other the moon and the plant world, and that was run across a track called the Milky Way—the course upon which the sun and moon "raced" each day. Similarly elaborate ritual preparations accompany the race, and once more the Great Spirit is invoked.[8] Such sporting ritual may seem a very long way from contemporary sporting endeavor—though, as we shall see, there are also good reasons to compare them carefully and reflect upon that comparison. Modern sport has become, for participants and spectators, highly ritualized, and some athletes speak about their own competing in religious terms.

More familiar to most readers will be the ancient Olympic Games, often ascribed a special place in the history of Western thought and certainly narrated in the ideology of amateurism from the nineteenth century onwards. Homer tells us that the Olympic Games had been played for some centuries earlier, but they are traditionally dated to 776 BCE.[9] This coincided with a population expansion and the founding of new city states, and some uniform organization was needed in order to allow competition that was not merely based on local conventions. Similar universalizing needs drive the development of modern sport in the eighteenth and nineteenth centuries. As athletes from all over gathered in one place to compete, each bringing their own local version of the race, or the bout, some standardization was necessary. Again and again this is the reason for the codification of rules: to allow people from different

7. See Miller and Taube, *Ancient Mexico*, 43–44.
8. Guttmann, *Whole New Ball Game*, 19–21.
9. Harris, *Sport*, 15.

localities to compete with one another. It was necessary to set the parameters of a contest (most basically, what counted as a legitimate win) when prize money and betting were involved. In disconcerting ways, given the generally idyllic view of historic sport, money raises its head even on Mount Olympus, and later more modern sports such as cricket also saw the codification of rules for such motives.

The ancient Greeks staged several cycles of games, each with a similar but distinct pattern. There were games at Delphi, Corinth, and Nemea as well as Olympus, and even then the games at Olympus were held every fourth year. The origin of the Olympus cycle of games is ultimately mysterious, though the subject of many a mythological explanation. Initially the games site was undeveloped with minimal spectator facilities and largely improvised competition space. But a stadium of some sort seems eventually to have been built here and in every Greek city of significance. Typically, they were rectangular, two hundred yards by forty yards with a starting line at each end and a divider up the middle with a turning post at each end of track. In mountainous countryside they usually had to be artificially created. But commodious conditions for athletes and spectators took a long time to develop.

Olympus had become a shrine to Zeus in about 1000 BCE and the games that developed there were probably held in his honor.[10] Religious ceremonies were interwoven with the games in a pattern that became fixed around 450 BCE and that continued for many hundreds of years until their eventual demise in the disintegrating Roman Empire. The first day was one of religious ceremonies, with athletes and patrons making offerings and taking oaths. On the second day chariot-racing was followed by horse-racing in the morning, and the pentathlon was held in the afternoon. Day three had massive religious ceremonies in the morning and foot-racing events in the afternoon. On day four the combat events took place—boxing, wrestling, and the particularly violent *pankration*—a kind of no-holds-barred fighting. Then on the fifth and final day prizes were awarded, thanks offered to Zeus, and a huge celebratory banquet brought the games to a close.[11]

The crowds who watched the games brought money to spend, and the glory of winning proved transferable—from competitors to sponsors

10. For an outline of the complex religio-sporting etiology of the games at Olympus see Drees, *Olympia*, 21–32. Harris, *Sport*, 16–17, plays down the religious importance of these games.

11. Baker, *Sports*, 16–21.

and supporters. Athletes would often be seen to represent wealthy patrons (who in earliest times received the prize rather than the athlete, as modern-day racehorse owners do) or even their city states. As winning brought glory and customers, participants began to be paid for their endeavors and a class of professional sportsman emerged. According to a nostalgic view, Greek sport *decays* into professionalism, and the standards of skill and fitness drove the amateurs out of competition (exactly the reason why some rugby union officials opposed professionalism, believing, rightly, that it would take the game at the highest level away from the ordinary players who would not be able to compete with those who had leisure and resources to train). But another theory suggests that such a view merely perpetuates the amateur ideology of nineteenth- and twentieth-century ruling bodies, and that "an ancient amateur is an anachronism."[12] Indeed, the ancient prizes were already very valuable: the winner of the boys' race in Athens received a prize one scholar estimates as the equivalent of $45,000.[13] With prize money, inevitably, came corruption. Races were fixed with bribes; collusion provided draws and shared prize money. Yet spectators remained passionate.

Scholars disagree on exactly what part religion played in the classical games. Certainly Greek sport thrived at religious festivals where large numbers assembled. But was it just a matter of the games coinciding with religious festivals, or was it—as was generally believed until more recently—that the games themselves had some continuing religious purpose, were a kind of offering or expiation, something given to please the gods? It is difficult to be definitive on the question of whether the games or the religious ceremony had initial and continuing priority, and whether or when there was a change in their symbiotic relationship. Religion was so enmeshed in ancient life, in social, political, and other practices, that it may be misleading even to pose the question in this way.

There appears to be a temptation for some contemporary scholars to downplay the religious element, perhaps reflecting the lesser social significance of contemporary religion in our society. The modern Olympic movement established by Pierre de Coubertin tries to distance itself from the more overtly religious interpretations,[14] and talks instead of its *moral* vision, of helping to build "a peaceful and better world by educating

12. Golden, *Ancient Greece*, 142.

13. Golden, *Ancient Greece*, 142.

14. See IOC, "Ancient Olympic Games."

youth through sport practiced without discrimination of any kind and in the Olympic spirit, which requires mutual understanding with a spirit of friendship, solidarity and fair play."[15] It omits to tell us that de Coubertin had strong views on the role of women in sport (that they should be present only to applaud the men)—such information would be as unhelpful today as would favoring any religion. The Olympic Charter states that "Olympism is a philosophy of life, exalting and combining in a balanced whole the qualities of body, will and mind. Blending sport with culture and education, Olympism seeks to create a way of life based on the joy found in effort, the educational value of good example and respect for universal fundamental ethical principles."[16]

It has to be said that "promoting ethics" sounds rather vague: *whose* ethics? De Coubertin actually spoke of a "religion of sport,"[17] but it is clear also that he understood the religious element to be principally found in the taking of an oath to the spirit of fair play and amateurism.[18] Sport has a history, and it is a history constantly written and rewritten from the perspectives of those with an interest of one sort or another.

Whatever has become of the ancient Olympics in their more modern iterations, in the ancient examples of sport that we have scanned we have seen sport fulfilling some sort of religious function. Sport and religion are congruent. It would be foolish to object to sport in such religious practice—they belong naturally together. This sport is a vehicle for, or manipulator of, divine energy, activity or communication. We have nothing quite like this in our contemporary sporting landscape. Perhaps the discourse of American evangelical sport comes closest. An American speed skater in the 2010 Vancouver Winter Games spoke of how he was "competing for God."[19] Milan footballer Kaka has "God is faithful" stitched into the tongues of his boots, and celebrates goals by raising a pointed figure to the sky as an act of praise. Countless footballers cross themselves when entering the field of play. Such rituals might seem mere superstition to the skeptic, but it would be wrong to dismiss all such practice out of hand in this way. Can sport be an expression of faith, an

15. IOC, "Commission for Culture."

16. IOC, "Charter," 12.

17. See his 1935 essay "Philosophic Foundations," 131, in Carl-Diem-Institut, *Olympic Idea*, and quoted by Parry in "Olympism and Peace," 208.

18. De Coubertin, "Opening Address," 17, and quoted by Parry in "Olympism and Peace," 207.

19. Fairchild, "Trevor Marsicano's Faith."

offering to the gods/God? Can sport be a means by which its participants, and perhaps even its spectators, reach for the heavens? Is it right to think of sports in these ways? And if it might be, what could we understand spectators to be doing as they sit in their thousands around the great shrines of contemporary sport—is there some vicarious, transferrable process taking place that allows them too to offer something to, or receive something from, a higher force? To these and other questions we will return.

"Keeping Company with the Devil"?

As we move away from the classical period and into the Middle Ages in the West we see a change in the relation of organized sports to religion. We can probably begin to trace this change to a more ambivalent and at times much more negative attitude in the Roman Empire with its "bread and circuses." This famous phrase was penned by Juvenal in his tenth *Satire* to suggest that the mass of the Roman population had abnegated its political influence and activity and cared now only for food and entertainment. Entertainment, at least by their own standard, was what they got. Roman politicians competed with one another to outdo their rivals in games of increasing ostentation and cost for the first four hundred years of the Christian era. The stadia in which sporting events were staged in the later years of the empire were of staggering size, dwarfing Greek venues. Rome's Circus Maximus, for instance, is thought to have held between 150,000 and 250,000 people. Like the Grecian games, Roman sport appears to have originated at religious festivals.[20] But they became a means of amusing a proletariat in danger of being bored or otherwise stirred to dissatisfaction with the regime. The games were used as a safety valve and a distraction. While Greek games clearly had some kind of military flavor, the Roman games valorized full-blooded warrior combat. Life was cheap in Roman sport. Centuries later Marxist critics would suggest that sport was a tool of capitalism in suppressing the masses; others would suggest, more neutrally, that sport served the vital function of social safety valve.[21] Both of these interpretations of sport find some *prima facie* support in the Colosseum and Circus Maximus.

20. Köhne, "Bread and Circuses," 9.
21. Guttmann, *Spectators*, 147–48.

The chariot races divided supporters into partisan tribes of followers, and inscriptions have been found that show a dedication to one of the four (later two) main teams that appears to go beyond rational explanation and approximate rather eerily to modern football fanaticism.[22] Charioteers were injured and even killed in their hectic races—but it was the gladiators who epitomized Roman attitudes to sport. Gladiatorial combat originated at funeral ceremonies as a way of celebrating the noble life of the departed, and proved such a compelling spectacle that it grew into a major sporting event attended by tens of thousands, with heroes and villains, and copious amounts of blood. Unlike most sporting competitors, these men (and sometimes women) were quite literally fighting for their lives in the arena. The combats proved useful not only as a means of controlling a restive population, but also as a way of disposing of certain undesirables. Because nearly all gladiators died eventually (they had to survive three years to have a chance of being allowed to leave the arena), criminals and prisoners of war could be sentenced to the gladiators' schools in what the authorities regarded as a win/win—it was the equivalent of the death sentence in reality, but gave the illusion of hope: the combatants received training and were given weapons, thereby getting more of a chance than those who were condemned to unarmed combat against some starved wild animals kept specifically for the purpose.

As well as criminals and prisoners of war, slaves were sometimes used in these games—especially if large numbers were required, as for Claudius' mock-up sea battle (though the deaths were real enough).[23] Some of the crimes punishable by the arena seem trivial to us, but others will sound more serious. High treason, for instance, could land a defendant in a gladiatorial school, and Christians were among those who were charged with high treason when they failed to comply with the requirements of the imperial religion. It is not surprising then that Christians were in the forefront of opposition to Roman games. They were not quite alone, and some Roman intellectuals carped that the games were barbaric and inhuman. But Christians, who might be said to have had a vested interest in opposing the Roman games, were consistently vehement. Around the turn of the second century CE, Ignatius wrote of them to

22. Guttmann, *Spectators*, 28–30.

23. Nineteen thousand combatants participated in this typically extravagant Claudian event: *Guttmann*, Spectators, 20.

the church in Rome as the "cruel tortures of the devil"[24] and Clement probably has martyrdom in the arena in mind when speaking of "many indignities and tortures."[25] The most sustained attack came from Tertullian in his *On Spectacles*, written about a hundred years later around 200 CE. He has little respect for the spectators: "See the people coming to [the circus] already under strong emotion, already tumultuous, already passion-blind, already agitated about their bets. The praetor is too slow for them: their eyes are ever rolling as though along with the lots in his urn; then they hang all eager on the signal; there is the united shout of a common madness. Observe how 'out of themselves' they are by their foolish speeches."[26]

Tertullian's concerns about a crowd taking on the character of a mob, blinded to rationality, driven by gambling, echo through the centuries of Christian commentary on sport. What happens to people when they gather in large numbers to watch sport? Are they somehow enlivened and exalted by this common experience, or are they diminished and degraded by it? Tertullian saw the choice as stark—Christians should avoid the games: "How many other undoubted proofs we have had in the case of persons who, by keeping company with the devil in the shows, have fallen from the Lord! For no one can serve two masters. What fellowship has light with darkness, life with death?"[27] Far from a means of reaching for the heavens, Tertullian and others saw these games as a descent into hades.

Tertullian also judges the contestants harshly. "I suppose [the boxer] received these caestus-scars, and the thick skin of his fists, and these growths upon his ears, at his creation! God, too, gave him eyes for no other end than that they might be knocked out in fighting! I say nothing of him who, to save himself, thrusts another in the lion's way, that he may not be too little of a murderer when he puts to death that very same man on the arena."[28]

24. Ignatius, *Romans*, 5:3.

25. Clement, *First Epistle*, 6:1.

26. Tertullian, *On Spectacles*, XVI.

27. Tertullian, *On Spectacles*, XXVI.

28. Tertullian, *On Spectacles*, XXIII. A *caestus* was a glove worn in hand combat competitions such as boxing or pankration. Made from strips of leather, it often also contained metal plates or spikes giving it a rather more aggressive purpose than a modern boxing glove.

The games' origin in, and continued connection with, pagan religious rites were damning, and Tertullian saw them as an indication of the abuse of God's creation by God's creatures.[29] All in all, and not least because of the bloodshed, "these [games] are not consistent with true religion and true obedience to the true God."[30]

It must be said that, Tertullian's objections notwithstanding, Christians did not always avoid the games. In fact, away from Rome where instances of Christians being martyred in the arena were less conspicuous, they often made their compromise with them. Even after Christianity became the religion of the empire in the fourth century the games were not banned but at first only prohibited on Sundays. It is often suggested that the games at Olympus were condemned by Theodosius (emperor from 379 to 395) because of their associations with pagan cults, but there is no official record of this. They did cease after the 392 games and it is possible that he had brought them to an end.[31] However, when games did stop altogether through the empire, it is likely that the causes are to be found as much in the changing economic circumstances and general disintegration of the empire as in any genuine religious objections.

It would be wrong, however, to suggest that all the evidence of early Christian attitudes to sport is negative. There are the well-known allusions of the apostle Paul to sport in his letters. While it is true that Paul does not explicitly support sports in using the imagery of running the race, or wrestling with evil, winning the prize, and so on, there does seem to be an implicit approval in his references.[32] It is almost certain that he has in mind the "purer" Greek forms of the games rather than the Roman crowd-pleasers. Clement of Rome, while referring negatively to the games as we have seen, is also among those borrowing its language to celebrate Christian martyrs whom he refers to as "those champions who lived nearest to our time."[33] Here there can be no doubt that the more barbaric Roman games shape the imagery in question.

It will seem obvious to us that Christians should oppose a sport that involved state-sanctioned killing, and opposition to gladiatorial combat in particular seems unexceptional. But we should also note the attacks on

29. Tertullian, *On Spectacles*, III.

30. Tertullian, *On Spectacles*, I.

31. Some connect his opposition to the Olympics with his concern about the role of women in pagan cultic practice. See Gill, "Chapters."

32. See the discussion of Paul's athletic imagery in chapter 4.

33. Clement, *First Epistle*, 5:1.

the games more generally. They often focus on what is seen as an abuse of God's creation by those made in God's image,[34] and upon the dangers inherent in spectating—mob mentality, gambling, drunkenness and other vices (brothels were usually sited close to the arenas). Both of these lines of attack will resurface after the Reformation but in the meantime, as in the Roman Empire, Christians often made their peace with popular entertainment, and even (as with Paul) appear to have nodded approvingly in its direction or given mixed messages on the subject (Clement).

As the religious festivals of Greece and Rome had been hosts of sport, this was to be the pattern in Christian Europe through the Middle Ages, though our knowledge of games and sports in the period is sketchy. There was something like bowling in Germany, something like shinty and hurling in Scotland and Ireland respectively, and judging from the comments of the Bishop of Clermont, something like football in France as early as the fifth century. As Christianity spread throughout Europe during this time its missionaries were by no means encouraged to stamp out local pastimes, even when linked with older pagan practices. According to Bede, writing in the eighth century,[35] Pope Gregory wrote in 601 to Abbot Mellitus, who was about to join the mission to England, that pagan temples should not be destroyed but only the idols in them—suggesting a policy of accommodation, of recycling pagan practice as Christian. The church in France, we know, adopted some ancient ball games into its Easter celebrations.[36] But more generally the church appears to have provided the framework for the playing of games through the sequence of holy days and Sundays.

The variety of games played in the Middle Ages is striking, though few of them could properly be called sports at this time, lacking the necessary bureaucracy and uniformity. Perhaps the tournament jousting of the aristocracy and gentry comes as close as anything, though following a number of fatalities which provoked ecclesiastical opposition the game of quintain began to take over in which knights jousted against a shield mounted on a rotating arm. The wealthy hunted, with the king often

34. Tertullian, *On Spectacles*, II.

35. ". . . the temples of the idols in that nation ought not to be destroyed; but let the idols that are in them be destroyed; let holy water be made and sprinkled in the said temples, let altars be erected, and relics placed. For if those temples are well built, it is requisite that they be converted from the worship of devils to the service of the true God." Bede, *History*, Book I, chapter 30.

36. Baker, *Sports*, 45.

closely controlling the land on which hunting could take place. Games rather like hockey, football, and other ball games such as bowls; combat of various sorts (including archery); sports involving animals that could be extremely cruel to our modern eyes; and various racing games—all these and more were regular occurrences. They were also, however, very local affairs with no fixed rules, and without common patterns of play. Sport as a separate category of *thing* was unknown: contemporary accounts will, as late as the seventeenth century, speak of dancing and the theatre and games as if they are the same kinds of activities.

But games, alongside other forms of leisure, thrived on church occasions and often on church property with the church yard or cloisters often used for this purpose especially if there was no suitable common land. It is true that there seems to have been an ambivalence about the church's attitude here, though it may be going too far to say that it was merely tolerated and that the church in general had little time for it.[37] There were sporadic attempts to discourage clergy from playing dice, and wrestling, as well as hunting and hawking, but these attempts were rarely successful.

Gloucester Cathedral has a medieval carving of what appears to be football, and its fourteenth-century great east window has a depiction of an early form of golf—or is it hockey? Their inclusion in this sacred space does not suggest hostility to games, and might even be taken to suggest the blessing of some of them at least.[38] Churchyard gates served for the locals as football goals, church walls were used for ball games, and churchyard yews were plundered by archers in need of a bow. In the middle of the fourteenth century the Archbishop of York banned "wrestlings, shootings or plays," and a hundred years later a far broader list was issued, including bowling, tennis, handball, football, stoolball, and "all manner of other games."[39] Perhaps the church authorities were less enamored than the ordinary clergy on the ground, but none of the interdictions seemed really to stick, and their protestations will have a familiar ring to contemporary church councils who have tried to prevent damage to the parish hall by the youth club. The authorities in general favored archery, and anything else that might help ready a man for military service. But the ordinary people just liked to have a good time on their day off.

37. As Brailsford suggests: *British Sport,* 12, passim.
38. See Gloucester Cathedral, "The Gloucester Golfer."
39. Brailsford, *British Sport,* 14.

Early forms of football are particularly colorful, and, it must be said, violent. Often played over vast areas, with "goals" miles apart, they were mass participation events. One of these games, the Haxey Hood, was played in Lincolnshire since at least the fourteenth century, and has recently been annually reenacted.[40] A quaint story was probably superimposed upon an ancient fertility game, and historians now generally consider that its origin lies not in the chivalrous recovery of m'lady's garments, but in "the conflict over an animal or even human head, whose blood would be held to make fruitful the fields of the victors . . . or to prosper their fishing."[41] Played over a dozen acres of land, with thirteen named characters and a boozy cast of hundreds, the winning team has to get the "hood" to their pub while three other teams have similar ideas. There were few rules beyond that, and the result appears to have been pretty chaotic. Football, like all these games, was always a local phenomenon, sometimes more orderly but usually sprawling and tending towards the rough. We find some stories of how such games could be used to settle local scores, and hide nefarious intent. The record of a game at North Moreton in Oxfordshire in May 1598, for instance, describes the sort of primitive football game that would have been common all over the country during the preceding centuries. But at this game two players were killed by an opponent, and there was cause to suspect that it may not have been entirely accidental.[42]

Where the church did have clear misgivings was not so much with the games themselves as with what often came with them. Football games were inevitably rough but sometimes, as at North Moreton, worse. Sometimes the game was not so rough, but an admixture of alcohol could quickly change that. Some games could damage property, including church property. Attracting large numbers of people, crowd problems could easily follow. The notion of "spectator" is often inappropriate here—the traditional football matches, for instance, did not really have spectators, everyone played in one way or another. But the crowds who gathered tended to drink, gamble, and otherwise cavort. When women

40. Peacock, *Hood-Game*, 331–32, suggests that at the end of the nineteenth century there were concerns that the traditional game might be fading. The game, which set neighbor against neighbor with its slogan "Hoose agin hoose, toon agin toon, and if you meet a man knock him doon" (341) appears to have revived, even if in a tongue-in-cheek, and more civilized form. See YouTube video: "Haxey Hood 2012."

41. Brailsford, *British Sport*, 2.

42. See Sharp, *Bewitching*, 14–19.

took part in racing they often slit their dresses at the side so that they could run more easily, or made other brazen adjustments to their clothing. Some worried that it was not just running that was made easier by such adjustments. Games on a saint's day could become raucous and get out of hand. But it is a mixed picture, and the church liked to have it both ways, often sponsoring these events as "Church Ales" that would raise money for the parish.

While Gloucester Cathedral's artwork might suggest an acceptance of games, even a blessing of them in some quarters, it is difficult to suggest that they had any recognized or valued sacred element to them. Medieval game players were not engaged in the same sort of activity as the Mayan ball players, the athletes at Olympus, or even the Cherokee and Apache "lacrosse" players and runners. They did not appear to be reaching for the heavens in their games so much as enjoying a break from the more grinding routines of their lives. But the authorities saw that, while games were usually as socially stratified as the societies in which we find them, they could also seem somewhat anarchic—dangerous to persons, property, morality, and good order. It is with this in mind that we see some interesting and opposite developments in the fifteenth and sixteenth centuries.

The rediscovery of classical culture in the Renaissance brought a new appreciation of the aesthetics of the human body, including a positive evaluation of athletic exercise. It may be helpful to speak of a north/south divide here, with Southern Europe having a more inclusively aesthetic and Northern Europe a more strictly intellectual perspective.[43] Certainly this seems to reflect the contours of the Reformation, and others can decide on cause and effect here. In Italy in 1528 Castiglione published *The Book of the Courtier*, in which he recognized that life at court required an easy facility with both recreations and manners, as well as a certain military preparedness. In England Sir Thomas Elyot had probably read Castiglione and warmed to his theme in *The Boke Named the Governour*, first published in 1531. He was particularly interested in the education of gentlemen, and suggested that all study and no exercise would exhaust "the spirites vitall," affect digestion, and increase vulnerability to sickness.[44] There seems to be a basic, intuitive physiology in Elyot's advocacy of wrestling, swimming, fencing, riding, hunting, archery—and dancing.

43. See Baker, *Sports*, 72–74.
44. Elyot, *Governour*, 74.

He quotes Augustine in his defense of dancing, who, he argues, was not against dancing as such but only its pagan forms that could lead to fornication. Elyot thought that cards and backgammon could quicken a man's wit, whereas dicing was likely to lead to vice.

Richard Mulcaster, in a treatise on education in 1581, appears to go further than Elyot or Castiglione, and seems to have read and digested a good deal of the argument of another Italian, Girolamo Merculiale, who had published on the subject a dozen years earlier. Mulcaster was interested in the education of all social groups, and spent quite a considerable time on games. He describes the soul and body as "co-partners in good and ill, sweete and sowre, in mirth and mourning"[45] and as such should be trained together. Mulcaster tries to define the nature of health and sickness with a primitive biology based on the four elements, and argues that exercise has a role in maintaining equilibrium. Different kinds of exercise can achieve different results. He includes wrestling, walking, fencing, running, leaping, swimming, riding, hunting, shooting, and ball games in his exercise curriculum before going on to argue that football too had considerable potential. He suggests that tutors should act as referees to curb the violent tendencies often associated with the game. Perhaps through Merculiale, he seems aware of the Italian game *calcio* (still the Italian word for soccer) that was played each year in Florence and was more closely regulated than traditional football in England—with equal teams and a clearly marked pitch.[46] Mulcaster appears unique as an Elizabethan advocate of football in England.

But among these various attempts to suggest a usefulness in games we do not find much attempt at a theological vindication of them. Strangely, perhaps, the nearest we come to this is in the infamous *Book of Sports* published by James I in 1618.[47] Puritans in Lancashire had been making life difficult for their fellows who enjoyed traditional pastimes after church on Sundays and on other feast days. To the Puritans all this seemed blatant Sabbath-breaking. James' response may not be profound theology, but it claims a missiological motive. Catholics of the county will think Protestantism entirely without enjoyment if they may not even play their games on Sunday afternoons and saints' days, he argues, and so

45. Mulcaster, *Training Up of Children*, 51.

46. To watch a reenactment of *calcio* see YouTube videos, "Calcio Storico Fiorentino."

47. James I, *The Kings Majesties Declaration to His Subjects Concerning Lawfull Sports to be Used* is colloquially referred to as *The Book of Sports*.

will be less likely to convert. But a second reason sounds more sinister: ordinary people will be prevented from the exercise that they need to be ready for military service. He is also afraid that, if prevented from play, the poor especially will simply be idle and drunk—an interesting objection given Puritan concerns. After all, if they cannot play on these occasions, when can they, being otherwise always at work? The existing Sunday laws should be enforced, James insisted, and if Puritans did not like the laws of the land they could find another land. Violent recreations were still banned, as was—curiously—bowling for "the meaner sort of People."[48] But church remained the first Sunday duty, and those who did not attend were also to be denied lawful recreations. James ruled that his book was to be read from pulpits across the land, causing uproar with many clergy refusing to comply. His book became a continued source of resentment among Puritans.

The opposite movement to that in Renaissance humanistic education did, however, come from a decidedly theological source. The Puritans have become known for a sour objection to any form of pleasure, including games and sport. The reality is, as might be expected, more nuanced.

While the continental Reformers stood on the northern side of the Renaissance divide mentioned above, their attitude to games was by no means wholly negative. Martin Luther and Ulrich Zwingli both valued physical fitness: Luther commended gymnastics and wrestling among other pursuits, and Zwingli saw the military value of exercise. Calvin was more cautious: he played quoits and bowls, but took a hard line on cards, dice, and gambling generally.[49] But while Calvin inherited a seedy Geneva waiting to be cleaned up, all three operated in their pomp in contexts where they could set the tone. The English Puritans, by contrast, found themselves in a more contested situation. As early as the sixteenth century, with the English Reformation not going far or deep enough for their convictions, Puritans were beginning to have an influence on lifestyle matters that was disproportionate to their numbers.

There were two principal types of objection to games articulated by the Puritans, and we see them clearly in Phillip Stubbes' *The Anatomie of Abuses*, published in 1583. The first relates to the breaking of the Sabbath in particular, but also relates to more general calendar issues. For

48. James I, *Declaration*, 8.
49. Brailsford, *Sport and Society*, 38; Hill, *Society and Puritanism*, 170.

Stubbes and his fellows the Sabbath was a day for listening to God's Word in sermons, marveling at the Creator and his creation, and for resting. It was not a day, therefore, for feasts (including the Church Ales organized by the church itself), or playing any kind of game—or indeed for "reading of lacivious and wanton books, and an infinit number of such like practices and prophane exercises used upon that Day, whereby the Lord God is dishonoured, his Sabaoth violated, his word neglected, his Sacraments contemned and his People mervelously corrupted, and caryed away from true virtue and godlynes."[50] Some recreations showed pagan or popish aspects, and the Puritan opposition to games on the Sabbath also included all the saints' days when ordinary people refrained from work, and played. There were a considerable number of these in the year, and there may be an interesting socioeconomic aspect to Puritan opposition: Puritans tended to be urban and were more likely to be in business or commerce.[51] They defended their right (and that of their employees!) to work six days each week without interruption from saints' days—and after six days' hard work, rest was an appropriate way to spend the Sabbath. Sabbath observance was already on the statute book, Puritans wanted existing laws enforced, and as their influence grew court records show that they managed to ensure this in a patchy way across the country.

The other main objection to recreations was, again, less to the recreations themselves but more to do with the type of behavior that often accompanied them. For Christians to play cards or bowls together, without gambling, was acceptable to Stubbes—but those who won money were no better than robbers in taking money that they had not earned.[52] But despite this concession Stubbes called bowls "brothel bowls" and complained that it leads to swearing, blaspheming, and "Whordome, Thefte, Robberie, Deceipt, Fraude, Cosenage, fighting Quareling, and Sometymes Murder . . . drinking, beggerye."[53] Football attracted particular censure as one of those practices that lured men into sin. It is better described as "a freendly kinde of fight, then a play or recreation. A bloody and murthering practice, then a felowy sporte or pastime. For doth not everyone lye

---

50. Stubbes, "The Manner of Sanctifying The Sabaoth in Aligna," in *Anatomie of Abuses*.

51. See Hill, *Society and Puritanism*, 153–59, 191.

52. Stubbes, "Cards, Dice, Tables, Tennisse, Bowles, and other exercises, vsed unlawfully in Aligna," *Anatomie of Abuses*.

53. Stubbes, "Cards, Dice, Tables, Tennisse, Bowles, and other exercises, vsed unlawfully in Aligna," *Anatomie of Abuses*.

in waight for his Aadversarie, seeking to overthrowe him and picke him on his nose, though it be upon hard stones, in ditch or dale, in valley or hill, or what place soever it be, hee careth not so he haue him down."[54]

The inherent violence of football creates particular problems, and is not unconnected from the energetic opposition to sports such as cock-fighting and bear-baiting, though the Puritans seem to have been more concerned with public than with private recreation, and more with the recreation of ordinary working people than with those of the gentry: hunting, for instance, escaped lightly. One kind of behavior to which any of these recreations might lead was idleness. Time was a precious gift from God for the Puritans, and had to be invested carefully and with an eye to its productive outcome—whether for the soul or the pocket.[55]

Stubbes' polemic has one other feature worth noting. He records a number of disasters interpreted as divine judgment for Sabbath-breaking in particular. There was a considerable popular appetite for such stories, and while there may be some exaggeration in Stubbes' accounts they seem generally accurate. One such instance is the collapse of the spectator gallery at the Paris Gardens Bear Pit in London on a Sunday in January 1583. Other contemporary accounts suggest that the wooden supports were rotten, but Stubbes sees the cause of this disaster in divine vengeance.[56]

There are more moderate voices than Stubbes'[57] but the general drift is similar, and retains the ambivalence we see in Stubbes on bowls, for instance: acceptable sometimes, "brothel bowls" another time. In fact, we might make sense of much of this ambivalence by understanding the Puritans as favoring moderation in recreations, and noting that they are less intrinsically opposed to many pastimes than they are either to their occasion (Sundays, saints' days), their accompaniment (drunkenness, gambling, general moral laxity), or their consequences (vice, idleness).

---

54. Stubbes, "A fearful Iudgement of God shewed at the Theaters," *Anatomie of Abuses*.

55. George Herbert reflects this fear of idleness among the wealthier in his *The Country Parson*, the earliest pastoral theology written in English, published posthumously in 1652.

56. Stubbes, "A fearful Iudgement of God shewed at the Theaters," *Anatomie of Abuses*; see also Pearson, "Composition," 323–24.

57. For instance, Lawrence Humphrey, whose *The Nobles* cautiously advocated moderate exercise.

This note of moderation is also clear in the new American colonies. Benjamin Colman could sound balanced in speaking of "sober mirth," but his long list of unacceptable behaviors was set against a shorter one of the mirths that were acceptable; John Winthrop's journal, like Stubbes' *Anatomie* in England, interpreted disasters as judgments on the ungodly.[58] Many of the traditional pastimes of England were brought to New England but ball games at first did not prosper. There was some horse-racing, and also hunting and fishing—partly, no doubt, due to their utility value, but perhaps also because they were not sports that encouraged spectating. But even hunting on the Sabbath could lead to a whipping in 1630 Massachusetts, and the colony outlawed shuffleboard in 1647 and bowling in 1650.[59] The harsh conditions provided another reason to frown on idleness, and the Massachusetts court explicitly forbade it. It is something of a caricature, but one that seems well-founded, that by comparison with New Englanders the typical Southern colonist was more likely to engage wholeheartedly in outdoor sports. In the South a much more positive attitude developed to recreation, perhaps more akin to Restoration England, but imbued with a distinctive code of honor and masculinity.[60]

In England when the Puritan party was in the ascendancy after the Civil War, many popular recreations were effectively outlawed—though once again, the geographical effectiveness of this varied quite considerably. Robert Dover's "Olimpicks" perished, as did maypoles and other popular pastimes. Parliament passed new Acts against recreations on Sundays in 1655 and 1657, and divided England and Wales into eleven regions under army supervision to enforce the legislation. But still success was not universal, and after the restoration of the monarchy in 1660 the pendulum swung back with the authorities then promoting traditional pastimes vigorously.

At the end of the century John Locke published *Some Thoughts Concerning Education*. He began by quoting the pre-Socratic wisdom of

---

58. Daniels, *Puritans at Play*, 18–19.

59. See Guttmann, *Whole New Ball Game*, 27–28. Guttmann suggests that, in general, New England leaders took a lead from the old world's divines: and while Edward Elton wrote in 1625 of the value of exercise for refreshing the body and mind, and John Downame wrote that "honest recreation is a thing not oenly lawfull, but also profitable and necessary," his list of appropriate recreations included hunting, hawking, fishing, archery, running, wrestling, and fencing. Richard Baxter later wrote along similar lines in his *Directory*.

60. See Gorn and Goldstein, *Brief History*, 27–30.

Thales that advocated a healthy mind in a healthy body. It would be a while before *mens sana in corpore sano* would become a sports apologist's battle cry, but the world was changing. In 1660 the Royal Society was founded, and while science was in its infancy we can trace a trajectory towards technology and industrialization that gathers pace. With these innovations come dramatic changes in employment and communities, and all of these had an effect on traditional games. While the Puritan influence waned, it did not die, and we see some of their concerns surface again in widely different locations.

Puritan influence on British national policy never again reached the heights of the Cromwellian period, but it did remain a conditioning factor on attitudes to games and leisure in general on both sides of the Atlantic. In Catholic Europe a much more relaxed posture can be seen regarding leisure on Sundays; the USA inherited both the British Protestant attitude to Sundays and the more accepting continental European one. The tension was visible in the differing regulations and practices relating to Sunday baseball in the diverse leagues—a tension only uneasily resolved in the 1930s.[61] In Britain legislation caught up with actual practice more slowly. Lord Wyatt, speaking in a House of Lords debate as recently as 1987, drew attention to the way in which members of the Royal Family and government ministers had routinely broken the law by attending sporting fixtures at which the public were charged admission.[62] References are made to Sunday legislation going as far back as 1625, but the 1987 attempt to reform the law failed because of particular concerns about horse-racing and betting on Sundays. The Puritans cast a long shadow.

Concerns about the accompanying behavior at sporting events and the possible consequences of exposure to sports also continued. The

61. Gorn and Goldstein, *Brief History*, 209–10. See also Kirsch, *American Team Sports*, 230–32.

62. In the House of Commons debate of the same bill, Andrew MacKay, MP, stated: "Even my most severe critics would concede that the current legislation is arcane and outdated. The Sunday Observance Act 1780 expressly forbids sporting events for which the public are charged admission to be organised on a Sunday. Those who organise the men's finals day at Wimbledon, the final rounds of most of our major professional and amateur golf championships, the British grand prix, athletic meetings, professional football matches and professional cricket matches on Sunday are breaching the law." See Hansard, Sunday Sports Bill. House of Commons Debate. February 17, 1989. For Lord Wyatt's address see Hansard, Sunday Sports Bill. House of Lords Debate. November 5, 1987.

evangelical movement that breathed new life into an increasingly moribund and self-serving church both revived individual devotion and made new inroads into the everyday culture of ordinary people. But this movement also brought with it many of the Puritans' sensibilities. In particular, as Dominic Erdozain puts it, "seemingly hardwired into the evangelical psyche was the assumption that secular pleasure was the enemy of vital religion; that you could not have one and keep the other."[63] In reaction to forms of Christianity that seemed cerebral or formalized, Evangelicalism preached a gospel that laid claim on the whole person. This gospel provided all that was needed for personal fulfillment—it was its own enjoyment and no other sources were needed. In fact, other, competing claims on human affection were imposters to be driven out. Sport, like alcohol, and most other leisure pursuits, competed with Bible reading and prayer and these devotionals ought to have provided recreation enough. While Evangelicalism did introduce a new sense of pleasure into faith the source of that pleasure was always to be found inside the practices of the faith, not outside of them.

Conversion to Sport?

It might be said, therefore, that a Victorian morality was emerging before Victoria's reign had begun. Popular recreations were held in grave suspicion and, combined with a gradual urbanizing of the British population and the need to police an increasingly industrial workforce, some traditional pastimes were beginning to disappear. Before and apart from Evangelicalism, clergy were becoming more socially aloof from their people, less benign patrons of popular amusement and more distant gentlemen content to hunt and shoot. The ardent Methodists, however, went further—actively banning attendance at local feasts in the 1820s, and evangelical clergy were now campaigning against the old festivals, local race meets, and prize fights.[64] The social reformers, who felt that they knew what people needed—if not actually what they wanted—came up with various improving schemes, but none of them involved games: libraries and institutes, lectures and, in time, open space and public parks, but not games. Quite the contrary; a surgeon told a parliamentary committee in

---

63. Erdozain, *Problem of Pleasure*, 42.

64. See Brailsford, *British Sport*, 60–62.

1818 that children did not need leisure; and a Scottish minister claimed that a factory was the best place to discipline the youthful mind.[65]

Not that traditional sports completely disappeared, just that they were increasingly frowned upon by many in the establishment and in the church, and a wedge driven between the emerging sports and the faith. In fact, through the eighteenth and nineteenth centuries some sports began to be increasingly regulated, cricket and horse-racing most notably. Both of these sports were popular on both sides of the Atlantic.

Cricket is an interesting example because it both reflects more common trends and contradicts them. In 1611 two Sussex men were prosecuted for playing cricket when they should have been in church, but the sport is not mentioned in James' *Book of Sports*, suggesting it was not widely played. But by the end of the seventeenth century games played for significant stakes were not uncommon. In 1646 a game was played for a wager of candles, and at the end of the century for a winning prize of £75 per player, a huge sum which, if increased in line with retail prices index might be £8,000 in today's terms—and a dozen times that if increased in line with average earnings.[66] This was becoming big business, often stimulated by the entrepreneurial initiatives of inn-keepers who wanted an audience that would give them trade. Some games were billed as between representatives from counties, such as Kent and Surrey, while other more local games were played between village teams on local greens. By the early eighteenth century crowds often numbered in the thousands, and were as socially mixed as the teams. Players often included gentry and workers together, and cricket is notable for the way it has both allowed different social groups to come together and yet also found ways of separating them—by facilities for changing, by designation on scorecards, and by function.[67] The caricature of the laborer toiling over the hard work of bowling while the gentlefolk specialized in batting has lingered even until today. Some laborers were hired by the squire more for their facility on the cricket pitch than for their skills on the estate, and the squire wanted a good team because of prize money and wagers. Cricket matches could take a long time, and in 1743 the *Gentleman's Magazine* reflected a Puritan attitude in suggesting that workers

65. See Brailsford, *British Sport*, 65.

66. See Birley, *English Cricket*, 14. For conversion of historic values in pounds sterling to today's values see *Measuring Worth*.

67. See Ellis, "Play up!" 250–52.

should not be distracted from providing for their families' livelihoods by playing. They might also have been concerned at the money being wagered on some results. Such betting did, however, have an interesting side effect: in order to avoid disputes about what counted as a fair result, rules needed to be agreed that might be the same from game to game. By 1744 several such rules were in place, and some grounds (like the Artillery Ground in London) had started charging admission, perhaps as much to keep out the riff-raff and prevent unruly behavior as to generate income.

It is generally accepted that ball games were not a significant part of early American games for a variety of reasons, including the rural nature of society; a tradition of individualism; and the religious objections to such amusements. When they were played they were often seen as children's rather than adults' recreation.[68] The religious objections are not unimportant. The tide began to turn in the middle of the nineteenth century, but in America as in Britain remnants of old objections lingered. Puritans continued to give off mixed messages: accepting restrained amusements that equipped one to work more heartily, but very suspicious of idleness and implacably opposed to gambling. Many of the elite, including those in the church and other opinion formers, still frowned upon physical recreations considering them at least potentially immoral, and also socially unacceptable. Even in the 1850s some American churches brought their members under discipline for taking part in ball games, including cricket.[69] Cricket was, in fact, very popular in pre-Civil War America. Clubs blossomed around Philadelphia and New York. The first international match in cricket took place between the USA and Canada in 1844, and local games were reported in the press. But after the Civil War cricket was eclipsed by baseball. Some said that cricket was unsuited to the American temperament, taking too long and being too formal.[70] It certainly wilted in the face of an intentional and commercialized promotion of baseball by Albert G. Spalding and others. As baseball became respectable, professional, and socially mixed, cricket in North America became increasingly the preserve of the elite, who jealously guarded its amateur status and traditional trappings as a way of protecting their own superior social status in a more socially fluid society.[71]

68. Kirsch, *American Team Sports*, 3.

69. Kirsch, *American Team Sports*, 11–12.

70. This was the argument of Albert G. Spalding in *America's National Game*.

71. See Kaufman and Patterson, "Cross-National Cultural Diffusion," 97–99.

As more games, like cricket, begin to be more regulated and made more uniform—become more like modern *sports*—the previously chaotic football games also begin to be ordered. Joseph Strutt, writing at the very beginning of the nineteenth century, describes how the lower classes of London had diverted themselves with football a hundred years earlier. But by his own time football appears to be taking on a more recognizable appearance for us. He describes a game with teams of equal size playing on a pitch a hundred yards long with a marked goal at each end. They "drive" the ball, an inflated bladder cased in leather, into their opponents' goal in order to win the game. It can be still be a violent activity: "the players kick each other's shins without the least ceremony, and some of them are overthrown at the hazard of their limbs."[72]

This more regulated football then proved a useful tool in the education of young men. What happened in the English public schools[73] was part of a wider social trend, but other factors were also at work: social control, and in time a particular idea of what makes a gentleman, and, indeed, a Christian. For in the nineteenth century something remarkable happens to Christian attitudes to sport.

In the nineteenth century public schools' behavioral standards were poor, as middle-class teachers tried to constrain upper-class pupils. These pupils, left to their own devices, played the traditional games, letting off steam and breaking heads. So teachers began to suggest more regulated versions of these games, in time played on marked pitches with even teams, and so on. The boys enjoyed them, and teachers found them useful: they helped discipline, created team spirit, and channeled energy. Unruly boys now became lauded for achievement and responded well to praise. "Football" (understood very loosely) became the natural vehicle for this social molding because it was *relatively* free of associations with drinking and betting, and because it was fading in the cities due to practical difficulties with traditional formats and so had escaped censure from the new moralists.

The Victorians, or some of them, began to dissociate games from their traditional puritanical reservations, and see sport as virtuous, character-building, worthy. Sport was seen to have come to acquire positive moral qualities: embracing equal competition between equal numbers to well-known and published rules that had to be justly upheld. With

72. Strutt, *Sports and Pastimes*, 79.
73. In practice, places of private education.

the amateur ideal that provided much of the early ideology, sport had to be pursued for its own sake, without any pecuniary consideration. (Amateurism was never really about money as such: but about control and social separation.) Yet, played for itself, as a world entire to itself, part of the vision was that games, whether honestly won or lost, promoted individual strength of character and so served a national need. It is worth observing that, when the public schools were playing sports, physical education in schools for the less privileged provided only drill: what these pupils needed to learn was how to obey orders. The education system mirrored and reproduced the wider social system. While masters in public schools sought to inculcate manliness, strength, discipline, loyalty, and leadership, those in working-class settings were content to produce "troops who would be dutifully regimented and led."[74]

Public-school boys wanted to play their games after they left university and, from the middle of the nineteenth century when the new pastimes trickled down the social hierarchy, workers increasingly had Saturday afternoons free.[75] Various technological advances assisted the "sportification" process: the availability of travel, for players at first; the development of a sporting press to communicate results and speculation; the development and mass production of sports equipment.

Away from the schools the evangelical movement looked to parliament to legislate on a variety of recreational matters, including blood sports—and Sundays. Public museums and parks closed on Sundays, and Sabbatarian regulations were enforced. However, at the very moment of their greatest successes some evangelicals began to have second thoughts: could people be converted to Christ merely by being warned off vice, by a predominantly negative message about giving things up? Would the church lose its already tenuous connection with working people if it cramped their Sunday style? "Sport—a word that conjured up images of contemptible dissipation in 1830—was reinvented in the period after 1850. That it was not only accepted but grafted into a leading role in the Victorian assault on irreligion can only be described as revolutionary."[76]

74. See Brailsford, *British Sport*, 97.

75. The mill workers of Manchester were the first to win their Saturday afternoons off, in 1843 following a campaign begun by William Marsden. Over the next few decades the half-holiday became established and public parks (three in Manchester by 1847), libraries (following the Free Libraries Act of 1850 which allowed municipal authorities to support them), mechanics' institutes' lectures, choral societies, and church outings soon followed. See Hibbert, *The English*, 621–25.

76. Erdozain, *Problem of Pleasure*, 85.

The movement that became known as "Muscular Christianity" distanced itself from evangelical negativity about sports and drew on ideas from romantic writers, German and English. Like Coleridge, they came to see play as a sphere of moral growth. Like Schiller, they believed that play and the use of an aesthetically oriented imagination provided a check on reason which when left to its own devices produced the terrors of the French revolution.[77] The movement's leader was Charles Kingsley, but its most well-known manifesto now is Thomas Hughes' *Tom Brown's Schooldays*, published in 1857. Kingsley challenged what he saw as the Manichaeism of evangelical thought, and made a connection between physical and moral well-being. The term Muscular Christianity was first used by an anonymous reviewer of Kingsley's novel *Two Years Ago* in 1857.[78] It was not intended as a compliment, and Kingsley did not warm to the description. His friend Hughes was more positive and deployed the term in his sequel to *Tom Brown's Schooldays*, the 1861 novel *Tom Brown at Oxford*.[79] The key ideas are, however, present in Hughes' earlier work.

Hughes' portrait of school life at Rugby connects games with moral fiber, heroism, and manliness, and (even if tenuously) with Christian virtue. In the actual schools, games had become embedded with remarkable rapidity, and sometimes seemed to take on a higher importance than the formal curriculum. Football became very important in this process, though with different variations at each of the schools initially: in one form the ball was mostly handled, whereas in another it was mostly kicked. Soon, far from being condemned by the church as "a freendly kinde of fight . . . A bloody and murthering practice," it was promoted as character-building and virtuous.

Muscular Christianity was an extreme expression of a newfound confidence in sports, and this confidence was soon pervasive. The American narrative of Muscular Christianity takes a slightly different form, more obviously rooted in revivalism and more pragmatic rather than idealistic in its use of sport.[80] One of its key manifestations was in the Young Men's Christian Association (YMCA). Founded by the London draper, George Williams, in 1844, its international spread began after the Great

77. Erdozain, *Problem of Pleasure*, 92–94.

78. *The Saturday Review*, February 21, 1857, 176–77.

79. *Tom Brown at Oxford* was first serialized in *Macmillan's Magazine* before being published in book form.

80. See Ladd and Mathisen, *Muscular Christianity*.

Exhibition of 1851. Williams had been influenced by a leading American evangelical, Charles Grandison Finney, and exporting the YMCA to the USA could not have been a difficult process.

The YMCA began as a distraction from worldly recreations, but within ten years lecturers there were beginning to advocate the use of physical recreation as a way of providing an improving alternative to other readily available and less wholesome activities. God had given us all things to enjoy, they argued—the problem was not with sports but with their inappropriate use. Sports, properly understood, could be a weapon in the armory of the missionary. In 1864 the YMCA built its first gymnasium in Britain, and the USA would follow in the next decade. We are within reach now of positions that suggest that sport can be a way of glorifying God through celebration of the body. Luther Gulick urged the YMCA to adopt "body, mind, spirit" (recalling Deut 6:5) as the Association's motto, and his thinking was that sports promoted a wholeness of development.[81] Under Gulick's direction, YMCA sports coach James Naismith created basketball in an effort to find a wholesome all-weather outlet for the energies of young men. Modern sports have usually evolved from primitive traditional games, but basketball was created *ex nihilo* and, it is worth noting, "for the sake of the gospel."

The YMCA came to construct physical training as a religious activity, and trainers increasingly thought of themselves as essential workers for the kingdom of God.[82] Churches in all the major denominations caught the mood too, making recreation a key tool of mission strategy. Such attitudes, though clearly of their time, nudge us towards considering sport in new ways theologically. However, when we come to consider the theological issues in a more focused way we will have to examine Erdozain's suggestion[83] that something more sinister was going on here—in effect, sport supplying its own soteriology and becoming implicated in the processes of secularization. Was sport ceasing to be a means and becoming an end?

As well as its rehabilitation in religious or theological terms sport appears to be fulfilling a particular set of social or cultural needs in the later nineteenth century in the United States, and probably also in Britain,

81. Gulick is described as the YMCA's greatest philosopher by Putney in *Muscular Christianity*, 71.

82. Putney, *Muscular Christianity*, 72.

83. See Erdozain, *Problem of Pleasure*, 203–11.

such as the redefining of masculinity. Of course, it might be suggested that these social and cultural needs are some kind of unconscious driver in the religious or theological rehabilitation. Most of the developments in sport described so far took place initially at all-male schools or colleges. Just as games in the Southern colonies of America before the Revolutionary War seem associated with honor and masculinity, it would appear that nineteenth-century sport seems to be offering a new kind of articulation of what it means to "be a man." *Tom Brown's Schooldays* shows something of this, but it is no surprise that women were discouraged from engaging in sport because it was thought unfeminine. Sometimes brutal, sport could even be seen as a kind of proxy for war. As Gorn and Goldstein put it, "Athletics offered an opportunity for young men to get their first taste of glory, and for older men to renew the tingle of heroic combat."[84] At Harvard, a donor contributed money for a sports ground called "Soldiers' Field" to commemorate the dead in Civil War battles.[85] With faith under siege in the age of Darwin, it seemed to some as if all that was left was faith in a man's honor, in the willingness to sacrifice for a good cause. Sports were like war: demanding duty, sacrifice, and all-out effort. After the frontier has been tamed, fortunes made, how are men to get in touch with vigor again, find something worth striving for? For some it might be in leading industry, through government office, and for others through participating in sports.[86] In Britain the rise of sports can be easily associated with elite schools and the expansion of leisure time; in the USA a case can be made that sees the rise of sports as meshing with a certain kind of entrepreneurial and pioneering spirit connecting with religious and patriotic themes.

By the 1860s a number of sports clubs had been formed on both sides of the Atlantic. In England, many of these had been founded by former public-school boys, and some also by churches. Peter Lupson credits this in part to the number of nineteenth-century clergy who had themselves attended the elite schools, as well as to the more pervasive adoption of a Muscular Christianity ideology. Writing in 2006, Lupson showed that about one third of the teams who had by then played in the

84. Gorn and Goldstein, *Brief History*, 140. In this regard Gorn and Goldstein refer to George Fredrickson, who argued that sport was becoming a moral equivalent of war in the 1890s.

85. The NFL stadium of the Chicago Bears was renamed Soldier Field in 1925 and originally had a similarly distinctive U-shaped design like the stadium at Harvard.

86. Gorn and Goldstein, *Brief History*, 143.

Football Association's Premier League had originated in churches, and about a quarter of all the football clubs founded in Birmingham between 1876 and 1884 had similar beginnings.[87]

The eleven clubs who met in London in October 1863 to form the Football Association (FA) and to agree the first set of FA rules were making an attempt to address the need for greater uniformity. In time this led to the codification of both association football and rugby football—though in the early days clubs would often field teams to play by different sets of rules from week to week.[88] Something similar was happening in the Ivy League institutions in the second half of the nineteenth century in the USA. Harvard, Yale, Princeton, and Rutgers played variations of soccer and rugby including games against touring English teams—sometimes playing with oval balls and sometimes with round ones.[89] The Americans found cricket less pliable, and turned increasingly to baseball.[90] But even after the 1871 publication of rugby union football rules brought some order and coherence to their games in England, the American players and coaches felt further improvements were possible—from 1880 additional changes saw the game evolve into what soon looked like modern American football.[91]

Through all these developments we see a different, positive attitude to sport from within Christian communities. The attack on sport made in the early church and by the Puritans clearly identifies issues over which we might still register some concern, and many of these were also known to the classical Olympians. The suspicion that sport fritters time away, is accompanied by other undesirable activities, and inculcates bad habits, is still not difficult to sustain. But from the middle of the nineteenth century onwards we see a potent counter position. Now sport is seen as an important tool in character formation for both individual and community,

87. Lupson, *Thank God for Football!*

88. These rules curbed running with the ball in hand, but some clubs played under both FA rules and the emerging "rugby" code. Football was the first pastime to use the Saturday afternoon slot—which lucky opportunism might partly account for its world dominance today.

89. Baker, *Sports*, 127f.; Guttmann, *Sports Spectators*, 93–94.

90. Kirsch, *American Team Sports*, 28–42.

91. It may be no coincidence that Canadian football seems to have originated in Montreal and is associated with McGill University (i.e. a French rather than British city and university). The Canadians decided in 1882 to play on a larger pitch with twelve rather than eleven players per team, and the Canadian game still has these distinctives.

and as a vehicle for communicating the Christian faith. It is true that there is also a whiff of the desire for social control about some of this, and some Marxist critiques of sport often home in on this. But far from seeing sports as inherently bad (a position that even most Puritans did not occupy), they come now to be seen as at worst neutral vehicles through which social problems and personal development can be addressed, and faith nurtured; more positively, they could even be seen as divine gifts for human fulfillment or opportunities for a total dedication of mind and body to God's purposes. The "sports ministries" which are so much a feature of the contemporary sports-and-Christianity scene have their roots in the "conversion" to sport in the nineteenth century.

Conclusion

This chapter has not attempted to give a detailed and exhaustive account of the development of modern sport and the relationship of Christianity to it. Rather, the sketch offered has sometimes been impressionistic and always edited. It might be objected that what has actually been offered is not so much a history of sport as a prehistory, because (by my own definition) recognizably modern sport takes shape from the middle of the nineteenth century and this account has tailed off at precisely this point. Two justifications for this can be briefly put forward. Firstly, in the descriptions of the contemporary scene offered in the next chapter there will be an opportunity to look at aspects of the history of sport in the twentieth century that will effectively extend the narrative given here. Secondly, in terms of the church's general disposition toward sport little changes significantly after the late nineteenth century. It is true that some of the trajectories established there go in interesting directions as we shall see, but the basic qualified approval of what we might call the "Victorian religious settlement on sport" holds. The history of religion and sport up to our own time is marked by the three principal attitudes that we have observed in this narrative: one in which sport is seen as the vehicle for divine communion, a predominantly pre-Christian perspective, though one that has its parallels in the devotion often shown today to sport and in the quasi-religious way in which sporting experience is sometimes experienced by our contemporaries; another in which sports or, to be more precise, those practices which tend to come with sports, are treated with suspicion and even suppressed; and finally one in which sports are seen as opportunities for character-building, community cohesion, and evangelism, as shown in Muscular Christianity or in a multitude of twentieth-century secular initiatives, often publicly funded. These three attitudes continue to exist, often unreconciled. An adequate theology of sport will perhaps see the valuable insights (and warnings) they each offer.

From the end of the nineteenth century, and remarkably soon after the beginnings of recognizably *modern* sports, the sporting experience begins to divide into elite and (often but not yet exclusively) professional sport on the one hand, and a more popular participatory sport on the other. Perhaps in truth, something like this divide is also as ancient as most sporting precursors. Elite sport is marked by large numbers of spectators, and by an escalation of commercial support. More popular and participatory sport might sometimes have seemed innocent but becomes increasingly competitive, commodified, and mimetic, being shaped by the experience of elite sport. Any theological account of sport will also have to discuss both of these different, though connected, manifestations of the sports phenomenon. It is to the experience of sport in our contemporary world that we must now turn.

2

A Question of Sport

Sport in Contemporary Society

IN THE FIRST CHAPTER we took a chronological perspective, examining the history of sport and religion's relationship to it—especially, the ways in which the beliefs, practices, and organization of the church have interacted with that history. In this chapter we will look more carefully at our contemporary world and at the place sport has assumed in contemporary British and American society. While the previous chapter had a constant religious reference point, in this chapter the religious content might appear more obscure. However, as we shall see later, an examination of the place of sport in our social context(s) will prove an essential aid to theological reflection on sport, and as we discuss sport in contemporary society theological questions hover around the edge of the discussion continually. In the next chapter we will be pressing that analysis a stage further in asking whether contemporary sport has to some extent taken over some of the functions or meanings of religious belief and practice.

One of the truisms that will become clear as we proceed is that sport reflects the society of which it is a part, though not necessarily in an uncomplicated way.[1] The values, sometimes the conflicting values, of society manifest themselves in sports. If society is racist, or consumerist, or dominated by visual media, sports too will display these features to a

1. See Donnelly, "Sport and Social Theory," 19–22.

greater or lesser extent. What is more complicated is assessing the extent to which sports reinforce these values or, sometimes, contradict or challenge them. The relation of sport to social class and race are interesting examples of this.[2]

One of the most popular and long-running TV quiz shows in the UK is the BBC's *A Question of Sport*. It began in 1970, and has had only three different presenters and sixteen resident captains in its remarkable run. Competitive but lighthearted in tone, celebrity sportsmen and -women answer questions on their own or other sports for points and laughs. The audience at home tries to do better. The presenter gives the audience the opportunity to see a human side to the celebrities, and a recent injury or triumph is discussed in undemanding and unthreatening terms as the teams are introduced. Good clean fun. In 1970 when the show began it was recorded on a Sunday morning in a "converted" church building.[3] In the forty years none of the regular captains has been a woman, and none of them black, though the most recent presenter is a woman and the black footballer John Barnes has acted as guest captain—but no woman has had that high accolade. Here in the safe place of family light entertainment we see indications of some of the most powerful and interesting ways in which sports make their presence felt in our world: the power of broadcasting, the cult of the sporting celebrity, the invisibility of women and of women's sports, the failure of black sportsmen and -women to reach places of "responsibility," and the original venue's hint at the "sportification" of Sundays, to name but a few. It would, I think, be wrong to suggest that *A Question of Sport* is doing anything other than reflecting the way sports are, and in turn the way society is—though we could ask questions about reinforcement or subversion.

We will now examine aspects of sports and society under a series of six headings. The order adopted in discussing these issues is somewhat arbitrary, and some overlap between the areas identified may be observed. We will not specifically look at questions of sport and social class or socioeconomic group, though this relationship will come up a number of times. Finally I will make some very brief preliminary observations about sport and religion before drawing some tentative conclusions.

2. References to cricket in the previous chapter and later in this hint at the way that these relations are exemplified in interesting but far from unique ways. I briefly discuss social class in relation to cricket in Ellis, "Play Up," 250–52.

3. See BBC, "The History of the Show." Only the thirteen regular captains, and no guest captains, are listed on the official site.

Sport and Business

Sometimes an idyllic picture is offered of "sports before the fall." Played on some Elysian Fields the vision is one of purity: the sports*man*ship of participants (and the players would have been men), rich and poor from the village cheek by jowl, spectators engaged but convivial, weather warm, a tight competitive game but not taken too seriously, and no danger of the sullying presence of money. Today's fans complain that "money is ruining the game"—whether their game is football, cricket, baseball, American college sport, or almost anything else. While money may or may not threaten the true nature of our beloved sports it is certainly true that to imagine a time when money did not—at the elite level of play most obviously—have a considerable impact on them is to live wholly in the imagination: such idyllic visions are entirely illusory. Money has always threatened to ruin the game.

For the ancient Greeks at Olympus and their other great sporting venues, prize money threatened to distort (though this choice of vocabulary hides a value judgment) the event. While we might be more familiar with idealized pictures evoking the distinctive sound of cricket bat on ball on the village green, or the baseball pitcher preparing to pitch a match-winning curve ball on the sand lot, the idealizing tendency is seen in much discussion of the ancient Greek games. As indicated in the previous chapter, the ancient Greek games were themselves commercialized and professionalized. Irrespective of what some will see as the morally corrosive effect of prize money, it is certain that the games, with their many visitors, would have required local tradesmen to rise to the challenge. There is a thin line here, to be observed in much modern sport, between business interests meeting the legitimate expectations of the public, and beginning to shape those interests and even the game itself.

In Roman times these lines are even more blurred. The major games probably had a more overtly political rather than commercial *raison d'être* but the commercial exploitation was more marked. The considerable financial investment involved in the Roman games brought a political rather than monetary return. Julius Caesar provides a good example of this practice. As well as a payment from the public purse, politicians wanting to make an impression on peers and gain popular support would add private funds to create a greater spectacle. Julius Caesar's games in 46 BCE were funded by debt (providing an interesting reference point for modern professional sports clubs, and the debt-leveraged takeovers often mounted), and the lenders were also drawn into a gamble on the success of the events. The games went on for weeks and surpassed in extravagance all previous games.[4]

By the Middle Ages local sponsorship was exercised through enterprising publicans, but perhaps the most noteworthy of sporting impresarios were the clergy themselves. Often referred to as Church or Parish Ales, these were occasions when the church exploited the business potential of local recreations, including games and primitive sports, for its own pecuniary advantages. The church here is in the forefront of sports sponsorship. Whether it is the inn-keeper who makes the cricket match, or the New York newspaper editor who promotes sports on the edge of legality, business has often proved the engine that has driven sport development.

The case of Richard Kyle Fox, who emigrated from Belfast to New York and became editor of the *National Police Gazette* in the 1870s, is particularly interesting given the way that the new visual media have shaped modern sport in the last sixty years.[5] When Fox took over the *Gazette* it was failing but he led it back to profit through a diet of sport and scandal. Soon it was selling 150,000 copies each week, a trailblazer of tabloid sensationalism. When extensive background reporting on a major boxing bout in 1880 gave his circulation the liftoff he had been looking for he decided not to wait for the next event to happen but to take responsibility himself for *making* it happen. Boxing itself was to benefit from Fox's investment: his money curbed the worst of the corruption, and also saw the establishment of weight divisions. Business has not always been a malign force, even when serving its own interests.

Walter Camp led the reform of the rules of rugby that in due course morphed it into American football, but there does not seem to have been a business *motivation* for this so much as a business influence on his approach to thinking about the game. Camp, who had played and then continued to coach with great success at Yale through almost thirty years up until 1909, rose to seniority in the clock industry. As Baker puts it, "Camp's affiliation with a clock company was a fitting coincidence, for he embarked upon revisions of the rugby game largely because it seemed to him to be disorderly and unpredictable."[6] But perhaps it was not so

---

4. Köhne, "Bread and Circuses," 16–17.

5. See Gorn and Goldstein, *Brief History*, 114–22.

6. Baker, *Sports*, 129.

much of a coincidence. He often compared football's tactics to those of business[7] and his teams took on the characteristics of the new industrial workforce, with division of labor and the use of timing, measuring, and other management tools. It was in the north of England and in Wales, industrial strongholds both with working-class players, that a similar division of labor process occurred first in rugby union.[8] Camp's analogy between sport and business might represent one of the more surprising connections, but we see here another way in which sport reflects the society of which it is part.

Camp's near contemporary, Albert G. Spalding, is an appropriate example of an early sporting businessman: in his own person he united sport and business in a way not often seen until much more modern times. Spalding moved from Boston to Chicago in 1875 as part of William A. Hulbert's building of a formidable team and business enterprise at the Chicago White Stockings.[9] But as well as being a very fine pitcher, Spalding was also astute in business and, having been made playing manager and captain, he proceeded to open a sporting goods shop in Chicago to sell mainly baseball paraphernalia, and indeed founded a company to make the equipment. Selling equipment to the White Stockings helped, but he soon acquired a monopoly on supplying balls and publishing the statistical records for the newly formed National League. He made wearing a catching mitt fashionable—and sold the gloves to all who wanted one. By the time he reached his early thirties Spalding was a millionaire, and retired from playing after only three years in Chicago. The modern link between merchandising and sport can certainly be traced back to Spalding, and the story of the glove may be an example of business benignly leading sport. Of course, many sporting innovations in the nineteenth century relied upon technological developments—such as the manufacture of rubber balls—and without business exploitation of such developments many a sporting history might have been curtailed early.

Spalding played but generally took the side of management in the disputes between players and owners that marked the early history of baseball, and indeed football in England. Early restraints on players now seem draconian, with capped wages and restricted movement, though

7. See Gorn and Goldstein, *Brief History*, 158.
8. See Richards, *Hooligans*, 59, and Erdozain, "Revival as Cultural Spotlight."
9. Baker, *Sports*, 146–47.

such measures may have been necessary to allow the economic base of professional sport to be securely grounded.

Another business-related motive is evident in the late nineteenth century in England. The football codes divided into association football and rugby rather messily. Sometimes clubs would play both codes alternately, or switch from one to the other. The adoption of generally binding rules by the Football Association (FA) in 1863 and the Rugby Football Union in 1871 (though there had been earlier iterations of both) marks the clearest demarcation of the codes. But whereas association football was, with some more changes to the rules, to develop without further division, the rugby rules proved insufficient to head off two different splits. In North America, Harvard, Montreal, Yale, Princeton, and Columbia had all adopted rugby football by the mid-1870s, and formed the Intercollegiate Football Association. But, as Huw Richards says, "almost as soon the rules were adopted, the Americans started altering them."[10] Relevant factors here were the physical distance of the USA from Britain, and the felt need to allow a kind of indigenization process—the kind of process denied by the nation's cricketers, incidentally. But in the north of England the rules could not hold either.

The issue there was not a desire to change the rules as such—though rule changes did follow—but the need to compensate predominantly working-class players for missed wages ("broken time"), together with a greater appetite for organized competition. The southern power block of the Rugby Football Union considered the latter unseemly and likely to lead to abuse of the game's true spirit. They feared paying players would, over a period, lead to a professional class that would effectively mean that "gentlemen" would no longer be able to compete at the highest level. When rugby union finally became professional in 1995 they were proved right. But as with other disputes over amateurism (and most sports had them towards the end of the nineteenth century in England, at least, though American baseball allowed payment of players in 1868) what was really at stake was control by a social elite. As Dunning and Sheard describe the "monetization" of rugby in the north of England it involved:

> charging for admission, the arrangement of matches which would attract large crowds, the payment of money to players and the use of material inducements to lure them from one club to another. Proletarian values were expressed in the use of

10. Richards, *Hooligans*, 52.

Rugby as a source of material rewards, the perception of teams as representative of working-class communities, and in the stress which began to be laid on the game as a spectator sport. In short . . . Rugby in Lancashire and Yorkshire began to emerge as what we would nowadays recognize as a "professional" sport.[11]

When the split came, with northern clubs breaking away to form the Northern Rugby Union in 1895, it was traumatic in a number of ways. But the breakaway clubs discovered that in order to compete effectively with association football for spectators—for in paying players they now *needed* the admission money to remain viable—the game had to become more attractive as a spectacle.[12] A number of rule changes followed with precisely this in mind. While rugby union set its face against such "compromises" until the professional era, it too eventually came to be influenced by the need to please spectators.[13]

The need for businesses to please spectators places some elements of the relationship of business to sport in a new light—though increasingly it is television rather than stadium audiences who are being courted. It is worth bearing in mind when tempted to become sniffy about the way current business interests—notably television—shape modern sports, that the stories of Richard Kyle Fox, Albert G. Spalding, and the new game of rugby league, show in different ways that business has been a driver of sporting change for a long time.

The modern business of sports merchandise and event promotion is sophisticated and hugely profitable. One can trace a good deal of it by watching the rise of Adidas, the sporting goods manufacturer. Beginning in a Bavarian family kitchen, Adolf Dassler and his brother Rudolf made running shoes at a time when the notion of such specialization was unheard of. Adolf had begun the manufacture and Rudolf came to join him to help grow the business. In an indication of an urgent and targeted marketing policy, Adolf drove to the Berlin Olympics to persuade Jessie Owens to wear his spiked running shoes and, following Owens' four gold medals, orders for the lightweight shoes poured in from around the world. After the war, and after some bitter family feuding, the brothers went their separate ways, dividing the Dassler Brothers Shoe Company into two: Adolf founded Adidas (combining parts of his given and family

11. Dunning and Sheard, *Barbarians*, 125.
12. Dunning and Sheard, *Barbarians*, 184–86.
13. Dunning and Sheard, *Barbarians*, 200.

names) and Rudolf began his own company that soon took the name Puma. The fractious story of these companies is the story of sports merchandising in the twentieth century: from a family kitchen to a huge multibillion-dollar industry. Repeatedly design innovation makes money for the brothers (and sometimes their rivals) and also enhances sport, as with the lightweight football boot Germany wore when they won the 1954 FIFA World Cup (the English dismissed the lighter boots as a passing fad). Barbara Smit records many instances of the companies sailing close to the edge of the amateur regulations for the Olympics through their relationships with players who were wearing their products.[14]

By 1988 Adidas led a global market with sales of $1.8 billion; Reebok were in second place with $1.7 billion, and Nike—not founded until 1972—third with $1.2 billion.[15] By 2006 Adidas' sales had risen to more than €10 billion and it had swallowed up Reebok and Taylor-Made along the way.[16] It spent more than $80 million sponsoring the Beijing summer Olympics in 2008,[17] and sponsors teams in rugby, association football (including in Major League Soccer [MLS]), cricket, National Association Stock Car Racing (NASCAR), and other sports.[18] Its sports goods range is extensive, but it also sells (on the back, so to speak, of its sports interests) leisure wear, watches, and toiletries. Adidas, and companies like them, are significant in so many ways: they supply elite teams and provide sponsorship—but sports sponsorship is a form of advertising rather than a charitable activity. This investment in elite sports yields a non-elite payoff: ordinary golfers, footballers, cricketers, and so on, buy the equipment endorsed by, or similar to the equipment they see the stars use, and they wear T-shirts with the Adidas logo, or slap on Adidas aftershave, because of the associations the brand has with a particular image of athleticism. The sporting goods industry is a key player in what we might call the mimetic process of elite sport, and we will return to it shortly.

Most elite clubs now rely heavily on merchandising, and "gate" money from paying spectators is comparatively less important. *Time* magazine assessed the growing commercial significance of English Premier League football in 2007 and suggested that, across the league's

14. E.g. Smit, *Pitch Invasion*, 92–98. The rise and rise of these companies is well documented by Smit.

15. Smit, *Pitch Invasion*, 263.

16. Smit, *Pitch Invasion*, 347–75, 356.

17. *New York Times*, "Adidas bets on Beijing Olympics."

18. For example: ESPN, "Adidas to sponsor MLS through 2018."

twenty teams, match-day revenue accounted for 31 percent of revenue. The National Basketball Association (NBA) was slightly higher at 33 percent, but the National Football League (NFL) lower at 23 percent. Of the balance, Premier League teams obtained 26 percent from commercial revenue including sponsorship and merchandise and 43 percent from broadcasting—a telling indication of the importance of the game-changing (literally) Sky TV deals from 1992. The NBA figures were 44 percent and 23 percent, and the NFL's 35 percent and 42 percent respectively.[19] Detailed figures for clubs in the Premier League in 2010–11 show how the global figures mask substantial differences between individual clubs.[20]

Sponsorship deals are increasingly important for sporting teams. A Formula 1 motor-racing driver, for instance, looks rather like a walking billboard. World Champion Jenson Button displayed eight sponsors' logos on his chest alone for the 2010 British Grand Prix at Silverstone, and like other drivers cannot appear out of his car on race days without wearing the sponsor's baseball cap. His McLaren team's website lists eight major "corporate partners" as well as a host of associate partners and official suppliers, apart from Vodafone and Mercedes. The BBC estimates that more than 80 percent of a Formula 1 team's revenue is derived from sponsorship.[21] According to Isabelle Conner of ING, the attraction of Formula 1 to a sponsor is its global reach—geographically and socio-economically—and its increasing profile in the East.[22] It would be extraordinary, however, if those who had invested so heavily did not have any influence on the development of the sport in some way. The least we might expect is that the teams who are so heavily dependent on their sponsors will have their interests in mind, however obliquely.

A comparison of the value of shirt sponsorship deals in English football gives an indication of the relative marketing worth of the different

19. Smith, "The Goal Rush."

20. Conn, "Premier League finances." Arsenal's relatively high turnover (£245m) is made up of 38 percent match-day income, yet Manchester City's similar turnover (£231m) has a contribution of less than 10 percent from match-day revenue. Commercial revenue for City is more than half of its income, and across at Manchester United commercial income is about 37 percent of a substantially higher turnover. Elsewhere in the league, Everton, hardly a weak club but having had some financial challenges in the last few years, have a turnover (£85m) around one third of Arsenal's and one quarter of Manchester United's—but TV income makes up more than 60 percent of it.

21. See BBC Motorsport, "Sponsorship Guide." In the current sporting economy sponsorship income is under pressure in Formula 1: see Benson, "Formula 1 teams."

22. Formula One.Com, "Interview with Isabelle Conner."

teams. Liverpool Football Club (FC) signed a shirt deal with Standard Chartered in 2010 worth some £20m in each of the next four years, and they hoped to renew and increase it according to press reports in 2012;[23] West Ham United FC had to settle for a deal worth £2m over 18 months,[24] and in 2013 a new deal will bring in £3m each year. In short Liverpool's shirt seems to be worth about seven to ten times West Ham's. Even within elite sport, business value is sharply differentiated. Given that Liverpool's average attendance[25] in the 2009–10 season was about 42,800 and West Ham's was 33,600 it could be argued that the different value placed upon these two teams by sponsors is distorting football finance. While broadly speaking, there does seem to be a correlation between average attendance and sponsorship value (though it may be coincidental), the value to sponsors appears to increase exponentially at the top of the range. The enhanced value offered to sponsors through a club's greater visibility nationally and internationally (and crucially, through TV coverage) is a decisive factor.

There are those, including within the church, who become exercised by the large sums of money involved in sponsorship and prize money. But without launching a full-scale assault on the advertising industry, and perhaps on capitalism itself, it is difficult to be convinced for long by such scruples. In sport, it seems, as elsewhere, the market decides value.

However, perhaps an assault on advertising and capitalism ought to be contemplated? Even those readers who would be reluctant to consider a Marxist critique of sport might do well to ponder the perspective offered by it. We have noted already the general point that sport reflects society, and the more specific point about Walter Camp's clock-factory workforce and the way it is reflected in American football teams. The Marxist critic wants to push this analysis one step further. "Sport socialised individuals into work discipline, hyper-competitiveness and assertive individualism. In other words sport not only reflected capitalist society, but also helped to reproduce it, to reproduce dominant social and cultural relations in society as a whole."[26] One does not have to be a communist revolutionary to find this an appropriate consideration on sport in society. Sport may

23. Bascombe, "Liverpool Eager."
24. Upal, "West Ham Tie up."
25. See ESPN FC. "English Premier League Stats." In the 2012–13 season both teams were showing a slight increase in attendance, as can also be seen from this website.
26. Donnelly, "Sport and Social Theory," 21.

have the effect described, and recognition of this may lead us to be alert to the ways in which it might be abused or unhelpful. Jean-Marie Brohm presses the matter further still, arguing that in the great blossoming of sport internationally between 1880 and 1900: "Sport was directly linked to the interests of imperialist capital."[27] Sport functioned in this period, he says, as an ideological cover for "imperialist international organisations," and since World War II the International Olympic Committee especially has been bound inextricably with such bodies as the United Nations and UNESCO, and with "American imperialism" generally. In international sports the class struggle hides beyond the facade of "brotherhood," whereas in fact sport is a "grim analogue for the permanent state of war under imperialism."[28] The point made in Donnelly's summary of the Marxist perspective is made forcibly by Brohm who argues that the ideology of sport, propagated by the capitalist-controlled mass media, is a key element of ruling bourgeois ideology. "*Sport has the function of justifying the established order.*"[29] In totalitarian countries sport simply becomes part of the mechanism of oppression, and in capitalism sport treats the athlete's body as a machine, as if it were a factory component. Sportsmen and -women become commodities like any other, being bought and sold according to supply and demand, and sport becomes a means of regimenting and dehumanizing the mass of the population. In a manner reminiscent of the Puritans, some Marxist critics object not to sport as such but what comes with it—and its hidden ideological baggage.

To many Western readers this analysis will seem convoluted and perhaps slightly paranoid. But there is at least food for thought here. Some of the assertions must be uncontroversial—for instance, the buying and selling of sports stars as commodities will be familiar to anyone who has watched the NFL draft or heard tales of lower-league English footballers being transferred more or less against their wills to a rival club. Moreover, the very close relationships between business and sport that sponsorship and merchandising arrangements have produced make it necessary to consider the way that sport not only reflects the capitalism of wider society but may also get caught up and borne along by it. If religion used to be thought of as the opium of the people, distracting them from the grind of their oppressed existence, is it not worth pondering

27. Brohm, *Sport*, 45.
28. Brohm, *Sport*, 47.
29. Brohm, *Sport*, 178, italics his.

whether sport is doing this for many today? Could sport be the bread and circuses of modern capitalism?

This is something like the argument offered by Roman Catholic theologian Eugene Bianchi:

> More than twenty-five million Americans fostered their own dehumanization each weekend last Fall as fans of big-time football. Fixed to TV sets or huddled in the great arenas across the land, the spectators reinforced in themselves the worst values of our culture. Through these autumnal rites of passage, we avidly introduce our young into the saving knowledge of adult life: brutality, aggressive competition, profit-greed, male chauvinism, and the discipline of dull conformity to the status quo. As the frenzy of the grid-iron season reaches paroxysmal proportions with the bowl games, football affords an excellent opportunity to study the dark side of America.
>
> Collegiate and especially professional football reveal the fascist streak in our society . . . Fascism means the control and domination of others by a forceful repression of personal and communal freedom. Football in the most blatant way manifests this tyranny by brute force over the wills of others."[30]

Bianchi goes on to make his case, arguing that the values externally manifested in football, and internalized by players and spectators alike, both reflect and reinforce cultural values of which Christians and others should be wary. His critique is not far from the Marxist analysis. It may be objected that this Marxist analysis, and Bianchi's own critique, have a somewhat patronizing air, as if these writers alone can see what is truly happening, and as if they alone are able to determine what is in our best interests and what we truly want or need. We might say, to anticipate some of the discussion of consumerism to which we will come in due course, that there is insufficient allowance made here for reflexivity, for the ability in Bianchi's football fans (for example) to stand back and be aware of what is happening in some kind of critical way. Bianchi, in other words, might not be alone in seeing "what's really going on." However, we would also have to recognize that there is a thin line between such reflexivity and collusion, between obtaining a knowing critical distance and being content to be drawn into a negative process that we attempt neither to change nor to mitigate.

30. Bianchi, "Pigskin Piety," 31.

In closing a slightly different—perhaps contradictory—point about the relationship of sport and business might also be made, that, insofar as sport is itself a business, it often seems to have functioned according to different rules from those which apply in business more generally.[31] For all the complaints from fans that the club's owners or board of directors are preoccupied with the bottom line, it is also the case that owners of sports clubs have often tended to operate them in a different way from, say, clock factories and sports good firms, and their "customers" have also usually behaved differently. Sport, even for many hard-nosed owners, appears to be governed by more irrational attachments and passions. Chairmen of football clubs have been accused of using their club as a vehicle for their ego, or as a rich man's hobby, and measured logic has not always been in evidence.[32] The club's supporters, meanwhile, are not like the customers of a business—a West Ham United FC fan, or a supporter of the Boston Red Sox, is not likely to take their business elsewhere in the same way that someone buying a clock or a leisure jersey or tennis racket can seek an alternative product if they get fed up with their current one. "Brand loyalty" works in a qualitatively different way in sports. Whereas the clock manufacturer can make more clocks when public demand for the product increases, sporting clubs are more circumscribed in the way their demand can be met—though in some leagues the arguments for a *reduction* in fixtures in order to improve quality of play and/or player recovery time are beaten off by more or less thinly veiled financial concerns.[33]

Ironically, at just the time when elite clubs came to see themselves as brands, and began offering a range of merchandise and credit cards, mobile-phone deals and TV stations; just at the moment when advertising becomes more prominent and sophisticated inside stadia; as many of the stadia are named after commercial backers (Reebok, Emirates, Sun Life, etc.); still "it is almost impossible, by legal means, to make a football club profitable."[34]

31. This may be changing now that more football clubs, for instance, are publicly listed or leveraged with international debt—Manchester United fans apparently say sometimes that the Glazer family takeover of the club in 2005 was intended to take money out of the club rather than pour money in, the more traditional expectation of club owners. See for instance James, "Glazers Brothers' Latest Move."

32. See Kuper and Szymanski, 59–89 and 90–112.

33. See the discussion in Robinson, "The Business of Sport," 174–75.

34. Goldblatt, *Ball is Round,* 685. Goldblatt also observes here that "it has become

The relationship of sports to business is complex, mutual, ancient, and by no means entirely reprehensible. Indeed, some genuinely good advances in the development of sports have been driven by business backers, or shaped by a business imagination. The church has tended to be wary of what can be seen as a corrupting influence in general and of the very large sums in particular, but the picture is more complicated than easy slogans suggest.

Sport and the Media

While business interests have expressed themselves through sport since the earliest days, there can be little doubt that modern sport's indebtedness to business is fueled by broadcasting and the media in general. Once again, however, we find that "it is as well to remember . . . that the role of the media in sport is only novel in its intensity."[35]

The emerging modern sports had generated the beginnings of a sporting press[36] by the end of the eighteenth century in England, and the still thriving *Sporting Life* appeared in 1821. Early in the nineteenth century regular newspapers began to offer an occasional page devoted to sport, as did the the *London Morning Herald* from 1817; London's *The Times* did so from 1829. It was some time before newspapers offered regular sports coverage—one of the first to do so was in Germany in 1886, the *Muenchener Neuesten Nachrichten*. In America sports periodicals at first closely followed English publications, often reprinting chunks of copy from across the Atlantic. *American Farmer* reported horse racing in 1819, and the *Spirit of the Times* (1831) and the *New York Clipper* (1853) followed. Subscribers were in tens of thousands. In France *Le Sport* began in 1854 and in Austria, *Allgemeine Sportzeitung* in 1880. When the market possibilities for daily sports papers were understood sports journalism went up a gear: *Le Velo* was among the first daily sports papers to appear in 1891, and within fifty years Spain would have two dedicated daily sports publications and Italy would have four; Japan, in thrall to baseball, had five. The print media fulfilled a social as well as a sporting function. In days when spectator behavior was not always exem-

---

apparent that football flouts many of the core assumptions of rational choice theory and neo-liberal economics."

35. Brailsford, *British Sport*, 131.

36. See the discussion in Guttmann, *Spectators*, 85–86.

plary, the press helped spectators understand what sort of behavior was expected of them. They also helped them to be more discerning spectators. In addition they stoked the fires of interest—creating in time the "fan" phenomenon. Newspaper proprietors have understandably sought to maximize circulation as well as provide a public service. In some local newspaper coverage there is also the phenomenon that Kirsch calls "urban boosterism"[37]—the use of sports to enhance the profile of local communities.

In July 1921 a boxing match was radio broadcast from Jersey City by WJZ, quickly followed by coverage of a team sport, the baseball game between the Pittsburgh Pirates and the Philadelphia Phillies in August 1921.[38] Two months later the same KDKA station was back at the same venue for a college football game. WWJ in Detroit had begun reporting results—boxing title fights, and baseball's World Series—even earlier.[39] In Britain the BBC offered radio commentary in 1927 on both the Oxford/Cambridge University Boat Race and the FA Cup Final[40] and so ushered in a new era. For the Cup Final there was a numbered grid in the *Radio Times* to help listeners follow the ball around the pitch as the commentators referred to the action in "such and such a square." But there was considerable caution from the English football establishment who feared a detrimental effect on gates: the commentaries were discontinued in 1931, except for the FA Cup Final that has been broadcast every year since 1930. Hockey Night in Canada began radio coverage in 1931, and was popular in the northern USA when CBS relayed the show.

Radio offers a special kind of intimacy for its audience, and for the modern listener a portability not matched by television—though streaming to mobile phones is beginning to change that. But as television has more and more usurped its preeminence radio has, in the USA at least, tended to concentrate on the local rather than the national. Even in the UK local radio provides a service in covering local teams and events that national networks cannot hope to emulate, though national coverage of cricket, football, tennis, golf, and other sports is still significant on radio.

The Berlin Olympics, controversial in so many ways, were the first televised sporting event—though broadcasting was restricted to

37. Kirsch, *American Team Sports*, 202–6.
38. Guttmann, *Spectators*, 132.
39. See Covil, "Radio."
40. Goldblatt, *Ball is Round*, 185–86.

twenty-seven "TV locales" in the city.[41] The BBC began to experiment with television coverage soon after those games, and broadcast the Oxford/Cambridge Boat Race in 1938.[42] A little later in the same year US broadcasters entered the field with a baseball game between Columbia and Princeton. Boxing followed soon after. Screens were small, pictures not always crystal clear, and early coverage was certainly influenced by the available technology. Baseball, for instance, played on a large field with a small ball which did not always follow the players, was not ideal. Boxing, with two men in close proximity, was more televisually appealing.

In 1954, glad of the free publicity they thought would follow, FIFA gave away the rights to broadcast the 1954 World Cup in Germany. In 2010 the television rights for the FIFA World Cup in South Africa were worth $1.9 billion.[43] A similar story is found with the Olympics. Avery Brundage, President of the International Olympic Committee (IOC) from 1952 to 1972, apparently doubted that the TV networks would pay anything for the broadcast rights. There were experiments in 1956 at the Winter Games, and in Rome in 1960 the Italian National Olympic Committee sold the rights. In 1964 NBC paid $600k for the Tokyo Games. Twenty years later ABC was charging almost as much for a one-minute advertising slot during the Games.[44] The broadcasting rights for the 2008 Games raised $1.73 billion for the IOC,[45] and NBC paid $2 billion for the US rights alone for the 2010 Winter and 2012 Summer Games.[46] There are similar stories to be told about rights for domestic competitions, with the Sky TV deal for the English Premier League in 1992 (and subsequent renewals) commonly thought of as the game-changer in Europe.[47]

But to concentrate on the remarkable increase in the values of TV rights masks a shifting symbiotic relationship. With television as with radio, initially sports administrators saw TV as a threat to ticket money—why would people pay to see a game if they could watch for free at home? In the US baseball attendances were in a postwar decline mirrored by British football gates, and anything that might further dent

41. Guttmann, *Spectators*, 134.

42. Jacob, "First University Boat Race Radio."

43. Saadi, "World Cup TV." US broadcasters paid a combined $425 million for US rights.

44. Guttmann, *Spectators*, 136.

45. Santo and Mildner, "Political Economy and the Olympic Games."

46. See *Sports Business News*, "The 2008 Beijing Summer Olympics."

47. See Horne et al., *Understanding Sport*, 51.

them was considered unhelpful. In American football there was a similar trend: the LA Rams' home attendances plummeted when home games were broadcast in 1950; the following year only away games were broadcast and attendances rose again.[48] But American football, baseball, and basketball were transformed by large injections of TV cash that led to a liftoff in salaries. Soon networks had to group together to bid. A similar specialization to that seen in print media developed, with sports-only channels setting up in Europe and the USA. Britain came relatively late to the big bucks party, but BSkyB's exclusive deal with the new FA Premier League in 1992 proved mutually enriching. The subscription package the broadcaster sold to viewers facilitated huge growth in customers allowing them to begin to dominate the pay-TV market. The income the Premier League received financed a massive growth in wages, and soon the league was being spoken of as the best in Europe as high salaries attracted the world's best players. Stadia were improved and, despite the increasing cost of tickets, attendances rose: Manchester United, to take the most impressive example, fill their 75,000 capacity stadium regularly. The exclusivity of the Sky deal was broken by EU competition law in 2007, but for the three years up to 2010 BSKyB paid the lion's share of the £1.78 billion deal for three years' rights to the FA Premier League.

The massive investment in time and money that broadcasters bring to sport inevitably comes at a price. It also changes the way we see and participate in sport. The scheduling of games in the twenty-first century is a fine example of this. In England, virtually all weekend football games kicked off at 3.00 p.m. on a Saturday before 1992. Since the injection of cable and satellite cash many games now do not start at this time. Initially this might have been to protect the gate receipts of clubs playing in the traditional time slot, but more and more it is to suit the TV network's perception of their audience's convenience, the most saleable advertising times, and to get as many matches on air as possible. The Rugby Union European Six Nations competition now has its kickoff times varied so that every game can be shown live; rugby contests between southern-hemisphere sides are sometimes arranged for the convenience of the lucrative northern-hemisphere audiences. Events in the Olympics and FIFA World Cup are arranged for the convenience of European or North American viewers. Television's effect on scheduling (day and time) is considerable.

48. Guttmann, *Spectators*, 137.

But television has also affected the way we see the game in another way. Cricket provides a particularly good example. In the nineteenth century in England it was the press who pushed the cricketing authorities towards an official championship for the counties and regular international matches between countries. Following the introduction of Sunday games on BBC in the 1960s, and Kerry Packer's intervention into international cricket in the 1970s, television has given cricket new competitions, new costumes, and floodlit matches. But at any game, the TV cameras are positioned behind the bowler so as to give the viewer a superb view of the delivery and shot. No one attending a cricket match live is ever likely to have been able to have this view before—the batsmen would have complained about a distraction in their line of vision—but TV has delivered the impossible. Slow-motion action replays, reverse angles, overhead "spider-cameras," mean that viewers on their sofas can get a much better view of the action in certain respects than spectators in the stadium, better even than the match officials. This in turn has led a number of sports to introduce various TV/computer-based technologies to resolve tennis line calls, cricket leg-before-wicket decisions, rugby touchdowns, and also allows disciplinary action to be taken against players after the game has finished. All this makes for an absorbing viewing experience at home, but it can also in some circumstances lead to a sense of missing out for those in the stadium. These changes tend to underline the shift in interest from the fan in the stands to the fan in the armchair. The televising of elite sport in high quality (and high definition) with lots of special effects and expert commentary has also put pressure on support for professional sport below the elite level.

Television, much more than print media, has also fueled a process of mimesis. I am using this word rather more loosely than it is sometimes used in philosophical or cultural discussions, to mean the process whereby individuals or groups mimic, imitate or reproduce the behavior and values of others. David Stead makes a similar point when he says that the media "acts as a key socialisation agent and is integral to framing, determining and influencing our picture of reality. Our experience of sport has become increasingly constructed and ordered through television output."[49] One need only take a turn around a school playground to see how this mimetic process is at work from television sport. I once heard one of my sons, about ten years old at the time and playing football alone

49. Stead, "Sport and the Media," 185.

in our driveway, "commentate" aloud saying, "Let's see that goal again from the reverse angle." And we did. Television affects the way we experience sport—the competitive and technological values we see represented on the screen are internalized by viewers so that the behavior (good and, regrettably, bad) of professional sports stars is reproduced domestically. The competitive father who urges on his son from the touchline, with colorful language and abuse of the referee, is migrating values from elsewhere into a sphere where they are clearly inappropriate. Without realizing it, he is mimicking elite sports. We need the best equipment, to look the part, before we can play our littler games. Some of this, I grant, may be a knowing mimesis: it may come with an ironic realization that we are pretending to be professional in our winner-takes-all attitude, or our designer gear. But while some mimesis may be knowing, we seem oblivious to it at other points.

However, the reality of this mimesis ought at least to generate a hermeneutic of suspicion. When the media present their versions of sport—and they do present their versions, for every presentation must inevitably involve editing and value-calls—with what "spin" do they do so? Whose interests are represented in the way they cover routine and major fixtures—those of the clubs? The players? Their agents? Or their own owners? Stead again: the media also "transmit the values and support the political and economic objectives of their owners and controllers . . . the challenge is to examine the degree to which . . . the media audience is exposed not to a neutral and objective presentation of reality, but rather to a packaged representation and construction imbued with ideological content and reflective of the practical and professional interests of the production staff involved."[50]

One of the consequences of media coverage is certainly the magnification of sports stars. To be sure, there were stars before TV. Babe Ruth, Stanley Matthews, and others, made their names without the help of the television cameras. But the modern cult of the celebrity has certainly featured in the TV presentation of sports.

One area where celebrity culture impinges on other things is through marketing and sponsorship. Television places star players in the spotlight, gives them air time "earned" by their talent. It therefore also stimulates the merchandising endorsements that make sport so lucrative for top players, agents, and the heirs of Adolf Dassler. In 2005,

50. Stead, "Sport and the Media," 192.

David Beckham, English celebrity footballer and "soccer trailblazer" in the USA, earned more than €25 million—two-thirds of this was from off-the-pitch earnings (perhaps including his endorsement of the Adidas predator boot). Babe Ruth made a fortune from endorsements before the TV;[51] Stanley Matthews had the first endorsement deal for boots in English football in 1950;[52] but they were unusual in their day, and next to what they might have earned with the help of NBC, ESPN or BSkyB, their incomes pale. While the situation is more complicated when networks are publicly funded, as with the BBC for instance, we also have to recognize that commercial networks are parts of large multinational conglomerates with diverse interests. The Marxist critic may have a point, for it is certainly true that modern sport is inextricably linked with capitalism at the elite level, and when one considers why a player endorses their boots, drivers, rackets or energy drinks, we realize that participation in sport is tied up with it too.

There is a considerable overlap between the issues covered in the first two sections of this chapter, because the media are, after all, business. Again we see how sport's relationship to the media is one of mutuality: sport has shaped, sometimes created, media platforms, and has in turn been shaped by them. The increasing economic importance of the armchair fan at the expense of the stadium fan has galling consequences for the latter who finds start times rearranged and their interests sidelined. But the media have also provided important scrutiny of sport and helped expose corrupt practices—the recent cricket betting scandals come to mind. They have also raised standards through support of such technology as "hawkeye" in tennis. At the same time, the creation of sport-only TV channels has brought the possibility of saturation coverage of sports in ways that would have seemed impossible a generation ago. In ways more insidious than print media, these channels offer the theoretical opportunity to watch sport all day every day. The Puritan concerns about the use of time and about unhealthy habits might come to mind. A more general remark about Christian concerns in this sphere might note the way in which the ever-greater availability of sport, borne by many media pathways, seems to be another factor putting pressure on religious observance of one kind or another. Media coverage of sport, especially TV though we have not even mentioned the internet, may figure in

51. Gorn and Goldstein, *Brief History*, 191–92.
52. Smit, *Pitch Invasion*, 52.

the displacement hypothesis we are examining: that sport is displacing religion in contemporary Western culture. The media, and its business engines, are also converting players and spectators into sporting consumers, and to this we now turn.

Sport and Consumerism

The phenomenon of consumerism is not simply the obtaining and accumulation of goods and services. Rather, it should also be considered to be a meaning-making activity. As we have seen, sports spectators and players have bought and sold goods and services around their play since time immemorial, but the modern (or perhaps, postmodern) significance of this is relatively new. Spalding's use of his Chicago club base for the sale of merchandise, such as the previously unfashionable glove, may have been the first presentiment of consumerism in sport. Since Spalding's time "sport has become more and more of a product that is manufactured, bought and sold."[53]

At the turn of the twentieth century Thorstein Veblen wrote about the way in which, within all human societies, objects are consumed in order to express identity and status.[54] Beyond mere subsistence, objects have always had a cultural value. At the meal table ostentatious or high quality food was a way in which individuals and groups both nourished their bodies and reinforced their view of themselves. The "conspicuous consumption" (the phrase was coined by Veblen) of expensive items which are *perforce* exclusive makes a statement about social status and self-understanding. Veblen thus not only described the excesses of a social group but also highlighted "the social significance of their consumption, which provided a way to establish class identity amid the fluid social boundaries of the United States. In the intervening century, conspicuous consumption has spread to the masses"[55] and across the Western world.

So, for example, from earliest times clothes did not simply keep one warm but could also be decorative: a clasp fastened on a cloak against the wind became also a piece of decorative jewelry and so laden with other significance. It was almost inevitable in a world increasingly plural and

53. Stead, "Sport and the Media," 189.

54. Veblen's *Theory of the Leisure Class* was first published in 1899. See the discussion in Lynch, *Popular Culture*, 60–64.

55. Miller, *Consuming Religion*, 9.

in which old social hierarchies were challenged that a hierarchy of commodities would develop that taken together indicated a person's social status and self-image. Such hierarchies of commodities function in our day, though they are context-dependent, with the same objects giving off different messages according to setting: the height of cool here is the nadir of naff there. Clothing offers many examples of this social signaling.

In the late nineteenth century a general increase in prosperity was allied with developments in image-based advertising.[56] Shoppers were encouraged to buy products not (just) for their utility value but also because of the lifestyles and identities they suggested. These purchases suggested a symbolic value beyond mere use. Text-based advertising had generally relied upon worthy claims about how a product might be better than its competitors, or might solve a particular problem for the shopper, that is, in terms of what it *did*. Now, image-based advertising began to suggest that shoppers might aspire to correspond to the images that represented the product. Television was to play an important role in this during the twentieth century, and linked to this is the phenomenon of the modern brand. In the late twentieth century this interest in and awareness of brand increased. Big brands were built up earlier, but brand awareness associated with image has become more and more important. A brand has associations: Adidas, Apple, Audi, Amex, and indeed Alpha—all these brands convey certain messages and images, and people like (or not) to be associated with them. The capacity of consumers to reclassify products and adapt them for their own consuming purposes adds some complexity to this process. *Bricolage* is the term sometimes used to describe the way that social groups consume a range of products, altering the "meaning" of them as they do so. The consumption of some items of luxury clothing and cars illustrates this process, and *bricoleurs* can also have political and/or theological motivations for their practices such that *bricolage* has been suggested as a Christian mode of consuming.[57] "People accomplish socially and politically significant things through consumption. Perhaps they accomplish religious tasks as well."[58]

Increasingly shopping has become a leisure activity that performs a wide range of cultural functions. Certainly there is an element of simple

---

56. The move from word to image and its implications for the media and popular culture is memorably analyzed in Postman, *Amusing.*

57. See Miller, *Consuming Religion,* esp. 146–63 and Bretherton, *Politics,* 190–92.

58. Miller, *Consuming Religion,* 8.

"reproduction" here, as we shop to maintain our domestic or working lives so that we have clothes to wear and food to eat. The extent of this utilitarian function of shopping is difficult to determine, and many who would feel tainted by the consumerist label will protest (unsuccessfully, I think) that most or even all of their shopping falls into this category. But shopping, or "consumption" as we should start to call it, is also an important way in which people in the prosperous West express, experiment with, and reinforce ideas of what kind of people we are and with which social groups we identify—in other words, who we are. The French theorist, Jean Baudrillard, put it like this: "consumption is a system of meaning like a language . . . Marketing, purchasing, sales, the acquisition of differentiated commodities and objects/signs—all of these presently constitute our language, a code with which our entire society communicates and speaks of itself and to itself."[59]

An example of this is a study of 1980s British working-class men buying themselves cashmere Armani sweaters: they are not just keeping warm but also making statements that redefine their identity.[60] Commenting on the study Angela McRobbie says that their working-class masculinity is "undergoing a transition, a renegotiation and perhaps even a feminization."[61]

The acquisition of goods is nothing new, and neither is the investing of these goods with certain social indicators. What appears to make the phenomenon of consumerism is a combination of the mass availability of goods produced for the mass market, allied to an aspirational context for advertising and the media, and the sense that—with the breakdown of older sources of identity—individuals are constructing their own identities through the things that they choose to consume. Some theorists go so far as to suggest that in consuming such commodities we no longer attend to practical value at all, but only consume for meanings that may be conveyed: "such matters as branding, packaging, fashion, and even the act of shopping itself are now the central meaning-making acts in our postmodern world."[62]

We may need to make allowance for the "knowingness" with which many of our contemporaries engage in this consumption: "When we

59. Baudrillard, *Consumer Society*, 79.

60. Mort, "Politics of Consumption," 160–73.

61. McRobbie, *Postmodernism*, 33.

62. Twitchell, *Lead Us into Temptation*, 14, quoted by Lynch, *Understanding*, 62.

look at adverts or commercial products, we're conscious of the fact that we're being manipulated and sold something. In fact, part of the pleasure of being a consumer is the very fact that we're conscious and self-aware as we consume. We're knowing. This reflexivity is part of the consumer package, and it's used by advertisers and by the media in general. They know that we know, and they pander to our knowingness."[63] *Bricolage* can be one practice in which this reflexivity is expressed, but we should be aware that what we sometimes regard as reflexivity may be a thinly disguised form of collusion with the practices of consumption fostered by contemporary capitalism. As Baumann puts it: "the way present-day society shapes up its members is dictated first and foremost by the need to play the role of consumer, and the norm our society holds up to its members is that of the ability and willingness to play it."[64]

Every aspect of human life in the West seems to have been to a greater or lesser extent made available for consumption as a commodity, and consumption of these various goods and services seems an important, perhaps the important, way in which twenty-first-century Westerners express, construct or know who they are. Sport and recreation have not escaped this process, and sports clubs and competitions became big brands in the late twentieth century. As sports have been commodified, "the sports organisations have gone along with this and, increasingly, have used agents and marketing companies to get their particular products into the media sports marketplace."[65] The commodification of leisure and sport needs to be seen in this perspective along with all manner of unexpected commodities offered up for consumption. Consumption is not just a matter of coats and cars, or sofas and suits. Experiences of all kinds are commodified, packaged, and sold for our consumption. Sport and leisure through gym membership, football season tickets, and package holidays; heritage, through the "Oxford Experience," Smithsonian membership, and a stately home tour; education through courses of life-long learning; religion through Alpha courses, and the consumer mentality manifests itself in our "shopping around" for churches.

We have already thought about television and sport, and I hinted then about the relationship between celebrity status, endorsements, sponsorship, and consumption. Television's effect here works on a

63. Ward, "Colonising the Adult Church."

64. Bauman, *Work*, 24.

65. Stead, "Sport and the Media," 189.

number of levels. The advertisement that shows us top sports stars using shaving products or sports shoes suggests that while we cannot play like Tiger Woods we might be able to shave like him. In doing it we somehow identify with him. The same applies when we see him wearing branded polo shirts on the fairway. The Ford car advertisement that "bookends" Sky Sports' Premier League football coverage in the UK reinforces ideas of "blokishness" and associates the quality of the cars with the quality of "the best league in the world."

But television is not the only driver of this trend. Jennifer Smith Maguire notes how the fitness magazines which multiply on the news-stands subtly promote consumption of goods from lip balm to health clubs to sporting goods. To buy a magazine (even if not actually to *attend* a gym regularly) is to make a statement to oneself and others about one's identity. Maguire suggests that in advocating the purchase of a variety of fitness equipment even the American Heart Association is tacitly acknowledging the rule of consumption.[66]

To think of sport as consumerism is to recognize that we and our contemporaries construct our identities, in part, through consuming (or not) sport—through attendance at elite sport events, through participating in sport whether as "serious amateur" or "weekend dabbler," and so on. Christians have tended to denigrate consumption, with a kind of closet Manichaeism. Material goods have often been assumed to be bad. There will be alarm in some quarters at the suggestion that identity is constructed in this way, but it is nevertheless clear that the identities of many individuals and communities are bound up with sports.

One cause for alarm, quite apart from the making of identities through consumption as such, certainly presents itself. The price in dollars, pounds or euros of consuming sport can be considerable. A seat at an NFL or Premier League game, a replica jersey, a gym membership, one of the latest designer pieces of equipment—these cost serious money. We see that the creation of identity in contemporary society relies upon having the resources to be consumers. Those who cannot consume are nobodies. As James Twitchell puts it: "Knowing this, we can appreciate how poverty can be so crippling in the modern western world. For the penalty of intractable, transgenerational destitution is not just the absence of things; it is also the absence of meaning, the exclusion from participating in the essential socializing events of modern life."[67] Those

66. Maguire, "Body Lessons," 455.
67. Twitchell, *Lead Us into Temptation*, 31, quoted by Lynch, *Understanding*, 67.

who cannot afford to consume may find other strategies including fake brands, charity shops, and crime.

The challenges presented to the lives of religious communities and to theological thinking represented by the phenomenon of consumerism are too numerous to enumerate and examine here. While the church and its leaders have tended to express a kind of knee-jerk negativity about "things" and "possessions," such a simple response is almost certainly *too* simple.[68] If consuming is indeed a central meaning-making activity then calls to turn away from it are unlikely to be successful. Furthermore, the church has itself both succumbed to, and employed some of, the vehicles of consumerism itself. Increased mobility for congregations through the twentieth century has allowed worshippers to travel to a church that "suits" them and most congregations are less local than they were. This is consumer activity, choosing according to preference but also according to brand and image. In evangelical churches especially the familiar consumerist requirement for the new is evident in the way in which new worship resources are consumed and also in the technologies used to display and consume them. Like shopping, churchgoing is increasingly a leisure or spare-time activity. Some individuals and communities will of course claim to construct identity amid consumerism by resistance (to global capitalism, or materialism, or some particularly despised form of religion) rather than through conformity. But Taizé, Hillsongs, Alpha, and even Fairtrade, fit the definition of brand in this debate rather well. Perhaps the critical point is that of reflexivity, and the question of collusion raised earlier. Are we knowing, or do we just like to think that we are, when really we perpetuate and reinforce the values represented in consumerism? Sport reflects society, and there may be nothing more sinister regarding consumerism in sport than in other spheres, though it would certainly be worth developing a reflexivity about its pervasive influence which ponders what this is doing to us and our sporting passions, as well as an awareness of how consumerist pressures exclude and marginalize others.

68. For discussions of consumerism which avoid the knee-jerk negativity (and lack of self-awareness) so often prevalent in treatments of the subject from a Christian point of view see Miller, *Consuming Religion*; Bretherton, *Politics*, 175–209; and Percy, *Engaging*, 41–62.

Sport and Gender

In considering the question of sport and gender two issues require our consideration: women in sport (or the lack of them), and gender identities in sport. Our discussions of these related matters will overlap.

Among the archaeological record of the ancient Mayans only at one site is there any indication that women played the ancient ball game.[69] That is not to say that in the more informal playing of the game they were entirely absent, only that we have no record of women playing. In Greece the situation was more complicated. Women do seem to have competed in ancient games, notably those in honor of Hera where there was a foot race for young maidens in three age categories. When women did have their own competitions the course tended to be shortened (by one-sixth at Olympus). Women came to compete in equestrian events at some meetings against men, though this was unusual and potentially destabilizing: a women's victory here might be seen to upset the "natural order."[70] As for watching, married women were banned except for the priestess of Demeter, on pain of death. This was usually justified by the athletes' nakedness—though maidens were allowed to watch. Roman sport presents a similarly varied picture, though rather more bloody.

Traditional pastimes were often more mixed, with men and women taking part, insofar as we can tell: again the historical record is not focused on participation by gender. We know of instances where women played football (though this is very rare),[71] stoolball (an early form of baseball), and various other games, including the odd pedestrian race,[72] but again the record suggests that it was predominantly men at play. Dancing, with its slightly risky reputation, was certainly mixed sex, and it is as well to recall again that games were not always distinguished clearly from other recreations like dancing. John Stow and John Strype, writing in the early seventeenth and eighteenth centuries respectively, seem to refer—when gender is mentioned at all—to boys or young men; at the beginning of the nineteenth century Joseph Strutt refers to embroidery and needlework as women's pastimes though he does go on to say that

---

69. Miller and Taube, *Ancient Mexico*, 43.
70. Golden, *Ancient Greece*, 132–40.
71. Horne et al., *Understanding Sport*, 36–39.
72. Guttmann, *Spectators*, 62–64.

they sometimes enjoyed pastimes of a more "masculine nature" such as sports of the field.[73]

The nineteenth-century "renewal" of games, the growth of what we can truly call modern sport, is less neutral, however. The major developments occur in, or around, elite male schools and colleges. The other striking feature of these developments is that the games concerned are often violent. (Cricket might be thought by those relatively unfamiliar with it to be a gentle game, but those who play will know otherwise!) Out-of-control boys were being tamed through regulated if rough play. Further, that regulated roughness was being inculcated as virtue. In the USA in particular there was some real progress in women's colleges towards the end of the nineteenth century, with baseball, bowling, running, swimming, tennis, and other sports making an appearance.[74] But this was always somewhat problematic. The Victorians associated femininity with daintiness and gentility, and there were concerns that women's reproductive organs could be damaged by exercise even as their general musculature increased: in sharp contrast with an ancient Greek race that had all the marks of a kind of prenuptial beauty contest some Victorians feared a woman's marriage could be jeopardized by athletics.[75]

The extent to which the advocates of muscular Christianity were concerned to promote a newly acceptable model for Christian men can perhaps be gauged by the title of Thomas Hughes' later book on Jesus as a model for Christian virtue called *The Manliness of Christ*. The author of *Tom Brown's Schooldays* proposed an idea of what it meant "to be a man" that would resonate with his age. Hughes thought that "manliness" incorporated courage but also tenderness, determination, loyalty, and devotion to duty.[76] As Erdozain points out, by the 1870s in English elite schools "manliness" and "virtue" are becoming synonymous.[77] Much the same is true of their American equivalents, and furthermore, this manliness is the product in no small part of participation in sport. Given these associations it is hardly surprising that women's participation is going to be thought problematic. In the industrial Victorian era the roles of men and women are being redefined on both sides of the Atlantic. There is

73. Strutt, *Sports and Pastimes*, xlix.
74. Gorn and Goldstein, *Brief History*, 132.
75. See Golden, *Ancient Greece*, 129.
76. Hughes, *Manliness of Christ*.
77. Erdozain, *Problem of Pleasure*, 109.

an assumption (seen in *Tom Brown's Schooldays*) "that serious piety is a woman's work, confined to the bedroom and the nursery."[78] So women now stayed at home in the "private" sphere, earning nothing, but as wives and mothers becoming the moral and spiritual center for family life, raising spiritually tuned families, and with their tender feelings having a moral effect on their men that might make them open to God; men meanwhile inhabited the "public" sphere, and there they earned their wages and played their games, going out into the world and then returning to domestic bliss.[79] This manliness meant responsibility, self-control, steady habits. In the USA this move may have underlined and consolidated the older association of sports with masculinity in the southern states.

The development of the Olympic movement is revealing here, arising as it does, at least in part, from this same Victorian elite educational ethos. De Coubertin, the "reinventor" of the Olympic Games, infamously said that a woman's role was in offering applause for the accomplishment of male athletes. It is true that the participation rate of women in the Olympics has been rising steadily with just a few setbacks: less than 1 percent in 1904, 9 percent in 1932, just over 14 percent in 1972, and just under 29 percent in 1992. In 2012, according to the IOC's own statistics, 44.2 percent of the competitors were women.[80]

As well as the imbalance of overall numbers, the differing range of events open to women and men may also be seen as problematic. Not until 1928 were women allowed to compete in track and field events, after de Coubertin's retirement from the IOC. After several runners collapsed at the end of the 800 meters it seemed that their participation was once more in doubt, but after protests from male competitors women were back in 1932 but with participation in longer races shelved until 1960. Once more the concerns were vocalized as "biological." While the 2012 London Games saw women run the marathon and match men in most events, they did not race in a 50 kilometer walk; similarly they did not race in the pool over 1500 meters, though they did swim the "marathon" 10 kilometer in the same way as the men. Before the 10 kilometer swim was introduced Mark Golden could reflect thus:

78. Erdozain, *Problem of Pleasure*, 103.

79. Gorn and Goldstein, *Brief History*, 63–64.

80. IOC, "Factsheet: Women in the Olympic Movement—Update March 2013." The figures for the Winter Games are lower, rising to about 40 percent in 2010. These participation numbers also conceal the paucity of women in administrative and decision-making positions which still runs at less than 20 percent.

. . . neither women nor men swim very long distances—distances at which women, with their greater resources of body fat and ability to metabolize it, would likely excel. This has every appearance of a discourse of male supremacy, informed by the allocation of the virtue of endurance or toughness to men. Women are excluded on the grounds of their perceived weakness, and then admitted to contests at which they (predictably) do less well than men; neither sex competes in those events in which women's physiology provides a natural advantage.[81]

Certainly, the Victorians, with some exceptions, could not see beyond what they perceived to be biological differences though social reasons were also sometimes invoked for opposition to women's participation in sport. During a roller-skating craze of the 1870s and 1880s in the USA, men were considered to be at risk of wasting their money and their time; but women could be seduced by skating teachers, or run off with other skaters, and broken homes would follow. One writer in 1878 traces the decline of otherwise upstanding women through the playing of croquet. Absence from church and immoral conduct are the precursors to seduction, "a runaway match," poverty, disgrace, and ruin. Women's weakness was not just a matter of physical strength or stamina; they seemed peculiarly vulnerable to moral lapses even if they were often pictured as the tempted innocent rather than the beguiling Eve.[82] Perhaps the unacknowledged fear lurking behind such stories, and the general resistance to women in sport, was that of women somehow shrugging off male control.

Since the start of the twentieth century there has been some progress for women in sport, though often it has been in the face of male opposition. One can speculate as to the reasons for the opposition, the kind that meant that the English FA withdrew its previous support for women's football in 1921, or that the Title IX provisions of 1972 that were intended to ensure equal treatment for women in college athletic programs in the USA were progressively countered and worked around. The defense of vested interest and preference for the status quo goes some way towards explaining things, but only some way. In the twentieth century the traditional patterns of gender identity came under threat from various quarters, notably two world wars, changing patterns of work and family life associated with them, and more recently the feminist movement

81. Golden, *Ancient Greece*, 131–32.
82. Gorn and Goldstein, *Brief History*, 102.

more generally. We might surmise that male identity was less clear in 2000 than it might have appeared in 1900, and that the domain of sports was one in which more traditional and clear-cut notions of masculinity could still be nourished and reinforced. As Martin Polley has observed, stereotypical post-match cultures in rugby, and to a lesser extent football, with their obscene singing, ritual drinking, and the like, often celebrate a certain kind of masculinity, while seeming to deride or demean women. Football hooliganism, for so long a scourge of late-twentieth-century western Europe, has been linked to an aggressive masculinity often with tribal overtones, with young men using ritualized violence while "supporting" their football teams as a way of asserting their male identities. Alongside all of this is an uncomfortable relationship between sport and homoeroticism. The crude rugby songs that seem to express strong hostility towards homosexuality are taken by some as evidence of suppression, and of gender uncertainty.[83]

Quite apart from any opposition from men (and countless examples could be cited here) the participation of women in sport in postwar Britain and America has had another serious hurdle to surmount. For if sport is associated with masculinity, even if it were a subtle and vestigial association, this clearly does not encourage women to participate. As Horne, Tomlinson and Whannel put it, "women's identity, generally understood, does not easily include sweat, muscle, communal facilities, etc. The 'ideal' male body is muscled; the ideal female body is not."[84] As we construct our identity through consumption, so also our identities may be constructed, reinforced or challenged by participation in and consumption of sports. Playing a sport, watching a sport on TV or in a stadium, can be a way of saying who we are or want to be. It seems that most of the messages about the meaning of "sporting identities" are masculine ones, or have tended to reinforce particular social constructs of masculinity and femininity. Typically, women sports stars have been praised for elegance and beauty while men are praised for aggression and courage, and the ability to endure physical pain is idealized.[85]

The areas where the most conspicuous advances have been made are arguably in sports that most easily conform to these traditional stereotypes, including aerobics and jogging.[86] Interestingly, both have

83. Polley, *Moving the Goalposts*, 108–9.
84. Horne et al., *Understanding Sport*, 115.
85. Polley, *Moving the Goalposts*, 107.
86. Polley, *Moving the Goalposts*, 91–92.

been promoted commercially, neither are inevitably competitive and aerobics also includes elements that might appeal to "glamour" interests. Elsewhere progress has been chequered with some notable exceptions, especially at elite level. But what all discussions of such progress are in danger of masking is the issue that can remain hidden in a discourse that is dominated by male voices and perspectives: that sociocultural difference might be passed off as biological difference. "The *physical* body holds *social* meaning. It is not a natural thing, purely physical, but a part of culture. Physical sex differences become cultural—they are used, modified, reinforced and accentuated as part of cultural beliefs about the real and the ideal attributes of men and women. Culture projects certain images and influences ideas about gender difference."[87] Given the subliminal associations of sport with a sweaty kind of masculinity, for adolescent girls the choice often appears to be *between* femininity and sports. Choosing sports can be like choosing anti-girl. Sports are often tied up with and complementary to an emerging male sexuality. "Many teenage girls simply do not associate sports activity with the femininity to which they aspire."[88] In this world, women who are competitive and strong at sports can be branded "butch" or "unfeminine." Coakley is not alone in suggesting that new definitions of masculinity (that do not stress domination and violence, or use military metaphors, for example) and femininity (that allow for competition, striving, and visible strength) are needed for and in sport.[89]

Feminist theorist Iris Marion Young argued that women are culturally conditioned to experience their own bodies in ways that express and reinforce patriarchy. Working from an analysis of the way young girls, and then grown women, throw a ball, run, use a bat or racket, and even carry parcels, Young suggests that the tendency to be more restricted in movement (in throwing, for example, the whole body is not truly engaged in the act, but just the throwing arm itself: "they do not reach back, twist,

87. Horne et al., *Understanding Sport*, 137. Italics mine.

88. Kay, "Sport and Gender," 94.

89. Coakley, *Sports in Society*, 8th ed., 275–76. As an example, in an unpublished undergraduate dissertation in 2012, "Gendered Identities: How does Participation in Sport affect the Construction and Performance of Gendered Identifies among Young Girls," Oxford student Ellen Geddes suggests that adolescent girls construct an alternative femininity in sailing which is marked by skill and performance rather than appearance.

move backward, step and lean forward"[90]) expresses other sociocultural restrictions. Women, she argues, are more likely to experience their bodies as "other," and less likely to express themselves physically freely. "For many women as they move in sport, a space surrounds us in imagination that we are not free to move beyond; the space available to our movement is a constricted space."[91] This constriction is the physical expression of the "timidity, uncertainty, and hesitancy"[92] that has cultural roots in patriarchal relationships. We will return to these ideas, and to a more recent feminist critique of them, later.

The male discourse on sport expresses itself in the way provision is shaped and sport presented. A tiny percentage of media coverage of sport (typically less than 5 percent) focuses on women's sports. What coverage there is is sometimes patronizing (praising the ability of a female star to win a medal *and* be a mother) or titillating (as in major sports magazines in the northern and southern hemispheres). Female athletes are often trivialized and sexualized, either treated negatively because they do *not* fit male perceptions of femininity or glamorized because they *do*.[93] The nature of media coverage of women's sport, and particularly its absence from prime-time television, is not likely to make the possibility of choosing sport for teenage girls any less complex. Of course, the media is largely owned and controlled by men. Female sports presenters and commentators are now beginning to appear, but they do not yet even match the numbers of women watching professional male sport (itself an interesting phenomenon). Matters are not helped when the president of FIFA suggests that the appeal of women's football to the public would be enhanced if the players wore tighter shorts.[94] When we progress to consider the management and coaching of sports we often find elite women's teams coached by men thus perpetuating a lack of appropriate role models, and perhaps indicating a glass ceiling. Coakley's statistics for US collegiate sports show a worrying and significant *decline* in the proportion of women coaching women's teams in all National Collegiate Athletic Association (NCAA) sports between 1977 and 2002.[95]

90. Young, "Throwing," 32. The essay was first written in 1977.
91. Young, "Throwing," 33.
92. Young, "Throwing," 34.
93. Stead, "Sport and the Media," 194.
94. Christenson and Kelso, "Soccer Chief's Plan."
95. Coakley, *Sports in Society*, 8th ed., 254.

Until recently the public space of sports provision has been geared towards men's interests, and problems of access remain for women who tend to be less independently mobile and often with child care and other responsibilities. Women may feel vulnerable to harassment or attack in dark or relatively isolated sporting locations. Communal changing facilities can also be a deterrent. Participation rates for women in sport are unsurprisingly lower than for men. In the UK by 1986, 37 percent of females and 57 percent of males participated in indoor or outdoor sports, with considerable socioeconomic group variations.[96] These figures increased slightly to a plateau in the early 2000s with the differential between male and female participation appearing to narrow a little. By 2007 the numbers were dropping, with the differential between men and women widening a little once more: 58 percent and 43 percent respectively. Participation also drops off by age and social class, a reminder that gender is not a factor that can be treated in isolation.[97] As Jay Coakley remarks, ". . . sport participation among girls and women will not continue to increase automatically. Just as the participation of men has been nurtured and developed through support and popular images of men in sports, so must it be for women. Without continued support and encouragement, without powerful new images, some of the progress of the past could be jeopardized."[98]

If sport is considered a "good"—something that has intrinsic value, in forming character or in expressing creativity, or in some other way yet to be defined—social structures and stereotypes that act as a restraint on the participation of women have to be viewed with dismay. Some feminist critics would urge us to go one step further, arguing that the ways in which we think about and engage in sporting activity are in every way deeply ingrained with male assumptions; that is, not just assumptions about masculinity, but assumptions made by the men who have predominantly regulated, played, written about, reported upon, watched, and promoted games and sport since the Mayans played their ancient

96. Horne et al., *Understanding Sport*, 66.

97. See the 2009 edition of the UK Government's *Social Trends 39*, 192ff. The patterns in the data are backed up by a number of "Western" sources, though it is often difficult to compare like with like, e.g. Scottish Government, "Scotland's People Annual Report: Results from 2011 Scottish Household Survey," with previous years' statistics available for comparison; and Australian Bureau of Statistics, "Participation in Sport and Physical Recreation, Australia, 2011–12."

98. Coakley, *Sports in Society*, 8th ed., 250.

ball game. The discourse of sport, in other words, is patriarchal.[99] For example, one of the reasons often given to explain why women's elite sports events can be less well attended than men's elite sports events is that sport tends to be about hitting the hardest, running the fastest, throwing the furthest, lifting the heaviest, and so on; the "best" women tend to do each of these things a little less hard, fast, far, and heavy than the "best" men. But who stops to ask why this is the way it is? Why is the fastest, furthest, etc. deemed to be most important? What does it signify? How is it "implicated in the reproduction of the social relations of gender or male power and privilege in society"?[100] The American sociologist Jay Coakley remarked that "Many people continue to compare women and men in terms of performance *differences* and then go on to say that differences will never disappear because men are simply physically superior to women." He goes on, "Of course, most of these people never wonder what kinds of physical skills would be needed by athletes if sports had been shaped by the values and experiences of women instead of men. It is certain that if sports had been created by and for women, the Olympic Games motto would not be *Citius, Altius, Fortius* (faster, higher, stronger); instead it might be 'balance, flexibility, and ultraendurance'!"[101] For feminist critics "sport is . . . a cultural representation of social relations. It is not . . . neutral, objective and ahistorical. Rather, it is . . . a set of selected and selective social practices that embody dominant meanings, values and practices which are implicated in the creation and maintenance of hegemonic social relations."[102]

"Sport reflects society" we mused innocently at the beginning of this chapter. Considering gender and sport requires us to see how, in doing this, it also reflects all the ingrained patterns of prejudice and ideologies present in society. Any attempt to grapple theologically with sport must take into account the serious issues of gender we have discussed here.

Sport and Ethnicity

Since the 1968 Olympic Games, when American sprinters Tommie Smith and John Carlos gave the Black Power salute from the medal rostrum,

99. Dewar, "Incorporation of Resistance?"
100. Dewar, "Sexual Oppression in Sport," 158.
101. Coakley, *Sports in Society*, 5th ed., 226.
102. Dewar, "Incorporation of Resistance?", 20.

there has been an increase in both the public awareness of race and sport and the academic study thereof. Social scientists, with good reason, now prefer to speak of "ethnicity" rather than "race": the latter suggests but defies precision, and is increasingly seen (akin to gender) as a social construction rather than a simple biological given. Ethnicity, on the other hand, denotes shared cultural heritage factors as much or even instead of any suggested common genetic components.

Framed in this way, sport has displayed elements of ethnic conflict through its history. The Mayan ball game, sometimes played ritualistically, would often humiliate captured troops or kings from other tribes; the Greeks and Romans had a very strong sense of the "barbarian" other. If the theme seems largely absent from so much of the story of traditional pastimes in Europe it is surely because these societies were *relatively* ethnically homogenous for so long. The experience of non-white sportsmen in Britain between the twentieth-century world wars suggests that racism was not prominent in their experience in this period because "there was only a handful of colored here, anyway."[103] Whether or not this apparently widely held perception of the situation is accurate, things certainly began to change in Britain after 1945 with a rise in immigration from the commonwealth and particularly from the Caribbean.[104]

The situation in the USA is rather different. There were not a significant number of ethnic minorities in England when its elite schools were at the cutting edge of the new sports boom, or when Muscular Christianity was born. But in the USA there had been a significant black population since the first slaves were introduced in the seventeenth century, or earlier. The social status of slaves, and even of the small minority of black people who were free of slavery, did not make them natural leaders in leisure.[105] In the south, as was noted in the previous chapter, a white leisured class developed where sport became important as a signifier of social status and of masculinity. We have no reason to suppose that black members of the community did not participate in this culture in a way appropriate to their social status, but the culture was formed by its white

103. Larry Gains, a Canadian-born black boxer, quoted in Cashmore, *Black Sportsmen*, 25.

104. For a brief reflection on a related topic, cricket and imperialism, see Ellis, "Play Up!," 253–54 which considers C. L. R. James' formative cricket experience in Trinidad.

105. "Sports were a prerogative of patriarchy, but not all patriarchs were equal." Gorn and Goldstein, *Brief History*, 23.

hierarchy. After the Civil War, as might be expected, a more integrated society slowly develops, but the past and the way it shapes attitudes and identities, is difficult to cast off.

Sport reflects society, and we should expect to find in it the same ethnic tensions as we see elsewhere. A brief examination of aspects of the national games of America and England will show us this. In particular they both show us structural racism, the more contingent racism of players and spectators, a phenomenon known as "stacking," and what I am calling "problems of afterlife."

We have evidence that plantation slaves played something like baseball,[106] but given the evolution of baseball into the game we know it would be easy to be anachronistic here. After the Civil War black players began appearing in teams alongside white players as well as forming their own teams as "the New York game" took off. It certainly seems that the black teams played the white teams, and there is little to suggest any segregation in baseball until in 1867 in Philadelphia an African–American club was denied admission to the local association. Later in the same year the color bar became national when the National Association of Base Ball Players received a report at its convention recommending that clubs "composed of persons of color" should be refused admission to the association.[107] In professional baseball the bar did not become complete until the 1890s, and in the meantime baseball was as popular among black members of the community as among white with black players often playing in major or minor league teams with whites in the north and Midwest. However, when the bar was complete other strategies were needed and the so called Negro Leagues (with the "Lone Star Colored Baseball League of Texas" in 1897 among the first) became very important. African–Americans who were excluded from competition with their white counterparts were thereby banned from a meritocratic public space in which they might have appeared as equals—or even as superiors: at such moments we glimpse the potentially subversive nature of sporting meritocracy.

The segregation of baseball in the USA lasted until after World War II though African–American teams touring in Canada and Central America had had a foretaste of another possible social order. The men who ushered in a new era were Jackie Robinson and Branch Rickey.

106. Seymour, *Baseball*, 560.
107. Gorn and Goldstein, *Brief History*, 210.

Rickey was the canny team manager of the Brooklyn Dodgers. His wartime experience of multiethnic military service, together with a shrewd business sense for new markets and a hunch for its sporting utility, led him to make a deliberate decision to break the color bar. His protégé was Jackie Robinson, a superior college athlete who was making a name in the Negro Leagues. He agreed to Rickey's offer, which included a willingness not to rise to the many racial taunts that came his way. Rickey worked hard with the black community to gain their support and Robinson took the game by storm. It is difficult to underestimate the significance of this: "Robinson and Rickey integrated not only baseball, but the public space of American sports."[108]

There is no doubt that Robinson blazed a trail mapped out by Rickey, but despite the considerable success of African-American ball players since Robinson it would be wrong to underestimate the difficulties still experienced. It is often alleged that African-Americans receive lower wages than white players of comparable ability, for instance, and more revealing is the phenomenon of "stacking." This describes the way in which African-American players are *deployed* even when present and playing, for they tend to be kept out of the most strategically demanding positions: typically, quarterback in football, catcher and backstop in baseball. Behind such stacking seem to lurk certain stereotypes about ethnicity.

The imperialistic logic that justified slavery in the USA and colonialism in Britain tended to see African-Americans and Caribbean-British as possessing certain natural *physical* aptitudes.[109] These black athletes are typically prized for their agility, speed, strength, and reflexes. In track and field athletics, with some exceptions, black athletes from Western nations have tended to compete in the shorter and more explosive events. The attitude in practice is summed up neatly by an English football league club chairman speaking in 1991: "The problem with black players is they've great pace, great athletes, love to play with the ball in front of them . . . When it's behind them, it's chaos. I don't think too many of them can read the game. When you're getting into the mid-winter you need a few of the hard white men to carry the athletic black players through."[110]

108. Gorn and Goldstein, *Brief History*, 217.

109. See Coakley, *Sport and Society*, 8th ed., 282–323. In this chapter Coakley offers a sociological hypothesis to account for the strong performances of African–American athletes.

110. Ron Noades quoted in Kuper and Szymanski, *Why England*, 113.

In Britain an analysis of black players playing top-flight football in 1985 showed that the great majority of them played as forwards and only a small proportion in midfield or in goal: midfield in particular is considered a creative position, linking defense and attack. A study five years later came to similar conclusions. While in both of these studies about 11 percent of the total players were black, a similar study in rugby union around the same time found that only 2.4 percent of the players were black, and of these two-thirds played on the wing, quite literally, a peripheral position and one that emphasizes speed over decision-making.[111] These studies suggest that sport reflects society to the extent that it reproduces its crude racial stereotypes. They are further borne out by the low numbers of black players who go on to work in management or coaching. This is the "problem of the afterlife": for a larger proportion of black players, there is none. There are signs of improving prospects, and some high profile sportsmen and women have made careers in advertising and the media. But even in those sports where black athletes are thought to be well represented they have made little impact. There are always exceptions, some of them remarkable. Given the absence of African-American golfers, for instance, Tiger Woods' impact is stunning. Woods distanced himself at first from descriptions that identified him as a "black golfer," but in time came to launch various initiatives that drew criticism from some as being too "political."[112] Like Smith and Carlos he discovered that any comments or behavior that states or implies criticism of the status quo may be deemed "political," though anything that states or implies support for it is apparently not.

English football does not have its Jackie Robinson moment, but instead a record of a number of black players who have appeared in league football from the later part of the nineteenth century. The British Boxing Board of Control had a color bar on title aspirants until 1948, but none existed in football—though it is only since the 1970s that black players appeared in significant numbers at the top level. As their relative numbers rose, so did tensions and prejudice. Those in football management appear to have reflected a fairly typical range of attitudes to ethnic minorities over these forty years of significant black involvement in elite football, from a nonchalant refusal to see ethnicity as an issue to different degrees of racism that now seem as remarkable for their candor as

111. See Polley, *Moving the Goalposts*, 154–55.
112. Horne et al., *Understanding Sport*, 120–21.

their content.[113] Coaches often seem to have bought into the stereotyping of black players as having flair and "natural ability" but not necessarily football intelligence.

The treatment of the growing number of black players by some fans was sometimes nothing short of scandalous. Liverpool had graffiti daubed on their ground after signing John Barnes in 1987, and the player himself had bananas thrown at him while playing. His experience was not peculiar: Ian Wright recalls having peanuts thrown onto the pitch, others endured monkey chants. Some made light of it, others found it more difficult. Fans wrote to supporters' magazines demanding that their teams "remain white"; when England drew with Brazil 1–1 in 1984 some fans insisted the score was "really" 1–0 to Brazil because John Barnes had scored England's goal and "Nig goals don't count."[114] There were suggestions on such occasions that football fan groups had been infiltrated by those with far-right political agendas, but proof was difficult, and others warned that this was too convenient an explanation for the phenomenon in allowing mainstream football followers to pass the blame along too easily.[115] A number of anti-racism initiatives beginning in the early 1990s have addressed the problem in the stands with some success, though there is no room for complacency. There is still a concern that stewards do not always act when members of the crowd exhibit racist behavior. Given the problems with English football hooligans, and the distasteful behavior still evident at some games and even on the field of play,[116] the sight of English football authorities complaining about other European

113. Some examples: Kenny Dalglish, Liverpool FC manager, on signing John Barnes: "The only criterion guiding me during moves for players is, are they good enough? Colour or creed doesn't come into it." Dalglish, *Dalglish*, 152. Ron Greenwood, England manager, on selecting Viv Anderson: "Yellow, purple, or black—if they're good enough I'll pick them." Quoted in Polley, *Moving the Goalposts*, 150. Contrast these comments with the anonymous first-division manager invited to contribute to a TV documentary: "What do I think about the black bastards you mean?" Quoted in Fleming and Tomlinson, "Racism and Xenophobia," 305. There are more disturbing examples given in their article.

114. Quoted in Fleming and Tomlinson, "Racism and Xenophobia," 306.

115. Dunning et al., *Roots of Football Hooliganism*, 181–83.

116. In a recent notorious case Liverpool's Uruguayan forward, Louis Suarez, was banned for eight games for racially abusing an opponent, though he continues to protest his innocence: *The Guardian*, "Luis Suárez Banned."

national associations regarding anti-racist behavior sometimes seems to be paternalistic and a bit rich.[117]

Sport is one site where social and cultural tensions between ethnic groups are played out. Unless artificially segregated, the meritocratic nature of competitive sport tends to be a social leveler. It exposes myths of superiority to deconstruction. Hitler discovered this at the 1936 Olympics as he watched Jessie Owens beat members of the "master race" to four gold medals. White male masculinity is challenged in the sporting arena, the myth of white superiority resisted and disarmed. As Ben Carrington observes, "sports can therefore be seen at one level as a transgressive liminal space where Black men can attempt, quite legitimately, to (re) impose their subordinated masculine identity through the symbolic, and sometimes literal, 'beating' of the other, that is, White men."[118] bell hooks is correct to note that, historically, "competition between black and white males has been highlighted in the sports arena."[119] These factors might go some way to explaining the rancor and violence that has greeted increasing levels of black participation and excellence in elite sport.

However, while in certain elite sports black athletes appear "over-represented" compared to the population in general, at non-elite levels participation in sports by ethnic minorities in Britain continues to trail participation by the white majority population. But this fact masks a more complex picture: participation rates vary between ethnic groups and drop off markedly among women of ethnic minorities.[120] Much discussion of ethnicity tends to ignore this feature, succumbing to a reductionism that implicitly focuses on black and Asian males but overlooks women. Public policy has not always fared better, with various initiatives aimed at increasing participation struggling to gain a hold. Too often they appear to rest on a comfortable supposition that the problem is always to do with "their" culture rather than "our" sport and its structures.[121] A similar denial is at work when various reports mention race or ethnicity as a factor in participation but fail to make the correlative leap to identify racism as a problem in sporting structures.

117. Lowe, "Xenophobia."
118. Carrington, "Sport, Masculinity," 280.
119. hooks, *Outlaw Culture*, 31, quoted by Carrington, "Sport, Masculinity," 279.
120. Horne et al., *Understanding Sport*, 118.
121. Carrington and McDonald, "The Politics of 'Race'," 129.

An interesting example of "competition between black and white . . . in the sporting arena" that affects both sides of the Atlantic can be found in the story of Jack Johnson's proposed visit to London in 1911.[122] Johnson was the American boxing champion of the time, a womanizer and gambler, and controversy had followed him around the USA with fights occasionally having to be relocated after local opposition. His contests had begun to be filmed so that they could be shown around the country. A fight was proposed next with an English challenger in London, Matt Wells. At the time the legal status of boxing was uncertain, and it split church opinion in Britain with some groups supporting the fights (particularly the Muscular Christians) and other opposing it. One of the factors in opposition in the US was color: Johnson was black; many of his beaten opponents were white.

The Free Church Federal Council, for reasons that remain obscure, became embroiled in the debate and came down against the staging of the fight. In correspondence with *The Times* a leading Baptist, J. H. Shakespeare, suggested that the fight would pit white and black against one another "in anger, revenge and murder, especially in lands like America in which the Negro is the gravest of all problems." He went on:

> there can be no greater disservice to the negro race than to encourage it to see a glory in physical force and in beating the white man . . . It matters not to us if an Englishman is beaten, for we have proved our place in the realms of courage, endurance, service, art and learning. But to a race which has not yet achieved glory it is a crime to turn its ambition to such glory as can be found in a Prize Ring."[123]

Another, F. B. Meyer said, "you must admit that the present contest is not wholly one of skill, because in the one side is added the instinctive passion of the negro race, which is so differently constituted from our own, and in the present instance will be aroused to do the utmost that immense animal development can do to retain the championship."[124]

Then, the railway company which owned the proposed venue took out an injunction to prevent their tenants staging the fight (the Director of Public Prosecutions was about to take action to stop it on the grounds of a likely breach of the peace). The judge who granted the injunction

122. See Stuart Mews' excellent account in "Puritanicalism."
123. Quoted in Mews, "Puritanicalism," 324.
124. Quoted in Mews, "Puritanicalism," 328.

was a member of the same Baptist church of which F. B. Meyer was minister. Muscular Christians and the Anglican establishment did not believe that the opposition to the fight represented the mainstream of church opinion but a hardcore Puritan streak—once more, perhaps, exerting an influence out of proportion to its numbers. Mews considers that if the fights' opponents had argued against boxing *per se* they would not have won—the ethnicity element here was crucial.

The episode appears to suggest that church leaders in 1911 reflected some of the stereotypes and prejudices of their peers, and that such contests could be seen as a threat at a number of levels. We would be foolish to assume that we are necessarily wiser or more detached from our surrounding culture. As such, the challenges emerging in this discussion of ethnicity remain strong and potentially disturbing for those wanting to think about the religious and theological aspects of sport.

Sport and Politics

Following Nigeria's disappointing performance at the 2010 FIFA World Cup the country's president forbade the team to compete in international competition for two years. FIFA responded to this by threatening to ban Nigeria indefinitely from world football because of political interference, ending all financial aid from FIFA to Nigerian recipients, and even stopping Nigerian referees from officiating in international games. The Nigerian president reversed his decision and the crisis was avoided. So passed a recent episode in the story of politics and sport, which, apparently, should never be mixed.

The reality has to be different, of course. FIFA exists as a federation of national associations, each one defined by a political boundary. While the franchising system of elite American sport has loosened the connection between team and community, still there exists some elemental connection between the Yankees and New York, the Dodgers and LA, and even—in England—between Manchester United and Manchester.[125] At a basic level politics defines team sports to a considerable degree. Beyond the geographical identities of teams, however attenuated, the playing of

125. Manchester United has received constant jibes regarding the perception that its supporters mainly do not live in Manchester. In England the history of MK Dons FC, who began life as Wimbledon FC until they were moved by their owners following a dispute with the local authority, has thrown the relationship between club and community into sharp relief.

the "Stars and Stripes" before NBA, NFL, Major League Baseball and National Hockey League games is a clear statement of the political significance of these pursuits as signifiers of American identities. To suggest that politics can be separated from such sports seems very odd. The passion with which the Welsh national anthem is sung at rugby internationals is another indication of how sport can express an identity; the Scottish and Irish teams have both seized eagerly upon modern anthems that can be sung with gusto before games and channel a sense of national identity. In the case of the "Flower of Scotland" in particular, these musical foci often have the "other" clearly and even politically in view so that an identity is affirmed over and against something or someone.[126] Whenever England play Argentina or Germany at football it will not be long before a tabloid makes a headline reference to previous military conflict.[127]

Sport and politics have always been interconnected. The Meso–American ball game ritualized political domination and the Romans used sport to buy political support at home and humiliate beaten opponents. In the Middle Ages and early modern period sport was favored as a means of ensuring military preparedness, either directly through the skills of archery or the tournament, or indirectly through general fitness. The church was not conspicuous in its opposition to such usage, and sometimes Christian writers positively commended it. Political regimes of the twentieth century found it useful to use sport for ideological reasons. During the 1930s depression the fascist states in Germany and Italy invested a great deal in sports believing that this would prepare the nations' youth for service of their country (including military service) in body, mind, and spirit. Hitler prescribed an hour's physical training each day for young Germans in *Mein Kampf*.[128] Similarly, the Soviet regime believed that sportsmen and -women winning international competition showed the superiority of communism over capitalism—sporting victories were signs of ideological superiority.[129]

126. The song was written in 1967 by Roy Williamson of the Corries, and celebrates the victory over Edward II's English army at Bannockburn in 1314.

127. Following England's defeat by Germany in the 2010 World Cup, the *Daily Mail* led on June 28, 2010 with "If the few had defended as badly as England we'd all be speaking German now." Littlejohn, "Three Lions?" See also Stead, "Sport and the Media," 190.

128. See Baker, *Sports*, 246–56.

129. Baker, *Sports*, 266.

But sport in the democratic West has not escaped political manipulation either. Smith and Carlos were banned for life by the International Olympic Committee after their Black Power salute, but when George Foreman wrapped himself in the Stars and Stripes after he had beaten a Russian in a boxing final in the same Games this was not seen as a political gesture.[130] In 1972 eleven members of the Israeli Olympic team and a police officer were killed in a terrorist raid on the Olympic village—five terrorists were killed in a failed rescue attempt. In 1976 more than twenty African countries withdrew from the Montreal Olympics in protest at the New Zealand rugby tour of South Africa. South Africa was banned from the Olympics from 1964 until 1992. When the Americans boycotted in 1980 and the USSR in 1984 politics were again all too obvious. Such extreme events may not be useful guides to general political involvement with sport, but it is always there. Governments shape the environment within which sport functions, give tax breaks and pump-priming money for projects, and lend support to prestigious schemes—such as the British Government's support for the 2012 London Olympic bid. All this (local, regional, and national) government support and aid is negotiated in multiple contexts where issues of gender, ethnicity, sponsorship, and access are live.

We might also think of politics with a lowercase "p". Politics in this sense might refer to the way in which national sporting bodies govern themselves, relate to clubs and players as supporters, allocate resources, and to the power struggles which may often be observed in such groups. Or to the way local clubs decide on who may and may not join, or be selected to play. It may mean a type of body lobbying against government or company policies that affect them directly—as with the "rain tax revolt" joined by many sports clubs in England in 2008–9.[131] To think of politics in this way makes it patently obvious that it must be nonsense to see sport and politics as hermetically separated.

Sometimes an incident draws our attention to the many-layered reality of politics in sport and sport in politics. In Britain just such an incident occurred in 1968 a few months before the Smith/Carlos salute. The English cricket team was due to be selected for a controversial tour of South Africa. In 1968 the selection of the touring team was under the auspices of the Marylebone Cricket Club (MCC). The English side

130. See Baker, *Sports*, 293.
131. Percival, "Minister Orders Water Companies."

that had played during the home summer matches had included Basil d'Oliveira, a "Cape colored" who had moved to England in 1960 and subsequently qualified to play for his adopted country.[132] Despite d'Oliveira's excellent form he was not selected for the tour and there were cries of foul all around: the suspicion was that the MCC selection committee had succumbed to pressure from the South African authorities who had indicated that their team would not be permitted to play opponents including a non-white player. When, following an injury to a member of the squad, d'Oliveira was subsequently called into the team as a replacement the South African Government duly banned the tour claiming that the team was no longer the team of the MCC but of the anti-apartheid movement. The effect of the incident was to raise public awareness of racism at home as well as of apartheid in South Africa. Well-planned protests followed against the winter 1969 South African rugby tour to Britain, and plans for similar disruption to the 1970 summer visit by South African cricketers were laid. The public debate became heated—one of the arguments deployed was rather like that used in the debate over the Robinson/Wells boxing bout, that public order and race relations in Britain could be threatened. The government eventually asked the cricket authorities to cancel the tour and in a strange mirror image of the situation in 1968, amid some recrimination, the tour was cancelled. Was this a moral or a political campaign? Could it have been one without the other? Should cricketers, free tradesmen in some respects, have been free to make up their own minds about playing cricket in or with South Africa? That governments cannot always compel is shown by the inability of the British Government ten years later in 1980 to prevent a British team going to the Moscow Olympics. But in the many-layered episodes of dressing rooms, sports committees and government offices the tangled reality of political sport is played out.

The totalitarian states of the twentieth century may have been particularly flagrant in association of sport with politics, but they were by no means unique. Politics is how we are together, and one of the complex ways in which we interrelate is through sport. To pretend that this is not the case is to ignore one of the key factors in creating identity, and suggests the risible notion that sport somehow floats free and above such considerations as law, governance, power structures, and international

---

132. See Birley, *English Cricket*, 304–5.

relations. All sport, and perhaps most especially elite sport, is inevitably political.

Conclusion

This chapter has attempted to outline the way in which sport is experienced through six contemporary social lenses. The purpose of these accounts has been to give a more balanced view of sports as social phenomena than could be obtained by studying them simply as sports, i.e. bracketing out all the questions that arise about such things as power, control, disadvantage, and money. What emerges is a picture of sports that shows clearly how embedded they are within culture(s), and how they reflect culture in many ways, good and bad. In cultures that exhibit racism and sexism, sports will also reflect these things; in sports as in other spheres it is true to say "follow the money"; if society is increasingly consumerist in attitude, that will also be likely to show itself in sport; and so on. Theologically, there is much to ponder in all this and the most enthusiastic sports fan will surely find pause for thought. In some ways the caution about sport that has been shown historically by some of those Christian thinkers we reviewed in the previous chapter seems amply justified. Any adequate theology of sport will have to reckon with its reality in our world—a reality marked by issues like those we have considered here. There are certainly questions about the playing of sport itself—its competition, for instance, and its fundamentally antagonistic nature—that will need to be addressed. But this sport is *situated*, arising from and expressing itself in a commercially oriented, politically determined, consumerist, sexist, racist world, shaped by the media that is controlled by dominant interests. Every new sportsman and -woman, we might say, is born into this sinful sporting world. We turn now to consider sport and its relationships to another aspect of contemporary life—religion.

3

1851 and All That

Losing My Religion?

IN THE PREVIOUS CHAPTER we considered various perspectives on sport as part of the fabric of contemporary society. One angle we did not consider was sport's relationship to religion; that is the purpose of this chapter. There are several ways in which we could proceed. We could, as was the case in our previous chapters, move back and forth between Britain and America noticing similarities and differences as appropriate, or we could separate the focus on each in turn. The differences between the two countries are so significant and marked that it is this latter method that we will adopt here: first we will examine aspects of British experience before turning later in the chapter to an American perspective.

We could look at ways in which organized religion directly impinges upon the practice of sport, and vice versa. This would be to examine the concrete and explicit relationship between one culture and practice—"sport"—and another—"religion." A rather different approach would be to consider the relationship on a more formal level, asking about the functions of sport and religion. It is this latter method that will predominate in our discussion, but first a brief consideration of the more concrete reality is in order. While our discussion will concentrate on the recent and contemporary landscape we will also have cause to go as far back as the 1851 Census. Is there any significance in the coincidence of the decline in churchgoing since 1851 (which Robin Gill charts) and the rise of sport in the same period? To anticipate discussion later in this chapter, working from functional definitions of sport's significance in society I will suggest that sport has taken over certain religious functions in contemporary society. In this and subsequent chapters I will be referring at a number of points to my empirical research into the attitudes of those who attend and participate in sport.[1]

Sundays: "the Lord's day" or "a day at Lord's"?

The changing nature of sport and religion in early twenty-first-century Britain becomes evident when one pauses to consider the changing nature of Sundays. Not so long ago Sunday was a day upon which virtually everything, apart from churches, closed.[2] The historic Protestant, Puritan keeping of the Lord's Day was enshrined in statute and observed widely. Sundays were different, "special" as the campaigners later argued. But a process of cultural change began in wartime and accelerated later. It reached its most obvious early high point in cricket matches being staged on Sundays specifically for TV audiences. Sunday as the Lord's Day now could mean something rather different—a day out at the "home of cricket," Lord's. In the old regime organized, and certainly professional, sport was an activity specifically ruled out. It will seem to some now that the tables have turned completely, that sport predominates on Sunday and the church which previously attempted to curtail it lags in the battle for the attention of the public. The reality is a little more complicated, of course.

When we consider the rather chequered history of the church's relationship with leisure in general, and games and sport in particular, the contemporary situation seems to suggest that peace has broken out. Criticism of sport is seldom expressed by national or more local church leaders despite some reservations about the huge sums of money sometimes involved in contemporary sport. (There seems, incidentally, to be a double standard here with similar reservations rarely expressed about other parts of the entertainment industry.) For the 2010 FIFA World Cup English church leaders supplied their congregations with prayers for use on Sundays, and mission agencies used the opportunity of the

1. See Ellis, "Meanings."

2. For British radio listeners this was amusingly illustrated in the *Hancock's Half Hour* episode, "Sunday Afternoon at Home," first broadcast in April 1958.

competition to highlight aspects of their work; the 2012 London Olympics were treated similarly.

The beginnings of this rapprochement might be found in what we earlier called the Victorian settlement on sport. Victorian church leaders came to see that religion could not be the sole source of enjoyment for its adherents. What Baptist minister R. H. Marten called an "oppressive seriousness" was particularly damaging in the church's relations with young people, and when purged of undesirable accoutrements sport could be a positive force. Marten thought it wrong to believe that sports such as cricket were inherently "worldly" as had often been held hitherto, but worldliness consisted rather in "sanctimonious reverence for habits and customs, which may be nothing but 'traditions of the elders.'"[3] This view became widespread, and by the last quarter of the nineteenth century in England sport had ceased to be regarded as sinful, and became permissible and even essential in the missionary cause. Of course, such a sweeping summary blurs real distinctions: Erdozain identifies five types of religious attitudes to sport, ranging from the separatist attitudes of exclusive sects to the thoroughly appropriated attitude of Muscular Christians.[4] The Victorians enjoyed statistics and their new enthusiasm for sport was backed by analyses of populations and facilities in many cities. In *Tempted London* the ubiquitous power of moral temptation seemed more troubling than working conditions and housing, and conversion was seen as a means to empower individuals to resist this temptation. In the USA, W. T. Stead carried out a similar survey in Chicago. Some statistics are enlightening in a number of ways. A survey in Bristol in 1882 suggested that of a population of 206,000, 104,000 attended drinking places on the first Saturday night of the year. Total religious attendance in the morning and evening on October 30, 1881 was 116,000.[5]

The first purpose-built YMCA in New York, opened in 1869, was a response to a similar gathering of "scientific evidence," and the YMCA initially had greater freedom to develop its programs than churches, though churches soon followed where the YMCA led. Manchester YMCA led the gymnasium way in England in 1876, and facilities and opening hours expanded rapidly across the country. Before too long, however,

3. R. H. Marten in the *Baptist Hand-book 1879*, 78–80. Quoted in Erdozain, *Problem of Pleasure*, 147.

4. Erdozain, *Problem of Pleasure*, 157–62.

5. Erdozain, *Problem of Pleasure*, 169.

there was a suspicion that the tail was wagging the dog. The Cambridge YMCA may not be entirely representative, but serves as the indicator of a drift towards what may be regarded as a highly secularized provision. By 1922 it defined the work of the kingdom as helping young men keep their bodies fit and their minds alert, and improving the quality of social relationships, with little mention of more traditional religious activity. In November of that year there were 105 separate events in the branch but only two could be described as being explicitly religious in any way. One was a service for sportsmen and the other was a discussion entitled, "Must Christians go to church?" They focused on sports such as cricket and football and also "the greater game of life."[6] In an increasingly secularized world sport offered common ground and a way of speaking about "the kingdom" without the kind of "speculative" discourse traditionally associated with religious practice. Long before the Cambridge extreme described here statistics were showing that attendances at YMCA facilities were going up while conversions and other religious measures were going in the opposite direction. To mix the metaphor, the sporting sprat may have eaten the religious mackerel. The Victorian Settlement may have been bought at a high price.

But there was also a rich and enduring harvest from this change of attitude in the churches. In chapter 1 I referred to Lupson's research showing that a third of football clubs who have played in the English Premier League were founded by churches. The clubs include some illustrious ones: Aston Villa and Everton (Methodist), and Tottenham Hotspur and Manchester City (Anglican).[7] Many clubs outside this highest level might also be mentioned; Northampton Rugby Union Club was founded by a church group too. While the most famous cricketing cleric of the nineteenth century, C. T. Studd, spurned the game when he became a missionary and dismissed it as an idol of his youth, the most famous cricketing cleric of the twentieth century, Bishop David Shepherd, had no such qualms and played international cricket for eight years after his ordination. Up and down the land clergy joined golf clubs at charitable rates, became keen fans of local clubs, and more recently even their chaplains.

Where enduring tension did exist was over the issue of Sundays, and I touched on this also in chapter 1. The Puritans had fought hard for

6. Erdozain, *Problem of Pleasure*, 228.
7. Lupson, *Thank God for Football!*

the Lord's Day, and part of their legacy was that Sundays were largely free of organized sport. The Evangelicals of the eighteenth and nineteenth century had built on their success with the Lord's Day Observance Society campaigning effectively. One of the reasons suggested for Sunday schools being well attended in the middle of the twentieth century was the paucity of alternatives. While some sports did see Sunday play they were typically those played by the middle and upper classes in exclusive private clubs, such as golf and tennis:[8] the Puritans had also not come down too hard on the gentry. The extremes of wartime allowed some relaxation, at first for direct military purposes.[9] In both of the World Wars, restrictions were lifted for workers at home, needing some letup after an arduous working week, and for troops overseas. After World War I cricket began to be played more often on Sunday, and rowing too. Amateur football clubs found the move to Sunday in World War II so congenial[10] that many never quite went back, despite a Football Association rule forbidding Sunday games.[11] In 1960 the FA recognized the growing popularity of Sunday leagues by allowing their clubs to affiliate and by inaugurating a national competition specifically for Sunday teams. The government began a consultation exercise with sporting authorities in 1961 on whether and how to relax the Sunday observance laws. Cricket was the first major sport to change its practice at the elite level. Afternoon charity games led to a series of televised all-star charity games beginning in 1966, and then to a Sunday League begun in 1969 with a much shortened form of the game. But professional football in England, in contrast to "Catholic Europe," was not seen on a Sunday until 1974 when Millwall played Fulham. Strictly speaking, these fixtures remained illegal.

By the early years of the twenty-first century the picture had changed dramatically, with three major factors. The earliest of these to have any impact was the changing face of television. In the early 1960s, turning on your TV on a Sunday morning would yield a blank screen or, at best, a test card. But as the century wore on children's programming and more general interest programs (including church services) began to appear on

8. Brailsford, *British Sport*, 115. A concrete example is found in Horne et al., *Understanding Sport*, 59.

9. Brailsford, *British Sport*, 122.

10. Rippon, *Gas Masks*, 37.

11. Brailsford, *British Sport*, 123. One of the most well-known leagues, with games played on London's Hackney Marshes, began in 1949: see the website of the Hackney and Leyton Football League.

the schedules. Parents began not to send their children to Sunday school any more as alternatives began to appear, and critics observed that values were now absorbed from the "box" rather than Bible lessons. Television was also involved in the second factor. The founding of the FA Premier League in 1992 brought a huge increase in TV revenue, and the regular broadcasting of a Sunday game. In time, further games were shifted to Sunday and it is not unusual now for half the program of games to take place on Sundays. In English rugby union, the top competition can also see half of its games on Sundays, and in cricket the traditional pattern in international test matches of a Sunday rest day has long gone. The Wimbledon tennis and open golf championships have moved their final days from Saturday to Sunday—again led by television. This is a remarkable transformation of sporting practice, largely within two decades. The third factor was the decision to relax Sunday trading restrictions in 1994, presented as a move to a "Continental Sunday." Previous legislation in 1950 had allowed a very limited range of outlets to open on Sundays, but the 1994 Act allowed all shops to open for a substantial period. Soon Sundays in town centers resembled other days. While the shifts in sporting fixtures had occurred with very little church opposition, the Sunday trading legislation was more fiercely opposed. Forming an alliance with trades unions, church groups (many of whom combined under the Keep Sunday Special banner) did manage to win some concessions for workers and over opening hours. But taken together these factors have had a huge impact on the way the English experience their Sundays.

The Sunday Leagues had already been having an impact on churches, however. As well as attracting adult players, Sunday mornings became the time for youth and children's coaching. Clubs recruited enthusiastically. Sunday school was certainly no longer the only show in town. While churches may not have fielded teams on Sunday mornings, many did organize teams to play in local football leagues—or indeed, in church leagues. Football was particularly popular in this regard, and has often been presented as a mission tool, though there must be a lingering suspicion that for many it was just good fun. Other sports were more difficult to organize for, and this partly explains also football's rise to be the nation's premier game as well as the obvious missionary vehicle.[12] Youth

12. Rugby needs more players and can carry a greater risk of injury for the inexperienced, and it is more difficult to persuade someone to "have a go"; cricket needs special equipment and very high quality playing surfaces, and also carries some risk for the inexperienced if pitched against much better players.

organizations, like British Youth for Christ, adopted sports into their outreach programs.[13] Churches have also found it useful to promote the spectator experience with big football matches being shown by churches on large screens in an effort to create a communal experience similar too, but different from, that found in pubs and clubs. In playing and watching, the conversion to sports seems complete.

Religion and Sport in the UK: What the Numbers Tell Us

Every week more than three quarters of a million people pay to watch professional football in the top five English divisions,[14] while smaller numbers watch other sport. Football also has impressive TV figures. When England played Portugal in Euro 2004 more than one third of the UK population watched the game—the figure of 20.7 million does not include those watching in pubs or on other public screens.[15] In 2010, the audience for England's World Cup defeat to Germany peaked at 19.5 million,[16] and 18.4 million watched the final between Spain and Germany.[17] Sky's live Premiership football games on subscription channels attract 1.5–2.5 million,[18] but BBC1's *Match of the Day*, showing game

13. For instance, the organization says about one of its current initiatives that "Kick London aims to 'Transform young people's lives with God's love through sport', combining sports skills with life skills, underpinned by Christian values and teaching. It was established in 2003, as an extension of Youth for Christ's vision of a 'Kick' football ministry for London. YFC helped Kick London to be established with a clear mission and vision for London." Website of Kick London.

14. Source: website of East Midlands Football. In 2009/2010 about 341,500 watched Premiership matches every week, 215,400 watched Championship (i.e. second tier) matches, and about 195,000 watched Leagues 1, 2 and the Conference combined. The statistics are given in a slightly different form at Football Economy.Com. The conference average total of 41,879 needs to be added in to the totals for the lower two Football League divisions.

15. Source: Football Economy.Com.

16. Deans, "TV Ratings."

17. Deans, "World Cup Final."

18. In April 2013 Sky Sports had an audience of 353,000 for a Friday evening Championship English game; simultaneously they attracted 112,000 to a Rugby League fixture, while on the following day they had an audience of 179,000 for a rugby union broadcasts match. Source: BARB, "Viewing Data, Top 10s."

highlights free to air, had an average of 3.7 million viewers in 2007/2008, with peaks at more than 4.7 million at key points of the season.[19]

In a typical week the main terrestrial channels each broadcast several hours of sport. The cable and satellite channels add more specialist options that roll around the clock. Two million watch test cricket highlights,[20] the Olympics attracts many millions, with the 2012 London Games breaking all kinds of records,[21] and Andy Murray's 2013 Wimbledon win was seen by more than 17 million viewers.[22] We should bear in mind that these are not *all* the same people, and that all these figures are for *watching* sport: I have made no attempt yet to offer statistics for sports *participation* of various sorts, or indeed the smaller numbers who watch other sports. Local newspapers in every town and city list results in local cricket, rugby and football leagues each week, as well as some other sports: multiplying by the appropriate number of players per team and adding a few for officials, scorers, and refreshment providers suggests a significant number involved in non-elite organized competitive sport. Figures for many sports are not indicated, but local cricket statistics give some clues. Oxfordshire's club cricketers play in clubs associated with at least three different leagues, many running several teams. A conservative estimate of the number of teams involved week by week is 175,[23] suggest-

19. See Mosey, "MOTD Viewing Figures Up."

20. Highlights of the final day of the final game of the 2009 series between England and Australia were watched by around 2m on the terrestrial channel Five, while a similar number had watched the climax of the game on subscription satellite channel Sky Sports. In 2005, when a terrestrial channel had shown the final test live the viewing figures peaked at 7.4m. ESPNCricInfo: "Ashes Climax Watched by a Fraction of 2005 Audience."

21. The opening ceremony drew a record audience to the BBC coverage, peaking at 26.9m. Source: *Mirror*, "An Absolute Triumph"; the BBC itself claimed that 51.9m (90 percent of the UK population) watched for at least fifteen minutes at some point during the event. See BBC, "London 2012 Olympics Deliver." NBC, through its controversial time-delay broadcast, also secured its highest ever Olympic-opening audience of 41m—surpassing the numbers who watched the Atlanta ceremony in 1996. Source: Reuters, "London 2012 Opening Ceremony." The audience for the 2012 Games themselves peaked in Britain on the evening when three British athletes won gold medals in the main stadium culminating in Mo Farah's 10,000m victory watched by 17.1m: Rojas, "BBC Hails 'Stunning' Viewing Figures." To put the BBC figures in perspective, generally about 5m viewers are needed to penetrate the BBC1 Top Ten in any given week (ITV1 programs would need 6 million, other channels all lower).

22. Cooper, "Record TV audience."

23. This estimate is derived from scrutiny of the following websites: Oxfordshire Cricket Association, Cherwell League, Home Counties Premier League, Oxfordshire

ing that a county with a 635,500 population[24] has about two thousand competitive cricketers of various standards, as well as several hundred officials, scorers, administrators, supporters, grounds maintenance staff, etc. These figures, which might come to 0.4 percent of the population, would be exceeded by the football leagues in the winter by some margin.

A decade or so ago angling was reckoned to be the leading participation sport in Britain, but now it is swimming, with 20 percent reporting participation according to MORI in 2003.[25] (In Oxfordshire that would come to 128,000.) A National Statistics Survey in 2002 had given slightly different results, with swimming (35 percent) second to walking (46 percent). Significantly, 54 percent of men and 38 percent of women had participated in a sporting activity excluding walking in the four weeks before the survey.[26]

Behind all these statistics is an implicit comparison. While the 2001 Census of England and Wales reported that about 71 percent of the population describe themselves as "Christian,"[27] by the 2011 Census the number had dropped to 59.3 percent.[28] Commentators and academics have speculated about this drop but no firm agreed conclusions have been reached. To those who feel embattled as Christians in contemporary Britain, even the 59.3 percent figure seems extraordinarily high. Indeed, "church censuses" and other surveys suggest that church membership runs at not more than 10 percent while the figure attending church is more like 6 or 7 percent,[29] or about 4.2m. It is sometimes easy to feel that even that lower figure is an overestimate.

How does broadcast religion fare? "[The BBC's] *Songs of Praise* is now the only religious programme scheduled for peak-time viewing on

---

Cricket Board.

24. Figures from Oxfordshire County Council, "About Oxfordshire."

25. "The rising popularity of swimming ties in with other MORI research which shows a trend towards 'individualistic' leisure pursuits—solitary activities which involve little organisation and can be done at any time. For example, two in five people use or are members of a gym." Hasler, "Public Interest."

26. Office for National Statistics, *Sport and Leisure 2002*, 3.

27. Office for National Statistics, "Religion 2001 Census."

28. Office for National Statistics, "Religion in England and Wales 2011."

29. See, e.g., Brierley, *UK Church Statistics, 2005-2015*, table 13.7. Here he gives percentage figures for England as follows: 1998, 7.4 percent; 2005, 6.4 percent; 2010, 5.8 percent. There is significant regional variation, with South Yorkshire at 3.4 percent, Merseyside at 7.8 percent, and Greater London at 8.4 percent.

a free-to-air channel in Europe and possibly in the world."[30] It would be good to think that the rarity value of this program arises because the broadcasting rights are so expensive and competition so cut-throat, but the reality is rather different. As of 2005 ITV was committed to 52 hours of religious programming *per year*, and the BBC to 80; by 2010 the ITV output had shrunk to one hour in the year, while Five's was zero.[31] The BBC Governors noted in 2005[32] that religious coverage on BBC1 had declined in the previous three years by 14 percent, and more of the hours had been scheduled off-peak.[33] *Songs of Praise* was a casualty of scheduling changes, with average viewing down from 3.9m to 3.3m. The BBC Governors record that efforts to broadcast "high impact" religious programs had failed. The complexities of whether the BBC and other broadcasters mirror or create trends in religion and culture may be left aside for now—by 2010 BBC executives confessed to finding religious broadcasting obligations "tiresome."[34] *Songs of Praise* has fewer viewers than *Match of the Day*. It is true that more people are in church than watch professional football each week, but it is also true that weekly church attendance at around 7 percent is now about the same as the audience of *Match of the Day* and that the graphs may be going in opposite directions. Those paying customers at the elite football turnstile are in turn a fraction of those involved in sports generally as fans, spectators, and participants. A good proportion of them appear sometimes to have an almost religious devotion to sport. Something different may be happening in spectator as opposed to participation sport, but taken together we must at least ask whether sport has become a meaning-making exercise in our culture just as another meaning-making practice declines. I concede that these statistics *prove* nothing in particular and that my use of them is somewhat impressionistic, but I suggest that questions are raised by them: sport seems to be on the up, religion on the decline. Could there be a correlation between these two graphs?

30. BBC Press Office. "David Taviner Appointed."

31. Beckford, "ITV Will Broadcast."

32. BBC Governance Unit, "Governors' Genre Review."

33. This resulted in a significant drop in "reach" which measures the number of people who watch for a shorter time than the whole programme, sometimes defined as ten minutes or less.

34. Midgley, "BBC TV Executives."

According to Robin Gill, the high point of church attendance in England was around the time of the 1851 Census.[35] The census of that year was the first in which information had been gathered about church attendance.[36] In gathering this information or, at least, in interpreting it, the Victorian statisticians showed not only a desire to count the faithful but also to calculate the extent to which the population was being well or badly served by the number and distribution of churches. This is at the heart of Gill's interpretation of the decline of churchgoing in Britain in the nineteenth and twentieth centuries.

Determining the number of individuals who attended church on the census day (March 30, 1851) is not straightforward. Census returns were completed by incumbents and pastors, and there must be a suspicion that some numbers were "improved." There are certainly indications that some counted worshippers who were not actually there but might have been there on that day. In addition, with returns for morning, afternoon, and evening services there is no clear indication of how many individuals attended more than once—we are just given a total number of attendances for the day. The population of England and Wales in 1851 was just under 18 million;[37] the three services on the last Sunday of March had 10.88 million attendees:[38] if no individual went to church twice, this would represent 60 percent of the population. Horace Mann, a barrister appointed to oversee the religious census, gave an official report on it to the Registrar-General. He devised a formula for calculating the number of individuals represented by this 10.88 million figure and suggests that one half of those attending in the afternoon would not have been present in the morning, and one third of those present in the evening would not have been at either of the other services. This conjecture leads him to a final total of 7.26 million individuals, or about 40 percent of the population. However, what other evidence we have suggests that it is an optimistic number. In fact, 30 percent might be nearer the mark.[39]

35. Gill, *"Empty Church" Revisited*, 212.

36. The "Census of Religious Worship" (to give it its proper name) of 1851 was not *technically* part of the General Census but a parallel exercise with returns distributed and collected by the same census enumerators as the General Census. The results of this census have been digitized and are available online as part of the Google digitization project.

37. Mann, *Religious Worship*, 57.

38. Mann, *Religious Worship*, 86.

39. See the discussion in Bruce, *God is Dead*, 63f., and Hamilton, *Sociology*, 193f.

There are striking regional variations: Wales and Wiltshire, for instance, record proportionately double the rates of attendance in Durham, London, and Lancashire.[40] At first this seems to correspond with an urban/rural divide, but the situation is more complex, as the Welsh figures show. Also worthy of note is that 1851 appears to come at the apex of a period of sustained growth through the previous three decades powered by the evangelical revival.[41] The 1851 figures were a high.

Horace Mann used his report on the census to urge the building of more churches, particularly in towns and cities. He carefully counted the number of seats available in churches and their location in relation to the population, and then estimated how many in the population "ought" to be able to attend church at any given service time (about 70 percent, he thought). He concluded that neither rural provision at 66 percent nor urban at 46 percent was adequate. More than one and a half million more seats were required according to Mann's calculations, and through the arithmetic there is an innocent assumption that if the seats are provided they will be sat on. In fact, Mann can be a little more sanguine.[42] He speaks of "the alarming number of the non-attendants" and bemoans that "a sadly formidable portion of the English people are habitual neglecters of the public ordinances of religion." Within this general picture one feature stands out—the underrepresentation of the "labouring myriads of our country" amongst churchgoers (though in saying this he is not working directly from census evidence, which did not record social class).

Beginning in the early nineteenth century the Sunday-school movement had conspicuous success, and this continued through and beyond 1851. By 1900 it may have had contact with more than half of the nation's youth.[43] But even when working-class young people attended Sunday school, on reaching the world of work they became as "people of a heathen country . . . thoroughly estranged from our religious institutions in their present aspect."[44] Mann's ruminations here have two resonances that are worth observing because they appear to be true of a much greater tranche of time than this 1851 snapshot.

40. Mann, *Religious Worship*, 113–33.

41. Gill, *"Empty Church" Revisited*, 86.

42. The quotations from his report in this paragraph and the next are from Mann, *Religious Worship*, 93.

43. Gill, *"Empty Church" Revisited*, 83.

44. Mann, *Religious Worship*, 93.

While noting and admiring the success of the Sunday-school movement, it remains true that the transition from Sunday school to church remained problematic. Almost seventy years after the 1851 Census a survey of all ranks in the British Army at the end of World War I concluded that whereas 80 percent of men had been to Sunday school, 80 percent did *not* go to church. In fact, this may understate the problem even in 1918. The same survey estimated that 11.5 percent of English and 20 percent of Scottish troops were in what they termed a "vital relationship" with the church.[45]

At the same time, Mann suggested that it would be wrong to conclude that a turn from the church constituted also a turn from belief.[46] He called the mass of non-attenders "unconscious Secularists"[47] and believed that the continuance of social-class distinctions in churches alienated workers, as did the perception that the churches were not exercised by poverty and that ministers were primarily motivated by self-interest rather than concern for others and their eternal salvation. Finally, Mann suggested, it was difficult to find a space for solitude and reflection in cramped and unpleasant living conditions—a revealing insight both into lifestyles of the poor and into a particular kind of (bourgeois?) spirituality. But Mann's assertion that practice rather than belief was in decline is one that has continued to be discussed by sociologists ever since. Gill cites evidence that seems to support the contention,[48] but Davie and Bruce may be the best examples of polarized views of the evidence.[49]

However the statistics are presented, since 1851 church attendance in Britain has been in decline. There are some caveats to this: non-conformists, as Gill's painstaking statistical analysis shows, actually grew slightly for another thirty years after the census before beginning their (sometimes rapid) decline; Catholic attendance at Mass remained buoyant until after World War II. But as a general truth the statement is unanswerable. When Callum Brown insists that church membership declined seriously from sometime around 1960,[50] Gill is surely right to note that the decline had really begun more than a hundred years before. What

45. Gill, *"Empty Church" Revisited*, 132.

46. Mann, *Religious Worship*, 93–96.

47. Mann, *Religious Worship*, 93.

48. Gill, *"Empty Church" Revisited*, 132–34, 214–19.

49. See Davie, *Religion in Britain*; Bruce, *Modern Britain*.

50. Brown, *Death of Christian Britain*.

appears to have happened in the second half of the twentieth century is an acceleration in decline brought about by many of the factors that Gill had identified as active much earlier, including the problem of having buildings in the wrong place, and of these buildings being expensive to maintain, especially for Free Churches relying on local munificence. Structural and strategic problems, some self-inflicted by the contrasting policies of the established and Free Churches, conspired to empty churches even when there seemed no substantial and sudden loss of belief as such. But eventually the empty churches become if not dilapidated then unwelcoming and, combined with the kind of social critique of churches identified by Mann, they begin to seem peripheral to the lives of ordinary people.

But as our historical review of the growth of sport has noted, the middle of the nineteenth century in Britain is not just significant as the moment at which the church begins its still continuing decline. It is also the period during which what we may call modern sport begins to take shape. As organized religion has waned, though admittedly not in a straightforwardly linear way, so organized sport has waxed. But could these two facts be in any way connected with one another?[51] Recognizing that the notion of secularization is still a contested concept,[52] most scholars agree that pre-modern (that is, roughly, pre-sixteenth-century) Europeans did not have to think about whether they were religious or not; religious belief and practice were just part of the rhythm of life, of the assumed world.[53] By the mid-nineteenth century this rhythm, this assumed world, was beginning to unravel for more and more people. To identify these twin processes (the decline of religion and the rise of sport) with urbanization is too simplistic. Gill argues persuasively that migrants into towns not uncommonly formed new religious affiliations as well as losing their old ones,[54] and at any significant life-moment people are

51. The fact that at first churches seemed to have attempted to compete with sport is another interesting feature of this relationship. For an American perspective see Szymanski and Zimbalist, *National Pastime*, 21.

52. For example, see the discussions in Bruce, *God is Dead*; Davie, *Sociology*; and Hamilton, *Sociology*.

53. There is some debate about the "true religiosity" of the general population. See, e.g., Hamilton, *Sociology*, 189ff. Peter Berger argued persuasively that Christianity bore within itself the seeds of secularization and that,while Catholicism had resisted this tendency somewhat, the Protestant Reformation with its rationality, implied pluralism, and later splintering, hastened it. See *Social Reality*.

54. Gill, *Revisited*, 212–13.

more likely to (re-)connect with organized religion. But at just the moment when traditional ties were being loosened for many, urbanization is an important factor in the development of modern sport from its predominantly rural and primitive precursors. This sport is going to become one of the rhythms of life for many people in a way that religion often was in preindustrial Britain. Of course, in the increasingly consumerist West, sport is not the only such meaning-making activity on offer, and it may be foolish to suggest that it takes a place similar to organized religion in medieval times, for instance. But migrants moving homes and changing their whole way of life need to find ways of establishing and expressing their identities. Religion may no longer be a viable way of doing this for some, and other means must be located.[55]

In the mid-nineteenth century organized sport as we know it begins to take shape and rules for sports become steadily more regulated. Rapid industrial and economic progress brings ordinary people both more spare time and also some spare money to be spent watching sports as the development of transport and the media nourish these possibilities. After 1850 something very dramatic happens in the *consumption* of sport, just as something begins to happen to church attendance. So we might want to ask: does sport fulfill functions in our contemporary society not dissimilar to the functions fulfilled for previous generations by religious belief and/or practice? Before we reflect on this question, having principally concerned ourselves until now with the UK, we must consider the North American experience.

American Exceptionalism: Sport and Religion

The term "American Exceptionalism" was first coined in the context of discussing the socioeconomic peculiarities of the USA (and in particular analyses of the relative lack of radical, organized, left-wing, working-class groups in comparison to other Western industrialized nations) but was popularized by the American press in the 1980s as a term helpful to describe cultural and political features of American life more generally. More recently again it has been pressed into the debate on American

55. The rapid growth of Middlesbrough may illustrate this need to find new coherent forms of identity. From a population of 25 in 1801 and 154 in 1831, it grew to 5,463 in 1841 and more than 100,000 by 1901. During that time the football club, founded in 1872, became a major focus for the rapidly growing community. See Horne et al., *Understanding Sport*, 43.

religion and its resilience against secularization compared to European countries. It seems a useful term with which to discuss both sport and religion in the United States, even though it may turn out to be (in the latter case, at least) finally misleading.[56]

Even a sporting innocent would quickly notice fundamental differences between sporting life in the United States and most (perhaps all, with the exception of Canada) other countries. America seems exceptional. It is the place of association football ("soccer," as it is known in the USA) that demonstrates this most clearly. Soccer is "the world game," and is the leading sport in terms of cultural profile in most countries of the world, but in the United States it languishes, by comparison, outside the "big three and one half" of American sports: American football, baseball, basketball, and ice hockey.[57]

How and why Americans have come to be devoted to sports which—broadly speaking (and with a degree of inaccuracy, I accept)— are played by no one else is a complex and interesting story. I will say a little more in the next section of this chapter about the origins of baseball: it is a story in which commercial interest, historical accident, social class, and nationalistic feeling all combine. Baseball derives from much older games and almost certainly from the old English game of rounders most of all. But in its modern form it is an American invention; or rather, it is a game that evolved into its current shape in an American context, and in an American way. American football represented an American development of the rugby football code—an example of how rule-makers felt free to develop and change an inherited sport for their own indigenous purposes. If American cricketers had felt a similar freedom, it is possible that both American and English sportsmen and -women would today play a different and common game, but they did not. Basketball was "invented" in the way few successful games ever are: the masterstroke of a YMCA instructor looking for a way to occupy energetic young urban dwellers when space (and, often, fine weather) was limited. Ice hockey may be what happens to an old grass game when played by those who live in territories where winter's grip is unrelenting but see that as no reason

56. The beginnings of the expression are usually traced back to Alexis de Tocqueville in his *Democracy in America*, vol. 2 (1840). In its most jingoistic forms "American Exceptionalism" is equivalent to "American Superiority," but this is not a necessary aspect to its definition and it is most usually used in discussions of the sociology of religion in a purely descriptive way.

57. Markovits and Hellerman, *Offside*, 9–13.

to spoil a game, but a case could be made for a game played on ice in pre-modern Europe too, and the question of which version of hockey came first—field or ice—is moot, and probably unnecessary.

Of these sports, baseball is played in parts of Central and Latin America, in several European countries and Australia, and Japan. But outside North America it is a fringe sport—often with a lower profile than soccer has in the USA.[58] American football has a Canadian variant, but has also been exported to countries around the world. The latest surveys suggest viable leagues in more than a dozen countries. These are, however, amateur and of marginal importance within the sporting culture of each country. Participation in the UK, for instance, almost counts as an exercise in Americana as much as enthusiasm for the sport itself. Attempts to play NFL games in Europe have had mixed success, though the motivation here is generally to exploit commercial rather than sporting possibilities. The NFL Europa League ran from 1991 to 2007 before folding (interesting here was a willingness to tinker with the rules for a European audience), and in recent years one NFL game per season has been staged at Wembley Stadium.

Ice hockey could make a much more coherent claim to being a world sport than either baseball or American football. There is evidence that a game with ball and bat or stick was played on ice in Europe (especially the Netherlands),[59] but it is generally thought that modern ice hockey (or hockey as it is usually known in North America) developed in Canada during the nineteenth century. Played generally in countries with cold winters, it is an important game in many eastern European countries, and has been making sufficient inroads in the USA in the last few decades to merit being considered the "half" in the "three and one half" description of major American sports offered by Markovits and Hellerman. In some European countries ice hockey is second only to soccer/football in popularity.

58. A version of 'baseball' is also played in South Wales and Merseyside in the UK, in a variant which seems like a cross between cricket, baseball, and rounders. Those outside North America often disdain the title "World Series" for an event which concerns only Canadian and American teams, but it is worth noticing that the International Baseball Board, which governs the British game, has only two members: England and Wales. The British game was established formally in the 1890s.

59. See, for instance, Peter Brueghel the Elder's painting, *Winter Landscape with Skaters and Bird Trap* (1565), which appears to show ice hockey and curling type games being played.

Basketball, invented at the YMCA in the USA by James Naismith, is played all around the world. In some countries the profile of the game is high, and though for many years the USA has dominated international competition this has been challenged a few times more recently. In the UK the game is played quite widely in schools and youth clubs, but despite over twenty years of a professional national league, it has minimal media exposure.

The cases of basketball and ice hockey in particular indicate that the peculiarity of American sport is not so much about what is played and watched as what is not: soccer. In just about every other country in the world soccer is preeminent as both a spectator and participation sport (though it is true that the statistics here are more varied), and also in terms of the place it occupies in indigenous popular cultures. There are exceptions: Canada follows the American pattern with some variations; in India and Pakistan cricket is the national sport; in some Pacific islands, and in New Zealand, rugby union predominates. But these are exceptions. In North America soccer has struggled to establish itself, has often been seen as primarily a women's or children's game, has a history of aborted professional leagues, and commands relatively little media attention.

In sporting terms America is "exceptional." Why? A number of reasons have been suggested. A persuasive account is offered by Markovits and Hellerman in their *Offside: Soccer and American Exceptionalism*, in terms of a country's "hegemonic sports culture." This term refers to what people "breathe, read, discuss, analyze, compare, and historicize."[60] Large numbers of adults and young people might be involved with soccer in one way or another—but do they talk about it when they meet for a drink, are the newspapers they read full of it, does prime-time broadcasting show them this sport? The hegemonic sports culture is reflected by what people *follow* rather than what people *do*; the term relates to the sports that fill the cultural space given over to sports. Markovits and Hellerman argue that a nation's cultural "sport space" is finite, and that once it is full it is difficult to displace existing sports with new ones, or enlarge the given space to incorporate new sports. This latter point accounts for the slow and partially successful spread of ice hockey in the USA. Which sports come to fill a country's sport space is partly an accident of history as

60. Markovits and Hellerman, *Offside*, 9.

"timing matters immensely."[61] The processes of modernization are significant, as are contests involving the vested interests of various groups.

> However, one thing is clear: whichever sport entered a country's sport space first and managed to do so in the key period between 1870 and 1930, the crucial decades of industrial proliferation and the establishment of modern mass societies, continues to possess a major advantage to this day . . . Early arrival does not guarantee late survival, but it most certainly helps, because choices are very rapidly narrowed once sport spaces become filled . . . in that any newcomer must exert a great deal of power and expend major resources to [gain entry] . . . Tellingly, the window of arranging the sport spaces of virtually all industrial democracies roughly occurs in that crucial period between 1870 and 1930.[62]

In other words, if sports were not established by 1930, they face an uphill struggle to become the topic of conversations at all the nation's watercoolers, to become part of the hegemonic sports culture. The particular historical and sociological reasons why baseball (being spoken of by the New York newspaper *The Clipper* as America's natural game as early as 1860) and then American football became established in the USA will be considered later in this chapter.

A different, less sociological and more economic, approach is taken by Stefan Szymanski and Andrew Zimbalist. They analyze the different sports structures in the USA and the UK (with the rest of the world largely following the UK model), and the different business cultures of the nineteenth century, finding connections between them. In particular, British mercantile and commercial dominance led to the "export" of soccer/football along with industrial products. If American economic dominance had come forty years earlier, they muse, baseball might well be the world game that soccer is today.[63] These arguments, alongside the "sports space" arguments of Markovits and Hellerman, seem compelling. Relations between Britain and the USA in the second half of the nineteenth century were not always cordial, and this was exacerbated by some British support (however informal) for the Confederacy in the Civil War.

---

61. Markovits and Hellerman, *Offside*, 15.
62. Markovits and Hellerman, *Offside*, 15.
63. Szymanski and Zimbalist, *National Pastime*, 81.

Americans wanted to forge their own sports that were interpreted as expressing American values and the national ethos as distinct from British exports.

Those observing the European religious scene in the twentieth century have also often thought of the USA as exceptional. The extent to which this is actually the case is the subject of much discussion, and of polarizing views. Broadly speaking, the secularization thesis mentioned earlier has generally been held to be a poor fit in the USA. While the constitution formally separates religion and the state, the place of religion (specifically Christianity, though one would also need to take account of Judaism and, increasingly, Islam) in public discourse is more secure than in Britain and most of Western Europe. One cannot easily imagine an American political aide telling a President "We don't do God" as Tony Blair is said to have been told by Alistair Campbell.[64] Furthermore, church attendance in the USA appears resilient.

Church attendance in the USA has been thought to have been running at around 40 percent since the 1950s. This figure is higher than the 30 percent that might be a reasonable estimate from the 1851 statistics in Britain and considerably higher than the 7 percent often suggested for the contemporary scene. While the European figures are complicated, with variations particularly striking between former Soviet-bloc countries and, to some extent, north and south, America once again appears to be exceptional: an exception to the (contested) secularization rule.

However, an influential article that appeared in 1993 questioned the received wisdom on American church attendance.[65] While church membership in the United States may be at an all-time high,[66] its authors argued that the self-reported church attendance of most surveys had given a misleading picture and that the true figure among both Protestant and Catholics is nearer 20 percent. There may be a host of reasons for unreliable self-reporting: in a culture where churchgoing and religious affiliations are still, in general, positively perceived, it is natural for some

64. See Brown, "Campbell Interrupted Blair."

65. Hadaway et al., "What the Polls Don't Show." See also, Hadaway and Marler, "Did You Really Go to Church."

66. Roger Finke and Rodney Stark argue that in 1789 only 10 percent of Americans belonged to churches; that the figure had risen to 22 percent by 1890; and somewhere above 50 percent by the 1950s. By 1990 it was thought that about two-thirds of Americans report that they are members of a church or synagogue: *The Churching of America, 1776–1990.*

correspondents to over-report what might be considered socially desirable behavior. More significantly, it is likely that questions about church attendance are interpreted as being about religious identity as much as about "whether I was in church last Sunday." (This is how researchers in Britain sometimes make sense of UK census data.) In their helpful discussion of this data Mark Chaves and Laura Stephens observe that although weekly attendance at services in the USA appears to be less frequent now it is still true that Americans attend such services more often than others in the industrialized West. They report a survey in 2000 which found that the figures for monthly service attendance were: USA 55 percent, Canada 40 percent, Spain 38 percent, Australia, Britain and Western Germany 25 percent, and France 17 percent. Here, too, there may be over self-reporting—the British figure, for instance, looks high. However, they conclude that "as in other arenas, a kind of American exceptionalism holds when it comes to religion."[67]

As with American sport, noting the exceptionalism is easier than explaining it, and sociologists are at odds on this. Secularization theorists such as Bruce focus on the "American decline" implied in the previous paragraph and argue that America is simply a little slower than Europe in this regard. "Though Americans differ from Europeans in their fondness for their churches, those churches have changed. Radical sects have become denominations. The mainstream denominations have become tolerant and ecumenical. The gospel itself has been rewritten to remove much of the specifically supernatural. Conservatives . . . are now shifting in a direction which, for want of a better term, can be called secular."[68]

Others such as Grace Davie, weighing the negative influence of state religion, and Rodney Stark, suggesting that an analysis in terms of market supply and demand goes some way to explaining why American religion continues vigorous, speak of Europe as the exception, rather than America: after all, the church is growing in Africa, parts of Asia, and Latin America, we might recall.[69] Davie says: "America is indeed

---

67. Chaves and Stephens, "Church Attendance in the United States."

68. Bruce, *Modern World*, 164. Just as Bruce accuses some of defining religion in terms conducive to their argument, it is interesting to note those factors which Bruce considers "secular" as opposed to irenic (tolerance and ecumenism), and that he requires religion to be supernatural in a particular sort of way.

69. See Davie, *Europe*; Stark and Iannaccone, "A Supply-Side Reinterpretation." Davie has an excellent brief discussion of Stark's "rational choice theory" in her *Sociology*, 67–88.

'exceptional,' but with regard to religion it is very much like the rest of the world—namely, very religious. The exception is Europe. (To be precise, western and central Europe; the Orthodox east is a different story. And 'America' here refers to the United States; English-speaking Canada, as one might expect, is about half-way between the United States and Britain in terms of religion, while rapidly secularizing Quebec looks like a curious extension of Europe.)"[70]

Nevertheless, in terms of the comparison I am making here between the UK and the USA, Berger, Davie and Fokas go on to say that "the American picture differs sharply from the European one. Both behavioral and opinion indicators are much more robustly religious"—despite the suspect nature of much survey data already noted.[71] They go on to plot the differences between "religious America" and "secular Europe" by exploring eight interrelated sociohistorical factors: including the separation of church and state, a competitive "market" for religious institutions, and two quite different appropriations of the Enlightenment in the eighteenth century (with the American version stressing liberty against the French stress on reason).[72]

In this book we do not need to make a definitive judgment on whether America is exceptional when it comes to religion. Even if we were to judge Bruce to be correct that secularization already has its roots established in the USA, the American scene is still different; if, as Davie and others suggest, the situation is more complex than Bruce allows, the particular nature of American religious practice is underlined. The question I asked at the end of the previous section was: does sport fulfill functions in our contemporary society not dissimilar to the functions fulfilled in previous generations by religious belief and/or practice? Is this still a meaningful question when asked in an American context? If Americans still find the traditional instruments and institutions of religion meaningful, is it worthwhile asking whether sport can have appropriated religious functions?

My thesis therefore needs careful clarification. I am not asking whether contemporary Westerners have given up on organized religion and *instead* taken up sports as players or spectators. Many may, in fact,

70. Berger et al., *Religious America*, 9f.

71. Berger et al., *Religious America*, 12. It is worth adding that the authors also believe that survey data tends to exaggerate European secularity too.

72. Berger et al., *Religious America*, 16–21. See also Davie, *Sociology*, 48–49, 86, 89–91.

have done this, but that is not quite my hypothesis. Rather I am speculating that our Western contemporaries may turn to sport *as well as*, or *instead of*, organized religion in order to express certain feelings; experience certain emotions or states of mind; construct identity; dramatize important human instincts; inhabit a rhythm of life; participate in life-shaping ritual; and so on. Insofar as we might call these activities needs (and even religious needs), our ancestors will have fulfilled them largely (though probably not exclusively) through churchgoing and other religious practices. Some of our contemporaries will fulfill these needs in other ways and in other spheres.[73] Those who turn to sport may not do so consciously to engage in quasi-religious activity and may be surprised to hear their activity described in this way. However, sports exert a grip on the public imagination which is probably unique in contemporary culture, and this grip began to gain purchase at a similar time in the USA and in the UK.

Today Americans experience March Madness, the Super Bowl, and other such sporting high points with great fervor. One might dismiss these events as commercially driven and over-hyped, but this would not fully explain matters: after all, how are the advertisers, sponsors, and broadcasters able to hook us in so easily and so repeatedly? As Joseph Price notes, on a more regular basis every week through the season sports fans of college and pro-league teams juggle their schedules to catch a game. They memorize otherwise quite useless facts, wear team uniforms, and sometimes paint their faces and dye their hair.[74] In the week leading up to the game they will read, surf, discuss, argue, and hope, in preparation. Price recalls Santayana's description of religion as "another world to live in,"[75] and this is precisely the enveloping experience of many sports fans in America as anywhere else. Modern sports have taken on some of the functions of organized religion allowing human persons and communities to express and experience significant and necessary aspects of

73. The list of contenders here is a long one. For example, both clubbing and classical music might be considered. Conductor John Eliot Gardiner remarks that "If I have any religious feelings at all it is thanks to music. I believe very strongly in the synergy that happens when you make music in beautiful historical buildings, but I am not a card-carrying Christian." Conner, "John Eliot Gardiner: This Much I Know."

74. Price, "American Apotheosis," 215–16.

75. Santayana says of religion that "The vistas it opens and the mysteries it propounds are another world to live in; and another world to live in—whether we expect ever to pass wholly into it or no—is what we mean by having a religion." *Reason in Religion: III*, 6. Quoted in Price, "American Apotheosis," 216.

what it means to be human. My own survey of sports fans on both sides of the Atlantic would seem to give some support to this.[76]

Price goes on to discuss the views of those who have decided that sport ought not to be described in religious terms: some claim a lack of sacramentalism in sport, others fail to trace a convincing parallel between players and priests, or some such. These points are debatable, and some of them we will debate. But my argument has not been that sport has become a religion but a rather more subtle one: that sport has taken on, or taken over, certain religious functions, became an outlet for urges that once would have been met for more people through the religious fabric of life. This hypothesis will be examined more closely in the next section, but our brief consideration of religion in America is not quite complete.

A developing body of literature regarding the United States makes a persuasive case for the role of sport in American civil religion. Marxist critiques of sport suggest that sporting activity is a kind of legitimation of, and preparation for, capitalist ideology wrapped up as leisure. The characteristics that modern sport displays, such as discipline, competition, purposeful rationality, and so on, both mirror and support the ideology of capitalism.[77] Some critics link sport to the militarization of young people as well as suggesting that in sport "economic competition is presented metaphysically as an eternal given"[78] and arguing that it prepares "labour-power for capitalist industrial labour." [79] While it camouflages the class system, "sport operates in every social formation in the world as a new type of opiate of the people."[80] While such a view sees sport as providing legitimation (as well as distraction) for capitalism, Jean-Marie Brohm can also argue that it functions as a "justification of the joys of the 'American way of life' or the 'socialist system.'" While I have neither the space nor the competence to consider whether America is more capitalist than Western Europe in general and Britain in particular, I suppose that it may be sustainable to argue that America wears its capitalism on its sleeve in a way not seen in Western Europe, and that its self-understanding may be inextricably bound up with some of the same core ideas as capitalism: individualism, self-help, aspirational belief

76. Ellis, "Meanings," 178–80.
77. See Mandell, *Sport*, 2–4.
78. Brohm, *Sport*, 178.
79. Brohm, *Sport*, 179.
80. Brohm, *Sport*, 178.

in bettering oneself, competition, and more. It may seem at first a strange proposal, but a link between Marxist critiques of sport and the uses of sport in contemporary America to legitimize, consolidate, and ritualize aspects of American self-understanding (and so, civil religion), is not too outlandish.

According to Robert Bellah civil religion does not involve a substitution of a secular or civil rite or credo in place of the religious, but rather a seamless combination of the two. American "doctrines" such as freedom and democracy can be spoken of in religious ways.[81] Bellah spoke of civil religion as an apprehension of transcendent reality through the experience of the American people.[82] Such a civil religion manifests its own calendar, rituals, heroes, "hymnody," and symbols. While Bellah may have discerned a traditionally religious or transcendent origin of this system of signs and practices, others have tended to see (in a more Durkheimian way) a wholly social reality as that which is celebrated and perpetuated through such civil religion, i.e. the "American way of life." Durkheim's observations of Native Australians led him to speak of religion as a way of providing social cohesion and, more than that, for Durkheim God was, in effect, society. The totem represented the tribe to itself and was itself its own most sacred object. The more Durkheimian interpretation of civil religion may see in sport the kinds of symbols, signs, rituals, and myths which help legitimize and sustain the American Way.

Two recent books show how such an approach to sport may be found convincing. Craig Forney attempts to show how the "big three" of American sports (or as he calls them, the "holy Trinity" of American sports) reflect elements of the American psyche, and when one considers the prominence of national anthems and flags at these fixtures one sees their nationalistic resonance and the link to civil religion similarly begins to appear compelling. These three sports show, he argues, "three streams of thought foundational to the American worldview. Football portrays the element of realism in the national culture, generating concern for the recognition of harsh realities. Baseball illustrates idealism of the United States. It expresses strong imagination for an ideal life to come, while basketball presents the pragmatic philosophy of the country, considered

81. Bearing in mind the rhetoric of the "war on terror" these insights may make possible uncomfortable comparisons with the Crusades.

82. Bellah, "Civil Religion," 33.

relevant for the most common situations."[83] These conclusions follow a detailed, and at times speculative, appraisal of the playing surfaces and arena, balls and other equipment deployed, team uniforms and crowd behavior. Eric Bain-Selbo concentrates on a more particular region and one sport: football in the American South. In a Bellah-like account he does not so much suggest that sport is supplanting religion as that the two have melded together, and the civil religion that results in the South has football as the site of many of its symbols and practices.

> Civil Religion is music—hymns and Southern rock, country and traditional/folk. It is church (particularly charismatic and emotional) and community (and food, lots of food). It is a history of courage, shame, stubbornness, and honor. It is the Lost Cause: sometimes racist, despicable, and divisive, and sometimes uplifting and uniting. Woven into this civil religion is college football, drawing from and adding to these various elements and often holding them all together at once on beautiful Saturdays in towns and cities all across the South.[84]

Bain-Selbo offers empirical data that illustrate how football fans describe their game day experience in religious terms, and argues that the *social* experience of attending football fits a Durkheimian approach to civil religion.

On the basis of such interpretations of sport and civil religion one might make a slightly different type of case for American exceptionalism in sport and religion. While some of the things said about sport by these two writers might be said about any modern sport anywhere in the West, American elite sport is very self-consciously *American*, both in terms of its origin and its relatively self-enclosed playing context, and only in America are domestic fixtures always prefaced by the national anthem and accompanied by a national flag. Something particular does seem to be going on here, and the argument that sport plays a peculiar role in the creation and maintenance of the nation's self-identity seems persuasive. Add to this the analysis of sport in religious terms, notably Emil Durkheim's theories, and America might be said to be, if not an absolute exception, an extreme example of the entanglement of nationalism, identity, religion, and sport.

83. Forney, *Holy Trinity*, 206. Forney's work is also discussed in chapter 4.
84. Bain-Selbo, *Game Day*, 174.

Sport and the Functions of Religion

Defining both sport and religion is extremely difficult. In this section we will briefly consider some ways in which religion has been defined before pressing a little further the hypothesis we outlined earlier, that sport fulfills functions in our contemporary society not dissimilar to the functions fulfilled in previous generations by religious belief and/or practice.

What is religion? It is odd that a word used so often (and so often in this book) and, in popular speech at least, so easily, should be so difficult to pin down when attempting to define it satisfactorily. A not uncommon way to categorize definitions is to gather them into three more or less distinct groups described as intellectual, affective or functional.[85] An intellectual definition will attempt to define religion by what is believed; an affective definition by working from attitudes of faith or piety; a functional definition will focus on what religion *does*. Importantly, this latter group of definitions can be further subdivided—into definitions which arise more or less from the religions themselves (such as, "religion creates or maintains a person's relationship with a Supreme Being"), or those definitions which suggest that religion fulfills the psychological needs of an individual (Freud), or the needs of a society for cohesion (Durkheim), or of a culture for shared meaning (Geertz).

Each of these types of definition has its problems. Intellectual definitions struggle to encompass the variety of beliefs in the great religious traditions—or indeed to account for the lack of centrality that appears to be given to statements of belief at all in some religious traditions. The natural assumption of many Western religious believers that belief in God or a Supreme Being is essential, for instance, does not fit all Eastern traditions well. An opposite problem is that too broad a rendering of the intellectual content of religion risks including philosophies and worldviews whose adherents do not consider themselves religious at all—such as Marxism. Affective definitions similarly struggle to isolate one attitude or disposition common to all traditions. Like the intellectual definitions, they usually inadvertently reflect the tradition of the person proposing the definition. Functional definitions can seem to fail to take seriously the way in which religious people of all traditions regard their own beliefs and practices when the definition is expressed entirely in nonreligious terms, and attempts to define a religious function at the core of

85. See, for instance, Harrison, *Religion*, 15.

all traditions runs into the same problems as the intellectual or affective definitions, the sheer plurality of religious traditions.

It is not necessary here for us to resolve these questions which continue to perplex scholars, but it is important that, if we try to talk about the religious functions of sport, we have some idea of what we mean and that such talk avoids being nonsense. Many Christians (and this book is primarily concerned with *Christianity* and sport, though other very interesting books might be written about Islam or Judaism and sport[86]) would probably find it important to include both intellectual and affective aspects in a definition of what religion meant to them—while perhaps they would not immediately think in functional terms (though such a judgment might simply reflect my own religious tradition).

We should also note that some will argue that it is not proper to look for a definition of religion at all. They might do this for a number of quite different reasons. It could be argued that the very notion of religion as a noun which subsumes different religion*s* is a modern, perhaps nineteenth-century, invention and represents a form of intellectual colonialism—as Western intellectuals attempted to analyze Eastern beliefs and practices in terms of their own known traditions.[87] A more strident Christian voice, such as that of Karl Barth, might suggest that religion is the human attempt to reach, and even manipulate, the divine, and that it stands in contrast to revelation—God's reaching to us.[88] These critiques of religion raise interesting questions, but not ones that need delay us here. We are not trying to analyze non-Christian traditions and their attitudes to or relationship with sport, so theological colonialism ought to be avoidable; we will come on to a more considered Christian theological assessment of sport in later chapters.

Ninian Smart approaches the problem in a different way, and he will prove a helpful dialogue partner for our discussion.[89] Looking at religions in general he identifies a number of "dimensions" of religion. The dimensions he identifies are:

86. For instance, for Islam and sports, see Prince Ghazi's *Sports and Culture*; and for Judaism, ed. Ezra Mendelsohn, *Jews and the Sporting Life*.

87. See Byrne, " 'Religion' reconsidered."

88. Barth is at his most strident in his early commentary on *Romans*, e.g., his comments on 7:14–25 at 257–70.

89. Smart, *Religious Experience*, 3–8; and Smart, *World's Religions*, 13–22, in which he expands upon the six dimensions of the earlier work by adding the "material" dimension.

- *Ritual*: religion tends to be expressed through acts of devotion of one sort or another, at least some of which often take place in buildings designed for this purpose.

- *Mythological*: Smart is using "myth" in the technical sense in which it is often deployed academically, i.e. not as something that is false but as a universal truth or permanent significance expressed in narrative form.

- *Doctrinal*: where myth expresses truth in story form, religions also often express such truths with "system, clarity and intellectual power."[90] There is a complex relationship with, and overlap between, doctrine and myth or story, but also a distinction between these two types of expression. These dimensions of myth and doctrine may be said to approximate to what is identified in intellectual definitions of religion.

- *Ethical*: historically, religions have usually included some kind of ethical teaching or code. Though the ideal of such a code is often in contrast to the lived experience of religious believers, the ethics express core values associated with the religion.

- *Social*: religions are generally organized and institutionalized and have a communal aspect that often takes on a self-subsisting life through authority structures and communal arrangements. This social dimension manifests the way in which adherents' lives are shaped by the ritual, myth, doctrine, and ethics of the tradition.

- *Experiential*: under this category Smart hopes to describe both the Buddhist monk's hope of nirvana and his contemplative experiences, and the Christian's report of answered prayer and forgiveness. Religious traditions often trace their origin back to key moments of experience: the Buddha achieving enlightenment, Moses being addressed from the burning bush, and Paul's conversion on the road to Damascus. As Smart indicates, there is a problem in that reports of experience are likely to be shaped by the tradition in which they arise (though if that were always rigidly true, no truly new experience would ever have emerged, and the very existence of the great religious traditions would be more difficult to explain), and this draws our attention to the interaction of these seven dimensions.

90. Smart, *Religious Experience*, 5.

- *Material*: religious faith, life and practice are inextricably bound up with buildings and artifacts—for Christians, crosses, communion cups, vestments, art works, church buildings, and so on. Even austere Protestant traditions developed a particular approach to buildings that became sermons in stone, conveying meaning in explicit and implicit ways. The use of bread and wine, water, and oil, indicates a sacramental expression of Christian faith that does not simply express and convey beliefs but also enables worshippers to enter into and appropriate spiritual experience. Items of material culture become gateways leading us beyond the material, in the same way as icons function in Eastern Christian traditions. Smart would include complex locations and sacred sites under this aspect—the Ganges, and Jerusalem, for instance, and we might also add Walsingham and Iona. The material dimension overlaps with the ritual, experiential, social, and doctrinal dimensions most obviously, but once again we see how the dimensions overlap and interplay with one another.

One way of approaching religion inspired by the philosopher Ludwig Wittgenstein, recognizes that it is difficult to find elements common to all the great world faiths and so suggests that it is more satisfactory to look for "family resemblances." According to this approach, while Christianity, Judaism, Jainism, Islam, Buddhism, Hinduism, and other traditions, do not have any elements common to all of them they may be said together to share certain characteristics. Smart's seven dimensions function in a similar way. In Buddhism the doctrinal element may be less important than in Christianity, for instance, but both of these traditions share to some extent in each of these seven dimensions. According to Smart, movements such as Marxism are effectively denied religion status by his method for it could not be said to have a significant experiential dimension.[91] That may be so, though it is perhaps possible to sketch that dimension in sufficiently broad terms to include it.

This latter observation leads me to one more cautious note. Before we proceed to think of sport in terms of Smart's seven dimensions we should pause to consider another possible objection. In his sociological study of religion Steve Bruce laments the methodological errors of his fellows who, in their efforts to refute the secularization thesis, find religion in all kinds of unexpected places.[92] Those who do express interest

91. He is a little more equivocal about this in *World Religions*: see 22–24.
92. Bruce, *God is Dead*, 186–203.

in religion but report no religious practice are not challenged on their answers. Researchers use generalized, leading questions (about "meaning", for instance), and answers to them are interpreted as indicating an innate religiosity, begging the questions they seek to answer. There is a tendency to a kind of imperialism here too: a reported interest in values or significance is taken to be theological or religious. Some research finds religion by reclassifying the secular as religious, such as Thomas Luckmann's description of "self-realization" as a "modern religious theme."[93] The extreme of such moves is made, suggests Bruce, by Edward Bailey in defining "implicit religion."[94] Bailey identifies commitment, social belonging, and strength of feeling, as implicitly religious.[95] Such definitions include more phenomena under the religious banner, but end up being so inclusive as to be virtually useless. Methodological sloppiness, or nostalgia, or wishful thinking, result in such broad definitions of religion or religious that the definitions lose their meanings.

Bruce's withering critique of this research must be taken seriously as we prepare to discuss sport in religious terms. However, we might also suggest that some of Bruce's own concerns could be turned back upon him. He accuses scholars with a vested interest in the ongoing viability of religion of over-optimistic interpretations of the evidence, or in effect of rigging that evidence. He remarks that this is especially likely when religion is defined in functional terms. Indeed, he compares football and religion, asking whether it is possible to speak of football as a religion. He argues that if it were it would be a meaningless exercise telling us nothing useful about either. This claim is, as I think we shall see, spurious. But Bruce may be accused in turn of wanting to read the evidence of religiosity in a pessimistic way, and his insistence in defining religion narrowly also may be said to beg questions. While very broad definitions of religion run the risk of *including* inappropriate beliefs or functions, narrower definitions run the risk of *excluding* beliefs and functions that might at least be examined in religious terms. If religion, for instance, is defined as a search for meaning, that may not make all searches for meaning religious, but it does at least suggest a connection between such searches and religion which should be scrutinized. It is in this spirit that

93. Bruce, *God is Dead*, 199.
94. See, e.g. Bailey, *Implicit Religion*.
95. Bruce, *God is Dead*, 201.

we now move on to ask about the possibility that sport might be said to fulfill religious functions.

What happens when we consider the phenomena of modern sport in terms of Smart's seven dimensions of religion? Ritual dimensions seem obvious. Historically, the playing of sport and the ritual of religion have often been congruent—as in the Meso-American ball game or the ancient Olympiad. Modern sport's ritual may not be that of official religion in the same way, but highly ritualized it certainly is. According to Catholic theorist Michael Novak, religions begin with ceremonies, often performed by surrogates on behalf of the adherents, they wear sacred vestments and the action is highly formalized, there is concentration and intensity.[96] To compare such practices with modern sports is relatively commonplace. The highly ritualized nature of sporting action is obvious in the actual Olympic races as well as in the medal ceremonies which follow them. Football crowds respond to the local cantor in singing their barbed but often amusing canticles. Large numbers of Welsh rugby supporters, in a rather strange cultural exchange, will only ever sing hymns at rugby international matches. Clubs often encourage or promote the off-field liturgists. When listing the teams in the match-day program, English football clubs frequently list their home crowd in the team list and allocate them an imaginary shirt number to indicate the way in which the crowd though off-field does not merely spectate but participates in and affects the action. Musicians, like the drummers at London Irish rugby, are given pride of place in the grandstand by club officials so that the "liturgy" goes well.[97]

96. Novak, *Joy*, 29–31.

97. At the latter club's games, the pre-match rituals for the crowd follow a set pattern, climaxing in the singing of the team's song. But whereas this liturgy seems fixed, during the game the crowd is led to sing and chant as the circumstances seem to require in a more free-flowing, quasi-charismatic worship. In a lighthearted list in their magazine, Sky Sports listed ten rituals carried out by sports fans worldwide: 1 Chelsea fans throw celery on the pitch; 2 West Virginia University burn couches when they win; 3 Detroit Red Wings throw octopuses onto the ice; 4 Oakland Raiders go to games in fancy dress; 5 St Paul's Saints play the theme music from *Shaft* to inspire their baseball players and fans; 6 Cardiff City soccer fans celebrate goals (and more) by performing a dance known as 'The Ayatollah'; 7 Texas A & M University fans are led by five elected students in a series of action 'yells'; 8 Pennsylvania University fans throw toast onto the field (though some reforming types throw bagels or donuts.); 9 Turkish soccer clubs sacrifice a goat as part of a pre-season training ritual; 10 At the Phoenix Open Golf tournament fans boo poor shots on the 16th hole. Stelling, "Jeff Stelling's Stats," 12.

Novak's priestly view of the players and officials might seem to accord well with elite sport but not so well with the local park teams, but even here ritual is apparent: the tossing of coins, the way teams line up at the start of games, celebrations at scoring or disapprobation for misconduct, and for individuals the particular routines that they go through before, during, and after games. Bruce would doubtless object here that we are confusing routine with quasi-religious ritual, but there is enough intensity about these actions to warrant careful consideration. When players put on their kit in a particular order despite denials of superstition because they believe that such procedures bring good fortune, ritual does not seem an inapt description.

Religious rituals are often associated with sacred sites, and frequently involve special persons wearing special garments. They also commonly deploy very particular items with symbolic significance: we might notice the material dimension of sport at this point. It is almost commonplace to compare our sporting arenas with sacred sites. Richard Mandell considers that we may compare the awe-inspiring stadia of modern sports not only with great Roman edifices but also with medieval cathedrals. They offer sites where we may fulfill our needs for entertainment and commerce, and our spiritual needs too, he suggests.[98] Commentators frequently refer to "hallowed turf," fans dig up squares of the pitch or ask in their wills to have their ashes scattered on the grass; players cut up the goal nets or take cricket stumps; they kiss their medals and trophies; supporters wear colors proudly—scarves and hats, but also replica jerseys that make their identification with the on-field players more vivid.

At first sight sport may seem devoid of mythological content, but this is not the case. The significance of myth may vary from sport to sport, but in some it looms large. Baseball is a good example of this. The story that Abner Doubleday invented the game in Cooperstown, Pennsylvania, in 1839 was promulgated by Albert Spalding—who, as we saw in chapter 1, always had an eye for opportunities to promote the sport and, therefore, his livelihood. Henry Chadwick had written an article in 1903 in which he traced the origins of baseball from the English game of rounders. But this did not fit well with the image of baseball that suited the game's promoters, who wanted to portray baseball as an American game through and through, linked to American virtues and values associated with manliness and the national character. In response to enquiries from

98. Mandell, *Sport*, 295.

a specially established commission, a 71-year-old correspondent from Cooperstown claimed to have seen Doubleday invent baseball on a spring day in 1839. Basing his invention on townball (already a slight modification of rounders), he marked a diamond on the ground and made other innovations recognizably continuous with modern baseball. This "discovery" in the early twentieth century has no contemporary account, and is not referred to by anyone, including Doubleday (who was dead by this time) in the intervening period. Its historicity must be in considerable doubt; but its mythological value, with a narrative expressing the ongoing significance of baseball for Americans, has proved invaluable and incontrovertible. The story lives on long after being discredited. Kirsch remarks that "strictly speaking, modern baseball is a refined, United States variety of townball and therefore certainly is an indigenous sport. While its ancestry is English, its essence is clearly American."[99] But this really amounts to little more than a statement of the obvious, that the particular form of bat-and-ball game that we now call baseball evolved on American soil. What baseball's patrons needed was to distance the sport from English ancestry, and it had begun to do this much earlier and certainly during the Civil War. Baseball made ground then against cricket which was identified with Englishness, and the English were often seen to be supporting the Confederates in that conflict.[100]

Rugby union has a similar myth of origins, with the story of the game's invention located in an incident in 1823 when William Webb Ellis is said to have picked up the ball during a game of football at Rugby School and run with it instead of kicking it. But the story, once more, was not told until more than fifty years after the event when a former pupil wrote to the school magazine saying that someone had told him this story. Once again the protagonist never mentioned this incident during his lifetime, and had died by the time the story was in circulation. "Even though Victorian journalists might not have sought Webb Ellis out in the manner of their modern counterparts, it seems odd that, if he did play the pivotal role of legend, there is no record of his ever expressing an interest or claiming reflected glory, since he lived long enough to see his school's pastime become an adult sport with adherents across the British Isles, a ruling body and an embryonic international competition."[101]

99. Kirsch, *American Team Sports*, 53.

100. Baker, *Sports*, 143.

101. Richards, *Hooligans*, 25–26.

Following an investigation in 1895, a plaque was erected at Rugby School celebrating Webb Ellis—even though the results of this investigation were that no proof was available to substantiate the story. In the same year rugby football experienced its great schism, when northern clubs broke away to create a professional version of the game that became known as rugby league. There was, in other words, a battle for control of the game between the clubs who adhered strictly to a gentlemanly amateur ideology and those northern clubs that were countenancing payments for players and which had a working-class ethos.[102]

The story also shows a blithe ignorance regarding the nature of football in the period of the alleged incident. As we saw earlier a variety of football games existed at the time, some involving more kicking and others more throwing or handling, whereas the rugby myth suggests it was all kicking until Webb Ellis' magic moment. But, as with baseball, the story served an important mythological purpose. "By giving pride of place in their report to the Webb Ellis story, an origin myth which correctly locates the beginnings of rugby football in their school, they were, it is reasonable to suggest, attempting to consolidate their ranks and reassert their proprietorship in the face of a powerful 'alien' threat."[103] Apart from the sudden appearance of this story and the distance between the supposed event and the raconteur, "there are further grounds for doubt [in the veracity of the story]. It is just not sociologically plausible that a deeply-entrenched traditional game could have been changed fundamentally by a single act, particularly that of a low-status individual such as Webb Ellis."[104] A similar judgment might apply to baseball. Many of the key developments in rugby football, such as the oval ball, the H-shape posts, and awarding points for tries as well as goals, came much later in the nineteenth century. The legend showed "a characteristically Victorian belief that great events must be the doing of great men,"[105] and soon became established. In the Rugby Union World Cup, which began in 1987, national teams compete for the Webb Ellis Cup. The myth lives

---

102. The reasons why rugby union should have insisted on amateurism when football allowed a mixed economy of professionalism and amateur are complex, and may well (paradoxically) indicate the higher and more secure social status of football's elite compared to their rugby counterparts.

103. Dunning and Sheard, *Barbarians*, 52.

104. Dunning and Sheard, *Barbarians*, 52.

105. Richards, *Hooligans*, 26.

on, though, as with baseball's Doubleday myth, its legendary character is now widely recognized.

These two myths are perhaps extreme examples of the way in which the values associated with a sport come to be enshrined in narratives about that sport's beginnings. In other sports generalized patterns of behavior or particular incidents take on mythical status—the "giant-killing" acts of the English FA Cup, the bodyline bowling of 1930s cricket, the exploits of a great racehorse, the patter of Mohammed Ali: each narrative in different ways tells us something about the way that sport is understood by its adherents.

The doctrinal dimension at first may seem even more unlikely than the mythological one, but here too it is possible to detect elements in sport that could be said to have this character. Of course, doctrine itself is not an entirely uncontroversial matter—its nature, purpose, and form are widely debated. However, we will understand it for now, rather simplistically perhaps, as a statement or series of statements of things that are believed, when those things attempt to provide both a statement about reality which can invite assent (and sometimes, belonging or participation) and a conceptual framework or rationale for certain practices. It may not easily be possible to demonstrate a doctrinal element to all sports, but I believe that it will be possible for some.

We had cause to reflect on the origins of the modern Olympic movement in chapter 1, and it will be worthwhile at this point to consider the Olympic Charter. This document has gone through a number of iterations, with the most recent agreed in September 2013.[106] Before many pages of regulations governing the organization of the Olympic Games, the charter begins by stating the "Fundamental Principles of Olympism."[107] Subsequently it affirms that "The goal of the Olympic Movement is to contribute to building a peaceful and better world by educating youth through sport practiced in accordance with Olympism and its values."[108] The Fundamental Principles begin with a statement defining Olympism as "a philosophy of life, exalting and combining in a balanced whole the qualities of body, will and mind," before going on to speak of its goal as a "way of life based on the joy of effort, the educational value of good

106. IOC, "Olympic Charter."
107. IOC, "Olympic Charter," 11.
108. IOC, "Olympic Charter," 15.

example and respect for universal fundamental ethical principles."[109] Olympism is said to have a global reach, and the Olympic Movement to be a "universal and permanent action"—if this is not doctrine, it is something very close to it. Some of the beliefs that inhere in the charter may be implicit rather than explicit, but the basic tenets of a "philosophy of life" are also spelled out.

While the charter belongs to the Olympic Movement, it would also be fair and realistic to observe that the development of Olympism in the late nineteenth century shared a common ethos with other sports developing at the same time, most obviously those that strove to keep an amateur ethos. Dunning and Sheard, in their study of rugby union, note the way in which sports incubated in public schools by social elites in this period take on a "highly specific, elaborate and articulate ideology,"[110] and that the amateur ideology has three clear parts. The first is the pursuit of an activity for its own sake, resulting in playing down both competition and training. The Olympic Movement was beginning to move beyond this, aided by its reference back to the ancient games, where competition was highly prized. The second element in the emerging amateur ideology was self-restraint both during and after games—this meant keeping rivalry "gentlemanly," winning graciously, and "losing well"—still enshrined in the inscription from Kipling's poem above the players' entrance to the Centre Court at Wimbledon, "if you can meet with Triumph and Disaster and treat those two impostors just the same . . ."[111] The third element is a spirit of "fair play" which includes complying voluntarily with rules and codes. We see the residue of this when football crowds complain about players diving in order to gain a free kick, and in both rugby codes' on-field high regard for referees. But when this emerging amateur ethos was harnessed by Muscular Christianity, as we saw earlier, and had added to it certain beliefs about the benefits of sport (an *improving* activity) a sports ideology that sees it as expressing and promoting positive values takes shape. This ideology still supports many schemes where sport is used to enhance communities, or empower individuals, for instance.

We might find another example of this doctrinal element, though perhaps a little more obliquely, if we consider the Victorian poem "Vitai Lampada." Here one might discern a kind of proto-spirituality which

109. IOC, "Olympic Charter," 11.
110. Dunning and Sheard, *Barbarians*, 131.
111. Kipling, "If."

shows that sport has begun to generate, or expresses, a whole way of looking at life and the world. It was written after the heroic performance of the heavily outnumbered British army at Abu Klea in 1885 on their way to an unsuccessful attempt to reinforce Khartoum. The second stanza makes explicit reference to details of the battle. The refrain "Play up! Play up! And play the game!" connects the qualities and character of cricket at Clifton College where the poet Henry Newbolt was educated with the qualities necessary to win a war. But the poem also shows us how playing a sport can shape the way that life in general is viewed.[112] Sport may be being used here as the vehicle for ideology imported from elsewhere, but the metaphors of sport may also be said to come to exercise a shaping influence on that ideology. This seems, in short, to be rather more than an opportunistic use of sporting imagery; sport is becoming a way of looking at the world and what it "means to be a man" (quite deliberately using exclusive language here) in it.[113]

Much of what might be said about an ethical dimension now follows on naturally. The Olympic Charter includes clear statements of an ethical type. The fourth fundamental principle, for instance, states that "the practice of sport is a human right. Every individual must have the possibility of practicing sport, without discrimination of any kind and in the Olympic spirit, which requires mutual understanding with a spirit of friendship, solidarity and fair play." This carries implicit beliefs about humanity and sport, but it is expressed in highly moral language of rights and justice. Likewise, FIFA can say that "Fair play is a fundamental part of the game of football. It represents the positive benefits of playing by the rules, using common sense and respecting fellow players, referees, opponents and fans."[114] The Fair Play Code[115] has ten basic moral injunctions for all associated with football. With varying success FIFA seeks to enshrine the practice of fair play through such campaigns, with attendant codes and awards. Little League Baseball launched an "I won't Cheat" program in 2008 with similar aims,[116] and some local junior associations

112. Sir Henry Newbolt (1862–1938), "Vitai Lampada" (often translated as "They Pass on the Torch of Life").

113. For a longer reflection on the cricketing imagery of this poem and its ideological significance, see Ellis, "Play up!," 252–55.

114. FIFA, "My Game is Fair Play."

115. FIFA, "Fair Play Code."

116. See Little League, "I won't cheat."

have fair play codes for players, parents, and coaches.[117] Such campaigns gain legitimation by appearing to be self-evidently sensible and right, and being rooted in some indefinable part of the game's core historic ethos. However much ignored in practice, every modern sport would claim to have a code of ethics—often expressed in term of "fair play"—as an unwritten (and sometimes, as we have seen, a written) rule.

Part of my definition of modern sport relates to the way in which primitive games have been bureaucratized and organized—and here we move towards the social dimension of sport. The transnational organization of international soccer, the Little League Baseball association, the high school basketball team, and the village cricket team, are all in different ways manifestations of the social organization that makes modern sports possible. Without some kind of overarching organization there might be no agreement on rules, and therefore no matches. These various social entities also embody the values of the sports in which they participate: the commitment to fair play and the belief in the social good produced by baseball, cricket, hockey, and even boxing,[118] are often consciously articulated in the clubhouse and changing room, and frequently used as means to attract younger players. The key point here is that the social organization is the bearer of meaning, purpose, and value.

This brings us to Smart's final dimension—the experiential. Smart observes that this dimension includes a very diverse range of (sometimes apparently contradictory) reported experience, and the nature of religious experience is, of course, controversial.[119] In particular scholars may differ on what (or who) is being experienced. What is religious experience an experience of? Members of the major world religions would not necessarily answer it in similar ways, and it might seem that here sport fails to have any kind of religious aspect to it. Would it not require at least the possibility that players and perhaps spectators could and do experience a transcendent or mysterious "other" in their sport? These are questions to which we will return at some length in subsequent chapters. But for now we might suggest that an experiential dimension in sport *of a similar kind* might include elements such as awe and wonder, communion,

117. The South Jasper Place Minor Baseball Association in Edmonton, Alberta, is an example: "Fair Play Codes."

118. From a glance at the home page of a typical local boxing club, the St Pancras Amateur Boxing Club.

119. We return to the nature of religious experience in chapter 5.

commitment, or a feeling of ultimate concern (Tillich).[120] While it may be difficult to think of moments that may count as originating experiences (the sporting burning bush, as it were), it is possible to see how a tradition of spectating and playing shapes the experience of those who come after, and we ought also to factor in the way that the media has shaped this tradition of experience from the earliest days of print journalism.

Allen Guttmann suggests that sports arouse in us similar emotions to those evoked by Bach or Matisse. For some people sport is as close as they get to any aestheticism. He goes on: "the line between sport and art wavers uncertainly. The line between sport and religion is equally hard to draw." In fact, according to Guttmann, "many sports spectators experience something akin to worship."[121] It is true that this sporting "worship" sometimes expresses itself in a rather shallow-sounding hero-type worship, but it can also be less personal: one needed only to be a golf fan and not a Ballesteros fan to gasp in awe when Seve Ballesteros hit what is sometimes spoken of as the greatest golf shot ever on the eighteenth hole of the 1993 Swiss Open. Many players and supporters can wax eloquently on the aesthetic qualities of sport[122] and supporters can also feel a sense of communion with players, one another, their club or team. To those uninterested in sport this may seem unlikely or bizarre, but it is an accurate representation of the experience of the devoted (a religious word consistently used regarding sports fandom) following the Seahawks, the Red Sox, or Liverpool FC.[123] In some sports—notably but not only soccer—this identification and bond between supporters and their team sometimes appears to take on pathological dimensions when violence erupts in or around the stadium.

While religious experience sometimes takes adherents by surprise, so to speak, it is often associated with a commitment and intentionality: the act of seeking experience in worship, or personal devotion. Sports

120. I am aware that this list may appear arbitrary and that it is not without problems; however, for the purpose of this discussion I consider it legitimate and will return to some of these later.

121. Guttmann, *Spectators*, 177.

122. For such reports and further reflection upon them see Ellis, "Meanings," 182–83.

123. The relationship of one fan to his football team is described in overtly religious terms in Edge, *Faith*. The book's chapter headings are revealing: Baptism, Indoctrination, Confirmation, Communion, Confession, Penance. The book's subtitle is *Football as a Religion*.

fans often do not lack for commitment, and the set routines sometimes reported by spectators before a game suggest an intentional seeking after the experiences available.

Conclusion

In this discussion of the quasi-religious experiential aspects of sport I have sometimes had the players in focus, and sometimes the spectators. There is a difference here that needs to be borne in mind. However, there is evidence that players and spectators report similar and overlapping experiences that could be interpreted in the light of Smart's dimensions, as the empirical research I carried out in the summer of 2011 consistently demonstrates. No wonder Hoffman can remark that "sports are inherently evangelical; they compete for our religious sensibilities . . ."[124]

Bruce's critique of over-wide definitions of religion that end up evacuating it of meaning and utility rings in our ears, but nevertheless there does seem to be enough affinity between religion, generally understood, and the experience of sport to allow meaningful discussion. I am not suggesting that sport is, has been, or will become a religion. My argument is more modest: that sport may have, for some people, taken on some of the characteristics of religion, and that it may exercise functions in their individual, social, and cultural lives similar to the functions that were once exercised by organized religion. For some that organized religion still does exercise these functions, conceivably alongside sporting affiliations.

That these religious functions of sport are not a figment of an over-active imagination is borne out, I believe, though admittedly not in any final or definitive way, by the empirical research to which I have already referred. Players and spectators report attitudes and experiences that sound suspiciously religious, and the prominence given to sport in the lives even of very amateur sportsmen and-women suggests something more than a mere "hobby." What is now required, after the extensive preparatory work of the first three chapters, is some more explicitly theological thinking on the subject. To this task we now turn.

124. Hoffman, *Good Game*, 273.

4

Play and Sport

Initial Theological Explorations

A s I sit at my desk writing this chapter I am interrupted several
times. Poppy, the family spaniel, is trying to put her toy into my
lap. She wants me to play with her; precisely, she wants me to try and
take the toy off her. As soon as I show interest she will withdraw it, give a
snarl that might be found off-putting by those who neither know her nor
notice the wagging tail. After several such attempts I finally give in and
battle for the toy (on this occasion it is a squeaking rubber chicken, but
it might be a tennis ball or a rubber Santa). Several minutes later one of
us will give up (often it is me); she will go back to her slumbers and I will
return to my writing. Humans are not alone in enjoyment of play.

Poppy is an adult dog but she has not stopped wanting to play. When
she was a puppy, she wanted to play more often and more recklessly and
she could and did draw blood in her more boisterous moments. Teeth
and claws tested the limits of acceptability, learnt their own strength.
For a puppy play is part of the socialization process. Puppy care books
emphasize its developmental importance. For human children too play
is an important part of growing up. It exercises the imagination and
helps teach cooperation, coordination, and numerous other skills. The
expression "child's play" suggests that playing has often been thought of
as something that children (or perhaps puppies) need and do, but with
the often unspoken expectation that such childish things pass with the

passage to adulthood. Not for Poppy; not for most of us either, though the forms that play takes for us may be infinitely variable. I play board games at Christmas time, golf a few times each summer. I also play when I sing in a local choir or spend an afternoon with my photographic equipment. I am playing in a slightly different way when I watch rugby matches in the stadium or from my sofa, and also when I sit back with a glass of wine and a CD, or attend a concert. I play actively and passively, though sports spectating (as we shall see) is not really a passive pastime.

In this chapter we will begin to shape a theology of sport, but we must begin by thinking theologically about play. While we should resist the temptation to conflate sport and play this is a necessary first step, for sport is (whatever else it is) also play. Play, we might say, is a necessary but not sufficient requirement for sport. Too often those seeking to theologize about sport have stopped at this point, so in the next chapters we will focus much more on the second stage, on sport. In order for us to think theologically about play and sport we will also have to spend a few moments carefully defining and distinguishing them (a task that some readers might feel is overdue) and this is where the current chapter will begin.

There is another reason why we must begin our theology of sport with a theology of play. When we look first to Scripture on the subject of sport the natural reflex is to examine the apostle Paul's use of athletic imagery. While we shall see that this is not without some reward, it will also be seen that such a strategy provides too precarious a theological basis for a theology of sport. We shall therefore, having first defined play and sport, consider Paul's sporting metaphors before taking the broader view of play from a scriptural perspective that is necessary for our task. Keeping play and sport entirely separate in this discussion is neither possible nor necessary, but as the chapter proceeds we will find that more and more we talk about sport rather than play, and this will lead us into the more focused treatments of sport *per se* that will follow in chapters 5 and 6.

Biblical perspectives will thus have a central place in this chapter. Johan Huizinga believed that play lies at the heart of all human culture. With such an assertion in mind we will look to the Christian Scriptures to see whether this central place can be glimpsed there. Hoffman suggests that two overarching myths are required to give a sound theological account of sport—one is the notion of God as player; the other is the myth of eternity, where the play of sport is interpreted as a kind of anticipation of a paradisiacal end-time.[1] Both of these "myths" will be considered but as helpful as these suggestions are they both rely very heavily on play as the core of sport: they will only take us so far. We will want to explore other theological themes as we begin to ask: theologically, what is the point of sport?

Defining "Play" and "Sport"

Huizinga, in his celebrated study, argued that play is both more fundamental and more ubiquitous than the view which isolates it in childhood. He submits that "culture arises in the form of play . . . [culture] is played from the very beginning,"[2] and through playing a culture expresses its interpretation of life and the world. Such a statement may seem strange at first to those who immediately think of their next set of tennis, a family ping-pong competition or, indeed, the children's game of make-believe in the school playground. But it does not seem so strange when we recall the Meso-American ball game and other so-called "primitive" games. Huizinga proposes that the "play-factor" has produced the most basic cultural forms: ritual, poetry, music, dance, warfare, and even philosophy. Civilization, he argues, "does not come *from* play like a babe detaching itself from the womb: it arises *in* and *as* play, and never leaves it."[3]

Huizinga does not offer a definition of play as such, though he does identify some core characteristics of play: it is voluntary; it is separated from ordinary or "real" life; it is played out within certain agreed limits (it has its own rules), and is passed on as a "game" in this form; play creates its own sense of order; and play promotes the formation of social groups.[4] He also recoils from the notion that play can be explained in terms of its biological, social, psychological, or developmental functions. This is because Huizinga, like many who reflect upon play, wants to insist that play is an end in itself: that it is autotelic. Only this, he insists, can explain the intensity and absorption of play, the "power of maddening" that it possesses for us, the sheer fun of it that resists all analysis.[5]

1. Hoffman, *Good Game*, 280–81.
2. Huizinga, *Homo Ludens*, 46.
3. Huizinga, *Homo Ludens*, 173, italics his.
4. Huizinga, *Homo Ludens*, 7–13.
5. Huizinga, *Homo Ludens*, 2–3.

But a definition of play may prove useful to us, and will in turn allow us to elaborate on the very general definition of sport we gave early in chapter 1. Robert Johnston proposes a definition that has a clear debt to Huizinga, is lengthy, and also anticipates the theological use to which he will want to put it—as such it seems a little loaded. Thus he suggests that play is free and spontaneous, has its own order, is social, is separated from ordinary experience, and in its own time. The social nature of play is expressed in Buber-esque terms as creating I–Thou as opposed to I–It relationships.[6] While Johnston is willing to concede that sport has effects, like Huizinga he is clear that these must be considered accidental to play as such which "must be entered into without outside purpose . . . [and] is an end in itself." One of the effects of play, as well as any joy or release, is that the player reenters ordinary experience in a "new spirit of thanksgiving and celebration."[7] While this might be so of our best experiences of play it seems debatable and idealized to require it of all play experiences. Also, games that we may play on our own (solitaire, golf, climbing) would need further discussion as "social" in nature.

The philosopher Bernard Suits offers a tighter definition: "To play a game is to attempt to achieve a specific state of affairs (prelusory goal), using only means permitted by rules (lusory means), where the rules prohibit use of more efficient in favor of less efficient means (constitutive rules), and where the rules are accepted just because they make possible such activity (lusory attitude)."[8] This definition separates what he calls the *prelusory goal* (reaching the finish line, or hitting a ball into a cup) and the *lusory attitude* (in which we agree to place "unnecessary obstacles" in the way of achieving our goal; the *means* (running, or hitting with a club); the *constitutive rules* (no tripping your opponent and stay in your lane, or no moving your ball by hand or kicking your opponent's ball into the rough); and the *rules of skill* (lean into the finishing tape, or keep your eye on the ball and your head down while swinging). The lusory attitude is contrasted with that of a "spoilsport" (literally) who refuses to accept the rules and goals of play and keeps breaking the illusion of the game. (Our word "illusion" derives from the Latin *ludo*, I play. Literally it would mean "against play.") This acceptance of limitations in play allows Suits to offer what he calls a simpler and "more portable" version of his defini-

6. Johnston, *Play*, 34.
7. Johnston, *Play*, 34.
8. Suits, *Grasshopper*, 54–55.

tion: "playing a game is the voluntary attempt to overcome unnecessary obstacles."[9] We should notice that this definition seeks to explain playing a game as opposed to play more generally, and for this Huizinga's more general description of the characteristics of play may still serve us very well.

The beauty of Suits' definition is, as he demonstrates, that it works for tennis and snakes and ladders, for baseball and doctors and nurses. Sports are certainly a kind of game in which participants voluntarily accept limitations on their activity. The quickest and most sensible way to get a ball into a small cup is usually to place it there by hand having walked a few hundred yards with it safely tucked in one's pocket. But golfers accept that they are not allowed to do this. They must strike the ball with something part stick and part bat, and avoid various hazards laid out deliberately to entrap them on the path between the tee and the hole. No wonder the cynic says that golf is a good way to spoil a pleasant walk. Similarly, football players could probably find more efficient ways of crossing the line for a touchdown (driving in an armored vehicle, for instance), and ice hockey players could think of more direct ways to place the puck in the net. But even these games, which sometimes appear to casual observers to be relatively free of rules, are hemmed around with them. Players voluntarily accept limitations on their actions (they adopt a lusory attitude) in order to achieve their goal.

But while Suits' definition covers forms of play as well as sports, it does not exhaust sport. If it did then snakes and ladders, and indeed doctors and nurses would count as sports, when our intuition tells us that they are not. What additional features might we want to add to differentiate sport from play? I suggest that we need at least four, though we should perhaps add that a truly comprehensive and uncontroversial definition is probably impossible—there will always be arguments about certain activities and whether they should or should not be considered sports or just "games."

First, as already suggested in chapter 1, modern sport is a form of bureaucratized play. It is, the reader may recall, what distinguishes a kick-around on the beach with local rules from the game in the stadium with universalized rules. The bureaucratization of sport also results in regional, national, and international associations that regulate its play and its players. It is true that snakes and ladders also has universalized

9. Suits, *Grasshopper*, 55.

rules, but doctors and nurses does not: neither, so far as I am aware, has an international regulating body. (Dope tests by international agreement are not yet in force for snakes and ladders.)

Second, sport is distinguished from play by what we might call the element of *agon*. This Greek word meaning "contest" (or the meeting at which the contest takes place) gave us the English word "agony," a word suggesting the element of struggle and physical or psychological pain that attends such contests.[10] Snakes and ladders is a contest of sorts, but it is perhaps questionable whether it has the intensity to be called an *agon*. As Roger Callois has suggested,[11] games fall into one of four categories: games of chance (snakes and ladders, perhaps, and roulette); games of make-believe (doctors and nurses); games that stimulate exhilaration, disorientation, and even vertigo (climbing and skiing); and contests that require speed, endurance, and physical and mental skill. Some games in the third of these categories (which Callois labels *illinx*,[12] from the Greek for whirlpool), often feature in debates about the definition of sport with climbing one of those borderline cases. Competitive skiing is clearly a sport, but what of non-competitive skiing? However, those games that Callois identifies as *agon*[13] are certainly sports.

With this in mind, in case one comes across a particularly dedicated player of the board game, we will want to add third and fourth distinguishing elements: third, sport is an embodied contest of physical and mental exertion. If we are were to define such terms in a very broad way, the board and pieces of snakes and ladders and the physical activity required in shaking a pair of dice might appear to qualify the game as a sport once more. But snakes and ladders can only be called physical or embodied in an attenuated way. Even snooker or darts is more embodied, involves more embodied movement with hand–eye coordination, for instance, and certainly requires more mental exertion; football, rowing, running, and golf are much more embodied still, and have greater degrees of physical and mental exertion. Harvey Cox calls ritual "embodied fantasy,"[14] and I believe that we need to regard sport as an "embodied contest."

10. See the discussion at Huizinga, *Homo Ludens*, 48–53.
11. Callois, *Man, Play and Games*, 11–36.
12. Callois, *Man, Play and Games*, 23–26.
13. Callois, *Man, Play and Games*, 14–23.
14. "Our body places us. It came from our parents and through it we touch, punch,

Fourth and finally, sports are marked by a significant element of skill that can be refined by practice. Here, I think, snakes and ladders is in no danger of encroaching. Sport gathers up elements of the definition of play and adds to it that it is a bureaucratized embodied contest involving mental and physical exertion and with a significant element of refinable skill.

These four features distinguish sport from play in general ways, though the perspectives we examined in chapter 2 also add further characteristics that are peculiar to sport (or apply to it in peculiar ways) as opposed to play, such as particular socioeconomic relationships with the spheres of commerce, the media, consumerism; all these leave a particular print on modern sport.

If play, an essential component of sport, is so fundamental to all culture we might expect to find some evidence of it in the Christian Scriptures. According to Robert Johnston, "the evidence for 'play' in the Bible is extensive. Yet we have for the most part failed to recognise it or act upon it because our work-dominated culture has biased our interpretation."[15] We will now consider the passages in Paul's letters that are often taken to offer support for a positive evaluation of sport, and even to give themes that may inform such a theology. After this exercise we will turn to the Bible's creation narrative, to the notion of God as Creator and humankind as made in the image of God, consider some important texts particularly from within the Old Testament's wisdom tradition, and take note of the cycle of resting from work and celebration in ancient Israel before considering some further theological themes.

Sport in the Bible? Paul's Sporting Imagery

It is not quite true to say that there is no sport in the Christian Bible, but direct references are concentrated in the New Testament epistles.[16] Many readers will be familiar with a range of weak jokes that suggest that sport can be found in all sorts of places,[17] but the few true references have fre-

caress, and pass life on to the future." Cox, *Feast*, 73.

15. Johnston, *Play*, 123. In the section which follows I make extensive use of Johnston's work, though not following its pattern, or, always, his substance or conclusions.

16. Acts 20:24 is one of those found outside the epistles.

17. Stuart Weir gives a list of some of these circulating in the UK: the cricketer's joke, "Peter stood up with the eleven and was bold" (Acts 2:14) is one of the well-known ones he lists—and, I should add, lists in order to indicate that they should not

quently been assumed to give an implicit approval to the sports to which they refer. Special editions of modern translations have been produced that offer a sports reading of biblical themes and particular passages,[18] and many popular books and websites often also use passages such as Old Testament battle texts that speak of tactics or victory to make sporting points. Opinions will differ as to whether such methods amount to contextual Bible reading or crude eisegesis. But while they are relatively few and somewhat repetitious in content, a full list of the explicit references looks impressive enough with clear examples in 1 Corinthians, Galatians, Philippians, 1 and 2 Timothy, and Hebrews. It is not possible to examine all these texts in detail, but we will consider briefly one of the most significant ones as an exemplar, the imagery of the athlete and the boxer in 1 Corinthians 9:24–27. This is not only to gain a more secure theological handhold on sport from the Bible but also because prevailing or popular wisdom regarding Paul's attitudes to ancient sports has been called into doubt following an influential monograph by Victor Pfitzner.[19] Pfitzner's argument proposed two main objections to the way in which the texts in Paul's letters had tended to be read, one relating to the use for which they were deployed, the other relating to what was subsequently deduced from this use regarding Paul's own experience of and attitude to sports.[20]

The first objection need not detain us too long. Pfitzner argued, from a detailed analysis of the Pauline texts and their contexts, that Paul's words about "running the race," about the disciplined preparation of the athlete, and "winning the prize," and so on, should not be taken to refer to the Christian life in general but to context-specific aspects of Christian

---

be taken seriously. *What the Book*, 15. For American readers we might add: who are the Bible's two most famous baseball players? Rebekah, who went to the well with a pitcher, and the Prodigal Son who eventually made a home run. Enough said.

18. For instance: *Sports Good News Bible*, and *The Sports Bible*. Slightly different, with an emphasis on graphics rather than additional text, is *The Skateboard Bible*.

19. Pfitzner, *Agon*. For a briefer and more descriptive discussion of the subject see Williams, *Paul's Metaphors*, 257–92.

20. Pfitzner scopes the athletics metaphor passages in Paul as follows: Rom 9:16; 1 Cor 9:24–27; Gal 2:2; 5:7; Phil 2:16; 3:12–14. Other passages which he says may also contain the imagery are: Rom 15:30; Phil 1:27–30; 4:1,3,12–13; 1 Thess 2:2,19; and possibly also 1 Cor 4:9; Col 3:15. In addition there are a number of Pastoral texts including 1 Tim 4:7–10. While he does not regard the military metaphor of Eph 6:10–17 as likely to be Pauline, he says that there seems sufficient Pauline material in the Pastorals for him to warrant their inclusion. He also suggests that Acts 20:24 could recall Paul's actual words. Pfitzner, *Agon*, 76ff.

discipleship and mission.[21] In 1 Corinthians 9:24–27, for instance, it refers to Paul's self-discipline in denying himself certain practices and privileges so as not to offend the consciences of fellow Christians. One of the reasons this matters, apart from the desirability of accuracy, is that the more general reading of such texts tends to stress effort in Christian living and begins to sound rather works- rather than faith-oriented.[22] It is worth noting that a theology of sport needs to steer a careful path on this issue: achievement in sport is not a 'work' that might be thought to gain divine favor, however significant and valuable we might feel that this achievement is. Indeed, such an observation might immediately distance a Christian theology of sport from the pagan attitudes to sport in which winning was often seen precisely as a sign of divine favor. Pfitzner's reading of the use of these athletic metaphors finds wide acceptance among recent commentators.[23] Hays, for instance, speaks of the purpose of Paul's self-control as being for the sake of others and clearly relates the use of this image to a particular point Paul is making rather than suggesting it relates to the "struggle" of the Christian life in general.[24]

It is the second of Pfitzner's points that is of more interest. It has been a commonplace among those arguing for a positive (re-)evaluation of sport by the church to suggest that Paul's use of sporting metaphors indicates a familiarity with sports (in particular, with the ancient Greek Games), and therefore (as he is using them for illustrative purposes without comment) approval of them. But Pfitzner argued that the Pauline passages in which these metaphors are deployed need to be understood against the background of the rhetorical conventions of the time. In Paul's day the image had been widely appropriated by moralists such as Marcus Aurelius and Seneca.[25] Raymond Collins notes that the image of the athlete is in fact one of the oldest in Hellenistic literature and is widely used in Homeric, Stoic, and Cynic writings often to denote the struggle for truth and virtue, suggesting "a public contest in which the

21. Pfitzner, *Agon*, 87.

22. Pfitzner trails this case at *Agon*, 7.

23. Of two commentators working more or less contemporaneously with Pfitzner, Barrett's runs with a more general interpretation of the sporting imagery of the passage, while Bruce's brief comments suggest that Pfitzner's point has been taken. Barrett, *First Epistle*, 217; Bruce, *I & II Corinthians*, 89.

24. Hays, *First Corinthians*, 156.

25. See Johnson, *Timothy*, 431.

competitors vie for the attention and allegiance of the spectators in order to win them over to the truth."[26]

In 1 Corinthians 9:24–27 Collins identifies no fewer than ten separate items of sports-specific vocabulary many of which do not appear elsewhere in the New Testament.[27] This may appear to support the view that Paul is here drawing on a tradition of rhetoric with a specialized vocabulary rather than using his own vernacular. Certainly, biblical scholars are often put on the alert when "odd" vocabulary appears that does not seem to be the standard vocabulary to be expected of a given writer or situation,[28] The word Paul uses for "athlete" in 1 Corinthians 9:25 is not used by Paul elsewhere, though the word translated "runner" in verse 24 *is*. Paul does use the language of wrestling in other places (2 Tim 2:5, for example[29]) but only in 1 Corinthians 9:26f. deploys the image of the boxer. Could it be, therefore, that Paul is drawing upon language with which he is familiar through traditions of rhetoric but which does not reflect his regular and familiar speech or experience?

The alternative possibility, that some readers will find attractive in its simplicity, is that these words (though there are a lot of them here) are just particular specific instances of what Paul does elsewhere—plunder the games for illustrative material. The particular context of the letter may not be insignificant. Most commentators point out that "Paul's use of this imagery is inspired by the Isthmian Games, the great athletic festival held at Corinth every two years: the Corinthians would find Paul's

26. Collins, *First Corinthians*, 357.

27. In NRSV translation they are: "prize," "athlete," "exercise self-control," "wreath," "not aimlessly," "box," "beating the air," "punish" (Collins: "bruise"), "enslave" (Collins: "subjugate"), "disqualified." Collins, *First Corinthians*, 358.

28. University teachers today are often alerted to plagiarism in student work in much the same way.

29. The authorship of the Pastoral Epistles is still a matter of debate. Many scholars believe that a "Pauline school" lies behind the letters, i.e. a group writing pseudonymously after Paul's death (see Johnson, *Writings*, 381), though a claim for the likely authenticity of 2 Timothy is often convincingly made. Nevertheless, "in the final analysis," says Johnson, "it is difficult to make any assured claims about either the authenticity or the inauthenticity of the Pastorals as a whole or as individual letters" (*Writings*, 382). While the question of authorship may make this discussion of athletic imagery more complex it does not much affect the substantial question of how these images are used, especially if it is still maintained that the author(s) was a follower of Paul—though that does not mean that the same vocabulary might not be deployed in subtly different ways by the "school." For a comment on Pfitzner's position on this see note 20 above.

depictions of the runner and the boxer familiar, vivid, and compelling."[30] It could be argued that while Paul may not use this vocabulary frequently on this particular occasion it seemed especially appropriate. That these games were very much in his mind appears the more probable when one considers that the winners' prize at the Isthmian Games included a wreath made of withered celery[31]—a "perishable wreath" (v. 25) indeed, and one that has perished even before it is awarded.

Why might this distinction between the two ways of understanding Paul's use of athletic imagery be an important one? Pfitzner's case is that Paul's language does not in any way indicate familiarity with or approval of the games. He is merely drawing upon this rhetorical tradition, using language customarily pressed into service for moral argument, but language that has largely been evacuated of its original, vivid color. We might say that Paul is speaking of athletics in the same way as a contemporary of ours might say that someone "steps up to the plate" or that some situation is "a game of two halves." Someone who speaks in this way might have no knowledge of baseball and no opinion about football, but these phrases are current in everyday speech and might still be used. This is the crux of Pfitzner's argument, and if we accept it as correct we would be forced to concede that we can gain not the slightest assistance from Paul in terms of a positive approach to sports. Says Pfitzner: "With regard to the metaphorical strength of the terms concerned . . . In every instance the presence of a *conscious reference to a specific athletic image* must be regarded as *unlikely*, and a warning must be issued against the . . . error of over-interpretation . . . To what extent Paul's readers perceived an image behind his words cannot be conclusively determined by our own non-Greek ears."[32] A typical example of the case he makes can be seen by his discussion of another sporting image, that of the umpire prize giver in Colossians 2:18 and Philippians 3:14. He observes: "past philological studies have confirmed the view that the verbs have here lost their original point of reference to the game . . . there is a wealth of evidence to show that the verb was mostly used in the more general applied sense to rule, control, judge or arbitrate, and it is with this meaning that it appears in Col 3:15."[33]

30. Hays, *First Corinthians*, 155.

31. Murphy-O'Connor, *Corinth*, 15. The prize at Nemea was a wreath of celery, at Corinth a wreath of *withered* celery.

32. Pfitzner, *Agon*, 127; italics his.

33. Pfitzner, *Agon*, 155.

In fact Pfitzner goes even further than this, arguing that it is most likely that Paul would have strongly *disapproved* of the games that are referred to in such metaphors. This argument is more speculative, and is based on what Pfitzner judges to have been a typical Jewish response to Greco-Roman sports. Those interpretations which speak of Paul's feeling for the glories of the games and on his familiarity with their conduct, he says, "paint not only an idealised picture of Paul as a thorough-going hellenist, but also of the games of his time . . . In actual fact Pauline metaphors from the sphere of the games are so general in their lack of concrete details that it is not hard to imagine that any hellenistic Jew could either have written or understood them without himself having gained a first hand knowledge of the games from a bench in the stadium."[34] Pfitzner points to the considerable interaction that Paul would have had with Palestinian Jews in his Pharisaic training and after his conversion with Jewish Christians from Palestine. Palestinian Jews would have been opposed to the games with a particular vehemence. They were despised because they were seen as part of a deliberate process of Hellenization by successive authorities. Opposition would have had a number of motives: the nakedness of the contestants would have been seen as problematic; the dedication of the games to Caesar would have been alarming; the Roman gladiatorial contests were cruel and bloody; and the trophies sometimes gave offence because they were mistaken for images.[35] Yet such games, as well as other "foreign institutions," simply multiplied even in Palestine. "Considering the deep lying abhorrence of Palestinian Judaism for Greek athletics and gymnastics as typical phenomena of heathendom, one must question Paul's so-called love for, and familiarity with Greek sports!"[36] Pfitzner concludes that Paul's use of the imagery owes much less to personal experience and much more to a popular metaphorical use of the imagery especially in Stoic philosophy but in Greek rhetorical traditions generally.

Such a position would come as a hard blow to many popular theologies of sport currently in circulation. As Hoffman says, "the evangelical athletic community has been especially attracted to Paul's heavy reliance on athletic metaphors, viewing them not only as an apostolic blessing on the sports and games of his day, but as justification for their involvement

---

34. Pfitzner, *Agon*, 187.

35. Pfitzner, *Agon*, 74.

36. Pfitzner, *Agon*, 188.

in popular sports today."[37] Hoffman accepts Pfitzner's argument conceding that while Paul may have "played sports informally in his youth" it was "conceivable, but highly improbable that he maintained an interest in some of the public games during his ministry."[38] The bloodiness of the gladiatorial encounters and the pagan associations with the games are given as the reasons for this improbability, and Hoffman believes that 1 Corinthians 10:7, Galatians 5:19 and 1 Peter 4:3 may not be simply general condemnations of vice but have had the games particularly in mind.[39]

Against this last point, the "play" of 1 Corinthians 10:7 is a midrash on Exodus 32:6, and refers to the dancing and revelry around the golden calf rather than any athletic event,[40] and the other two references appear very general. On the question of Paul's familiarity with the games generally, and approval or disapproval of them, there is actually much less agreement with Pfitzner among commentators. Indeed, it seems striking that 1 Corinthians 9:24–27, one of the most developed instances of such athletic imagery, should be addressed to Christians in a city known for its tradition of games. Commentators note this conjunction without fail. It is true, as indicated in chapter 1, that every Greek city of note would have had some sort of games at some point in their history, but Corinth's Isthmian Games were particularly significant in the sporting calendar being held every two years and taking a particular place within the "Olympic cycle." Beginning in 582 BCE,[41] it is possible that they continued until finally suppressed by Emperor Theodosius (who is also thought to have put paid to the Olympic Games) in the late fourth century CE.[42] Commenting on 1 Corinthians 9:24–27 Collins makes so bold as to claim that "Paul demonstrates a fair amount of awareness of athleticism. He mentions two athletic contests, running and boxing. He notes the importance

37. Hoffman, *Good Game*, 41. He goes on: "It is not uncommon, for example, to see Christian athletes sporting T-shirts emblazoned with athletic imagery from Philippians 3:14 ('I pressed toward the mark for a high calling of God in Jesus Christ') or 2 Timothy 4:7 ('I have fought a good fight, I have finished my course, I have kept the faith')."

38. Hoffman, *Good Game*, 44.

39. Hoffman, *Good Game*, 44–45.

40. Hays, *First Corinthians*, 163.

41. Golden, *Ancient Greece*, 10.

42. The ostensible reason for this suppression was that the games were pagan rituals, though evidence is sketchy and, as mentioned in chapter 1, it is possible that the general disintegration of the empire, together with the economic problems which this would have brought, is at least as much to blame.

of training so as to be able to win. He is aware of the possibilities of failing to qualify and being disqualified (cf. 2 Tim 2:5). He knows full well that there is only one winner in a race (Phil 3:14; cf. 2 Tim 2:5) and that it is really necessary to press forward in order to win (Phil 3:14). He knows about the prizes (*brabeios*) and the crown (*stephanos*) of victory."[43]

Murphy-O'Connor suggests that Paul may well have been in Corinth during the games in April or May of 49 CE or 51 CE, and also notes that the many visitors to the games in Corinth were accommodated in tents in the city.[44] Corinth would, therefore, have been a profitable base for someone like Paul who made a living as a tentmaker.[45] Acts 18:3 records Paul's trade in the context of his stay in Corinth. Murphy-O'Connor also remarks that, while Palestinian Jews were certainly hostile to the games, those of the Diaspora (especially more Hellenized Jews) were less predictably so, and were often actually quite favorably inclined. Philo, a significant Hellenistic Jewish philosopher based in Alexandria, and more or less a contemporary of Paul, attended wrestling contests. In Miletus, due west across the Aegean from Corinth near modern Izmir, local Jews had specially reserved seats for the games.[46]

These observations make the case for Pauline abhorrence, for merely formal use of such imagery, for a lack of interest and familiarity, much more difficult to maintain. In directing our attention to Greek rhetorical traditions, Pfitzner appears to have gone beyond the evidence in claiming such negativity for Paul. It seems possible to make a case that is at least as strong and plausible for Pauline acceptance and even qualified approval and interest.

Hoffman does succeed in suggesting some sporting turns of phrase that have passed into common speech and now appear completely divorced from their original context and meaning. "Touching base" and "taking a rain check", both originally from baseball are the most obvious examples.[47] However, after a brief and admittedly unscientific survey of contemporary practice, I suggest that sporting analogies in use today are more likely to be deployed by those who are familiar with sports. Hoffman's examples do indicate that some metaphors become deeply

43. Collins, *First Corinthians*, 360.

44. Murphy-O'Connor, *Corinth*, 15.

45. The broader sense of "leather worker" sometimes given to Paul's trade derives from the use of hides in the making of tents.

46. Murphy-O'Connor, *Corinth*, 15.

47. Hoffman, *Good Game*, 44.

ingrained, and this must be taken seriously when assessing Paul's usage, but Pfitzner presses his case too hard in going on to argue for revulsion rather than approval in the face of the games. Would Paul have used such images if he strongly disapproved of and was revolted by the games? Pfitzner asks us to believe that Paul's use of language was unthinking, and he does his case no good when remarking that rabbinic literature makes very sparing use of metaphor and image drawn from the games because of the Jewish opposition to them—precisely what we might expect from Paul if Pfitzner is correct that Paul was trained in this tradition.[48] If Paul had positively disapproved of the games would he not, as with the rabbinic tradition, have exercised more restraint in using this rhetorical device, or indicated in some way distaste for the sporting sphere from which his language is drawn? Considering the number of times it is used, this would not seem an unreasonable expectation.

Pfitzner may be correct to argue that there is no clear evidence to confirm that Paul ever actually entered a stadium,[49] but the frequency with which the imagery is deployed, the rich illustrative support that it provides, and (most clearly in the case of 1 Cor 9) the aptness of the imagery for his readers, may suggest a deliberateness in use that goes beyond the habitual or routine. Paul deploys these metaphors without comment, though appears happy to apply them to himself as well as his readers. While skeptics may argue that it is hardly a ringing endorsement of sport, it is also difficult to see clearly any reservations about sports in the text, and extratextual arguments can be made to point both ways with some persuasive arguments on the "pro-sport" side.

It may be useful to compare Paul's use of sporting imagery with the apparent acceptance of other aspects of everyday life in his time such as inherited patterns of domestic relationships. In arguments that appear to parallel Pfitzner's in some ways, scholars sometimes argue that passages that regulate the behavior within Christian families such as Colossians 3:18—4:1 and Ephesians 5:21–33 were taken over from the "household codes" that would have been well known to contemporary readers.[50] What is of interest is the subtle tweaks given to them, tweaks

---

48. Pfitzner, *Agon*, 74.

49. Pfitzner, *Agon*, 187–88.

50. See, e.g., Witherington III, *Philemon, Colossians, Ephesians*, 181–96; Sumney, *Colossians*, 230–55; Keener, *Paul, Women and Wives*, 145–46. Suzanne Watts Henderson suggests that the use of these codes present a hermeneutical model: "the Colossians Code adeptly applies the logic of Christ's lordship to the writer's own cultural milieu,

that might be said to undermine them in serious ways. One might think, for instance, of the injunction to mutual subjection between husband and wife as an undermining of the kind of male headship assumed in Greco-Roman, and indeed Jewish, culture. One could also make the case, when referring to other texts such as Galatians 3:22, that other words of Paul found elsewhere destabilize some of these "accepted" aspects of ancient life under the *Pax Romana* and the old covenant. Some of Paul's discussions of life in community (e.g., Phil 2:1–11; 1 Cor 12) could in turn be seen to undermine the competitive drive that underlies sporting endeavor. This is a question to which we will return: bluntly, is sporting competitiveness a sign of, or an opening for, sin? But in the sporting references themselves it is not easy to see signs of any desire to alter the resonance they create. There is no destabilizing gloss in evidence in any of the sporting texts, unless one counts the contrast between perishable and imperishable prizes, and as we have seen this contrast is inherent in the Corinthians games so is hardly a gloss at all.

We know that later in Christian history individual Christians and perhaps groups thereof had different attitudes. That church leaders such as Tertullian felt they had to speak out against the games must be taken as an indication that some Christians (perhaps many) frequented them. Novatian, who lived a few decades later in the first half of the third century, was disappointed that some Christians used Scripture proof texts such as 1 Corinthians 9:24–27 to justify attendance at the games. "A struggling apostle paints for us the picture of a boxing match and of our own wrestling against the spiritual forces of wickedness. Furthermore, when he makes use of illustrations taken from the footrace he also mentions the usual prize—the wreath or garland. Why, then, should a faithful Christian not be at liberty to be a spectator of things that the divine writings are at liberty to mention?"[51] But Novatian is uncompromising: "it would have been far better for such people to lack knowledge of the Scriptures, than to read them in such a manner. Words and noble deeds which have been put down in writing to stimulate us in the practice of evangelical virtue are misinterpreted by them as so many incentives for the practice

---

actively engaging the prevailing worldview in light of the cross. In these words, we find neither wholesale endorsement of secular Hellenistic values nor a prophetic indictment of stratified social structures. Instead, the writer refracts prevailing assumptions regarding household conduct through the lens of Christian faith and, in so doing, offers a hermeneutical model that retains traction today." "Taking Liberties," 420–21.

51. Novatian, *The Trinity, The Spectacle*, 124–25.

of vice."[52] Novatian's negativity appears to be based on the opportunities afforded for vice around the games, and also on the pagan nature of the games. "[Scripture] has forbidden us to be spectators of whatever it has forbidden us to do . . . What spectacle is there without an idol? Is there a game without some sort of sacrifice? Is there a contest that is not dedicated to some dead person? If a faithful Christian really abhors idolatry, then what is he doing among such things?"[53] This sounds much more like the kind of attitude to the games that Pfitzner suggests Paul might have had, but for which we can find no direct evidence. Novatian's strong statement not only indicates that some Christians thought otherwise, but also suggests that if Paul had thought along these lines he might not have used the imagery in the first place.

We might also note that some commentators agree that Paul's use of these metaphors suggests a positive view of the body. As Hays comments on 1 Corinthians 9:

> Throughout this letter, Paul resists the Corinthians' tendency to deprecate the body, and the present passage is no exception. While Paul speaks of "punishing" and "enslaving" his body in order to avoid being disqualified (v. 27), the interpreter may need to explain that the body is not the enemy of the spiritual life; rather, it is the *instrument* of that life. The athletic metaphor continues to govern the sense of verse 27: the "punishment" of the body refers to the grueling training for the contest, seeking to bring the body to peak efficiency.[54]

Pfitzner's more negative reading is overdone and it is appropriate for readers to find in the many deployments of the athletic metaphors some kind of implicit approval for these sports. Further, sports appear to Paul to embody or recall some of the virtues that are required for faithful Christian life and witness. Theologians will want to create a theology of sport that is in some sense biblical, but "sporting texts" of Paul are unlikely to be a solid enough or sufficient base. "A contemporary Christian perspective on sports should have deep roots in Scripture and tradition,"[55] but how will these deep roots be identified? It will be wishful thinking to imagine that it may be grounded firmly on the athletic metaphors of Paul

52. Novatian, *The Trinity, The Spectacle*, 125.
53. Novatian, *The Trinity, The Spectacle*, 126.
54. Hays, *First Corinthians*, 156.
55. Kruschwitz, "Sports in the Christian Life," 1.

alone, and a broader biblically informed view of play must now be taken as a next step.

God the Creator: *Deus Ludens* and the Game of Love

The creation narrative(s) of Genesis offers both evidence of continuity between human and (other) animal life but also a striking contrast between them. This contrast is usually focused on the notion that women and men are created in the image of God. The meaning of this *imago Dei* has not proved straightforward to unpack, and many different interpretations of the concept have been offered focusing on human rationality, freedom, relationality, openness to God, creativity, and the status of humankind as "ruling" in God's place, or indeed a combination of these possibilities. The concept of dominion seems exegetically sound given that the Hebrew word translated as "image" is that used to refer to the idol or statue that an ancient ruler would place in one of his territories (cf. Ps 8:5f).[56] Such dominion as humankind is given "excludes arbitrary control or exploitation. It is like the work of the gardener, as in the second creation story (Gen. 2:15)."[57] It is not difficult, if beginning with this as the most basic interpretation, to identify some of the other themes mentioned above as unfolding naturally from it, themes such as rationality, freedom, and creativity. Harvey Cox sees a clear link between the *imago Dei* and creativity and play. "In [fantasy] man not only relives and anticipates, he remakes the past and creates wholly new futures." Out of fantasy, he argues, grows our ability to invent and innovate, it is the richest of all sources of human creativity. Here is the image of the Creator God in human beings: "like God, man in fantasy creates whole worlds *ex nihilo*, out of nothing."[58] In Cox's twin ideas of festivity and fantasy we see much of what we mean by play though together they evince a broader meaning. Festivity is life-affirming, superfluous, and a contrast to the everyday;[59] fantasy relives and anticipates, imagines new worlds,

---

56. Brueggemann, *Genesis*, 32.

57. Pannenberg, *Systematic Theology II*, 205. Pannenberg also discusses the exegetical issues and interpretations.

58. Cox, *Feast*, 59.

59. Cox, *Feast*, 22–23.

allows us to play new roles, bursting the bounds of the here and now with a creative imagination that is rooted in the *imago Dei*.[60]

God the Creator creates creative creatures in the image of God, and creativity is vitally associated with play. In playing the human being creates a world. The game is its own world, and boundaries are created or observed (that fence is out of bounds, this corner is the hospital ward) and the freedom of play is exercised within these boundaries. The bureaucratized play of sport hardens these boundaries in certain ways and those who play sports give themselves over to the givenness of the rules in order to exercise their freedom within agreed boundaries. The rules of a children's game of cops and robbers are set (whether informally or not) by those who play at the moment of playing; the same might be true of a group of adults improvising a game in the park with a football. But when sports proper are played the rules are set elsewhere, and even local variations are based on remote rules. In this sense, sport may appear to some to represent something of a corruption of pure play as the players do not set their own rules in the act of playing, or create entirely their own world. But if a characteristic of play is that it sets its own rules and creates its own world whereas sport proper works within rules set elsewhere, it could be argued that in play we are creators while in sport we are creatures. Sport in this sense may be said to be more truly creaturely than play, because sports players do not set their own boundaries even though they push at them constantly. The human creative task in general can be considered to be working as sub-creators within the givens of God's creation. This is what the sports player does in refining and extemporizing on a repertoire of moves to express their own creativity within the limits of their sport. For sports players are still creative in myriad ways, but they are so within obvious and externally set limits. From this perspective playing sport is a profoundly human enterprise.

Consider here Karl Barth on his beloved Mozart:

> our daily bread must also include playing . . . And in Mozart I hear an art of playing as I hear it in no one else. Beautiful playing presupposes an intuitive, childlike awareness of the essence or center—as also the beginning and the end—of all things. It is from this center, from this beginning and end, that I hear Mozart create his music. *I can hear these boundaries which he imposed upon himself because it was precisely this discipline that*

---

60. Cox, *Feast*, 59.

gave him joy. And when I hear him, it gladdens, encourages, and comforts me as well.[61]

It is possible to understand the act of creation itself as God at play. Jürgen Moltmann puts it like this:

> There is no purposive rationale for the proposition that something exists rather than nothing. The existence of the world is not necessary. Theology expresses this with its understanding of the world as "God's creation" . . . When he creates something that is not God but also not nothing, then this must have its ground not in itself but in God's *good will or pleasure*. Hence the creation is God's play, a play of groundless and inscrutable wisdom. It is the realm in which God displays his glory.[62]

Moltmann wants to distinguish divine and human creativity clearly from one another and notes that the Hebrew word for divine creative action is never used of human activity, suggesting that God's creativity is qualitatively different. God, we can say, sets the rules by which God plays entirely, whereas human players (especially in sports) are always working within givens. Rather as in playing sport, "man can only play with something which, in turn, is playing with him."[63] Some Indian traditions speak in similar ways, as with the Hindu notion of *lila*, the divine play through which the world is created.[64] According to Moltmann, in Proverbs 8:22–31 we see that creation has "the character of play, which gives God delight and human beings joy"[65] and, in the face of the terrible uncertainties of life, men and women can understand their relationship with God as a game God plays with them, just as through evolution creation is a game played by God, says Moltmann.

The playing of God in creation-through-evolution was a feature of Arthur Peacocke's 1978 Bampton lectures that attempted to bring theological insights into dialogue with reflections on then current scientific research. Peacocke also drew on Hindu thought and a range of other writers, and recalled Dante's description of the angels praising the Trinity

---

61. Barth, *Mozart*, 16–17. Italics mine.

62. Moltmann, *Joy*, 40–41.

63. Moltmann, *Joy*, 41.

64. See, e.g., Sax, *Gods at Play*.

65. Moltmann, *Creation*, 311. See the next section of this chapter for further discussion of this text.

in paradise as like "the laughter of the universe."[66] In his understanding, creation is the play of God, and the role that chance plays in the ongoing creation can be seen, he says, as a sign of "the overflow of the divine generosity," a sign of God's "displaying the delight and sheer exuberance of play in the unceasing act of creation."[67] The modern thus echoes the ancient, as this accords with Blowers' account of the use of play imagery by Maximus the Confessor (580–662 CE), which, he says, indicates "the excess of the positive attributes . . . wisdom, power and prudence of God."[68] Blowers goes on to say of Gregory Nazianzus and Maximus alike that "the Logos-at-play bespeaks the Creator's urge to cajole and 'tease' the creation toward its true destiny, using all created 'playthings' at his disposal."[69]

Playful Wisdom: Proverbs, the Song of Songs, and Ecclesiastes

As well as its prominence in discussions of play, Proverbs 8:22–31 has been significant in Christological discussions because of the way it appears to offer an Old Testament picture of Wisdom as separately hypostasized or (more accurately) personified.[70] The character of Wisdom appears separate from but alongside "the Lord" at creation. "Created" (as in most translations) or "formed" (with connotations of being pro-created)[71] first, before all else, Wisdom accompanies the Lord in creation like a "master workman" (v. 30). Wisdom continues, "I was daily his delight, rejoicing before him always." But there are issues of translation here. "Master workman" can also be rendered, as the NRSV margin indicates, "little child," and many modern commentators strongly prefer this reading.[72] This alternative fits well with the context, not least when the remainder of the verse can also be alternatively rendered. In the New English Bible verse

66. " 'Unto the Father, Son and Holy Ghost, glory!'—all Paradise began, so that the sweetness of the singing held me rapt. What I saw seemed to me to be a smile the universe had smiled." Dante, *Divine Comedy: Paradise*, 27.1–5.

67. Peacocke, *Creation*, 111.

68. Blowers, "On the 'Play' of Divine Providence," 203.

69. Blowers, "On the 'Play' of Divine Providence," 216.

70. See, e.g., Prov 1:20–33.

71. Waltke, *Proverbs 1–15*, 409. This distinction is significant, of course, in Christological debates.

72. Fox, "Ideas of Wisdom," 628; Waltke, *Proverbs 1–15*, 418–19.

30 runs: "Then I was at his side each day, his darling and delight, playing in his presence continually, playing on the earth." Where the NEB had "playing" in verse 30, other translations often give "rejoicing" (as in the NRSV), following the tradition established by the Septuagint translation that rendered the Hebrew Old Testament into Greek in the third century before the Christian Era. But again, many contemporary scholars favor the alternative "playing," arguing that Proverbs 8 portrays Wisdom during creation as playing like a little child before God who delights in her. Wisdom's play may be a delighting in understanding, intellectual exploration, and learning. "This gives an extraordinary picture of Wisdom—the noble, ancient sage, the stern disciplinarian and teacher—frolicking like a little child near her divine paternal guardian as he goes about his great work."[73] We may associate play with the act of creation more securely because of this memorable image. Creation is, we might say, made in play, or playfully made.

It is possible to describe both the act of creation and the divine life in terms of play. Hugo Rahner quotes a hymn by Gregory Nazianzus: "For the Logos on high plays, stirring the whole cosmos back and forth, as he wills, into shapes of every kind."[74] These words might call to mind Peacocke's notion of God playing through evolution. Cornelius a Lapide, a Flemish Jesuit writing a commentary on Proverbs in the early seventeenth century, could speak of the Son's eternal relationship to the Father as "in the dewy freshness and springtime beauty of his eternal youth he eternally enacts a game before his Father."[75] God is a player, *Deus ludens* creates and enters into relationship with *homo ludens*. As Gerardus van der Leeuw puts it, "the meeting of God with man, of man with God is holy play, *sacer ludus* . . . Play is the prerequisite for those forms of existence which strive toward a communion with the other, and finally for a meeting with God."[76] Given what we have already said about creation being playfully made, about play constituting creation's present goodness, and how play is in some way social, it should come as no surprise to understand that play becomes the vehicle for relationship—and not just

73. Fox, *Proverbs 1-9*, 288.

74. Hugo Rahner, *Man at Play*, 23, quoting a poem of Gregory of Nazianzus. For a discussion of play imagery in Gregory see Blowers, "On the 'Play' of Divine Providence."

75. Hugo Rahner, *Man at Play*, 23, quoting Cornelius a Lapide, *Commentaria in Proverbia* 8.31.

76. Leeuw, *Sacred*, 111–12.

the relationship of human persons with one another, but also between *homo ludens* and *Deus ludens*, between created and Creator.

This divine/human relationship can be characterized as play, or as a game. It is perhaps in this sense that one might make sense of Johnston's discussion of "play" in the Song of Songs "which should be interpreted in the context of the joyful play of lovers."[77] The Song of Songs is not straight-forwardly considered part of the wisdom tradition, though its links with Solomon connect it with texts like Proverbs that have similar traditional associations. The Song of Songs is, however, like the other wisdom texts, not a theological text in quite the same way as, say, Genesis, Psalms or 1 Kings. Wisdom texts sit separately from, or less directly connected to, the texts that speak of divine revelation in history, for instance. Wisdom texts *mention* God much less and seem more practical in orientation. The Songs of Songs is hardly practical in the sense of giving tips for lovemaking or courtship but, in an initial reading, the text appears more concerned with earthly delights than divine revelation. God is mentioned only once (at 8:6), and that mention is disputed and does not appear in all translations.[78] It seems legitimate for our purpose, therefore, to discuss the Song of Songs alongside these wisdom texts.

Leaving behind the allegorical interpretations of the book that have dominated Christian understandings since Origen, most modern commentators read the book more literally as a celebration of human love and also as a warning about its destructive power when distorted.[79] While being careful not to slip into allegorical crudities, at the same time it can also be read as illumining the "emotional intensity, intimacy, and exclusivity"[80] of the divine/human relationship. Johnston suggests that the opening verses of the book immediately strike a playful note in 1:2–4,[81] though there does not seem to be play here as such, unless one understands it in a very broad sense. We might be alert here to a distinction between "play" and "playfulness." While there is no game in 1:2–4 or elsewhere in the Song of Songs in an ordinary (or, we might

77. Johnston, *Play*, 107.

78. The NRSV translates the verse: "Set me as a seal upon your heart, as a seal upon your arm; for love is strong as death, passion fierce as the grave. Its flashes are flashes of fire, a raging flame." This "raging flame" is sometimes rendered as "the flame of the Lord," or similar.

79. Longman, *Song*, 61.

80. Longman, *Song*, 70.

81. Johnston, *Play*, 107.

say, technical) sense, the relationship of the lovers as exemplified in these opening verses does share many of the features of play that Huizinga identified: the intensity and absorption of the players, the separateness of the lovemaking from everyday life, its capacity for forming strong social bonds, the exclusiveness of the relationship constrains the "game" of love as rules order other games, and such ecstatic love is necessarily entered into voluntarily (though lovers may also speak of being driven by forces before which they feel powerless, and perhaps this resembles Huizinga's "power of maddening"). The delight of the lovers corresponds with the sheer fun of playing as Huizinga understands it. This said, a more obvious key with which to understand the Song of Songs' capacity to shed light on the relationship between God and humankind is probably that of lovers or married partners. To the extent that these relationships can be said to be playful they offer some assistance to our task.

Attempts to draw on Ecclesiastes are a little more promising. "I know that there is nothing better for them than to be happy and enjoy themselves as long as they live; moreover, it is God's gift that all should eat and take pleasure in all their toil" says the book's philosopher at 3:12–13. As well as the more world-weary observations and advice of the book there is a considerable amount of material extolling the pleasures of life and urging the reader to seek them out. Thus "eating and drinking" represent a host of other pleasures such as music and the human form (2:8), food and drink (2:24; 9:7) laugher and dancing (3:4), love and lovemaking (3:5,8), good works (3:12), relaxing (4:6; 5:12), material prosperity (5:19; 7:12f.), wine (9:7), one's spouse (9:9), and more.[82] Many of these kinds of activities or states we might legitimately regard as "play" even though the word is not used, and once again the characteristics of play suggested by Huizinga appear to apply to many of them. Even work is enjoyed: at 2:24 work and leisure are paired as equal enjoyments, and in reading the enjoinder to enjoy work and leisure alike we certainly encounter a more balanced attitude to life than has frequently been suggested within the Christian tradition.

Johnston is correct to suggest that the negative tone of the work can be explained as an attempt to puncture a sense of humanity's reliance on its own effort and a tendency to give ultimacy to that which is penultimate, to glory in creation rather than its Creator. To achieve this end the writer "exhorts his readers to play—to eat and drink with joy and to make

82. Fredericks and Estes, *Ecclesiastes*, 39.

love. For as we play, as we commune joyfully with creation and our fellow creatures, we become aware that life truly is a gift from God (Eccl 2:24)."[83] Play is not simply the mode of God's act of creation; it is also a means by which creatures become open to receiving life as the Creator's gift and so become open to the Creator in relationships and potentiality. Sport is a particular form of play, institutionalizing play in its bureaucratizing of it, and so takes it seriously in a new way. The ancients, in their use of games as ritual and liturgy as a means for securing knowledge of the divine will and favor, took it seriously in another way and that way also manifested an intuition regarding the significance of play as a means of being open to the divine. We might speak of sport as a kind of dramatization, a ritual form, of play. If so, and thinking as we have been of sport as a possible vehicle for an encounter with the Ultimate Player, it might also be possible to speak of participation in such sport as being a participation in God's playful creativity, or creative play, and so even a participation in God's self, participation as creatures bounded by but yet straining at the edges of the constraints within which human life is lived.

Many have claimed and do claim that sport is a positive good in society and, if we are correct about the significance of play in general, this might also suggest that the 'goods' of sport are not coincidental but inhere within them. Of course, like the sexuality celebrated in the Song of Songs, play and sports can be and sometimes are debased and distorted so that they become carriers of harm and manifestations of sin, but this is neither the full nor an adequate story about play and sport. Muscular Christians believed sport was character-forming in positive ways, and various research projects appear to substantiate this.[84] But if play and sport can be (though are not necessarily) a participation in God's playful creativity and even in God's self, then one might expect such goods to follow.

Sabbaths and Festivals: Playful Rest

The creation narrative is commonly said to reach its climax in the creation of humankind on the sixth day. However, the narrative in fact reaches its conclusion on the seventh day, the day of recreative rest from work, the

---

83. Johnston, *Play*, 100.

84. Tess Kay's research shows useful examples of this based upon careful empirical evidence.

Sabbath.[85] On the seventh day God rests from his creative work, and God's people are also to keep this Sabbath. This is a day when God's people are to cease from economic activity, from the potential exploitation of others through their labor or in trade, cease from the accumulation of wealth, and even from the task of looking after one's own and one's fellows' daily needs. There is a "lilies of the field" aspect to the Sabbath.[86] It is a day for different things, for rest and for re-creation. The moving of the "Christian Sabbath" to the first day of the week may have obscured this sense of the week culminating in rest. To suggest that play is an appropriate way of describing what might occur on the Sabbath day (let alone that play is its true purpose) is to enter controversial territory, as our earlier historical summaries would indicate. We have, of course, just suggested that the "work" of the first six days can be understood as divine play, and to see the Sabbath then as *for* play might seem like wanting to have one's cake and eat it. But, as Bernard Suits suggests, there is a sense in which any work can become play. This might be the "game-playing" of the employee who attempts to do a certain amount of work in a certain time or by a certain method; more fundamentally, work is often taken to refer to an activity that is *instrumentally* valuable, while play is *intrinsically* valuable. Suits insists that "by 'play' I mean nothing more than all of those activities which are intrinsically valuable to those who engage in them."[87] This may seem a broad definition but people do sometimes say of their job that "I can't believe that they pay me for doing this." Equally, as in professional sport, sometimes play can become work (though whether it ceases to be play in so doing we will ask later). It is also clear that "rest" need not mean reclining or reposing, but can be active and even energetic. The Sabbath rest should not be assumed to be inactive, and at the end of this chapter we will also consider how the "rest" to which creation moves might also involve movement and activity.

The play of the first six days, the "working play," is a play that expresses creativity, freedom, and rationality, among other characteristics. The Sabbath play of the seventh day is a "re-creative play" that restores balance and refreshes. That these two forms of play belong together may be indicated by Ecclesiastes 2:24. Johnston contrasts the Greek model (where only the elite have leisure), the Protestant model (that saw work

85. Brueggemann, *Genesis*, 35.
86. Matt 6:27–34.
87. Suits, *Grasshopper*, 146.

as a vocation and downplayed leisure), and the more wholesome Hebraic model in which *everyone* worked, and then rested together following a divine pattern.[88] While the Sabbath command in Exodus 20:8–17. roots its justification in the creation narrative, the version found at Deuteronomy 5:12–21. reaches back to the liberation of Hebrew slaves from Egyptian bondage. As Johnston remarks, the Israelite who does not joyfully refrain from their work on the Sabbath is placing their confidence in their own work rather than God's liberating action.[89] This twin grounding of the commandment is significant. On the one hand, the rooting in salvation history connects the Sabbath rest with redemption, and points forward to final and complete salvation. On the other hand, the rooting of the Sabbath command in the creation narrative suggests that rest and play are not just experiences to which we look forward in a promised, redeemed future. They are also part of the created world, the world pronounced "good" by its Creator, and therefore part of properly ordered human lives now.[90]

Israel also rested and played on other occasions. While the Sabbath is the weekly rest rooted in the narratives of creation and redemption, there are other moments in ancient Israel when God's people set aside the demands of work and engage in restorative activity. The religious festivals of the Old Testament provide shape to the year with intervals in which the history of the people is made available to the present and celebrated. These festivals "keep defining memories derived from critical moments dynamically available in the community."[91] Just as the Christian year is dominated by the three festivals of Christmas, Easter, and Pentecost, so the Israelite calendar had three principal festivals: Passover (marking the liberation from Egypt), Sukkot or "Booths" (recalling the trek through the wilderness that followed), and Shavuot or "Weeks" (celebrating the giving of the Law at Sinai). Later there followed the Day of Atonement, and Purim. Celebrations include feasting (and, it must be said, often fasting) and other playful activities. The Festival of Booths creates a week of playful camping out, and Purim offered opportunity for "a day of gladness and feasting" (Esth 9:19) and the exchanging of gifts. This was the moment to celebrate how their mood had been changed "from sorrow

88. Johnston, *Play*, 89.
89. Johnston, *Play*, 94.
90. Johnston makes a similar point, *Play*, 95.
91. Brueggemann, *Reverberations*, 84.

into gladness and from mourning into a holiday" (Esth 9:22). A notable feature of these festivals was a drawing of attention away from human achievement (such as a harvest well gathered) and towards God's saving activity in history, a movement from works to grace. Play, from some points of view unnecessary and superfluous, must be understood in terms of grace and gift, and any encounter with God that results from play is similarly gift. We shall consider in subsequent chapters how any divine encounter through the play of sport should be construed as divine grace rather than a human work. The worship of the festivals are not attempts to manipulate God into showing up and blessing, they are the free offering (the voluntary play) of love that may be met by the freely given gift of divine presence and blessing. We recall the Song of Songs: the love of intimate human relations is freely given and cannot require or force any response.

In acts of devotion such as pilgrimage and sacrifice there may appear to be actions that are intended to regulate the relationship of worshippers with God, but all of these festivals show many of the characteristics of play. They match Cox's marks of festivity and fantasy perfectly: life-affirming, superfluous, a contrast to the everyday, reliving and anticipating, imagining new worlds, allowing new roles to be played, and bursting the bounds of the here and now.

But, as Johnston points out,[92] as well as festivals there are feasts. Abraham celebrates the growing of Isaac (Gen 21:8), wedding feasts celebrate nuptials (Gen 29:22, John 2:1–11), the welcome home party for the prodigal (Luke 15:23), the entertaining of guests (Gen 24:22–33; Deut 23:4), and Jesus' own partying (Luke 7:34). And as well as feasts there is dancing: Pss 68; 149:3; 150:4; Judg 21; 1 Sam 18:6f.; 2 Sam 6:12; and so on.[93] Sometimes there are also indications of the distorting effects of disordered play too, as when the fleeing slaves bow before the golden calf and enter into drunken revelry. The word that the NRSV translates "revels" in Exodus 32:6 has sexual connotations and probably points to orgiastic mayhem. However, in the strand of celebration that is marked by these festivals and practices we see a playfulness close to the heart of the life of God's people. As Johnston remarks with respect to Nehemiah

92. Johnston, *Play,* 114–16.

93. "God moved, and he set us upon this earth in motion. That is sublime and impressive. It is the beginning of his work in creation and salvation. It is also the beginning of the dance." Leeuw, *Sacred,* 74.

8:9–12, "the call to festivity assumes that holiness is better associated with joy than solemnity, with happiness rather than gloom."[94]

Play, "Signal of Transcendence"

Few theological discussions of play in recent decades have felt able to ignore Peter Berger's suggestion that, in the face of a secularized culture that robs traditional theological accounts of revelation of their plausibility, play offers an opportunity for re-establishing the possibility of faith by inductive means. Berger is writing as a sociologist and not expressing any opinion about the truth or otherwise of the claims of revelation, but is observing that late-twentieth-century Westerners find claims about revelation difficult. Berger has in mind the Neo-Orthodox reaction to theological liberalism in the earlier part of the twentieth century. Barth insisted that theology could stand only on the rock of revelation (on "Thus says the Lord . . .") and that there was no way "up" to God from human experience. Statements about humanity and its experience could be made only on the basis of revelation: "an anthropology could be theologically deduced, but there were no inductive possibilities *from* anthropology *to* theology."[95] Barth's more extreme position was modified to some extent by others but the resultant anthropological themes were gloomy, as might have been expected given the carnage of 1914–18 and then Europe's descent into an abyss following the rise of Hitler. Berger looks for an anthropological starting point in "fundamental human experience"[96] that will not be so susceptible to changes in mood occasioned by current circumstance. As such he says, "I would suggest that theological thought seek out what might be called *signals of transcendence* within the empirically given human situation. And I would further suggest that there are *prototypical human gestures* that may constitute such signals."[97]

Berger identifies five of these signals of transcendence, which are phenomena found within our everyday and natural experience but which appear to him to point beyond that experience and reality. As such they transcend the normal everyday world and may be described as pointers to a supra-natural reality. The "proto-typical human gestures" are

94. Johnston, *Play,* 111.
95. Berger, *Angels,* 67, italics his.
96. Berger, *Angels,* 69.
97. Berger, *Angels,* 70, italics his.

repeated actions that "express essential aspects of man's being" and which "belong to ordinary everyday awareness."[98] The five he identifies are: the human propensity for order, the intuition that things make sense and that all is well; the pervasive power of hope; the sense of outrage at gross acts of cruelty and injustice (which he calls the argument from damnation); the human capacity for humor; and play. Berger's inclusion of play in this series of proto-typical human gestures is echoed by Hoffman's remarks that "all forms of play are expressions of the same characteristic human response to the world, a response so universal—evident in animals as well as humans—that it is difficult not to believe that it is part of God's design."[99]

Berger begins his discussion of "the argument from play" by reviewing Huizinga's work, remarking that Huizinga appears to show that culture without play is an impossibility. He is taken in particular with Huizinga's suggestion that in play human persons create their own world. In this world a new universe of discourse is established, rules willingly adopted (and other normal rules therefore suspended), and a new sense of time experienced.

> When one is playing, one is on a different time, no longer measured by the standard units of the larger society, but rather by the peculiar ones of the game in question. In the "serious" world it may be 11 am, on such and such a day, month, and year. But in the universe in which one is playing it may be the third round, the fourth act, the *allegro* movement, or the second kiss. In playing one steps out of one time into another.[100]

Berger's inclusion of a musical example is in keeping with the broader understanding of play with which we have been working, and it suggests interesting comparisons between play and music. According to Rowan Williams, music "forces us to rethink time,"[101] and the same might be said of play. Like music, play alters our experience of time, and can be said to create its own time. Music is an inexorably temporal phenomenon: not only does it have duration and pace, but also a rhythm given largely in its time signature that sets the number of beats in each bar and the way that accenting determines the predominant beat—that which makes the

98. Berger, *Angels*, 70.
99. Hoffman, *Good Game*, 274.
100. Berger, *Angels*, 76.
101. Williams, "Keeping Time," 248.

listener or performer tap their feet. The listener who claps along but "out of time" has missed this essential beat, and when enough players in the orchestra succumb to a similar problem the musical experience disintegrates. Proper time holds back chaos, it allows a creation to unfold. As well as the familiar experience of time dragging or flying according to the extent to which one has been "grasped" by the music, this sense of music's own temporality lies close to the heart of its power to move and entrance us. In more sophisticated music, sometimes a number of different temporalities coexist, yet ultimately coherence depends on an underlying or ultimate unity. Play also has its own rhythms. Chronological duration is most obvious in sports where records are set by time, and the fastest athlete to a given point is the winner, but the duration of a game's four quarters or two halves, or in the case of a cricket test match five days, all give a certain pace to play. Urgency is required at some moments, patience at others. Just as musical form (the sonata form, for instance, often employed in symphonic composition) gives a shape to the piece that has temporal aspects, so the shape of play and sports also have core temporal dimensions. God created time in creating the universe *ex nihilo*, time is God's creation and gift and in making music and playing humans engage in making time too, and this time has a complex relationship to ordinary chronologies outside or beyond them. Drawing on the work of Barth, Jeremy Begbie suggests that the window onto eternity that it is often suggested that music offers is not simply a lack of time, a simultaneity in which all sense of sequence is set aside, but a rich conjunction of the two.[102] Like play, music makes time stand still and gives us a glimpse of another order with a different time, but it does so without losing its own sequence and direction. Theologically, this is significant in understanding God's time, and God's time for us. Eternity is, according to Barth, the form of God's time. It is not a lack of temporality, but instead:

> the fact that there is in [God] no opposition or competition or conflict, but peace between origin, movement and goal, between present, past and future, between "not yet," "now" and "no more," between rest and movement, potentiality and actuality, whither and whence, here and there, this and that. In him all these things are *simul*, held together by the omnipotence of his knowing and willing, a totality without gap or rift, free from the

102. See Begbie, *Theology*, 153. His discussions of music and time in chapters 2 and 5 are both helpful.

threat of death under which time, our time, stands. It is not the case, then, that in eternity these distinctions do not exist.[103]

Like music, play is absorbing, and in it the experience of time is often strange. Children lose track of "proper" time when absorbed in a game. The teenager spends an evening trying to reach the next level on her X-Box when she had only meant to play for a half hour, but time flies. Being engrossed in a book under the covers at bedtime can be a similar experience. Adults too have a different experience of time when playing—it can "stand still," or pass too quickly, or drag. "I thought that the final whistle would never sound" says the footballer hanging onto a lead against the odds. In the moment, with "normal" time ceasing to matter or be noticed, the concerns, cares, and horizons of the "normal" world have also ceased to matter. Playing is an escape from this world into a new world, freshly made, with different horizons and mores and chronologies. This escape into another world, Berger suggests, is a signal of an actual "other world" or, rather, of a reality beyond the present everyday reality in which we live most of our lives.

Berger maintains that play is meant to be, and usually is, an enjoyable experience. The joy of play has an effect on the way that time is experienced during play. Joyful play turns time into eternity. Berger concedes that this is true of all joyful experiences but maintains that it is particularly true of play because of the way in which play creates its own temporal structure, and its own self-contained world. Moreover, "even as one remains conscious of the poignant reality of that other, 'serious' time in which one is moving toward death, one apprehends joy as being, in some barely conceivable way, a joy forever. Joyful play appears to suspend, or bracket, the reality of our 'living towards death' (as Heidegger aptly describes our 'serious' condition)."[104] This, he suggests, explains the sense of liberation and peace that often accompanies the playing of adults and children alike. It was Wordsworth who described this losing of the sense of wonder as the child becomes adult:

> Heaven lies about us in our infancy!
> Shades of the prison-house begin to close
> Upon the growing Boy,
> But He beholds the light, and whence it flows,

---

103. Barth, *CD II/1*, 612. All except the last sentence quoted by Begbie, *Theology*, 153.

104. Berger, *Angels*, 77.

He sees it in his joy . . .
At length the Man perceives it die away,
And fade into the light of common day.[105]

Berger is proposing that when adults truly play this also has the effect of dispersing the "shades of the prison-house" and transforms the experience of time.

A complementary understanding of this phenomenon is offered by psychologist Mihaly Csikszentmihalyi. He calls this experience "flow"— "the state in which people are so involved in an activity that nothing else seems to matter; the experience itself is so enjoyable that people will do it even at great costs, for the sheer sake of doing it."[106] His research testifies that the experience is not peculiar to people in the West, or in industrialized cultures, and he gathered reports of the phenomenon from Thailand, India, Tokyo, the Navajo shepherds, and Alpine farmers as well as Chicago factory workers. At moments of flow we enter a state in which we feel in control and yet also begin to feel ourselves become so absorbed in the activity as to become one with it: "people become so involved in what they are doing that the activity becomes spontaneous, almost automatic; they stop being aware of themselves as separate from the actions that they are performing."[107] The toddler absorbed in her game, the jogger who strikes just the perfect rhythm in the park, the musician engrossed in a demanding but beautiful sonata, the artist who suddenly sees their vision begin to emerge from the canvas, the cricketer building a long innings who becomes oblivious to distraction and begins to see the ball big and hittable, all these know flow. The character Billy Elliott expresses it well in the film of that name. The boy is quizzed by tutors at the Royal Ballet School. One asks, "What does it feel like when you're dancing?" Billy struggles to articulate his answer: "Don't know. Sorta feels good. Sorta stiff and that, but once I get going . . . then I like, forget everything. And . . . sorta disappear. Sorta disappear. Like I feel a change in my whole body. And I've got this fire in my body. I'm just there. Flyin' like a bird. Like electricity. Yeah, like electricity."[108] Billy is reporting an intense experience of flow. In flow, says Csikszentmihalyi, time no longer seems to pass in the usual way but generally to pass much more quickly, although

105. William Wordsworth, "Intimations."
106. Csikszentmihalyi, *Flow*, 4.
107. Csikszentmihalyi, *Flow*, 53.
108. *Billy Elliott*.

occasionally the reverse happens so that the ballet dancer's difficult turn takes a second, but seems to last minutes. Most flow activities have their own pace, their own sense of time.

While this is true of all play, it is true of sport in particular ways. Sport generally creates not only its own time but its own space, ordinary boundaries dissolved and new ones created. The new created world of sport is often marked out and bounded by white lines, and created in a peculiar timeframe measured in minutes or innings or sets. New special regulations govern behavior, the "constitutive rules" identified by Suits, and set boundaries of another kind. Generally we are told "it's good to share," but when ordinary time gives way to football of any code the ball is not to be shared but guarded jealously, fought over, prized with a ferocity that would make no sense when one considers its monetary value or ease of replacement. This is no ordinary world.

In addition, "games are played in the timeless present; they carry a 'spark of eternity.'"[109] Berger pictures girls playing hopscotch. Time stands still for them, they become unconscious of normal chronology in the flow of the moment. And with this stepping outside of ordinary time "pain and death, which are the law of that [ordinary] world, have also ceased to exist. Even the adult observer of the scene, who is perhaps all too conscious of pain and death, is momentarily drawn into the beatific immunity."[110] Here Berger gives us a glimpse of vicarious play, a glimpse that points us towards the experience of the sports spectator. What both the spectator of sports and children's hopscotch might tell us is that these experiences themselves have the capacity to become a kind of play. They do not, perhaps, match all of the characteristics of Csikszentmihalyi's flow entirely but there is certainly some common ground.

For Berger play constitutes a signal of transcendence "because its intrinsic intention points beyond itself and beyond man's 'nature' to a 'supernatural' justification . . . which cannot be empirically proved." As such it could be seen as a "merciful illusion" or as a regression to the kind of wish fulfillment of which Freud speaks so that "the religious justification of the experience can be achieved only in an act of faith."[111] But this faith is inductive, not resting on a mysterious revelation from beyond but on everyday common experience. Hans Küng says something similar about

109. Hoffman, *Good Game*, 276.

110. Berger, *Angels*, 78.

111. Berger, *Angels*, 79.

the listener's experience of Mozart's music. Taking the slow movement of the clarinet concerto as his example, he remarks that "here are cyphers, traces of transcendence. *One need not perceive them, but one can*—there is no compulsion here. If I allow myself to be open, then precisely in this event of music which speaks without words I can be touched by an inexpressible, unspeakable mystery."[112] Openness to the experience and to the Other who may come to us in it gives the music, and the play, the possibility of being a vehicle for divine encounter. Here we have a hint of something that we will pursue later: that experiences such as those identified by Berger may not simply be windows through which we can catch sight of another world, but might also be apertures through which the reality beyond comes in to encounter us.

Berger's five signals have some common elements such that they may be said to tessellate with one another. Berger's propensity for order, of which the prime illustration is the parent reassuring the child crying in the night that "everything is all right,"[113] and the arguments from hope and humor fit most obviously with his discussion of play. To play is to create a new world that points beyond itself to another, and in so doing brackets out pain and death, the bleakness of the "ordinary" or everyday world. This is also a demonstration of a kind of hope, though again this can be recognized only by the eye of faith. To a skeptic it may look merely like denial. All play then really would be illusion, and *homo ludens* would become *homo illudens*: the human person whose nature is to play becomes the one who at the core of their being is deceived (*illudens* in modern Italian) and even mocked (*illudens* in Latin) in his or her most basic cultural reflex, play. But the eye of faith sees that the illusion turns out to be the reality.

In just this vein, for Berger the comic element of human life, our pervasive and ubiquitous humor, is based on a discrepancy, an incongruity, with the punch line of the joke flipping meanings to create the effect.[114] All the minor discrepancies that humor celebrates are reflections of the one basic discrepancy between humanity and the universe, between the way things are and the way things might be. Every joke and every comic moment "*reflects the imprisonment of the human spirit in the world.*"[115]

112. Küng, *Mozart*, 34. Italics mine.
113. Berger, *Angels*, 72.
114. Berger, *Angels*, 89.
115. Berger, *Angels*, 90, italics his.

This accounts for the oft-noted close relationship between comedy and tragedy, and perhaps why humor can so often cross a line into cruelty. Our sense of the comic is a sign of our finitude or, in existentialist terms, our "thrown-ness." Like play and hope, humor has the effect of bracketing out for a while the bleakness of life as it laughs at the tragic and the limitations of finitude. "Humor mocks the serious business of the world and the mighty who carry it out."[116] We are not so far now from Harvey Cox's notion of Christ the Clown. "The clown is constantly defeated, tripped, humiliated, and tromped upon. He is infinitely vulnerable, but never finally defeated." Considered in such a light Christ's pathos, weakness, and irony can be seen in new ways—as highlighting the fundamental discrepancy which Berger identifies. "Only by learning to laugh at the hopelessness around us can we touch the hem of hope . . . [Christ] is the incarnation of festivity and fantasy."[117] Every good joke turns out to be a kind of protest against the human condition of thrown-ness in finitude. Every good joke points beyond, signals transcendence.

Play is usually enjoyable, and enjoyable things will make us smile and laugh. Humor is a close cousin of playfulness. We noted in chapter 1 how ancient games were intimately related to religious rituals. Playfulness and the means of relating to the higher force(s) that governs the world are connected. While the play of ritual is usually solemn, the playfulness of worship can often be glimpsed. It too creates its own world, space, and time. It too appears to be an end in itself, to be of no earthly use. The central moment of Christian worship is (depending on one's tradition) the preaching of Christ crucified and risen and/or the celebration of the same in bread and wine. The word and sacrament thus present another great discrepancy, or perhaps several: that God should be killed, that the dead should be raised, that death is not the end, that a death can restore and vivify. The discrepancy is so great, the joke is on the universe. Moltmann recommends that we should "leave the cross out of the game" for understandable reasons given the conflagration of World War II. He is quite properly aware of the difficulty of theology after Auschwitz, let alone playful theology. "In spite of Bach, the dying agonies of Jesus do not fit the categories of song . . . Jesus did not die as a 'fool.' After all, Golgotha was not Oberammergau." While Easter "begins the laughter of

116. Berger, *Angels*, 90.
117. Cox, *Feast*, 142.

the redeemed" the cross can never be a subject for humor.[118] But David Jenkins' critique of Moltmann hits the mark here.[119] He laments the lack of interpenetration that sets up crippling theological dualisms. Suffering and joy must not simply be held in contrast, as Moltmann appears to be suggesting in this particular case, but somehow held and known together. Without this holding together, joy and play will just be a distraction from the world's woes rather than an undermining of them, a pointing beyond them. Barth believes that Mozart captures just this "holding together" in his music. "There is no light which does not also know dark, no joy which does not also have within it sorrow; but the converse is also true: no fear, no rage, no plaint which does not have, far or near, peace at its side. No laughter without tears, no weeping without laughter!"[120] This is not a sign of demonic indifference but an awareness of the ambivalence of creation, though the end of his final work, the opera *The Magic Flute*, avers that "The rays of the sun *drive* out the night."[121]

To joke about the important, Cox reminds us, is to be free for a moment. "Christ the harlequin . . . is the spirit of play in a world of calculated utilitarian seriousness," and prayer becomes a kind of exercise in fantasy and festivity, in play. Christ is "the prayer as joke or the joke as prayer."[122] In play a new world order is created, but "playful" prayer envisages something similar. In supplication we imagine and long for an as-yet nonexistent but richer reality. In intercession, we do this on someone else's behalf, an analogue to the make-believe playing so common in childhood and institutionalized in the theatre. All our proper thanksgivings are "the whoops and hurrahs of a creature who is glad about something. As such they are expressions of play."[123]

The playfulness of the liturgy that celebrates these holy mysteries was noted before Huizinga by Romano Guardini. Guardini noted, as we did earlier, Proverbs 8:22–31. Here, "the Son 'plays' before the Father" and Guardini sees this as characteristic of the life of the "highest beings, the angels, who, without a purpose and as the Spirit stirs them, move before God, and are a mystic diversion and a living song before Him."

118. Moltmann, *Joy*, 50.
119. Jenkins, "Liberation," 21–25.
120. Barth, *Mozart*, 54.
121. Barth, *Mozart*, 55.
122. Cox, *Feast*, 145.
123. Cox, *Feast*, 148.

In our creaturely sphere two activities approximate to this: the creativity of the artist and the play of a child. The liturgy approximates the latter "in which everything is picture, melody and song . . . in a supernatural childhood before God."[124] Guardini here concentrates on the *form* of the liturgy, with Berger we might point to its *content* also, the play of worship as it celebrates God's discrepancy, the incongruity of resurrection. Play: basic to human culture, a signal of a reality that transcends our everyday life, appropriately expressed in liturgy as God's people celebrate God's joyful play of creation and redemption and pray for a new world order.

The End of Play

Play creates a world, and playful prayer longs for a world that is yet to be created. Play's fantastic creation of a world is not simply a sign that humanity is creative, for this play is an anticipation of the end when all shall join with Dante's angels in the "laughter of the universe." Play anticipates the good end of God. In the playground, on the court or the diamond, during the andante or the waltz, earthly realities become transitory and passing, to be left behind, sloughed off as a snake sheds a skin. Instead, the playful mind imagines a new world with different rules, and whose time is somehow tangential to our ordinary time. As Hugo Rahner puts it, "man at play is reaching out for . . . that superlative ease, in which even the body, freed from its earthly burden, moves to the effortless measures of a heavenly dance."[125] Or to tweak Barth on Mozart once more: whenever I play "I am transported to the threshold of a world which in sunlight and storm, by day and by night, is a good and ordered world."[126]

The joyful experience of time during play of which we spoke earlier, a new created time with complex relationships to ordinary chronologies and in which we might glimpse something of God's time, eternity, also allows us to speak of play as an anticipation of God's good end in which our time is "healed." This term, that Fiddes borrows from Barth, is used to suggest how, in God's eternity in which simultaneity and sequence somehow cohere, God always integrates past, present, and future within

124. Guardini, *Spirit*, ch. 5.

125. Hugo Rahner, *Man at Play*, 65–66.

126. Barth, *Mozart*, 22. This, we might note again, is once more a *vicarious* experience. Barth is here listening to music, perhaps on his gramophone before launching off into another day's work on the *Dogmatics*, rather than playing (and certainly not writing it).

perfect love.[127] Fiddes goes on: "we are absorbed in a piece of music or in reading a piece of poetry" or, we might add in playing a game, "and we do not notice that an hour has slipped by. But though we may call this a timeless moment, it is not strictly so. It is not even a 'relative simultaneity'. The whole effect of the music or the poetry" or the game "depends upon a sequence of time in rhythm, repetition and variation. We have not escaped from time but experienced a new relation to it."[128] Our new relation to time experienced in play is an anticipation of the end when God heals all our times, and sport is a particular form of play in which rhythm, repetition, and variation, a storied past and an aspired-for future, become concentrated in the special time of the game.

"And the streets of the city shall be full of boys and girls playing in its streets." In Zechariah 8:5 one of Scripture's pictures of heaven shows us boys and girls playing in the open, careless, safe, and free. Heaven, the good end of God, is a place of play. The end of play is the playful end. Christian visions of the end, whether in Zechariah or elsewhere, have tended not to portray what Moltmann calls "a kind of retirement" or inactivity, but an existence focused on enjoyment of God and (implicit in most accounts) a sense of the joyful fellowship of such enjoyment. In ways that evoke Zechariah's picture, Moltmann argues that Christian eschatology has "painted" the end in "the colours of unhindered laughter, devoted vision of the marvellous riches and goodness of God and of new innocence"[129]—a kind of new and playful childhood. At creation Wisdom played before her father in delight, and in the new creation all God's people will join in this playing before God.

As the final day of creation the Sabbath anticipates another "final day," the end-time when God's people will be gathered to share in the "laughter of the universe" and in the play of paradise. We considered earlier how the Sabbath can be understood in terms of play, and the playful Sabbath also anticipates the good end of God. Through the creation narrative of Genesis 1, after each day's work God sees that "it is good." But only the seventh day is made holy because God rests in it: the "play" rather than the work is sanctified. "The sabbath is . . . the promise of future consummation built into the initial creation."[130] This Sabbath, this

---

127. Fiddes, *Promised End*, 138.

128. Fiddes, *Promised End*, 139–40.

129. Moltmann, *Joy*, 55.

130. Moltmann, *Coming*, 264.

play, is "the dynamic presence of eternity in time" because in the Sabbath *Deus ludens* rests with those God has created.

Particular sports may be said to have particular eschatological resonances. One thinks here, in particular, of games such as cricket and baseball. It is surely no coincidence that these are summer games, and offer a visionary idyll of green sward and shirt-sleeve relaxation. As for cricket, the game on the village green is part of the English rural idyll, a certain kind of English vision of paradise.[131] Craig Forney describes baseball as the "Sacred Story of American Eschatology,"[132] and it is a description that will not be found strange by many American sports fans. Forney's details sometimes stretch our imaginations. The baseball diamond is apparently the perfect shape, and the ball supports baseball's portrayal of the "American mythology of the perfect world to come", in its "ideal" color of white resembling so many American monuments. "Oftentimes, it travels too fast for the naked eye to follow, bringing vision of a world to come when objects will travel instantaneously."[133] Baseball, says Forney, suggests a future of unlimited freedom that is shown even in the longevity of the careers of its players who carry on far longer than their peers in the NFL or NBA. Because baseball games are relatively error-free they suggest a future time free from mistakes, and its non-violent form suggests a future harmony in human relationships. Forney has more to say, not all of it entirely convincing. His contribution is somewhat experimental, as he admits, in seeking to give an account of sports as a particular ritualized outworking of American civil religion, and without a grounding in empirical data some of his correlations seem fanciful. In summarizing his argument he does succeed in bringing out contrasts between baseball, football and basketball that seem intuitively sensible. Football signifies gritty realism, battling against adversary; basketball signifies a kind of pragmatic spirit of compromise, everyday American living; baseball suggests an idealism with a "strong imagination for an ideal life to come."[134]

There is, of course, a forward-looking element to most sports. In a way that is not true for all play, the playing-to-win of sport means that participants are always aiming for something and not satisfied without it.

131. See Ellis, "Play up!" 245, 248–50.

132. Forney, *Holy Trinity*, 66ff.

133. Forney, *Holy Trinity*, 67. Forney does not elaborate on this remarkable future prospect!

134. Forney, *Holy Trinity*, 206.

Often, even when they attain the prize it needs to be won again. There is a kind of restless hope to sport. The best performance always lies in front, pitchers and batters seeking to drive up their averages, golfers looking to connect in just that perfect way, personal bests always in view. Dutch footballer Denis Bergkamp says: "Well, you set yourself goals, targets. And once you've got there you want to move on and go further. You keep raising the bar and therefore it's never good enough. You want perfection. It's never good enough but it's within your reach. You climb one mountain and see the higher one."[135] Sport often appears fundamentally eschatological. The restless hope of sport, with its constant drive for improvement and unwillingness to be satisfied with achievement, recalls theological debates about whether heaven itself might be marked by a continuing, though different and transformed, desire and growth. Macquarrie speaks in this way about the destiny of the cosmos:

> The end would be all things gathered up in God, all things brought to the fulfilment of their potentialities for being, at one among themselves and at one with Being from which they have come and for which they are destined. But this end too could not be thought of as a point that will eventually be reached, for at every point new vistas will open up . . . A static perfection, achieved once for all, would be frozenness . . . [heaven is] the goal of human existence. We may think of it as the upper limit, but . . . every attainment of this limit would disclose further possibilities beyond it."[136]

If sport often appears eschatological, there are other themes associated with the end in Christian eschatology. Not everything is peace, joy, and play. There is also judgment, and sport also offers moments of judgment in a way in which play in general may not. In a contest there is a winner and a loser. The loser can seek excuses in misfortune, but sometimes such remedies do not even convince those who offer them. The strong meritocracy of sport allows no hiding place for the less competent: for those whose skills are less honed, whose fitness is less refined, whose mind is not quite in the zone, whose tactics have fallen short. There are many reasons for defeat that are not excuses, but defeat nevertheless hurts and is public.

135. Bergkamp, "You Climb."
136. Macquarrie, *Principles*, 359, 366.

Joseph L. Price compares the college basketball "Final Four" to the Final Judgment. These teams do not face absolute rejection; they are already the elect, the best of the best. Rather than condemnation their fate is better thought of as akin to the disciples of Jesus asking who will get to sit at his right hand![137] This is an appealing parallel, recognizing the relative success of the final four teams in the competition who have seen off all other opposition. However, it may not be a view that would find favor in a losing dressing room. As Billy Beane remarks when taking the Oakland Athletic to the American League Elimination game in 2002, unless you win the last game of the season, the final, you've done nothing.[138] In some ways, to fall at the final hurdle hurts more than to fall at the first. Defeat *feels* like a judgment, and in some ways really is a judgment. As the cliché goes, the scoreboard does not lie. Could the moment of defeat also point us towards other less welcome eschatological realities, and could it also help prepare us for the moment when we are seen for what and who we are, when everything is laid bare before our Creator and Redeemer? To carry on after defeat, to bear it well and begin again, is there not here some hint of grace?

From a theological point of view, it could be considered idolatrous to portray and promote sport *as* heaven, or as the perfection of experience rather than a groping towards and anticipation of perfection. Some of the soteriologies that we noted during our historical review as emerging in the prime of Muscular Christianity might give this impression. But with due caution there is much in our experience of play that may point us to God's final purposes. In these concluding considerations we have increasingly looked to sport rather than more general play for our material. The time has come now to focus more clearly on a theology of sport, building on aspects of a theology of play that we have explored here.

137. Price, "Final Four," 172.
138. *Moneyball.*

5

"A Matter of Life and Death"?

Playing and Winning

E VERY SPORT, AND EVERY sporting culture, throws up its larger-than-
life characters whose actions and *bon mots* find their way into the
vernacular of players, commentators, and supporters. British football has
its share of these personalities, and among them the former Liverpool FC
manager, Bill Shankly, shines as brightly as any other star in the firma-
ment. The club had fallen on hard times when they appointed him in
1959, having been relegated to the then second division with their stadium, playing staff, and morale in a poor state. Shankly gathered about him
the people with whom he would transform the club into one of Europe's
strongest. Alongside the many stories that abound about Bill Shankly, his
name is always associated with "that quotation." Like many such quotable
quotes, one comes across it in a number of forms, but the most commonly heard is perhaps, "Some people believe football is a matter of life
and death, I am very disappointed with that attitude. I can assure you it is
much, much more important than that."[1] For Liverpool FC and its fans,

1. *Mirror Football*, "Wit and Wisdom." Interviewed on local commercial TV in
1981 (seven years after his retirement) Shankly is recorded as saying, "Someone said to
me, 'To you football is a matter of life or death!' and I said, 'Listen, it's more important
than that' "—which somehow has a less compelling cadence. There is some speculation that Shankly may have been adapting something said by the American college
football player and coach, Henry Russell Sanders. While at UCLA Sanders is reported
to have said that "Beating USC is not a matter of life or death, it's more important than

tragically, football was associated with life and death too often in the years following Shankly's death in 1981: in the Heysel Stadium disaster of 1985, when thirty-six Juventus fans were killed following crowd disturbances, and at the Hillsborough Stadium disaster of 1989 when ninety-six Liverpool fans died in a crush while getting into the ground. These awful events leave their continuing mark on football across Europe, and on the people, city, and football clubs of Liverpool. The controversy following the Hillsborough deaths still rumbles on more than twenty years later.[2]

But aside from such grim moments, many sports fans will know the extreme passions that often come with the territory of playing and watching their sport. Losing can be, as we shall hear Michael Novak suggest, a little like a death.[3] Winning can be, as Francesco Duina observes, like an affirmation of the whole of life.[4] This strange sense of the "importance" of sport, of our desire (could we say "need"?) to win, or to improve, and the effects upon individuals and communities of defeat or failure will be an important focus for theological discussion in this chapter. Why does it seem so useless, facile, to receive the well-meant consolation of "it's only a game"? While we might not want to go so far as to suggest that Bill Shankly (whether or not he had a twinkle in his eye as he made his remark) was correct, is his famous line pointing to something important?

Arousing great emotions, and affording almost spiritual moments, sport is also potentially problematic. The culture of the sporting world has been described by Shirl James Hoffman as "narcissistic, materialistic, self-interested, violent, sensational, coarse, racist, sexist, brazen, raunchy, hedonistic, body-destroying, and militaristic."[5] Even if we consider such criticism to be overstated any theological assessment of sport must come to terms with sport's faults and failings and not idealize its theory and

---

that" (*UCLA Magazine*, Summer 2004, "Rah-rah Boo-hiss").

Interestingly, in this sometimes apocryphal world of sporting one-liners, Sanders has also been credited with saying, "Winning isn't everything, it's the only thing," another quotation which occurs in different forms—including this *Sports Illustrated* version from 1956 (Sayre, "He Flies"). But "Winning isn't everything, it's the only thing" is usually associated with Vince Lombardi—though no version of it is ascribed to Lombardi until 1959 (Maraniss, *When Pride*, chs 21 and 22.)

2. See David Conn, "Hillsborough Service." The report of the independent review of the Hillsborough disaster chaired by the Bishop of Liverpool is also available online.

3. Novak, *Joy*, 20, 47.

4. Duina, *Winning*, 8.

5. Hoffman, *Good Game*, 11.

practice. A theology of sport must be rooted in the actuality of our sport; its realism must recognize the reality of sin. The importance of rooting a theology of sport in its actuality is also a reason to be inductive, and to work to some extent from the reports of those who play and watch sport, correlating these reports with theological observations from other sources.

The theological account of sport that I will offer in this chapter and the next will go further than a theology of play. Too many theologies of sport are, in effect, theologies of play, whereas I believe that we must distinguish between the two more carefully. Play is certainly a part of sport but we have not exhausted what we want to say about sport when we have spoken of play, as the definition offered in the previous chapter attempted to show. In this chapter we will continue the move already begun towards the end of the previous one and shift our focus much more clearly onto sport rather than play. In trying to answer this question I will propose in chapter 6 that a central place be given to the notion of transcendence. This will not be unproblematic—for we will see that a number of the "problems" associated with sport also present themselves as we explore this theme. But first we will ask here why men and women play sport at all, and when they do why winning appears to matter as it does. Attendant questions of competition will also come into focus.

Why Play Sport? What the Players Say

It is difficult to get away from sport, even if one should want to. Television, radio, and other media are saturated with reports of elite sport, and local newspapers offer coverage of amateur sports. A drive through any British city will reveal not only sports centers and clubs, but also enticements to join—"more players welcome" at this football club, "under-11s fun cricket" at that venue, assurances that this gym membership package represents excellent value for money, and so on. Every school curriculum makes some space for physical education and sport. When the sun is out (and very often when it is not) my local park is full of more or less organized games—some in local leagues, others much less formal. The number of men, women, and children regularly occupied by sport in some way is so great that it is difficult to measure, even after one reckons on those whose gym membership pricks their conscience rather than tones their muscles.

Why do people play sport? There are many, many answers to this question. Some of the reasons for playing sport will be conscious, others exert their pressure at more subconscious levels. Some of the reasons have been hinted at already in this book, and it will useful to reflect on them briefly. We will address more explicitly later the question of why people *watch* or *follow* sport. That phenomenon, the spectatorism that we saw develop in chapter 1, will be described as "vicarious sport." This description does not capture the whole of what might be said, to be sure, but it is worth keeping in mind as we ask the more basic question as to why people play.

A good place to start is by listening to what sports participants themselves say. As related earlier, in the spring and summer of 2011 I undertook a survey of sports players and participants in the UK and the USA. Among the almost five hundred respondents were more than a hundred who reported on their direct participation in sports (as opposed to their spectating), most of whom gave reasons for their participation. We need to bear in mind that these sportsmen and -women were (with the possible exception of the odd track-and-field athlete) all taking part in local sport rather than elite sport, and mainly but not exclusively team sports.[6] The range of answers is considerable, though it is possible for analysis to group them into a smaller number of categories. The most commonly reported responses fall quickly under five headings: fitness and health; relief of general stress; social motives; enjoyment of competition; and just simple enjoyment. This latter response, pervasive in the survey responses, is the vaguest of these answers but it resonates with a repeated refrain from our discussion of play. Play is fun, and respondents to my survey played sport because it was fun, because they enjoyed it. Some answers suggest a playfulness about their sport, though others suggested a seriousness even to local sport.

Physiologically, *the enjoyment of sports* may be a by-product of the release of endorphins. The release of these hormones is triggered by a number of human activities including excitement and exercise (though also fear and pain). Their effect is said to be similar to an opiate, and they not only offer an analgesic effect but also a feeling of general well-being and even euphoria. The analgesic effect may help explain why some athletes are able to endure severe discomfort, whereas the fear-factor

6. More information about this survey, including its use and limitations, can be found in Ellis, "Meanings," 170–73.

may explain why some are motivated to overcome discomfort in other endorphin-producing contexts (a fight, for instance), the accompanying sense of well-being seems sufficient explanation for sports participants. There is evidence, incidentally, that when sporting discomfort is endured by a group or team simultaneously then the human powers of endurance can be stretched even further.[7]

In popular parlance one sometimes hears talk of an "endorphin rush" and this phenomenon is related to the "flow" experiences we discussed in the last chapter, though our knowledge remains incomplete.[8] Roger Bannister, the first man to run a mile in under four minutes and himself a neurologist, finishes his book relating his athletic career as follows:

> I now understand more about the sources of pleasure and pain and the strange, some say mystical, experiences that come to those who extend their physical powers to limit. Many recreational runners report experiencing a sense of well-being that has astonished them. Science and medicine cannot yet explain quite why exercise and sport give us deep satisfaction, perhaps for some the most real satisfaction they have in life. With our increasing knowledge of brain chemistry and endorphins, I feel confident that, in the next 50 years, we shall come much closer to understanding this paradox.[9]

One track-and-field respondent to my survey reported that he ran "because it gives me serenity in an occasionally turbulent world and gives me a daily opportunity to feel at one with nature and to feel a spiritual hold on life." This appears to be the kind of motivation that Bannister has observed in "recreational runners."[10] Roger Bannister begins his book

7. "Physical exercise is known to stimulate the release of endogenous opioids (endorphins). Psychologically, endorphin release is experienced as a mild opiate 'high', a corresponding feeling of well-being, and light analgesia, reflecting the role that endorphins play as part of the pain control system. Endorphins have been explicitly implicated in the processes of social bonding, especially in primates and humans, although the mechanisms involved remain unclear. However, there is evidence to suggest that engaging in coordinated physical exercise with another individual gives rise to a heightened sense of social bonding compared to engaging in less energetic activities . . . " This is the first paragraph of Cohen et al., "Rowers' High," 106.

8. From hereon I will dispense with the quotation marks when I refer to the concept of flow.

9. Bannister, *First Four Minutes*, 228–29.

10. It might be argued that recreational runners are "playing" rather than engaging in "sport," as the rules of their "game" are not properly bureaucratized. They certainly do strain the definition, but many aspects of their activity will point towards

with a description that is often quoted by those writing about flow experiences in sport:

> In this supreme moment I leapt in sheer joy. I was startled, and frightened, by the tremendous excitement that so few steps could create. I glanced round uneasily to see if anyone was watching. A few more steps—self-consciously now and firmly gripping the original excitement. The earth seemed almost to move with me. I was running now, and a fresh rhythm entered my body. No longer conscious of my movement I discovered a new unity with nature. I had found a source of power and beauty, a source I never dreamt existed.
>
> From intense moments like this, love of running can grow. The attempt at explanation is of course inadequate, just like any analysis of the things we enjoy.[11]

This is probably a description of flow, and we note also his words in the first quotation that indicate reports of those at the non-elite level who attain similar feelings. We will return to the "mystical" description he tentatively offers presently, but for the moment it is the leaping in "sheer joy" that we take note of and set alongside the many respondents' reports of the joy of playing sport.

Aside from this physiological explanation, the content of the "fun" referred to may be clarified, if not completely explained, by reference to the other common answers. Another answer so frequent as to be nearly universal referred to *the social importance of sport*. Typical among the responses were "to have fun with friends," "a sense of community," "feeling part of a unit," playing is "fun and I enjoy the bond with players," "it's about being and doing things as a team." Another says that "much of my social life revolves around sport." As indicated here, the social side of sports enjoyment has a double aspect: there is the sense of being part of something bigger, such as the team, "on the field"; but there is also the general camaraderie and opportunities to meet and stay in touch with people "off the field." The research of Cohen et al. suggests that bonds made firm off the field can improve performance on it. A number of correspondents also valued the conversation that sports participation offers.

---

the appropriateness of describing their activity as "sport," including the conventions of running which they will observe, the kit in which they run, and a sense of the importance of their own performance, time, etc. Further, many will regard their regular running as training for a larger public event which is at least in form a race.

11. Bannister, *First Four Minutes*, 1–2.

The footballer who said that the enjoyment derived from talking about the game was almost as great as playing it seems not atypical. The social motivations for recreational sport can easily shade into a kind of instrumentalism. The executive who does business on the golf course is just an obvious example of other social reasons why men and women might find sport socially useful in a broader sense.

Another reported motivation for sport that is pervasive, and often used in conjunction with words such as "enjoy," is *the enjoyment of competition*. A cricketer reports that "success with bat or ball is addictive"; a footballer reports that nothing beats the sensation of scoring, and that the sport gives him a sense of achievement; a runner reports "enjoying my competitive successes"; a player of netball and badminton enjoys them because she is "very competitive." Among participants of competitive and non-competitive sports this enjoyment of competition can be found also in terms of competing against oneself. A player of multiple sports, including football, tennis, and rowing, reports that they like to challenge themselves physically and mentally, while a caver reports on the sense of achievement of succeeding in an arduous expedition. The concentration required for this allows her more easily to "let go of work burdens and just have fun," again suggesting a cross-reference to reports of flow. Alongside these reports we should also note similar ones such as "I enjoy the challenge of trying to run faster," and "I want to play well." One respondent speaks of the importance of "pushing myself beyond the limits of comfort." Competition, in recreational sport at least, is not just about winning tournaments or games but also about measuring and testing oneself. This must also be the case in at least some elite sports events. If one thinks of a golf tournament, while players will always try to win, and keep coming back year after year in an effort to do so, the zero-sum experience here is particularly harsh: 156 players competed in the 2013 Open Golf Championship at Muirfield; there was one winner and 155 "losers." While individual teams will win games from one week to the next only one team wins a Champions League, a Super Bowl, or a World Series. Winning is, as we will soon discuss, very important. But unless sports players are fantasists it cannot be the only thing, or the vast majority of players would not turn up to compete, especially bearing in mind what we will hear said about the effect of losing. Competition has to be calibrated more broadly for it to make sense, though this is not to say that the *hope of winning*, or of doing well, or one's best, does not remain important.

A frequently reported motivation for sports participation was its *perceived advantage in reducing stress*. One respondent spoke of playing in order to "escape the daily stress" (the word "escape" is used regularly in this and other contexts), and another of the "de-stressing side effects" of running. Related to this, a number of those who responded reported "letting off steam" or (notable in the case of contact sports) of "channeling my aggression and anger in a positive way," or of their (non-contact) sport being a "good vent for aggression."

These latter remarks are interesting bearing in mind the debate about the cathartic value of sport. Some kind of cathartic function in sport—both playing and spectating—is often assumed or reported, as by a number of my own respondents. However, what empirical data there is does not offer much support for the theory. Wann and his psychologist collaborators put it particularly strongly: however widely held and intuitive, the catharsis theory does not stand up to empirical scrutiny. But, as we shall see later, the evidence is more damning when it comes to spectating than playing.[12] While some Marxist theorists argue that sport has a cathartic function because capitalism needs to provide a safe place in which to express the aggression that its own operation inevitably builds up,[13] there does appear to be some evidence that players often are less aggressive after a game—though not necessarily immediately. Perhaps because of pumping adrenaline, aggression levels sometimes go up immediately after a victory, for instance.[14] However, it is difficult to gainsay what Guttmann calls a modified version of the theory that observes that it is much more difficult for most people to experience certain kinds of excitement and risk in a socially acceptable way. Dunning and Sheard, writing about the way in which violence in sport has been historically moderated in their classic work on rugby, make a similar point about the possibility of expressing violent frustrations with hemmed-in lives that are otherwise socially taboo. The need to express this aggression can be satisfied "vicariously by acting out or witnessing violence in the mimetic sphere, e.g. in sport or the theatre."[15]

There is clearly some debate to be had about the actual de-stressing effect of playing sports but, interestingly, the stated reasons for playing

12. Wann et al., *Sports Fans*, 52–53, 115.

13. Guttmann, *Spectators*, 148.

14. Guttmann, *Spectators*, 154–55; Guttmann, *Ritual*, 130.

15. Dunning and Sheard, *Barbarians*, 236.

sport in my survey discussed so far are common to both players *and* spectators. However, there is another very common, almost universal, reason reported by sports players for their participation, and it relates to *the perceived fitness or health benefits* of participation. "To keep fit" reports one runner, "enjoyable exercise" says a footballer, it "keeps me fit" claims a rugby player, a tennis player modestly reflects that they "enjoy feeling a little fit," and so on. One multi-sports participant responds: "Having been a chubby asthmatic until I reinvented myself as a rower at age nineteen, I am convinced of the medical, psychological, physiological, and myriad other benefits of regular exercise." Short of carrying out extensive tests on my respondents, it is difficult to assess the actual health and fitness benefits that come to these recreational athletes. They are certainly show-ing themselves in tune with current health orthodoxy. The UK National Health Service website summarizes the "Benefits of Exercise" under the photograph of a pair of training shoes as "it can reduce your risk of major illnesses, such as heart disease, stroke, diabetes and cancer by up to 50% and lower your risk of early death by up to 30%." It goes on, "exercise is the miracle cure we've always had, but we've neglected to take our recom-mended dose for too long. Our health is now suffering as a consequence. This is no snake oil. Whatever your age, there's strong scientific evidence that being physically active can help you lead a healthier and even hap-pier life."[16]

While these are clearly the most frequently reported motives for engaging in sport, other reasons are given for playing recreational sport, and some of them several times. Some refer to such considerations as the more aesthetic aspects of sport, some to its family resonances ("my granddad passed away this year and he was a great cricketer so I prom-ised myself to get back involved"), and some speak of the social side as experienced in a sense of duty to teammates or local club.

Closely linked, perhaps, to de-stressing and health functions, is another motivation not explicitly reported in my survey but frequently encountered in anecdote and press report. One such feisty testimony is found in Jamie Doward's account of his "conversion" to running about ten years ago. The word conversion is used deliberately, it is his own word and, as he suggests in his article in *The Guardian* newspaper,[17] running

16. NHS, "Benefits of Exercise." Some of the "harder" science may be found here: Wu Xifeng et al., "Minimum Amount."

17. Jamie Doward, "Running."

and religion appear to have certain common elements—his account is shot through with religious vocabulary. His motives for running include some of those already reviewed plus an element of cleansing or catharsis. The catharsis that Doward describes in his running is linked for him to a very specific event, the death of his "pain-racked" mother from cancer. Now he runs "for her," and indeed also for others who have died similarly prematurely. The tone of his piece is, in theological terms, decidedly and almost aggressively secular, but the therapeutic nature of his running is clear. Running heals him of a dreadful hurt or, at least, it is palliative care for the symptoms of this disabling grief. Speaking of the tens of thousands of runners in the 2012 London Marathon he writes:

> Each runner will have their own reason for attempting to go the distance. Some run to honour dead loved ones; some because their physical efforts may help charities working to alleviate the conditions of those less fortunate . . . some people like to dress up as superheroes in front of tens of thousands of people . . . We run because much of life is frustrating and futile, and only by countering it with some sort of painful, time-consuming, hard-won conclusion to months of repetitive slog—which has kept us from friends and family and beer and sanity—are we able to make an act of defiance to the Fates who conspire over our lives . . . We run because it allows us, albeit briefly, to enter another world. Often this may involve discomfort or even pain, a sense of alienation from our normal comfort zone that reminds us of our mortality and makes us respect our capabilities and limitations. In turn, we are rewarded for our exertions with a form of release, a smoothing out of those toxic feelings of anger, anxiety, injustice and sadness that plague our everyday lives. In short, we run to achieve a sense of inner peace, a recalibration of our souls. If this sounds as if I am suggesting that running is a quasi-religious experience—one that comes with the added bonus of an endorphin rush providing your knees hold out—then that is because I am. Running is the secular equivalent of the Sunday service. The marathon is modernity's equivalent of the medieval pilgrimage.

While each and every daily run appears to be "for" someone's memory, Doward himself runs the major public events in memory of his mother and also to raise funds for charity. The major city marathons around the world attract three types of runner: elite professionals, serious amateurs, and less serious runners for whom a main point of participating is to raise money for charity. About 35,000 runners take part in the London marathon each year (having been fortunate in a ballot open to about three times that number). The vast majority of these will use the event to raise money for a favored charity. Doward's article nicely shows the balance between an altruistic motive (raising money for charity), and the more private ones (some kind of personal therapy). As such it is a reminder that human beings rarely do anything for just one reason. And one hardly needs to be a psychiatrist to guess that sometimes we do things without being able, easily, to articulate *why* we do them. This observation is not meant in any way to diminish the reported reasons from any surveys, nor the testimony given in any piece like Doward's. On the contrary, such reported motives must be taken very seriously. However, it does suggest that we should not stop with these reported reasons for sporting participation but probe further.

Why Play Sport? Sociocultural Factors

Accepting Huizinga's argument that play is a basic form of all human culture we should not be surprised to find that men and women, and indeed girls and boys, have some kind of innate need to play. Sport is one context for the expression of this need. We might be, as some have suggested, "hard-wired" to play,[18] and this would be consistent with what was suggested in the previous chapter about creation and *homo ludens*. Huizinga's argument, however, restricts itself to more anthropological or cultural considerations. As Overman puts it, sports "socialize novices into the values of the society, reinforce behaviors, and reaffirm social values."[19] There may be physiological explanations for play and sport but in terms of the developmental needs of maturing and matured persons the case for play as an essential component in the repertoire of our social interactions seems overwhelming. Exactly how social and psychological forces exert themselves upon us, so that we play without wholly realizing that we do so, say, in order to refine our social skills and oil the wheels of social intercourse, we could speculate about on another occasion. For now we note that there appears to be some deep reason, perhaps not quite

18. Susan Saint Sing, in "Energy," suggests that play constitutes the physical make-up of the universe and us as part of it.

19. Overman, *Sport and Recreation*, 6.

within our normal conscious reach though present to us in moments of deeper reflexivity, why we play.

In terms of our social interactions, some of the ground we covered in chapter 2 suggests other reasons why we might play sports, but of which we may not often be wholly conscious as we do so. Gender identities and sports are related in a complex way. For some men, their identity *as* men is established or reinforced through sport. When a rugby player responds to my survey by saying that playing his sport satisfies "my need to compete physically" one might legitimately speculate about what kind of need this is. Clifford Putney's account of the Muscular Christianity movement in the USA describes it as, in part, a response to a perceived "crisis of masculinity." What some saw as a feminizing of American culture had constructed an ideal masculinity that emphasized stoicism, gentility, and self-denial. In response to what was seen by many as a soft passivity, some argued that a more authentic masculinity should be promoted rooted in activity and channeled aggression. At the turn of the twentieth century when women's participation in sport was advocated the reasons given were often telling. Some argued that participation would help to develop a "graceful carriage," while others spoke in more eugenic terms, of making women fit and healthy so that they could be good mothers. Some simply objected to women participating in competitive sport on the grounds that it could damage their femininity and threaten their reproductive capabilities, or that women would simply become too "masculine" through the experience of competition.[20] These early polarized attitudes to gender and sports show that the way in which our gendered identities are created or expressed in sports has long been significant. We noted earlier the problems of sporting participation for women in terms of gender identity. It is neatly summed up in one study as the "Serena Williams/Anna Kournikova dilemma." Though Kournikova had never won a Grand Slam, her "ideal feminine figure, beautiful face and overall cover-girl looks" meant that she garnered far more off-court attention than Williams and "perhaps the message is that for girls success is won via sex appeal, not athletic contests."[21] I referred earlier to suggestions that some women might try to construct an alternative femininity that looks beyond the very masculine "faster, higher, stronger,"[22] but much

20. Putney, *Muscular Christianity*, 5, 48.
21. Deardorff II and Deardorff, "Escaping," 196.
22. Coakley, *Sports*, 275–76; Geddes, "Gendered Identities."

evidence we possess would suggest that while men may reinforce their gender identity by playing sport, women may do so by *not* participating in sport.

We also considered earlier the way in which sports have become a product to be consumed. While this may appear to be more obvious in terms of paying spectators, it is true also of participation. Veblen observed wryly that "it is noticeable, for instance, that even very mild-mannered and matter-of-fact men who go out shooting are apt to carry an excess of arms and accoutrements in order to impress upon their own imagination the seriousness of their undertaking."[23] Whether shooting, or running, or playing cricket, or football, or baseball, few players compete without the proper kit. Team uniforms may come centrally supplied, but much gear does not. Albert Spalding really started something. As sport is increasingly commodified, and as "branding, packaging, fashion, and even the act of shopping itself" become "the central meaning-making acts in our postmodern world,"[24] it seems likely that our need to construct our identities through consuming will extend to our participation in sports too. In a sense that intriguingly abuts discussion of religion and sport; sport is recognized as a meaning-making activity through the manner of our participation, through the ways in which we consume sports participation.

Why Play Sport? Sport and "Religious Experience"

In seeking to determine whether it may be possible to speak of "religious" reasons for playing sport we first need to clarify a little more carefully what such reasons might involve, and in particular to differentiate between possible kinds of "religious" reasons. A Durkheimian interpretation of religion would render such an assertion relatively uncontroversial: we have ample evidence for the ways in which sports encapsulate and express society's values, and for the way in which sport can bind communities together. But the most obvious kind of religious reasons we might expect to find, perhaps, would be a conscious approach to sport that appears to be seeking (or, at any rate, resulting in) something like religious experience. Even discerning this is much more complicated than it at first sounds. What does "religious experience" look like?

---

23. Veblen, *Theory of the Leisure Class*, X.
24. Twitchell, *Lead Us into Temptation*, 14.

In discussing religion earlier so that we could map sport on to it, we followed Ninian Smart's identification of seven aspects of religion that might be likened to family resemblances. But we did not at that point attempt to define a religious experience. Such a definition would not be entirely uncontroversial. Many of the definitions of religion offered by those who reflect upon religion and sport appear to indicate that religious experience must purport to be an experience of what might be called a supernatural being. However, a crude use of the term "supernatural" is problematic by the standards of much Christian theology, raising many questions about its meaning.[25] It is often those scholars who most want to demonstrate the decay of the significance of religion (like Bruce) or to challenge any kind of religious content in sport, who want to tie the definition of religion down most closely and use such crude definitions. Higgs and Braswell, for instance, grudgingly allow Joseph Price to define religion without any necessary reference to divine beings, though with a necessary reference to a rather more vague "ultimate force or pantheon of powers."[26] Even this is, I believe, too restrictive a definition, offered too often by those who want to close down discussion to suit their own polemic. With Eric Bain-Selbo, I prefer to work from the position "that human beings act religiously in ways other than those restricted to institutionalized religion, and that the sacred is not restricted to one's church, and that spiritual communities can be formed outside of stereotypically religious congregations." Bain-Selbo himself offers something like a set of "family resemblances," though a little different from Smart's, and concurs with Eliade that "human beings are *homo religiosus* through and through, not merely on Sundays, or whatever day one stereotypically worships."[27]

But if it may be proper to speak of sports as a locus for religious experiences we then encounter a further difficulty. If the "religious" part of "religious experience" seems adequately addressed, what about "experience"? A good deal has been written that compares moments of sporting intensity with mystical experience. Some, like Watson, distinguish between "nature mysticism" and what they would regard as truly religious

---

25. For example, see Tillich, *Systematic Theology* I, 72–73. Also: "without diminishing the holiness or reality of God, we have nevertheless escaped the crude supernaturalism of supposing God to be a kind of *deus ex machina*"; also Macquarrie, *Principles*, 155.

26. Higgs and Braswell, *Unholy Alliance*, 18. They refer here to Price, "American Apotheosis," 228.

27. Bain-Selbo, *Game Day*, 232.

experience.[28] While Watson never defines religion in his essay on mysticism he does make clear that he is attempting to explore his subject from within a "mainstream Christian theological worldview"[29] and accepts the caution of Higgs and Braswell on this issue about such experiences appearing to have a "supernatural root."[30] If one prejudges in this way what is likely to count as a religious experience it is not surprising that one might come to the conclusion that experiences of unity with all things (to caricature somewhat) are nature mysticism rather than the kind of mystical experience that might be recognized as religious from within a mainstream Christian framework.

But we need at this point to pause and ask again, what does religious experience look like? We might distinguish five types of experience that are sometimes classified as religious. The mystical, the charismatic, the regenerative, the communal, and the nurturing.[31] Almost always in discussions of sport it is the first of these that features prominently. William James, in his classic discussion, identified four elements to mystical experiences: they were ineffable, noetic, transient, and passive.[32] It is significant to note, for our purposes especially, that James regarded mystical experience as the true core of religious experience. Here, religious experience in general had its "root and centre."[33] In this opinion he appears to have been followed by many who write upon religious experience and sport. The enlightenment gained from an exploration of mysticism would illumine every other aspect of his enquiry, James suggested, and he regards mystical experience as a certain state of consciousness. The comparison often made is between flow experiences in sport and these mystical states, and there are clearly good reasons for asking whether these flow experiences might be considered in such a light. The four marks of mysticism identified by James seem to fit these moments of flow quite well: they are difficult to talk about, they often seem to give some special insight or knowledge, they "cannot be sustained for long"[34]

28. Watson, "Nature and Transcendence," 103–6.

29. Watson, "Nature and Transcendence," 97.

30. Watson, "Nature and Transcendence," 96.

31. Peter Donovan lists four types: the mystical, the paranormal, the charismatic, and the regenerative. I have omitted the paranormal but added the communal and the nurturing. See *Interpreting*, 3-20.

32. James, *Varieties*, 380–82.

33. James, *Varieties*, 379.

34. James, *Varieties*, 381.

with an hour or two being the outer limit but a half hour or less more usual, and while both flow and mystical experiences can be prepared for they always remain outside of the control of the subject.

Where critics in the sport/religion debate find particular difficulty is in the noetic aspect of the flow experience, in the claim that such moments might give some special insight or knowledge. This is partly why Watson insists that such flow moments might be described as "nature mysticism."[35] Certainly, Roger Bannister's description of discovering a "new unity with nature"[36] in running might give support to this view. Watson is concerned that, while the flow experiences may appear to have something in common with descriptions of experience in Asian religion, there is a pantheistic tinge to this—and this does not sit comfortably within what he calls a mainstream Christian theological framework.

John Macquarrie identifies ten common features of mystical experience, though they could be read as a Christian theologian's reflection on James' four.[37] The cognitive aspect is that which corresponds to James' noetic, and Macquarrie recognizes quite frankly (as most writers do) the difficulties involved in claiming a cognitive dimension to mystical experience, while still going on to give a robust defense of it. It should not be surprising, when the first thing James noted about mystical states of consciousness was their ineffability, that the assessment and communication of any knowledge gained will be difficult. It will be, as James put it, an insight "into depths of truth unplumbed by the discursive intellect."[38] But Macquarrie reminds us that there is more than one kind of knowledge, and more than one way of arriving at it. Emotions and feelings in other contexts carry some kind of direct awareness: "fear, for example, implies awareness of a threatening environment."[39] He notes that Kierkegaard's notion of *angst* brings with it a compelling knowledge of our finitude. We might know certain facts about a country or about a person, but this is not the same kind of knowledge we have from visiting a country or actually knowing the person. Whatever kind of knowledge the knowledge of God is, he reminds us, it is more like the knowledge of another person than the knowledge of a list of facts. Similarly, "the mystic knowledge of

35. Watson, "Nature and Transcendence," 104.

36. Bannister, *First Four Minutes*, 1.

37. Macquarrie, *Two Worlds*, 7–34.

38. James, *Varieties*, 380.

39. Macquarrie, *Two Worlds*, 10.

God is . . . of the kind that is gained through the experience of living."[40] Mystics also continually connect knowledge of God with self-knowledge "to such an extent that sometimes it is hard to say where the knowledge of the one leaves off and the other begins."[41]

In a later discussion of the Irish theologian of the ninth century, John Scotus Eriugena, Macquarrie tackles nature mysticism specifically. Eriugena, says Macquarrie, used the term "Nature" to describe everything that is, the material and spiritual worlds *and*, crucially, God. Unity with Nature here includes unity with God, it is not something that makes sense *apart* from God. More modern philosophers, suggests Macquarrie, might have used the term "Absolute" to do this work. Within what he calls "Nature" Eriugena distinguishes carefully between created and Creator, but nevertheless Eriugena has sometimes been charged with pantheism, and this probably led to his condemnation several centuries after his death. Macquarrie's view is that "Eriugena cannot justly be called a pantheist."[42] Instead, he is seeking to affirm strongly both the immanence and the transcendence of God, which all Christian theology should wish to do. For Eriugena, quite properly, God is present within Nature but also distinct from it in a way echoed centuries later by Wordsworth who spoke of

> . . . A presence that disturbs me with the joy
> Of elevated thoughts; a sense sublime
> Of something far more deeply interfused,
> Whose dwelling is the light of setting suns,
> And the round ocean and the living air,
> And the blue sky, and in the mind of man;
> A motion and a spirit, that impels
> All thinking things, all objects of all thought,
> And rolls through all things.[43]

Again, with reference to Wordsworth, Macquarrie insists that it would be a mistake to categorize *this* position as pantheism. Wordsworth is not saying that the natural world *is* God, but that God may be encountered through it. Similarly, John Keble articulates a nature-mysticism in the hymn that runs:

40. Macquarrie, *Two Worlds*, 10.
41. Macquarrie, *Two Worlds*, 11.
42. Macquarrie, *Two Worlds*, 109.
43. Wordsworth, "Tintern Abbey."

The works of God above, below,
Within us and around,
Are pages in that book, to show
How God himself is found.[44]

Views like those of Eriugena, Wordsworth, and even Keble may have frequently been viewed with some suspicion by the gatekeepers of Christian orthodoxy, but they have been more popular within what is sometimes called "ordinary theology,"[45] the theological positions held by those outside of the academy or the teaching office of the church. This can be put down to undisciplined sentimentality, or it could be more generously thought to reflect the "religious experience" of many believers unfamiliar with the nip and tuck of academic discourse. Many otherwise exemplary believers not versed in the dangers of natural theology will have inscribed around their garden pond the couplet from Dorothy Frances Gurney insisting that "One is nearer God's heart in a garden, than anywhere else on earth."[46]

It is still true that, in a more generous assessment of the "mystical" such as this, one has still not established what might be the source of such experiences or how any knowledge gained can be relied upon. The key difficulty is establishing what the experience of the "something" of which mystics speak, and perhaps also sports players in flow, is an experience of?[47] What I believe we can show is that to *dismiss* it as nature mysticism is unhelpful. Nature mysticism is not necessarily pantheistic, and it can be claimed to be an experience of God through nature. Taking a cue from Eriugena we might even venture to suggest that it is not impossible that a Bannister-like experience of "a new unity with nature" may also be in fact an experience of God. Higgs and Braswell object at various points that the function of sport is not to bring about an experience of the holy.[48] I concede that it is true that this is not the explicit or declared function of sport: one will not find it in the rules of the Football Association or the NFL.[49] However, one of the purposes of this study is to consider whether

44. Keble, "There is a Book, Who Runs May Read."

45. Astley, *Ordinary*.

46. Gurney, "God's Garden."

47. "For religion is in some way a response of the whole personality grasping, intuiting something through its own profound interest in its own fullest realisation. What, then, does it grasp? What is the content of the religious intuition?" Farmer, *World*, 42.

48. Higgs and Braswell, *Unholy Alliance*, 31.

49. Neither was it Moses' purpose in herding sheep (Exodus 3).

it might not be an implicit or subconscious purpose. My survey does give some grounds for believing that those who play sports regularly also have some experience of moments of flow, or something like them, and also of other experiences which may be regarded as religious—as we shall see presently. Though there are none quite so effusive or articulate as Bannister's account, it does seem that some people play sport in order to have the kind of experience that we have been talking about here. One athlete speaks of the serenity they gain through running, which suggests that the more positive side of "de-stressing" might be expressed in something like these terms. This respondent goes on to say that running gives them "a daily opportunity to feel at one with nature *and to feel a spiritual hold on life."*

But my objection to those who focus on the mystical in attempting to find, or discredit, religious experience in sport is based upon more than a critique of a tendency to denigrate it as nature mysticism. Rather, following James in his central position given to mysticism within an understanding of religious experience, such a view works with far too narrow a view of what counts as religious experience. This takes us back to my fivefold categorization of religious experience as the mystical, the charismatic, the regenerative, the communal, and the nurturing. We have considered mysticism; what of the other four?

Within the Christian tradition, and in the last few decades in particular, the subject of charismatic experience has often proved controversial. Pentecostal congregations are growing rapidly in many parts of the world, and charismatic evangelicalism has influenced many mainline denominations. The controversy usually focuses on "spiritual gifts" such as speaking in tongues, healing, and words of prophecy, but issues of leadership, spirituality more generally, and mission lurk near the debate. Charismatic experiences are not peculiar to Christianity, however, and Sufism in Islam, and some traditions of Hinduism and Buddhism could also be described in this way. It is difficult to think of glossolalia and healing in terms of sports participation, but it would perhaps be as well to note that Paul lists wisdom among the *charismata*,[50] and that the church traditionally has also spoken of charisms as divine gifts in less spectacular terms. This is reflected in the more secular use of the terms charism and charismatic to denote someone who is attractive and influential. Looked at more generally, it is certainly possible to see some individuals "come

50. 1 Cor 12:8–10.

alive" when playing sport, to see someone who is quiet and inarticulate off the pitch suddenly become animated, powerful, and dominant on it. Some sports players also think of their own ability to play as itself a gift, a charism. For instance, according to one footballer in my survey, "I have some level of God-given ability to play so it is rewarding to do so . . . I play because I feel that sport can be an arena to honour God."[51]

All evangelicals, for whom the language of "being born again" is so important, will know of the central place of the regenerative religious experience. Sometimes massive external changes take place in the life of someone whose orientation dramatically changes, and at other times the transformation is more internal or attitudinal. William James recognized the importance of this kind of experience also, and devoted two chapters to the subject of conversion. But regenerative experiences are not confined to conversion: healing, spiritual growth, moral progress, sensing a new vocation perhaps to ministry in the church or to some other new venture, and also the regular reception of the Eucharist might all be spoken of in this way. My survey is replete with responses that suggest that the playing of sport can be experienced as regenerative. We may recall the rower who "reinvented herself" through sport, and every testimony to refreshment known in sport, the identity established or confirmed through it, the "sense of achievement" gained through it, seem to point toward sport's regenerative powers. It does need to be said, in anticipation of a reasonable objection, that there are other spheres of human activity where regenerative experiences may be known, and that sport may not be peculiar in this regard. This is readily conceded. I am not trying to argue that sport is the only place where such experiences can be gained, nor even that sport is the only sphere of activity in which something like religious experience may be possible. For instance, Higgs and Braswell object that, if sport is a religion, then perhaps literature should be considered one too.[52] Perhaps, that is for other people to consider at another time. My claims for sport have never been necessarily exclusive. However, this current investigation is occasioned by the remarkable coincidence of so many indicators that appear to give sport something like a religious

51. This recalls Olympic sprinter Eric Liddell's often quoted line from *Chariots of Fire*, "I believe God made me for a purpose, but he also made me fast. And when I run I feel His pleasure," though this appears to be the screenwriter Colin Welland's attempt to encapsulate Liddell's belief rather than words which can be traced directly back to the sprinter himself.

52. Higgs and Braswell, *Unholy Alliance*, 4–5.

character. Indicators as diverse as ritual, myth, and experiences, to name just a few.

William James' views on religious experience were extremely individualistic and, as in so many other ways, this appears to have shaped much of the discourse on the subject that has followed him. When Alfred North Whitehead suggested that "religion is what the individual does with his own solitariness"[53] he not only showed signs of James' influence (Whitehead's philosophical and theological outlook was in other respects so notably *social* rather than individualistic), but he uttered a dangerous partial truth. While we may want to express the importance of the individual's relationship with God, and also of the individual's responsibilities in living as a Christian disciple, religion is a fundamentally communal reality. "Our experience of the life of faith comes . . . from participation in a community of faith."[54] Christian theology recognizes this immediately it gives any prominence to the notion of church. In scriptural terms, Jesus called the disciples into the Twelve, or the Seventy, and he bound together his close friend John and his mother Mary in reciprocal relationship recognizing (as Genesis puts it) that it is not good (nor indeed possible) for us to be alone.[55] Paul's letters speak of believers as the body of Christ, seek to build up the church, and are chock-full of personal greetings.[56] "Greet one another with a holy kiss."[57] We might further suggest that the importance of the communal in some way reflects or points toward the Triunity of God: Father, Son, and Holy Spirit. One does not need to hold a thorough-going social doctrine of the Trinity to see such correspondences. The Triune God created human beings in and for community as God may also be said to be "in community," and our experience of the reality of God is also likely to have this dimension. The notion of our play as a participation in the divine play also recalls the Triunity of God: I have deployed the term seeking resonances with the notion of Trinitarian participation outlined by Fiddes.[58]

The importance of the communal aspect of sport is easily seen from my survey responses, and this community is experienced as itself a source

53. Whitehead, *Religion*, 16. Compare James, *Varieties*, 31: "religion . . . [is] the feelings, acts, and experiences of individual men in their solitude."

54. Macquarrie, *Principles*, 5.

55. Luke 6:13; 9:1–6; 10:1–12; John 19:26–27; Gen 2:18.

56. 1 Cor 12:12–31; Rom 16; 1 Cor 16.

57. 1 Cor 16:20.

58. Fiddes, *Participating*, passim, but esp. ch. 2.

of healing, strength, and hope. Team sport is the most obvious source of such responses, with many speaking of the importance of "camaraderie" and of "bonding" with others, and the degree of mutual commitment that comes through from some rugby responses suggests that contact team sport may take this to another level again. Some responses indicate a different kind of community through time. A cricketer says, "I have always [played cricket]. I don't always enjoy it but my granddad passed away this year and he was a great cricketer so I promised myself to get back involved;" and a footballer says that playing "is so much part of my family." Overwhelmingly this community is experienced as positive.

It is also experienced as nurturing. H. H. Farmer, like Macquarrie, likened our knowledge of God to our knowledge of other persons rather than objects. Such knowledge immediately seems thereby relatively more intuitive and less discursive. Farmer himself affirmed that our knowledge of the personal reality of God was marked by two elements that would always be held in tension: the sense of the unconditional demand that God places upon us, and the sense of ultimate succor that God offers to us.[59] While each of these five dimensions of religious experience may be said to bleed into one another, I believe that Farmer was right to single out absolute succor. Furthermore, Farmer is also surely correct to suggest that authentic religious experience is always marked by a sense of a demand placed upon one's life that in different traditions may be experienced as moral, spiritual, ritual, or in some other way. The absolute demand may run through all kinds of religious experience like a seam of rock running through other strata. Ultimate succor, too, may have some similarity with regenerative experience most especially. However, it seems to me rather less bracing. A common experience of Christian believers is to know God as, in Farmer's own biblical allusion, their "refuge and strength."[60] The sense of self-worth and affirmation, often made more profound by a corresponding feeling of unworthiness, is a core element in Christian experience. The sense of receiving life as a gift, and of God's goodness being made real to us in a myriad ways that we have done nothing to earn, is part of what is meant by the term grace. This ultimate succor is articulated in Christian terms in John Newton's fine hymn that begins:

> How sweet the Name of Jesus sounds
> In a believer's ear!

59. Farmer, World, 23–26.
60. Farmer, World, 26.

It soothes his sorrows, heals his wounds,
And drives away his fear.

It makes the wounded spirit whole,
And calms the troubled breast;
'Tis manna to the hungry soul,
And to the weary rest.[61]

This nurturing is certainly closely linked also to the communal aspect of religious experience. Nurturing generally takes place in community, but the conviction is that it is Christ who nurtures through and alongside the care of others. The divine nurture is mediated. In the responses to my survey there is a strong sense of sport's nurturing qualities. Reading the responses one has a strong sense of sport as recreation, that is, as re-creative in the lives of its participants. Sport enlivens, supports, affirms, fulfills, heals, socializes, and broadens the horizons of those who play it.

No one of these arguments or parallels alone makes a case for people playing sport for "religious reasons." However, taken together they do begin to make a more impressive cumulative case. In particular, it is necessary to move away from a definition of religious experience that is shaped too much by a James-ian notion of mysticism and to think in a more comprehensive way, a way earthed more in the experience of actual believers.

A further caution is required. James' seminal study was profoundly individualistic in its approach, as already mentioned. This individualism was mirrored in an atomistic account of religious experience, which he understood to be fundamentally episodic rather than continuous. James, we might say, set about describing religious *experiences* rather than religious *experience*. This is also, I believe, misleading. A more complex and nuanced approach is suggested by Nicholas Lash. Lash argues that when, in ordinary speech, we talk about "experience," more often than not we do not mean a one-off occasion, a particular moment. Instead we usually have in mind an accumulation of such moments, a reservoir of experience upon which we draw and by means of which we make judgments and interpretations. Thus we say we will "put that down to experience." In the same way, religious experience is best understood as an accumulation of moments that enable us to react and respond and interpret the world in which we live and enable us to live with hope and faith. "Christian experience," Lash says, "is simply a complex of particular experiences that

61. John Newton, "How Sweet the Name."

have, for each Christian, the quality of being at one and the same time, their experience—lived, refracted, and interpreted in faith—and yet not strictly singular, because the interpreting faith is no merely individual affair." [62] The attempt to identify a single moment—the flow moment, for instance—and label it as the "religious" moment in sport is misguided or misleading. We need to focus instead on something much more like the *total experience of playing* (or spectating), though I suppose that we might want to suggest (in a way that Lash seems reluctant to do) that within the total experience there will be more and less significant moments in the whole that can for the purposes of analysis or narrative be separated out.

Lash also notes that James was "fascinated by 'religion,' but took no great interest in any particular religion." [63] James sought some core experience (singular moment) that might be said to be essential to all religious experience, and he believed fundamentally that all mystical experiences from every tradition were the same kind of experience. But in so doing James tended not only to abstract from particularities in religion (not being very interested in any particular one), but also to de-historicize human experience. The Stoic, Buddhist, and Christian in fact have different kinds of mystical experiences and these differences arise at least in part because of "their different modes of apprehending what they consider to be the divine" (in James' phrase). [64] These modes of apprehension are largely specified and determined by their varying social, historical, and cultural situations. The place I occupy in space and time is not a neutral or abstracted one, and my "religious experiences" do not come to me unmediated by culture, language, and tradition. [65]

Sport is not an isolated phenomenon but embedded in culture, and no sports player comes to their activity devoid of other experiences. In particular, they come from a culture that already has certain "religious" aspects within it, however secularized. The way in which they apprehend the religious dimensions of the wider culture may then impact upon

62. Lash, *Easter*, 174.

63. Lash, *Easter*, 25.

64. James, *Varieties*, 31.

65. William James tended to focus on the elite religious experience, on Moses, Jesus, and Paul, rather than ordinary believers. It has to be conceded to James that there is something about, say, the story of Moses at the burning bush (Exodus 3:1–22), which does seem to come in a more dramatic and discontinuous way. This may lead us to qualify Lash's point, but its main thrust remains and it has an implication for our consideration of religious experience and religious motivations in sport.

their experience of sport. For instance, the Muscular Christians of the nineteenth century interpreted their experience of sport in part at least in the light of their understanding of Christianity. To complicate matters, this appears to have been a somewhat reciprocal process. The shaping of American sport by the Protestant work ethic, outlined convincingly by Overman,[66] is an example of this. Taking these two aspects together we may say that the concrete sociohistorical actuality of any sport shapes the experience of the participant, including anything we might think of as "religious"; but also that any openness to such "religious" experience in sport will also be conditioned by the vocabulary available to reflect upon it and will be at least partly brought *to* sports participation. Speaking about religious experience in sport is not straightforward.

To this discussion we might add a brief word of a more functional nature. Discussions earlier in this book have suggested that many features of contemporary sport may have displaced those previously offered by organized religion. We are thinking here of such elements as the ritual or "liturgical" aspects of sport, its sense of seasonal time, and its provision of the kinds of myths and narratives that are common to religions. In the words of chapter 3, people may turn to sport as once they turned to institutional religion in order to express certain feelings; experience certain emotions or states of mind; construct identity; dramatize important human instincts; inhabit a rhythm of life; participate in life-shaping ritual; and so on. Taking all this together it seems that there are good reasons for saying that some people play sport for religious or quasi-religious reasons.

Why Winning Matters

There is, of course, another reason why men and women play sport. They play to win. This is what distinguishes sport from many games and from play in general. Some people, apparently like 2013 Wimbledon men's single tennis champion, Andy Murray, are fiercely competitive from a very young age.[67] Others may be socialized into the orientation more slowly. Winning, playing to win, is an important distinguishing factor in sport, and also, in the eyes of many Christian commentators, the source of many of its problems. Earlier we distinguished sport from play, or

66. Overman, *Sport and Recreation.*
67. BBC TV, *The Man Behind the Racquet.*

other kinds of games, by the bureaucratization of its rules, and by the element of *agon* or contest; this contest is embodied, involves physical and mental exertion, and the skills necessary for the successful playing of a given sport can be refined through practice. Implicit here, and made explicit now, is that sports are (with one or two exceptions that prove the rule)[68] contests with winners and losers.

My survey asked two questions about winning: one asked about its importance, and the other about its effects (coupled with a complementary question on the effects of losing). For many players of recreational sport in my survey winning was not the only thing that mattered[69] though it still ranked as important. Supporters in the survey also did not generally display a must-win mentality though there was some contextual variation: the identity of the opposition was a factor here. Generally, supporters were most eager to win in games against local or traditional opponents. In elite English football terms we are talking here of the major derby games such as Arsenal versus Tottenham Hotspur, or Everton versus Liverpool, though nothing, perhaps in the world, compares to Glasgow Celtic against Glasgow Rangers. In professional or top amateur sport such rivalries are often regional or based on a narrated history of memorable encounters (Manchester United have one kind of fierce rivalry with Manchester City and another with Liverpool, each with its own narrative). However, it is also true that away from the glare of the national media a game between local rivals at any level has a certain "needle" quality. Even at local sport level, clubs develop intense rivalries that can turn otherwise routine fixtures into grudge games with more at stake than championship points. Winning in these fixtures has a peculiar importance, and in the case of recreational sport the interest and intensity is much more focused in players than spectators.

What these rivalries often show is the way in which sports enable individuals and communities to establish and reaffirm identity. This identity is never more precious than when faced with the neighboring "other" against whom one community defines itself. This intense local

---

68. In terms of the exceptions which "prove," i.e. *test*, the rule we might consider climbing, recreational running, and other "solo" activities. A strong case can be made that many such activities are properly called sport though they do not fit straightforwardly into any agreed definition. However, in these two examples, for instance, it is still possible to speak of "winning" and "losing" even though the participants may not generally beat other participants. See note 10 above.

69. Compare Vince Lombardi's phrase: see note 1.

rivalry often surfaces in matches where the rivals are not even playing one another as supporters sing with derision of their traditional foes.

Some of my respondents predictably reported that "winning is everything. Losing isn't an option." However, another equally strident and devoted fan could say that "winning is important but so is knowing how to lose; you can't know the pleasure of one without knowing the pain of the other." This pattern recurred throughout the survey and through all sports. It does also need to be said that losing was acceptable only if one's team lost well, i.e. if it had played well and performed to a high standard, "done us justice," then defeat was manageable. We might again bear in mind the fact that, moving the focus away from individual matches, only one team wins a season's championship: most are destined to be losers in the bigger picture. Taking the longer view, sport's zero-sum games seem cruel.

However, slightly at odds with this more mixed picture, is one presented by the question about the impact of winning and losing—here even those who had declared that winning was not the only thing they cared about reported on the negative effects of losing and the positive effects of winning. There were answers that called for a sense of perspective or that reported that losing some matches is not as bad as losing others. As well as losing to local rivals, losing a match with a lot at stake such as a major play-off game, for instance, was hard to bear.[70] Terms such as "exhilarated," "depressed," and "gutted" are used regularly. To lose is to feel empty.

Michael Novak connected this awful feeling in sport with Christian life and worship. Sports possess great power to lift or lower us, and losing symbolizes death. "The same is true of religious symbols like Baptism or the Eucharist; in both the communicants symbolically experience death and are reborn. If you give your heart to the ritual, its effects upon your inner life can be far reaching."[71] Novak develops this theme, of what we might call the existential anguish of losing, claiming that "the underlying metaphysic of sports entails overcoming the fear of death."[72] This appears

---

70. A rugby league fan is not untypical: "winning a big game such as a grand final or a cup final has a knock-on effect for days afterwards. As does losing. Losing to Wigan is up there with the worst feelings I have ever had. *It makes me sick.*" From another sport we hear that "winning is the single greatest feeling in the world, and losing is the worst."

71. Novak, *Joy*, 21.

72. Novak, *Sports*, 47.

to be a bold claim, but it may go some way towards explaining the appeal of sporting encounters. Remember: even those who were relaxed enough to see that not every game must be won admitted that winning was important, and everyone reports the negative impact of defeat. Perhaps sport should be seen as a kind of continual reenactment of a battle for life itself, dramatized through the particularities of a given sport. Novak: it is "no use saying 'it's only a game.' It doesn't feel like a game. The anguish and depression that seizes one's psyche in defeat are far deeper than mere comparative failure—deeper than recognition of the opponent's superiority."[73] If it were simply a matter of recognizing that the other team or player is better, emotions would not run so deep—there must be more, suggests Novak.

> The [sports] game tests considerably more than talent. A game tests, somehow, one's entire life. It tests one's standing with fortune and the gods. Defeat is too like death. Defeat hurts like death. It can put one almost in a coma, slow up all of one's reactions, make the tongue cleave to the mouth, exhaust every fount of life and joy, make one *wish* one were dead, so as to be attuned to one's feelings . . . Consolation and comfort from others do not touch the depths of one's feelings. In decency, announcers do not usually visit the locker rooms of the losers. It takes enormous efforts of will for the dead to pretend to be alive, congratulating those in whom life still flows triumphant . . . Each time one enters the contest, one's unseen antagonist is death.[74]

Novak's argument here is similar to that put forward more recently by Francesco Duina. Duina is interested in why Americans "need" to win, why they are (as he puts it) obsessed by winning. Americans marvel that a cricket test match can last five days and end in a draw—no American game in any sport ever ends in a draw: there must be a winner. Duina explains it persuasively, and in a way that may help explain not just American attitudes. Winning, he argues, "often serves as an objective and external validation that we are *right*."[75] By a strange logic we seem to feel that winning means that we have a better grasp of the world, that we are right in all sorts of ways. Winning means that we are "clearheaded, correct, sharp." By contrast, losers are "wrong in a general sense." The loser has "soul-searching" to do. Research at North Carolina State University

73. Novak, *Sports*, 47.
74. Novak, *Sports*, 47–48; italics his.
75. Duina, *Winning*, 35.

revealed that losers give more causal and introspective reflections of their performance while winners are more matter-of-fact and less reflective. Duina concludes: "victory, in other words, is liberating."[76] Furthermore, winning makes us feel good about everything and losing makes us feel correspondingly bad. There are sociopolitical dimensions to this too that we hinted at in in an earlier chapter: both the Soviets and Americans saw sporting victory during the Cold War as demonstrating the superiority of their whole socioeconomic system, not just their athletes. Duina notes that the 1980 US hockey victory at the Olympics "was perhaps the single most important athletic event of the Cold War."[77] In the same way, "teams winning national titles in American football, baseball, and basketball make the residents of the cities and localities where they come from 'proud'—not of their athletic abilities but of their way of life."[78] Duina here demonstrates the very close relationship between players and spectators at elite level. The players might sometimes be characterized as journeymen, only performing for their pay check. And yet their strange reciprocal relationship with the spectators suggests that "spectators" may often not be the correct word with which to describe them. They are involved in the action as it unfolds and affected by it afterwards. We will bear this in mind when we come to "vicarious sport" shortly.[79]

Everything that Duina says finds an echo in the players' responses in my survey. All the footballers agreed that winning was very important, one adding that "if it all ends up in the team winning in the right way by playing some good football and overcoming the challenges well, then it doesn't get much better than that for me." A cricketer signals a change of tone when he says that winning is very important, "though if I lose but know I've played well, I am ok with losing." This is taken further in the more individual sport of track and field. In athletics the team winning is very important, and for each individual athlete the setting of a personal best is equivalent to a win. "Winning, *in the sense of achieving personal goals*, is very important. It is the main motivation behind my training." Here the *agon* is clearly against oneself as well as other opponents, but

76. Duina, *Winning*, 36.

77. Duina, *Winning*, 39.

78. Duina, *Winning*, 41.

79. These two respondents capture the identification with the team and the scope of that winning feeling: "I feel elated when my team wins as if I had played myself"; "when my team wins I feel a sense of community and accomplishment. This feeling of 'we did it' with both the team and fellow supporters."

there are traces of this attitude in many responses from many sports. A rugby player comes close to the nub of the matter: "you always have to focus on winning otherwise there's no point in playing, and losing every weekend is quite demoralizing." This contribution is significant because it reminds us that sports are oriented towards a winner. The *point* of playing is to overcome the opposition by scoring more goals, throwing more hoops, making more touchdowns, batting more runs, running more quickly, taking fewer shots. This respondent also bears out the effects of not winning. Losing on a regular basis is demoralizing. If it really were "only a game" there is no reason why this should be so, but something more is clearly going on here. As Novak put it, "a game tests, somehow, one's entire life. It tests one's standing with fortune and the gods. Defeat is too like death. Defeat hurts like death." Winning provides an affirmation of the self; it represents a successful (if provisional) dalliance with death and darkness; its taste is sweet. Winning must sometimes seem close to salvation itself, it is a trip to the edge and back. This rugby respondent also reports that "The important skill is learning how to win and lose well, making sure you get something from the experience each time you take the field." Learning to lose well is perhaps therefore an attempt to negotiate through the medium of sport a way through some of life's very biggest questions.

Winning and losing, then, take on metaphysical significance. They are tied up with questions of identity, self-worth, and self-esteem. If losing feels something like a death (the "loss" of defeat reflecting in some pale way the "loss" of grief), winning feels like an overcoming of death if only for a moment. Positively, we may say that defeat enables us to anticipate more grievous losses, perhaps indicating even the horizon of death itself. Winning and losing thus become so important that players and coaches will go to extraordinary lengths to succeed. Winning matters, and human beings are sinners. In due course we will have a more general discussion of *that* subject, but it is appropriate at this point to pause in order to give some theological evaluation of competition in sport.

The subtitle of Francis Duina's book suggests that winning is an *American* obsession. There is certainly *prima facie* evidence that appears to support this, though we also need to note again that the *point of anyone anywhere* playing sport is (usually) *to win*. Our theological discussion of competition will be informed by Duina's work. It will often seem that Duina is speaking particularly about sport, and many of his illustrations are from the world of sports. However, we should note that his analysis is of American culture much more generally, and he also uses many illustrations from commerce, politics, education, and other spheres.

Duina notes that as long ago as the early 1800s Alexis de Tocqueville described America as a restless nation, ingenious and bent on self-improvement, and that compared with other nations (the Danes are in view in the research quoted) Americans tend to have an unrealistically high opinion of their own abilities; in general surveys, the approval rating for competition in general is almost double that which is reported from western European countries.[80] But these observations need careful qualification. For one thing, if winning were enough in and of itself, then we might expect that we would choose "easy" opponents—but we do not. "Victory itself is not very interesting. Without close competition, very few of us would be eager to compete."[81] To beat opponents who represent no challenge is not satisfying. We tend to seek out opponents who will test us, push us, make us work hard to win, and thereby we will derive satisfaction from victory. The joy of winning is complex but it involves a differentiating of ourselves from our closest peers. The effort involved in winning requires a considerable investment of energy and labor, physical and mental exertion. We invest ourselves in winning, and that means that while loss is painful because of our investment, "winning vindicates us . . . Winning often serves as an objective and external validation that we are *right*."[82] This relationship between effort and reward is "central to American culture and its roots."[83] The battle to win is the battle to gain our proper place in the world.[84]

Duina is not alone in suggesting that there is something distinctively American about the need to win: the anecdotal evidence compiled by Warner from sports coaches[85] and Overman's thesis tracing extreme competiveness back to a particularly American appropriation of the Protestant work ethic are among complementary corroborating sources. Overman observes that "from its very beginnings, America was a nation held together by pitting group against group, state against state, region

80. Duina, *Winning*, 3–6.
81. Duina, *Winning*, 16.
82. Duina, *Winning*, 17, 35.
83. Duina, *Winning*, 17.
84. Duina, *Winning*, 182.
85. Warner, *Competition*, 85–86.

against region in competition."[86] The "Land Rush" both demonstrated and encouraged this and, with no state religion, individual denominations vied with one another in an open market so that religion too falls under the analysis. "The highly competitive American has viewed life as a zero-sum game in which someone always has to win, someone to lose. This love of competition has had profound effects upon individual behavior—as it has on institutions."[87]

We might remind ourselves that, by common agreement, modern sport is not an American invention but emerged (to abbreviate absurdly) in nineteenth-century Britain. At that time an amateur ideology mitigated the drive to win somewhat. We saw that in the USA especially, but perhaps also elsewhere, the emerging phenomenon of sport was connected with the search for a new ideal of masculinity; it also became entangled with notions of health, patriotism, and with Christian concerns for mission, among other things. It is true that in the USA sport was to some extent *re*invented. Whereas the sports that emerged in Britain had been through a long process of gestation, a more rapid development and appropriation of baseball and American football marked them out as American sports designed for American needs. Basketball is the most striking example of this (literal) reinvention of sport. But even in Britain the amateur ideology that moderated competition and valorized (among other things) restraint and "Olympian sportsmanship" was under threat, and from the first. Overman's account of developments in the USA give a reasonable explanation of developments in Britain too. In more middle-class circles, he observes, where social status is settled, the amateur ideal tended to downplay competitiveness. Here it was considered ungentlemanly to try too hard, and bending the rules or even preparation before competing, was frowned upon. But in working-class contexts, where social status was not already assumed or assured, competitiveness took precedence over sportsmanship. This ethic came to fashion that of professional but also amateur sport in the USA, and in time elsewhere too.

In chapter 3 I had cause to speculate that America may not be more "capitalistic" than Europe, but that it might bear its capitalism in a different way. The same might be true, therefore, of winning in sport. Winning is the point of playing sport, and American, British, French, and Brazilian sports men and-women play to win. Of course, if the Marxist critics

86. Overman, *Sport and Recreation*, 92.
87. Overman, *Sport and Recreation*, 93.

are correct, it may well be that their common capitalist cultures have socialized them in this behavior, though this does not explain the fierce competitiveness of the Cold War Communists. What does explain it is Duina's argument, echoed in many other writers (perhaps most notably Novak), that winning is not just about winning, but signifies something else. Perhaps then, the most we can say is that human players are all en-cultured to seek to win in different ways. There may be an American way, and it would contrast quite markedly with a British way circa 1860. The present-day contrasts are probably less marked.

Most theological discussions of competition concede that it is a mixed phenomenon, with positive and negative aspects. Gary Warner's popular but generally wise discussion tries to balance these carefully. On the positive side competition encourages individual and collective disci-pline and responsibility, self-control, endurance, the benefits of learning to win and lose well, fosters good relationships (with one's own team and one's opponents), and the "healing power" that comes through the sense of achievement when one has competed well. [88] It is notable that all of these appear to be extrinsic goods, that is, they arise from competing in sport but are benefits that may then be exported to other spheres. Nota-bly lacking in this list might be any sense of the physiological pleasures of exertion, or the health benefits derived therefrom. There is also no mention of straightforward fun. This latter especially might be said to be taken for granted in much of Warner's discussion, but it is interesting that it does not appear in this list. The instrumental feel of his list of benefits suggests that for Warner sport is not to be considered autotelic, in con-trast to play, and he therefore risks taking the play out of sport. Perhaps, some will argue, that is precisely what competition does.

On the negative side of the balance sheet Warner's list is headed by pride. Other dangers are the potential to be stuck in lifelong adolescence that never grows out of a certain kind of play, the dangers of hero-worship and idolatry, of greed and exploitation, and of violence and militarism.[89] If human beings are *homo ludens*, then it is unlikely that we are meant ever to grow out of play, but Warner's point stands as a caution against arrested development. Having a mature adult attitude to sport will be having an outlook that places things in proper proportionality. Warn-ings about greed and exploitation can be targeted at recreational sport

88. Warner, *Competition*, 51–117.
89. Warner, *Competition*, 119–86.

(with its consumerism) as well as at elite level. Here Warner expresses some concern about top salaries,[90] but it is difficult to treat sports stars in isolation from other entertainers or indeed anyone else. In the USA especially, perhaps, there is seldom coyness about the appropriateness of maximizing one's earning potential, and the athlete's career peak is usually short and always fragile. Warner's cautious note on violence is a timely reminder of what can happen to human beings in competition either when the adrenaline takes over and rational thought retreats, or when a sense of proportion about rewards is lost. We noticed in chapter 1 that the development of sport is tied in various ways to military action, and we recall these ties in the bellicose vocabulary often used to describe sporting events. It would not be a surprise if, the closer sport and patriotism become connected, the more insidious the dangers here.

Having created a balance sheet, how does one attempt to calculate credits and debits, and would such methods of accounting enable us to make progress? First, the dangers of competition in sport are very clear, and they could be rehearsed much more dramatically. I think that we should take judicious note of Marxist and similar critiques that appear to show us that sport in this regard as in others both mirrors and reinforces ideologies and social mores. Perhaps it is not entirely a coincidence that sport emerges not simply as institutionalized religion declines but when modern industrialization and capitalism begin to take shape. However, the historical record appears to give evidence of competitive spirit before modern sport, though it had to be channeled in other ways. Sometimes, one suspects, in just staying alive. Stuart Weir comes close to suggesting that we are created not simply to play but to compete when he remarks that God created us as those who could run, and kick, and catch, and with some desire to compete.[91] Even allowing for cultural variations, for the different ways in which individuals are socialized to compete, and the different spheres in which they decide to compete, there appears to be something here that cannot quickly be dismissed. Conceding that different cultures give different weights to competition and calibrate competition in different ways, we appear to be both created to compete and conditioned in the way that we compete. But let us not be under any illusions that sport is the only sphere in which we do so. If competition is an evil that Christians should avoid or discourage such a judgment would

90. Warner, *Competition*, 156–60.
91. Weir, "Competition," 108.

place a ban on a great deal more than our sporting activity. It would affect business (and the creation of wealth) and education very clearly, but its impact would have much wider reverberations. Seldom does this appear to be recognized by those critical of sporting competition.[92]

Second, the bad is a distortion of the good—and it is a good before it is distorted. Some presentations imply that, crudely, the first humans *played* in the Garden of Eden, but only *played sport* after the fall. Play is presented as an innocent pastime, in which men and women become creative and flourish; whereas sport is a human creation, bureaucratized and institutionalized, zero-sum in nature with some condemned to defeat. But such a view takes a naïve view of play while also adopting a partial and dismal view of sport. Any playground observer will know that even the innocent play of children can be distorted. Of course, sport, like all our play, is not now played in paradisiacal Eden, but like every other human enterprise is pursued in a murkier world. Sport is not inherently bad, but like many other intended goods (such as play and other gifts from God) it can become corrupted and distorted.

Much of this chimes with what Mark Hamilton calls his Augustinian critique of sport. Before considering his argument it will be instructive to look at one of the incidents to which Hamilton refers. Augustine's friend Alypius "had lost his heart and his head to the games in the amphitheatre" in Carthage.[93] He was, Augustine tells us, "wrapped up in this wretched sport" and "needed to be cured of this mania."[94] Alypius also attended lectures at Augustine's school of rhetoric. Through listening to Augustine, who made his points with illustrations drawn from the games, Alypius "hastened to drag himself out of the deep pitfall into which, dazzled by the allure of pleasure, he had plunged of his own accord. By a great effort of self-control he shook himself free of all the dirt of the arena and never went near it again."[95] But Alypius moved to Rome, fell in with the wrong sort, and was taken to the Gladiatorial Games there. Despite attempting to prove that he would be unmoved by this "cruel and bloodthirsty sport" when he attended the arena that was "seething with the lust for cruelty" he could not resist and succumbed to:

92. Weir is an exception.
93. Augustine, *Confessions*, vi/7, 120.
94. Augustine, *Confessions*, vi/7, 121.
95. Augustine, *Confessions*, vi/7, 121.

the roar of excitement from the crowd . . . When he saw the blood, it was as though he had drunk a deep draught of savage passion. Instead of turning away, he fixed his eyes upon the scene and drank in all its frenzy, unaware of what he was doing. He revelled in the wickedness of the fighting and was drunk with the fascination of bloodshed. He was no longer the man who had come to the arena, but simply one of the crowd which he had joined.[96]

It is no part of my argument to defend the Roman games, and Alypius' newly refound blood-lust appears to be indefensible. There is much in common here with Tertullian's concerns about the ancient games. There was an independent tradition of games that the Romans inherited from the Etruscans and perhaps others, and it would be folly to assume that such an inventive people could not create their own entertainment. In some measure the Roman Games followed on from and appropriated aspects of the Greek; however, while the etiology of the Roman Games is much discussed and it may be possible to see aspects of them as a distortion and corruption of the Greek Games that preceded them, there is nothing in the Greek tradition of the games which matches the barbarism of the Roman arena at its worst. While it would be easy to dismiss Alypius' frenzy and joy in violence as quite different from, say, basketball or cricket or tennis competitions today, we should be a little cautious about this. The "frenzy" that Augustine (and Tertullian) observed is familiar enough in modern fans. And while there may not be the same mortal conclusion to modern sport there is a tendency for combative vocabulary to be deployed in emotive terms: a coach might speak of his team "destroying" their opponents, or fans will speak of "annihilation." In contact sports the dangers are more obvious. Rugby and NFL players frequently acquire injuries that if not life-threatening can be life-changing. Players regularly retire on medical advice, and injuries inflicted *without* foul play can be devastating. But in the heat of battle, as it were, players can commit illegal acts that risk or give serious injury. The officials frequently have great trouble in determining whether any illegal intent was present in a given incident; such is the nature of the game.[97]

96. Augustine, *Confessions*, vi/7, 122.

97. Boxing, still arousing controversy long after nineteenth-century church authorities expressed their reservations, is a sport where the object is to knock one's opponent out. Boxing is a special and testing case for sport apologists in this context. I simply note here that it crystallizes issues about the acceptability of violence in sport

Alypius had extracted himself from the Carthaginian Games "by a great effort of self-control", but this self-control failed him. When he was delivered finally from his thrall to the Gladiatorial Games Augustine claims it as God's work: "You stretched out your almighty, ever merciful hand, O God, and rescued him from this madness, You taught him to trust in you, not in himself."[98] With this typically Augustinian reminder of the necessity of reliance on grace we might note that the "madness" that can come with sport, played or watched, and that can have the character of addiction, can be something from which we need deliverance with resources stronger than our own. We should not underestimate its allure and power.

However, the Gladiatorial Games are not, despite the similarities just conceded, modern sport. The Final Four, though a moment of judgment of sorts, is not designed to bring about loss of life, and contestants and spectators at the Super Bowl would likely be traumatized by life-threatening injury rather than energized by it. When David Busst, playing for Coventry City against Manchester United in April 1996 sustained compound fractures of the tibia and fibula in an otherwise innocent collision in the United goal mouth, the game was held up for some time and the pitch needed cleaning up before play could continue. The United goalkeeper Peter Schmeichel is reported to have needed counseling after the incident, and many fans still find the YouTube footage too difficult to watch.[99] We might also compare Roman chariot-racing with contemporary Formula 1 motor-racing. The latter may have, as part of its appeal, a sense of wonder that drivers keep their cars on the track at such high speeds, and there may even be among some spectators something like the phenomenon of rubbernecking seen on highways where other drivers slow down to view a car wreck on the side of the road showing a strange fascination for the macabre. But even after all this, we have to note the extraordinary progress made in safety provisions in Formula 1, and the devastating effect on fellow drivers, support teams, and spectators when there is a serious accident. Modern sport is *not* the same as Alypius' dreadful passion in the Roman arena.

---

in a particular way, and a full theological assessment of it must await another time.

98. Augustine, *Confessions*, vi/7, 123.

99. Robert Philip, "Busst Counts His Blessings"; YouTube, "David Busst Horrific Injury."

Hamilton highlights the self-deception in Alypius' attitude, and notes that modern sports fans can be equally delusional about the time and resources given over to sport. The problem is, he suggests, that this prevents us from analyzing our relationship to sport clearly. In particular, we begin to act out of disordered affections: we love sport too much, out of proportion to its real importance—though this, of course, does beg rather a lot of questions. How much is too much? And what is its real importance?[100] Augustine's argument that evil was a privation of good rather than a reality with its own actual existence was a significant affirmation bearing in mind his former Manichaeism with its dualistic understanding of good and evil, spirit and matter. Augustine could say that while "God is good, utterly and entirely better than the things which he has made," nevertheless "since he is good, the things that he has made are also good."[101] Evil is "not a substance" but a lack of good.[102] Puzzled by the behavior of evil men he concludes at last that "when I asked myself what wickedness was, I saw that it was not a substance but perversion of the will when it turns aside from you, O God."[103]

This fits well an understanding of human sin which distorts the enjoyment of sport—and indeed *any other sphere of human activity* that might be thought to be good in itself. But while Augustine certainly affirmed the good of God's creation, he still sometimes gives cause for us to wonder whether the Manichaean influence has been entirely shrugged off. The last quoted paragraph of the *Confessions* also speaks of higher and lower orders of creation: the higher orders, nearest to God, are the most spiritual, and Augustine elsewhere attributes sin to the body more than the soul. He "raises doubts about the extent to which the individual human soul can be held responsible for morally bad actions, responsibility instead being attributed to the body in which the soul (itself quasi material) is trapped. Although Augustine is vehement and at times merciless in his repudiation of the Manicheans, questions can still be asked about the influence the Manichean world-view continued to exert upon him."[104]

100. For instance, I wonder whether the fan respondent to my survey who opined that "You have many cars, pets and even wives, but you only have one team" had his tongue in his cheek? Possibly not, though experience of sports fans gives ample evidence for a knowing sense of humor.

101. Augustine, *Confessions*, vii/5, 138.

102. Augustine, *Confessions*, vii/12, 148.

103. Augustine, *Confessions*, vii/16, 150.

104. Mendelson, "St Augustine."

There may remain a kind of residual dualism here and sometimes one suspects that theological critics of sport have inherited it. For Hamilton, the distorted love of sport effectively *reduces* us to bodies, and this results in obsessive behavior.[105] It is not that I am unwilling to countenance the possibility that love of sport can be disordered, of course it can be and often is. Rather, I want to question an implicit assumption that the very embodiedness of sport, with its high risk competitive content, is somehow of necessity part of the "lower orders." There is something here also reminiscent of James' treatment of religious experience as unmediated and direct, as if experience that dispenses with the physical is somehow superior and even (as in some anti-sacramental Protestant traditions, perhaps) the only way of communing with God. Hamilton refers to C. S. Lewis (like Augustine a Platonist of sorts[106]) and *The Great Divorce*, recalling the artist who loved art but now loves only the recognition that is gained from it. The difficulty is that such objections can quickly turn into a different kind of zero-sum challenge: love art *or* God—choose. Our mediated experience of God enables us to love God through art, or indeed sport, perhaps, rather than having to choose between them—having to leave behind the "lower" for the unmediated "higher" and more spiritual experience.

It certainly does not appear to have been Augustine's intention to retain any part of this dualism. Andrew Cameron argues that the central place given to the incarnation is testimony to this.[107] Cameron agrees with Hamilton: "Evil happens when we lose perspective, when we *stop seeing things as they really are*, when some good thing is no longer enjoyed in its 'due place' but as an end in itself and we desert God for it. This logic of good things 'malfunctioning' brings Augustine to speak against what he calls 'concupiscence,'"[108] though even Cameron's summary of Augustine on concupiscence, which is much more than sexual lust, goes on to suggest that it "springs from within our bodies."

With Augustine we can affirm that "a good life is lived by a person who loves what ought to be loved properly."[109] All things in moderation, Aquinas' Aristotelian happy mean is anticipated. It is a matter of

105. Hamilton, "Augustinian Critique," 31.
106. For a sympathetic account of Lewis' Platonism see Allred, "Platonic Foundation."
107. Cameron, "Augustine," 35.
108. Cameron, "Augustine," 35, italics his.
109. Hamilton, "Augustinian Critique," 28.

proportionality and balance. Indeed, Aquinas, writing far removed from Roman gladiators though doubtless with other instances of cruelty near enough at hand, had encouraging things to say about play. He does not have our sport in mind (how could he?) but his insistence on balance and the need for recreation is significant. His illustration here is taken from the "sport" of archery: not to release the pressures of life through play would be like snapping a bow through over-tensioning.[110] Aquinas says that the proper place of playing needs to be qualified in three ways: that nothing indecent or harmful should result from it, that it should be appropriate for time and place, and furthermore, "we should take care not to lose our poise"—by which he appears to mean that in our playing we should not dissipate the personal formation established in our living Christian lives in other ways. So: playing sport should not be harmful or indecent, should have a care for context (over-competitive parents on the touchline of school sports, please note), and should not allow us to lose our identity "lest we dissolve the harmony made up by good works in concert."[111] As such, "a settled disposition to act accordingly is a moral virtue," to which Aristotle gave the name *eutrapelia*. The person who possesses this virtue is "a pleasant person with a happy cast of mind, who gives his words and deeds a cheerful turn."[112] There are clear glimpses of eutrapelian individuals in my survey, those whose competitive sport gives them a "happy cast of mind" and a "cheerful turn."

I have been suggesting that Augustine's own experience of "sport" through Alypius' frenzy at the Circus Maximus is only partially helpful in forming an attitude to modern sport that is—even at its worst—fundamentally less barbaric. Also, I am suspicious that some attitudes to sport bear something of what might be a tendency to be suspicious of or downplay pleasures of the body—and sport, while it has intellectual delights is certainly also an embodied pleasure. In much of the debate about sport one can see what Gorn and Goldstein describe as a tendency to label activities as straightforwardly either good or evil in a dualistic way.[113] Few will want to argue with Hamilton's description of Augustine's position, that "a good life is lived by a person who loves what ought to be loved properly." And, as Hamilton argues, many athletes do trip into nar-

---

110. Aquinas, *Summa Theologiae*, vol. 44, 217.

111. Aquinas quoting Ambrose, *Summa Theologiae*, vol. 44, 219.

112. Aquinas, *Summa Theologiae*, vol. 44, 219.

113. Gorn and Goldstein, *Brief History*, 251–52.

cissism[114] or an unhealthy desire to win: "when love of winning becomes more important than it ought, it creates a distortion, a disharmony, vice or evil."[115] But these errors are neither intrinsic nor peculiar to sport. Hamilton's critique is useful in exposing sports practices to the theological framework of a major thinker. Where it sometimes falls short is in its persistence in seeing sport as somehow isolated from other cultural practices, from the rest of human life, thus running the risk of singling out for opprobrium in sport what is equally pernicious elsewhere.

Competition can be destructive but, as Warner observed, it also has a peculiar effect on relationships. This can be shallow and instrumental, as it can in workplace or church. But it need not. When the British & Irish Lions rugby union touring team is selected every four years, the finest players from England, Scotland, Wales, and Ireland are melded into one squad to play high intensity matches against the leading southern-hemisphere rugby nations: Australia, New Zealand, and South Africa. Players from England, Scotland, Wales, and Ireland do occasionally play for the same club teams, but when chosen to represent one of their four rugby countries they are one another's opponents; on tour with the Lions they become teammates and the friendships they establish last by common testimony for a lifetime. Competition for places in the starting team can act as a curious bonding force. Sometimes great rivals can also become friends even though they never play on the same team, and for all the moments when behavior on the field falls below acceptable standards there are many, many occasions when players show great sportsmanship even at the risk of competitive disadvantage. On the 2013 British & Irish Lions tour of Australia, Lions player Johnny Sexton dropped out of an attacking move in order to check on an injured opponent and call for assistance. This is not an unusual sight. If there is a "problem of evil" in sport there is also ample evidence of good works, of Aquinas' poise being affirmed.

Between great opponents there is not only fear but also respect and camaraderie. For all the bellicose language generated around contact sports in particular there is a particular kind of fellowship that exists between opponents. One of the most obvious places where this is seen is in elite tennis. To be sure, not all players form close friendships with one another, but many do. Andy Murray, already mentioned as fiercely

114. Hamilton, "Augustinian Critique," 29.
115. Hamilton, "Augustinian Critique," 32.

competitive, has real friendships with most of his major rivals at the very top of the world rankings. After a number of near misses he won his first "major" in New York in 2012. Asked by a journalist whether he wished he could be playing in another era, away from his friends Djokovic, Nadal, and Federer, so that he could win more tournaments, he replied that while he might win more trophies that way he would not be such a good player: his opponents had made him the player he was by continually stretching him to new limits in his play. This is a helpful reminder of a truth most obvious in sports like tennis and golf where only one player wins each tournament, which is that "winning" has to mean more than what at its face value it appears to mean.

Weir reminds us that winning can mean different things to different people in different contexts. "There may be a greater sense of satisfaction for the runner who achieves a personal best and a national record, or for the runner ranked 20th in the world but who makes the final, than for the 'winner' who finishes first in a performance well short of his best."[116] Etymology is illuminating: "the word [competition] comes from the Latin *com* and *petere* which has the root meaning of striving together."[117] *Together.* Sport is fundamentally relational, and is a cooperative enterprise even between opponents. Few gain the clarity of thought of Andy Murray who prefers to test himself against the best rather than win more often. The existence of any league or conference, of international and local tournaments, is a very basic acceptance that in order to compete at all one needs opponents. The gladiators had no choice but to fight for their lives, but modern sport, like true play, is entered into freely and competition depends upon cooperation in arranging fixtures and tournaments, in agreeing rules, in developing and refining acceptable standards of sporting behavior.

Most players and spectators have a keen sense of right and wrong in playing, even when they commit infractions. This explains the outrage at a heinous foul, the sense of injustice when officials miss a crucial detail, the burning resentment that can turn workaday fixtures into grudge games. We may recall Berger's signals of transcendence: as well as the argument from play there was also an argument from damnation. Here Berger had particularly in mind the most atrocious of crimes that called forth a damning indignation in response, but the sense of fair play is

116. Weir, "Competition," 101.
117. Weir, "Competition," 101.

universally recognized—even, paradoxically, by those who deliberately set out to circumvent it. Duina observes how, even amid the obsession with winning, "the breaking of rules is tantamount to an affront to the very existence of competition itself."[118] This sense of fair play is sometimes written into the structural arrangements of sports as in the NFL draft that gives the previous season's weaker teams first pick of new college players for the next season, or in the handicapping systems in golf and horse-racing.

Weir casts this cooperative competition in terms of "loving one's neighbour,"[119] suggesting that the challenge is to love the teammate who is selected before you, the opponent who abuses you, and the referee whose mistake costs the match. This recalls Martin Luther's very grounded way of explaining this commandment. Commenting on Galatians 5:14 ("for the whole law is summed up in a single commandment, 'You shall love your neighbour as yourself.'") he says:

> Paul knows how to explain the law of God. He condenses all the laws of Moses into one brief sentence. Reason takes offense at the brevity with which Paul treats the Law. Therefore reason looks down upon the doctrine of faith and its truly good works. To serve one another in love, i.e., to instruct the erring, to comfort the afflicted, to raise the fallen, to help one's neighbor in every possible way, to bear with his infirmities, to endure hardships, toil, ingratitude in the Church and in the world, and on the other hand to obey government, to honor one's parents, to be patient at home with a nagging wife and an unruly family, these things are not at all regarded as good works. The fact is, they are such excellent works that the world cannot possibly estimate them at their true value.[120]

Luther's concept of love for neighbor is an accessible one, not at all the kind of reading that is only available to the professionally religious or the incurably saintly. It is earthed in the day-to-day realities of living in the *polis* and in the family (where husbands can nag as well as wives, of course). Loving one's neighbor through playing sport is therefore a potentially rich notion. The cooperative competition that lies beneath all sport is a form of neighbor-love in its everydayness, and love for jostling

---

118. Duina, *Winning*, 172.
119. Weir, "Competition," 112.
120. Luther, *Galatians*.

teammate, dissembling opponent, and incompetent official are a gritty kind of love for neighbor.

Weir goes further by picking up the same theme as struck by Andy Murray.

> Perhaps the way to love one's neighbour is to give him the hardest tackle one's body can produce—fairly and within the rules. By doing that I am forcing him to be the best player he can be. Similarly, I need the opponent to nail me when I get the ball and to play the most brilliant tactical game he can so that I have to take my gifts and use them to the best of my ability against him. That is to love my opponent in the heat of competition. It is wanting the best for your opponent, in order to get the best out of yourself.[121]

In the "mutually acceptable quest for excellence" whereby "opponents cooperate to bring the best out of one another"[122] we have returned to Duina's observation that winning itself is not really anything of note. It is the contest, the competition that matters. Of course, in practice achieving this gritty neighbor-love on the field or court is not easy. But sport is not unique in such challenges. Where it perhaps offers a dimension that is not available to the competing businesswoman or student is in the physical contact and opportunity for harming one's opponent (and being harmed) that accompanies it. Once again, a sense of proportion is needed. Without trivializing the awful incidents or downplaying the most wicked participants, given the opportunity for harm in regular sport it might be considered remarkable that the injury list is so relatively small—which is not to say that officials and governing bodies should not give further thought to any evidence that evolving patterns of play do appear to be causing harm.

Abusing Ourselves to Win: Competition's Dark Side?

Where the obsessive need to win *does* show itself may be not so much in the abuse of one's opponent as in the abuse of one's own self. Here we may encounter competition's dark side, perhaps. Watson and White give a disturbing, but not exhaustive list: "performance-enhancing drugs, surgical

121. Weir, "Competition," 113.
122. Watson and White, "Winning," 63. They go on to express severe reservations about this notion.

enhancements, injured players competing through pain and assuming serious risks to body and mind, unhealthy eating habits (and disorders, e.g. bulimia and anorexia nervosa) and drastic weight reduction among some women gymnasts, wrestlers and jockeys, and extreme training regimens among endurathon-type athletes, exemplify the kind of action of" a winning-at-all-costs perspective.[123]

Elite sport is a high pressure business. Part of sport's appeal is its very uncertainty. Few people would want to watch many contests where they can easily predict the result. But the margins are small, the prizes are huge, so every little piece of extra preparation could make a difference, and anything that gives confidence a boost is useful—elite sports, it is often said, are as much about the mind as the body when one reaches the highest level of competition. As athletes are propelled to the top, as they make more and more money, as endorsement deals become dependent on a profile in the public eye, the stakes rise. Gorn and Goldstein put the matter starkly in discussing basketball in the USA: "The rewards of making it in college and professional sports are entirely too seductive for anyone to expect adolescent males to resist them. That is why the issue of performance-enhancing drugs is so conceptually straightforward. As long as there remain disproportionally valuable prizes for those who win games, people who play them will break the law and endanger their health."[124]

This bleak assessment is followed by the assertion that drug-taking is routine in college sports such as wrestling, weightlifting, and football, and even in these sports at high schools too. Reliable data for performance-enhancing drug use is, by the very nature of the problem, difficult to obtain. It seems obvious that it is more widespread than simply those who have been caught in the dope-test programs. Some dope-test positives appear to show that some athletes may come under pressure from their coaches or whole systems of sports management—in such cases it may not be the athletes who succumb to temptation but those around them who control training schedules and contracts. The revelations of performance-enhancing drug use in elite cycling show how complex and ingrained such practices can become.[125] Gorn and Goldstein note, ironi-

123. Watson and White, "Winning," 64.

124. Gorn and Goldstin, *Brief History*, 245.

125. See, e.g., Hamilton and Coyle, *Secret Race*, and Vinton, "Fight to Expose Cycling's Doping Culture."

cally perhaps given our earlier positive evaluation of the body, that such practices show the extreme objectification of the athlete's body that this entails.

At elite level some sportsmen and -women may begin to feel themselves invulnerable and above the rules. Their sudden wealth cushions them from the kind of decisions that most people have to make. They are treated with a respect that sometimes turns into veneration, and because confidence is so important they are frequently told how good they are. Many of them "suffer" in this way from adolescence and receive huge financial rewards at an early age. No wonder then that sometimes they appear to believe that rules apply only to other people. This may entice them into performance drug use, or it could land them in trouble because of their relationships, their unguarded speech, or their driving. The abuse of the body lurks as a temptation for some to maintain or gain advantage.

Temptations to cut corners exist in every competitive environment: the exam candidate who cheats on a test, the dealer who is economical with facts, the politician who taps the conversations of his rivals in order to outmaneuver them strategically. However, sport does seem peculiar in the way in which such opportunities involve the willingness to hazard the health of oneself or those under one's charge. Two decades ago Eastern European sports management routinely inflicted such treatments on aspiring athletes as part of a political propaganda war,[126] and we recall Duina's observation that winning on the sports field appears to us to say something about how we are winners in other spheres too. Here indeed we see an ugly side to sport.

Winning in sport confers various benefits to the fortunate few. For the elite, great wealth. For many, status in a given community. For most, the warm glow of satisfaction. Even when winning is understood more broadly, as doing one's best, its rewards can seem highly felicitous. The connection between winning and esteem is worth pondering. Duina remarks that we believe that the outcome of a competition tells us something important about ourselves, that is, it tells us something about our *worthiness* not only in this competition but in general.[127] In the USA, a culture that does "do God", we find that

> according to the General Social Survey, more than 75% of Americans believe that God plays a role in shaping one's success

126. Costello, "East German Athletes."

127. Duina, *Winning*, 143.

or failure in life. With the victory, thus, comes the belief that God was instrumental in shaping our performance and, by reflection though seldom acknowledged, in punishing our opponent with defeat. We then reason that God's favorable treatment of us must have a reason. We consciously or subconsciously assume that God must be rewarding us for something that we are doing right, not in the particular realm in question (politics, a sport, etc), of course, but in life and as people in general. We must somehow be worthy of God's grace. We must be living a virtuous life that is in line with God's desires.[128]

Once again, we might remind ourselves that Duina is not just speaking about sport, but competition in every sphere of American culture. Even so, this report seems most worrying theologically. While British and European respondents may not put it quite like this, one can imagine a similar sense of self-justification and self-worth arising from achievement.

Should we not feel and enjoy a sense of achievement when we do things well? When we perform a fine sonata, create a garden, design a prototype, paint a remarkable picture, or many other successes? Perhaps even, score a home run, or make a touchdown, score a goal, beat our previous best golf round on our home course, or even get picked for the team at all? The difficulty is not with a proper sense of achievement, but with proportionality and balance. *Eutrapelia* knows nothing of an identity that is founded only in what we do in any sphere of activity. We are not "justified," do not earn esteem and worth by our performance, but through some other means. When Aquinas speaks of retaining our poise in play he is suggesting that whatever we gain from sport we also take some sense of identity to it that must already be robust because grounded properly. Human persons are not valued by how well they perform Mozart or write a novel, cook *cordon bleu* or knit a sweater or kick a goal. They are valued because they are made in the image of God and are loved by God, because through Jesus Christ they may redeemed from the disease of sin that corrupts and distorts all things, including our sport. As Weir says, "it is important to remember that God does not love an athlete any more on a day she wins than on a day she loses. If, as an athlete uses her talents, her attitude is above all to please the God who made her, then God can rejoice in this particular aspect of his creation."[129] This construc-

---

128. Duina, *Winning*, 145.
129. Weir, "Competition," 109.

tion both shows the thin line between an approach based on grace and one based on works ("above all to please . . . God") and also may suggest that an appropriate attitude to sport is impossible for a non-believer, which would be unfortunate. What emerges is the importance of attitude. Crudely put, and by analogy with orthodox teaching on good works, the sportswoman or -man should play out of their sense of self rather than to gain it through achievement. But even this may be putting it too strongly. Is Mozart's sense of self not properly partly realized through his music? If so, one might expect it to be the case that for some people their sense of self *will* be realized through sport. A dialectic of being formed by sport but also expressing ourselves through sport is held in necessary tension.

An attitude to sport that seeks self-justification and self-aggrandizement through it is, however, not the same as one in which a person expresses themselves or realizes their full personality or potential through it. Competitive sport must not be instrumentalized as a crude lever on our egos. Insofar as competitive sport *is* used in such ways it would appear to be sign of what the Christian tradition has understood to be a replication of Adam and Eve's sin. In eating from the tree of the knowledge of good and evil they no longer trusted God but sought to be god-like. Watson and White expound the basic sin, the pride that drives the need to win at all costs. From Reinhold Niebuhr's classic account they hear this: "man is insecure and involved in natural contingency; he seeks to overcome his contingency by a will-to-power which overreaches the limits of human creatureliness." They stop the quotation there but we can usefully continue a little further: Niebuhr goes on, "Man is ignorant and involved in the limitations of a finite mind; but he pretends that he is not limited. He assumes that he can gradually transcend finite limitations until his mind becomes identical with universal mind. All of his intellectual and cultural pursuits, therefore, become infected with the sin of pride. Man's pride and will-to-power disturb the harmony of creation."[130] I have elongated this quotation for two reasons. The linking of the seeking of transcendence with sin should be noted in readiness for our discussion in the next chapter. But also we note again the assertion that *all* human "intellectual and cultural pursuits" are infected with sin. Sport is in good company.

---

130. Niebuhr, *Nature*, 178–79, the first sentence quoted in Watson and White, "Winning," 68.

From Niebuhr, Watson and White turn to C. S. Lewis, and an account of the sin of pride from *Mere Christianity* that appears to speak adroitly to a competitive environment. The source of every other vice, our sense of pride competes with the same sense in others. Lewis makes pride sound like a zero-sum game. Watson and White give a long edited quotation, though their selection is as interesting for what it omits as for what it includes. I am also going to offer an edited quotation from the same Lewis passage, but I will omit most of what they include and introduce some material they omit (this latter material denoted by italics). The result reads similarly, and yet differently in significant ways.

> Two of a trade never agree. *Now what you want to get clear is that pride is essentially competitive—is competitive by its very nature—while other vices are competitive only, so to speak, by accident.* Pride gets no pleasure out of having something, only out of having more of it than the next man. *We say that people are proud of being rich, or clever, or good-looking, but they are not.* They are proud of being richer, cleverer, or better looking [or better at sport] than others . . . It is the comparison that makes you proud: the pleasure of being above the rest. *Once the element of competition has gone, pride has gone* . . . For, of course, power is what pride really enjoys: there is nothing makes a man feel so superior to others *as being able to move them about like toy soldiers.*[131]

Watson and White use their quotation to make their point and resource their discussion of winning at all costs in sport; my quotation is significantly shorter even with quite a bit of added material. Their omissions are interesting because, in general terms, they would seem to make the case against competition *per se* even more strongly. Pride is, for Lewis, "The Great Sin"—this is the title of his chapter. And the great sin is "essentially competitive." Without competition there is no pride, and therefore (presumably) competition is at the root of sin.

It may be that Lewis' argument against competition in this fuller form is just *too* strong for Watson and White. Their prime purpose is to argue against "winning at all costs," and while that phrase is frequently used in discussing sport and its problems it is seldom examined closely. *All* costs? Winning through bending rules on the field is unlikely to prove successful for long. I concede that the use of performance-enhancing drugs signifies an unhealthy and hazardous obsession with winning,

131. Lewis, *Mere Christianity*, 107–8.

but most of those who take these substances voluntarily (unlike the East German athletes of the Cold War, for instance) usually do so because they have made a calculation of gains and losses. However unwisely and misguidedly, they have decided that the risk of any possible damage to themselves is outweighed by the enhanced performance and greater opportunity for prizes. A cost-benefit analysis is not actually quite "winning at *all* costs." This slang vernacular is a hyperbolic expression that rarely describes accurately what is going on even among the most obsessive players.

Those who decide to cheat may be winners, but they are so in an attenuated way once their cheating is exposed. The loss of respect, and the withdrawal of rewards, can be swift and devastating. Drug cheats, betting scammers, official-bribers, and more, once exposed, are held in contempt. Berger's argument from damnation operates, there is outrage. Sometimes there is some sympathy for players who have allowed themselves to be compromised by those who have exploited them, or may even have been powerless to resist the control of others. But the fall from grace is usually hard. Standards of vigilance do vary from sport to sport, and more does need to be done,[132] but once exposed those who have won through cheating are dramatically transformed into losers.

One might argue that, in Suits' terms, they have failed to exhibit the necessary "lusory attitude" to their sport. Sport (like play) is marked by the acceptance of certain artificial obstacles, we recall, and these include constraints on and off the field. Without the appropriate lusory attitude it can even be charged that such cheating players are not really playing, and not really winning. They have broken the illusion of play and distorted it into something else, a parody of itself.

But in seeing the Lewis quotation in a little more detail we can also ask how convincing his argument really is. Theologies of sin that work from pride, Niebuhr's being another, must always go back to Genesis 3 and the garden. Is the narrative there about competition? It is not self-evidently the case. Niebuhr's presentation of "the great sin" is less horizontal and more vertical than Lewis'. If there is competition in Niebuhr's account it is between humankind and God, not, primarily at least, between human persons. The will-to-power and the desire to be god-like will certainly have implications for social relationships, but the primary orientation is elsewhere.

132. E.g., Majendie, "Drug Cheats."

Human beings do spend a lot of time comparing themselves with one another. The "keeping up with the Joneses" dynamic that has often been thought to drive consumption and materialism is some kind of evidence for this. However, we might question Lewis' certainty that no one is happy unless they have *surpassed* the Joneses: the phrase "keeping up with" suddenly seems illuminating even if still problematic. To be sure, some individuals (and some of these will be involved in elite sports) will want this experience of surpassing all others, but I question whether it accurately describes the attitude of all. Even in sport, as we considered earlier, most are—"at the end of the day" to use the sporting cliché—losers, not winners. Most compete knowing that they will never be champions, but the enjoyment of trying and doing as well as they might hope is enough. It might be argued that for some, in sport as in other spheres, the sin is in *not* competing, in not aiming high enough, in being content with mediocrity, rather than in recklessly competing.

This suggests that a strangely paradoxical thing about sport *for the vast majority* of those who play and those who watch, is that *sport is terribly important but also utterly unimportant.* My survey showed just this ambivalence repeatedly—in the number of respondents who said that winning was not important but then reported feeling lousy when they lost, for instance. Like play, sport is a kind of serious irrelevance. Worship is often described in similar ways.[133] Perhaps it is only because of this that it can be a vessel for the most serious metaphysical issues that Novak wants us to see resting in it. We play with sport, as it were. Elite sport stars recognize this paradox themselves in their cliché-ridden discourse. Winning is their total focus. In the end it is about "who wants it most," indicating the mental toughness and dedication required to attain the final prize. But reaction to natural disasters such as the earthquakes in Christchurch, New Zealand, in 2010 and 2011, or to the terrorist attack on Sri Lankan cricketers in Lahore in 2009 shows also that elite athletes can change perspective with remarkable speed. The involvement of elite players in charity events and such occasions as visiting hospital wards testify to this sense of perspective, as does the minute's silence before matches that remember the death of someone connected to the club. A random search on the internet while writing this paragraph turned up several relevant stories in quick time: English footballer Trevor Francis' heart attack

---

133. One recalls the title of Marva Dawn's book on worship, *A Royal Waste of Time: The Splendor of Worshipping God and Being Church for the World.*

"puts football in perspective again";[134] a similar reaction to the story of Tito Vilanova, coach of Barcelona FC who had to stand down because of a recurrence of cancer;[135] the sobering impact of a visit by England footballers and management to the holocaust museum in Jerusalem;[136] and the plea to "pray for Muamba" in the wake of the young Bolton Wanderers footballer's heart attack during a game at Tottenham, when according to the then Tottenham manager, Harry Redknapp, "football is the last thing on anyone's mind when an awful situation such as this happens. All we are thinking about now is Fabrice and his family."[137] These are typical stories, no less important for their relative infrequency. After reviewing various sentiments about football as a religion, a matter of life and death, and the obsession of fans, the first of these pieces continues: "That is how it feels to football fans at times. In reality, it's a load of old tosh." Sport is terribly important but also utterly unimportant.

Lewis has made the case for "pride" particularly strongly, and it often occupies a central place in accounts of sin. Tillich's account of sin as estrangement is rather more rounded. He finds three elements, one of which is *hubris*, a Greek word deployed by Augustine and Luther but which he concedes cannot be easily translated. *Hubris* is the condition in which "man is outside the divine center to which his own center essentially belongs. He is the center of himself and of his world."[138] *Hubris* is "most distinctly expressed in the serpent's promise to Eve that eating from the tree of knowledge will make man equal to God."[139] In a more subtle and sympathetic way than Lewis seems to allow, Tillich proposes that *hubris* is a risk precisely because human beings are capable of great things, that in stretching and reaching we might over-stretch and over-reach. *Hubris* is possible, he declares, in acts of humility as well as pride. Pride is, in fact, *not* a good translation of *hubris*: self-elevation is better. It can be an act of self-elevation by an individual or by a collective, and so understood *hubris* may indeed be seen as the root of all human sin. But the notion of sin is rounded by Tillich with two further elements gleaned from the historic theological accounts. The first is unbelief, which is not

134. *Total Football*, "Trevor Francis."

135. Hayward, "Villanova Illness."

136. *London 24*. "Hodgson puts English."

137. *Sky News HD*, "Players and fans pray."

138. Tillich, *Systematic*, II, 56.

139. Tillich, *Systematic*, II, 57.

so much an unwillingness to believe the church's doctrines as a total turning away from God. "Unfaith" might better describe this, he ventures, because unbelief seems too cerebral. It is "the disruption of man's cognitive participation in God" but also "the separation of man's will from the will of God." It has elements of disobedience and self-love within it, but these terms already imply a separation of the self from God and it is the total turning from God, estrangement from God, which is denoted by unbelief. While in unbelief we remove ourselves from the divine center, and in *hubris* we make ourselves the center, in concupiscence, the third element of sin, we draw everything else into our center—we desire the other in a disordered way. "The classical name for this desire is *concupiscentia* 'concupiscence'—the unlimited desire to draw the whole of reality into one's self. It refers to physical hunger as well as to sex, to knowledge as well as to power, to material wealth as well as to spiritual values."[140]

Rather than an over-cooked account of pride, Tillich's account seems more faithful to the tradition of a richer theological debate, and also to make more sense of the fall narrative in Genesis. It is also a challenging account for considering sport. It fits well with our previous discussion of disordered desire and the necessity of balance. Many of the individual sins of sport arise from the selfishness of the mis-centered center, and the concupiscence that attempts to order and even possess the world around us. Cheats take this to extraordinary lengths by putting themselves so much at the center that even the rules now do not matter: they are bigger than the rules. Their concupiscent need to possess the prize results in an act of self-elevation. Their breaking of the lusory attitude might be said to show that they have demonstrated a kind of unbelief in sport itself, breaking their own selves away from the center and "point" of the competition. The cheats have ceased to be *homo ludens* and become *homo delusans*.

Feminist writers would often want to demur to these kinds of account, however. Sin is gendered, they argue. What might appear to be sin for a man may not be sin for a woman. "Given women's ongoing gender socialization toward self-sacrifice and subjugating their needs, desires, and will to others, the sin of pride (understood as the self-exalted ego or the 'will to power') . . . widely misses the mark of most women's lives."[141] It may not *so* badly miss the mark of men's lives however. Denise

140. Tillich, *Systematic*, II, 59.

141. McDougall, "Sin," 221. McDougal offers a typology of feminist approaches to sin, and an attempt to offer a new direction which, among other things, seeks to restore what I described earlier as a vertical dimension to a usable definition.

Carmody says that "in recent analyses of the peculiar characteristic (or at least stereotypic) failings of men and women, two sins stand out. For women the failing, the sin, the vice that gets most attention is weakness, cowardice, diffusion—having no self. For men, the vice that gets most attention is the old, standard, most capital sin: pride."[142] Carmody believes that the testosterone-fueled pride, "a Neitzchean dreaming to become a superman, a blazing intensity of will that might blow away all obstacles to creativity or rule,"[143] gives reasonable purchase on male behavior. Like Tillich, however, she sees much that might be described in this way as positive, with the bad being a distortion of the good. Drawing on the work of psychoanalyst Dorothy Dinnerstein, she likens the male of the species to a minotaur: half human, half beast, a bull fixated on strength and lust. The female of the species is more like a mermaid: watery, insubstantial, unreliable, confused, unproductive. While such a contrast is an exaggeration, there is enough to alarm us. Further, she believes that men and women have colluded "to perpetuate our aberrations, generation after generation"[144] through the socialization processes that shape our gendered identities.

Such analyses are common among those who scrutinize the human condition from a feminist angle, though some will seek to absolve women entirely from blame rather than posit collusion. Patriarchal societies are themselves a product of the fall. The narrative records God's words to Eve as "yet your desire shall be for your husband, and he shall rule over you" (Gen 3:16), and so appears to locate the subjugation of women in the consequences of a fallen world. Wherever we live out the domination of men over women we live out our fallenness. The possibility then that sin would look and feel different for a man and woman (and, possibly, for other cultural variations in a fallen world too) must be taken seriously. Looked at from this point of view, entering into competition might not appear to be a sign of overweening pride, or even of disordered desire, but of an assertion of self. The opposite of sin, potentially.

In closing we might briefly note that original sin is often lacking from discussions of sport. This may betray the individualism of contemporary culture, and possibly of the evangelical Protestant assumptions of some who write on the subject, but it ought not to go unchallenged. The

142. Carmody, *Feminist*, 153.

143. Carmody, *Feminist*, 154.

144. Carmody, *Feminist*, 155.

doctrine of original sin is logically and theologically problematic for various reasons,[145] and it is not my purpose to defend a literalistic account of Augustine's views. The truth in the doctrine that we need to recognize is that there is something of sin that precedes and exceeds our individual wills. The whole is greater than the sum of its parts. In a real sense we are born into sin, the choices of others and the warped nature of the institutions our ancestors created before we were born work their dastardly consequences upon us before we come to think and act for ourselves. Indeed, our thinking and acting for ourselves are hopelessly slewed towards sin before we have begun.

Sport is not simply a locus for sin, but for original sin. We sin in sport, but the sin of other individuals and collectives surrounds us in it before we have thought and acted for ourselves as sportsmen and -women. None of this, as the Christian tradition has always paradoxically asserted, takes away our own responsibility for how we think and behave but it needs to be recognized nonetheless. In this, we beat the familiar drum: sport resembles every other sphere of human activity. It goes some way to account for drug abuse, and for many of the more egregious wrongs of sport, but only some way.

Deus Ludens, Deus Victor: God the Winner

In considering theologically the importance and place of winning in sport, there is one more issue that necessarily arises. We have already characterized God as *Deus ludens*, "God the player." Should we not also be ready to name God as *Deus Victor*, "God the winner"? And if so, what are the implications of such a naming?

A number of mainly popular American writers on sports and Christianity have sought to make such a move, though sometimes it has appeared facile and unconvincing. Nelson Price is often mentioned here. A former college basketball coach and later Baptist pastor, he wrote that "Competition means to have an opponent or adversary. The title 'devil' means adversary. Jesus and the devil went head to head. Their teammates still do."[146] Price talks about the story of Jesus' temptations at the beginning of his ministry as "the Wilderness Games." These showed Jesus to be

---

145. Niebuhr's discussion highlights most of these difficulties: *Nature*, 241–64.

146. Price, "Jesus," quoted in Warner, *Competition*, 191, and in several other sources.

a competitor of "discernment, diligence, and dedication," and contemporary competitors should emulate him: the imitation of Christ-the-athlete. Jesus out-thought his opponent but also managed the perfect combination of "mind, muscle, and morals." Price goes on to discuss other competitive situations and other opponents: the money changers in the temple show Jesus to be "gutsy," while the clash with the "intellectuals" showed him to be "gritty."[147]

Price is not alone in using such imagery or themes, and their deployment is not confined to evangelical circles. In the Archdiocese of Baltimore's *Catholic Review* under the headline "Jesus is the Quarterback on the Gridiron of Life," Brent Heathcott writes: "Jesus is there for every battle, every struggle. He calls the plays, shows us the way to success and happiness. He challenges us to be the best we can be, puts us in position to succeed by honoring him with our thoughts, words and deeds and expects us to work for the common good of the team—our families, friends and the greater community of believers."[148]

Players and former players are not shy of such language either. Baseball player Fritz Peterson affirmed that "I firmly believe that if Jesus Christ was sliding into second base, he would knock the second baseman into left field to break up the double play. Christ might not throw a spin-ball but he would play hard within the rules"; San Francisco pitcher Dave Dravechy said "if I could put Jesus Christ into my shoes he would be the most aggressive and intense performer on the field. He would win every time."[149] This kind of approach is reflected in fiction too. Elmer Gantry, in the movie of that name, puts it memorably: "Jesus had guts! He wasn't afraid of the whole Roman army. Think that quarterback's hot stuff? Well, let me tell you, Jesus would have made the best little all-American quarterback in history. Jesus was a real fighter. The best little scrapper, pound for pound, you ever saw. And why, gentlemen? Love, gentlemen. Jesus had love in both fists."[150]

It is interesting to note that all of these examples come from the USA, and we may have encountered here another form of American exceptionalism: exceptional not only in religion (possibly) and sport (probably), but also in the combination thereof. Picturing Jesus as an

147. Price, "Jesus," quoted in Warner, *Competition*, 192.
148. Heathcott, "Jesus is the Quarterback."
149. Quoted in Weir, "Competition," 106.
150. *Elmer Gantry*.

aggressive major league player or a scrapping quarterback (let alone with love in both fists) will seem to many a step too far, a co-option of the figure of Jesus that lacks the kind of self-awareness necessary for proper reflection. The Jesus described here seems rather like a reflection of the coach's ideal of a good baseball or football player in a way reminiscent of Günther Bornkamm's characterization of the failure of the Quest for the Historical Jesus "because it became alarmingly and terrifyingly evident how inevitably each author brought the spirit of his own age into his presentation of the figure of Jesus."[151] Perhaps this is an over-reaction to what might be thought of as an attempt to earth devotional and discipleship questions in the everyday reality of people going about their (sporting) business, but when such rhetoric fails to engage at all in what Jesus may or may not have said critically into these sports we seem to have lost touch with theological reality. As Warner says, "it is easier to follow a 'fiercely competitive Jesus.' *We make him just like us.* He understands why we lose control, get angry, and do whatever it takes to win."[152]

Warner goes on to suggest that, contrary to the portraits of Jesus referred to above, Jesus would have felt so secure in his own sense of self that he would not have needed to compete. This suggestion is attractive to a point, and may at first sight undermine any positive theological connection we might seek to make between winning and gaining a sense of self and self-worth. Lewis would surely find it an acceptable suggestion: if pride is the root sin, and fundamentally competitive, then Jesus would not have needed to compete to gain a sure sense of self and this would have absolved him from the need to prove himself better than others. Tillich's more nuanced account with a much less prominent place for competition might also work: Jesus, in whom the New Being appears, is not marked by the unbelief that is a separation of self from God, nor the concupiscence that desires to control and possess the Other; neither is he marked by the *hubris* that elevates himself at the expense of others. While such accounts suggest that Jesus does not compete because of a sense of insecurity or the grip of sin upon him, is that all that might be said?

Despite the rather crude account of the "Wilderness Games," Price has in fact touched upon a major gospel theme. Mark's Gospel does sometimes read as a battle, or competition, between good and evil, between Jesus and the devil(s) who pursue him. The early Fathers were fond

151. Bornkamm, *Jesus*, 13.
152. Warner, *Competition*, 193, italics mine.

of speaking of the significance of the cross as a victory over evil powers—sin, death, and the devil—but in this account the cross is not isolated from the rest of Jesus' ministry. Jesus might not need to win in order to establish his own sense of self, but the *fact* of his victory establishes his identity for those who follow him and affirm him as God's Son.[153] In the life, death, and resurrection of Jesus, God in Christ fights a decisive and victorious battle against evil forces. Humanity shares in this victory and enjoys its fruits. As a view of atonement it has the advantage of making forward and backward connections from the cross: backwards into the various conflict episodes of the gospels, and forwards to the victory of the resurrection. Many other atonement theories have lacked this broader compass. This set of images and stories was rediscovered and championed by Gustav Aulén in his book, *Christus Victor*, in the twentieth century, and still plays an important part in reflection on the atonement. The eternal victory of God's love is won once for all by God in Christ. As the hymn writer Timothy Rees puts it:

> . . . sin and death and hell can never,
> o'er us final triumph gain . . ."[154]

Macquarrie speaks of Christ's self-sacrificial victory over every demonizing idol—including the last idol, one's own self—and so attempts to rehabilitate *Christus Victor* for a contemporary audience.[155] In so doing Macquarrie reminds us of a central Christian mystery, that of death and resurrection. The victory follows a death, a defeat.

The purpose of this brief account of *Christus Victor* is to recall that locating the theme of competition in Jesus' life and ministry may not be so far-fetched or misplaced after all. This is not, of course, the competition of sport. Or even of the other competitive spheres of human life like commerce and education. It is something far more serious, deadly, and significant. If anything, it is more like the competition of war. We have noted at various points the connections between war and sport, and how the language of one seeps into the other. However, if our concern is with the need to win, with competition itself, there is still something of interest here.

Jesus the competitor is an interesting character. He is brutally uncompromising in conflict with evil, yet also willingly vulnerable in the

153. Rom 1:4.
154. Timothy Rees, "God is love, let heaven adore him."
155. Macquarrie, *Principles*, 318–27.

face of a threat to his own person. He casts out demons and wages war with sickness, though not always without some selectivity or prioritizing. He has a sense of the fittingness of certain conflicts, including the final one in Jerusalem. Thus, it is at a time of his own choosing that he sets his face for Jerusalem[156] and prepares for this ultimate competition. But in that competition, to the confusion, no doubt, of his friends and followers, he appears to have willingly walked into a trap. There may be a moment of wavering will in Gethsemane,[157] but Jesus gives himself over to death via a flawed judicial process with a strange mixture of active control and passive vulnerability. He always seems to be where he is because he has chosen to be, and yet he seems simultaneously powerless. The result of this competition is, by human standards at least, a crushing and cruel defeat. After mistreatment and corrupt practice he is crucified with common criminals and buried in a cold stone tomb. As a model competitor, Jesus, at this point, looks more like the glorious failure so often said to be valorized in Britain, than the all-achieving superstar of America.

Those examining the ministry of Jesus for guidance on competition can doubtless still find help here, perhaps in Jesus' self-possession, in his determination and focus, his choosing his battles with care, and so on. However, a recognition of the centrality of Jesus' self-sacrificial disposition might appear to fit ill with the kind of culture that we may recall Hoffman described as "narcissistic, materialistic, self-interested, violent, sensational, coarse, racist, sexist, brazen, raunchy, hedonistic, body-destroying, and militaristic."[158] Players could be and are encouraged to "take one for the team," and restless footballers in England during the summer transfer window are from time to time reminded that they are "not bigger than the club," with the implication that they must sometimes subordinate their own desires to the policies and priorities of others. Nevertheless, Watson and White suggest that for the Christian "the most distinguishing characteristic of the heroic is the sacrificial, that is sacrificing your needs, wants, and even life itself, for the good of others." This conclusion is drawn from "the ultimate act of heroic sacrifice . . . when God himself entered the world in the form of his son Jesus, and 'humbled himself and became obedient to death . . . even death on a cross' (Phil 2:8), so that we might know his love."[159] Living this "cross-carrying" at-

---

156. Luke 9:51.
157. Luke 22:42.
158. Hoffman, *Good Game*, 11.
159. Watson and White, "Winning," 73.

titude in sport is seen as problematic. It is one thing, we might say, to love one's neighbor by tackling them hard and bringing out the best in them; it is another to give up our own desire to be the best we can in order to do it. Is this what a sacrificial sporting disposition requires?

The gospel command, summarizing the divine will with regard to our horizontal relationships, is to love your neighbor, but to love your neighbor *as you love yourself*.[160] The bad is the distortion of the good, and loving oneself in a self-interested narcissistic way is a distortion of the proper love of self, it is a disordered desire. Concupiscence is the consequence of unbelief and *hubris*, in which our self's relationship with God is fractured and we become the center of our world. Language of self-sacrifice is dramatic and sometimes necessary. It also can be and has been used to protect the *status quo* by demanding that others give up their rights for some higher cause, and that women in particular put up with abuse by domineering partners because their suffering fits some higher pattern and somehow sanctifies them. It is not always problematic language, but sometimes it can be. Balanced with the love of neighbor *as oneself* a more nuanced picture of Christian service emerges. This Watson and White recognize when they see that in a sporting context it perhaps means "the moral strength to follow the correct path when easier routes are available."[161] This is still demanding, it will still test the player faced with the dilemma of doing the right thing during a game, but it no longer sounds quite so dramatic, no longer appears to require that players would prefer that the other team actually won.

The central position of the cross, of Jesus' *defeat*, still requires some thought. In another essay, Nick Watson articulates the challenge clearly and helpfully. Again thinking of the death of Jesus he directs us to the opening line of Moltmann's *The Crucified God*: the inner criterion of any theology that "deserves to be called Christian" is the centrality of the cross.[162] Moltmann certainly has made the cross of Christ a key anchor of his theological thought. However, it is not the only such key idea. The doctrine of the Trinity could claim pride of place, though it would, admittedly, be a Trinitarian doctrine informed and shaped by the cross. But Moltmann began his work elsewhere, and it could be argued that he ends it in that place too—with eschatology.

160. Luke 10:27.
161. Watson and White, "Winning," 74.
162. Watson, "Nature and Transcendence," 113.

Moltmann's first major work, *Theology of Hope*, attempted to rehabilitate eschatology as "not one element of Christianity, but [as] the medium of Christian faith as such, the key in which everything in it is set, the glow that suffuses everything here in the dawn of an expected new day."[163] The promised future conflicts with our experience of the present, and we are "drawn into the conflict between hope and experience,"[164] a conflict that is none other than the conflict between cross and resurrection. "Christian hope is resurrection hope."[165] Moltmann believes that our involvement in the conflict (can we say "competition"?) between present and future involves "self-surrender and sacrifice"[166] but the wholesomely restless drive is toward a future that God promises and will give. The resurrection discloses and promises this future.

Self-sacrificial love, yes; but hope and conflict, competition, yes. Moltmann certainly did not have in mind the competition of the Super Bowl or Little League, the Premiership or Sunday League cricket. But his own views on play, and the Sabbath, suggest that sport has its part in hoping for and actualizing God's promised future. Noting this orientation of hope in theology, and recognizing the fundamental role that hope with its future orientation plays in all human life, once more allows a nuancing of our topic. Berger's signals of transcendence, we may recall, included an argument from hope. "Human existence is always oriented toward the future. Man exists by constantly extending his being into the future, both in his consciousness and in his activity. Put differently, man realizes himself in projects."[167] The constant realizing in projects is a sign of the kind of restlessness that Carmody believed created great (usually male) explorers, inventors, and so on. But this need to "compete" against the elements, again the givens, against oneself and, sometimes, against one another, appears fundamental. It is a future orientation. Competition is a mark of hope. Many a sports player will know about the contradiction between hope and experience. Even though most do not win, hope is one major factor that makes us return to the game again and again.

The resurrection must count as a victory, however else it is understood. While the cross is central to theology we notice it only because it is not the end of the story. The defeat, while total and awful, proved not

163. Moltmann, *Hope*, 16.

164. Moltmann, *Hope*, 18.

165. Moltmann, *Hope*, 18.

166. Moltmann, *Hope*, 338.

167. Berger, *Rumour*, 80.

to be final. It was a victory won in a particular way, won with a strategy that was nearer to emptying than to self-elevation, but a victory. Traditional accounts of Jesus' self-consciousness believe that Jesus in fact always knew that he would be victorious, that though a painful death was to be feared for its agony, nevertheless Jesus knew that final victory was assured.[168] If this is taken to be true (and it has implications for our Christology, and our views of God and the future generally) it should represent some kind of qualification to set against Jesus' self-sacrifice. However, Jesus is, by any account, a winner. In the competition with evil upon which he was engaged he has emerged victorious: "God raised him on the third day."[169] This is not an easy victory, but the cross does not turn out to be the last word. Here, Moltmann will say, is the ground of all our hope. And this also must moderate the extent to which the cross can be allowed to be the *only* "inner criterion" of Christian theology. If it were, such theology would be a theology of (perhaps glorious) defeat, whereas a theology of hope yearns for what is promised but not yet, victory.

We spoke earlier of the self's affirmation and worth that comes through victory, the sense of being right and in the right; it contrasts with the feeling of dissolution of the self that can be the aftermath of defeat. At the heart of the Christian good news is a story of affirmation (God's "yes" to Jesus) that puts him, and those who through baptism are identified with him, "in the right," establishing their worth and their identity "in Christ." Paradoxically, it is a victory given in defeat. We recall Duina's remark that we believe that the outcome of a competition tells us something important about our *worthiness* in general. When human persons participate in the victory of Jesus they also share in this established identity, in this being in the right, they find here a ground spring for self-worth.

These considerations lead us to one final observation on this theme for the moment. The Word made flesh,[170] "the image of the invisible God,"[171] the manifestation of salvation,[172] "the reflection of God's glory and the exact imprint of God's very being,"[173] Jesus is important in

168. Luke 9:22.
169. Acts 10:40.
170. John 1:14.
171. Col 1:15.
172. 2 Tim 1:8–10.
173. Heb 1:3.

Christian theology because what we say about Jesus we say about God. Jesus the winner points us to God the winner, to *Deus Victor*. Indeed, properly, the victorious resurrection of Jesus is not Jesus' own act, but the act of the Father who raises the Son.

Scripture, often through various statements cast in the language and imagery of eschatology and apocalyptic, affirms God's final victory. Ephesians puts it like this: "he has made known to us the mystery of his will, according to his good pleasure that he set forth in Christ, as a plan for the fullness of time, to gather up all things in him, things in heaven and things on earth."[174] Theologians have (always) disagreed on what this final victory will look like. I am not thinking here of the décor of heaven, of the eternal occupation of the saints, or even of whether eternity will in some way be temporal or unchanging. Rather I am thinking of whether the final victory of God will contain within it some element of what may look to us like tragedy or defeat. When God wins, will he send others to defeat, or will God's victory encompass all? The Ephesians text quoted above is often read in this latter way, but the trading of texts on both sides of the argument can be heated, not to say attritional. Throughout Scripture God is portrayed as one whose divine purpose will prevail, as a winner. What that purpose is with regard to the eternal destiny of all men and women, and perhaps of creation itself, is another question for another day. The implication through Scripture and all-pervasive in the Christian tradition, that somehow fallen human beings are *competing* with God in the exercise of their sinful will but that God will neverthe- less prevail, must lead us to name God as victorious and to rest in this happy hopeful state of which the resurrection of Jesus is both illustration and pledge. God has won, is winning, and will win the competition for the glory of creation. How wonderful it would be if we could affirm that every (sporting) victory for which we press is in some way an expression of such a hopeful intimation.

174. Eph 1:9–10.

6

"To Boldly Go"

Sport as Divine Encounter?

THE TV SERIES *STAR Trek* and its spin-off movie franchise have
achieved niche cult status. Much admired and often parodied, the
series' creator, Gene Roddenberry, set out to help its audience reflect
upon contemporary issues by casting them into a sci-fi future. A number of its script lines have passed into the vernacular and among them is
what is often regarded as the most famous split infinitive in the English
language or, at the very least, in English language popular culture. The
opening line of almost every episode of the show was: "Space: the final
frontier. These are the voyages of the starship *Enterprise*. Its five-year mission: to explore strange new worlds, to seek out new life and new civiliza-
tions, to boldly go where no man has gone before." This famous prologue
is thought to have been inspired by a publication from the White House
in 1958 entitled "Introduction to Outer Space," in which a group of scientific advisors to the US President speak of "the compelling urge of man
to explore and discover, the thrust of curiosity that leads men to try to go
where no one has gone before."[1]

Roddenberry doubtless caught something of the spirit of the age,
with the arms race morphing into a space race, and the human imagination piqued by the possibilities of the deep recesses of space. As the
best writers of sci-fi have shown us, projecting our dilemmas onto future

1. White House, "Introduction to Outer Space," 1.

space can prove a fruitful way of examining them. But the space race also spoke to the exploring instinct. Everest had been conquered for the first time a few years before the White House document was published, and as "Introduction to Outer Space" says, "Most of the surface of the Earth has now been explored and men now turn to the exploration of outer space as their next objective."[2]

I began this book by sketching a history, and by characterizing one historic attitude to sport that saw it as a means of "reaching for the heavens." In using this image I pointed to attitudes to sport (many of which are very old) in which something like our "sport" appears to have been part of religious ritual. This sport was a dramatization of creation or of humanity's relationship with deity or deities, and it was often part of the apparatus deployed to manage that relationship. These primordial sports, if we may call them that, were a means whereby a given people sought and maintained a relationship with their god(s).

In this chapter I recall the phrase "reaching for the heavens" in moving on to a discussion of the notion of transcendence. Could this concept enable us to speak of players, and even spectators, reaching in some way for something beyond their immanent experience of the world? If play, and so sport, creates its own world with its own time and space, is this a location in which it is possible to encounter ultimate reality? This chapter will continue the ruminations of the previous one in moving from playing, winning, and competing to consider transcendence in sport. Having addressed this with the players in focus we will turn to consider the experience of spectators, before a more general discussion of sin and salvation in the context of competition and some concluding reflections on the theological account of sport I have offered.

Imago Dei: Further Thoughts

We must return briefly now to the notion of the image of God. In chapter 4 I suggested that the notion of *imago Dei* was best understood first by analogy with the statue of a ruler placed in a territory and giving a sign of their authority in that place. Dominion is the term used in Genesis 1:26. I also suggested that some of the other proposed meanings of the *imago Dei* might still be thought to be contained within such a primary interpretation. In putting it in this way I slid over a key exegetical detail.

2. White House, "Introduction to Outer Space," 1.

The verse reads, "Then God said, 'Let us make humankind in our image, according to our likeness; and let them have dominion over . . .'" The idea that understanding human beings as made in God's image corresponds to the statue placed in a governed territory raises the "likeness" question. The statue performs this function, in some measure, because it *looks like* the ruler of whom it is a representation. The statue is made "according to [the] likeness" of the ruler. This raises the question, in what might the "likeness" between humankind and God obtain, that it can be said that humans are created in the image of God? The biblical narrative does not elucidate, and so theologians have attempted to identify the theological foundation of such an affirmation.

One of the earliest conceptions was to see the *imago Dei* as the rational soul, a human *nous* corresponding with the divine *logos*.[3] This seemed to give an appropriate explanation of the difference between human persons and the other living creatures over which they were given dominion. One of the tasks given to Adam and Eve is the naming of the animals, hinting not just at dominion (for naming confers power), but also at rationality—for naming requires language, another distinguishing human feature. This naming of the other creatures also carries with it the classification of them into types of some sort, and here we see something of the capacity for rule-making and necessary generalization, as well as the creative impulse necessary for play and for sport. The idea that men and women alone among terrestrial creatures possess a soul has fed into various visions of the afterlife. But it does seem a decidedly Greek notion and not completely sympathetic with the more Hebraic idea of (in modern terms) a psychosomatic unity of the person. It was, of course, developed when Greek philosophical thought had considerable influence on Christian theology.

Much more recently Barth's imaginative exegesis focused on the plural form of the divine speech, "Let us make . . ." and suggested that it is in and as a community of persons that humankind corresponds to the divine community of persons, the Trinity.[4] In so doing Barth was drawing on a long tradition of Christian exegesis that related the plural first person form in Genesis 1:26 to the Trinity, though this is usually met with considerable skepticism by modern commentators.

3. Westermann, *Genesis 1–11*, 149.
4. Westermann, *Genesis 1–11*, 144.

However the more general notion that the text is signaling something of importance about human community is more widely accepted, not least because of 1:27: "So God created humankind in his image, in the image of God he created them; male and female he created them." Some scholars relate the text quite specifically to the question of gender;[5] while some go on to make political and ecclesial observations.[6] In particular, it is argued that human persons have a peculiar capacity for relationship with, or openness to, God. Such an interpretation goes back some way before Barth's reading and has wide support among biblical scholars.[7] God, as the Old Testament will go on to show, is a covenant God, that is, God is a God of relationship. God calls men and women into relationship, and in creating them in *imago Dei* human persons are in a sense God's "counterpart," as Westermann puts it, referring to Barth. To be made in the "image and likeness of God" designates the distinctiveness of human existence within creation in which humans are called into a particular kind of relationship with God and also stand accountable to God in relationship. Humans have the kind of "I–Thou" relationship with God that is unique according to this interpretation.[8]

A distinctively Christian reading of Genesis 1:26f. may also align it with texts such as Philippians 2:6; 2 Corinthians 4:4; and Colossians 1:15. In these texts Jesus Christ is said to be the image of God, or in the form of God. Irenaeus (*c.*130–202 CE) believed that the falling from grace in the Genesis story that we usually call the fall was not so much a moral failure by Adam and Eve as a lapse precipitated by immaturity. For Irenaeus, "the commandment [not to eat from the tree of the knowledge of good and evil] is an important and integral element in the economy of human maturation, preventing the newly-fashioned creature from laying hold of that which it is unable to bear, preserving the fullness of knowledge for a time—and there will be a time—when humanity shall be ready and able to partake of the full knowledge God offers."[9] This is still a disobedience, but in identifying the immaturity of Adam and Eve Irenaeus suggests that even though made in the *imago Dei*, humankind is not created perfect and complete. Rather, humanity is made open to God, as we have seen,

5. Brueggemann, *Genesis*, 33f.; Amos, *Genesis*, 11f.

6. Carmody, *Feminist*, 89–91, connects the text to politics, gender, and ecology.

7. Westermann, *Genesis 1–11*, 150–51.

8. Westermann, *Genesis 1–11*, 150. See Barth, *CD*, III/1, 183–206.

9. Steenberg, *Irenaeus*, 164.

and also open to its own growth and flourishing. This has proved a useful strategy in some discussions of theodicy that suggest that God's creation, while the best possible creation, is nevertheless still a work in progress.[10] Irenaeus insisted on interpreting the *imago Dei* in Christological terms. Adam's imperfect and immature response to the calling into relationship that God gives is perfected by Christ, who recovers and restores the good relationship between humankind and the Creator. It is into this mature, perfected, restored relationship that men and women are called and enabled in Christ.

If we work with an Irenaean reading of the *imago Dei*, we will read the creation narrative as suggesting that human persons are not created perfect but in potential. The image of God is the potentiality of maturity and fullness, and human persons grow into this potential (or, indeed, slip back from it). This potential is also a growing towards God, which could ultimately lead to a communion with God which ancient writers often described as deification, and that echoed the way some Scripture passages such as 2 Corinthians 3:18; 1 John 3:2; and 2 Peter 1:4 speak of growth in Christ. Says John Macquarrie:

> We must think of the *imago Dei* more in terms of a potentiality for being that is given to man with his very being, than in terms of a fixed "endowment" or "nature." Man is a creature, but as the creature that "exists," he has an openness into which he can move outward and upward . . . As the early Christian writer Theophilus of Antioch expressed it, "God gave man an opportunity for progress, so that by growing and becoming mature and furthermore having been declared a god, he might also ascend into heaven."[11]

There is in humankind made in the image of God, according to this understanding, an openness and potential, a continual reaching beyond itself, and reaching towards God, its counterpart. It is here that we may find the nub of a theology of sport, and we note another pointer to the theme of transcendence to which we now turn.

---

10. In recent times, John Hick (*Evil*) has been one of the most well-known adherents of such a position.

11. Macquarrie, *Principles*, 231; quoting Theophilus, *To Autolycus*, ii/24.

Transcendence and the Transcendent

We noted in the previous chapter and we need to recall now that sports players play in order to win. We made two main qualifications to this statement. The first qualification was that, however much the rhetoric points in another direction, sports players generally have a sense of perspective about what they are doing. Sport is both crucially important and yet also marginal, peripheral, to the "really" important things that are often defined in terms of health and welfare and human flourishing more generally. Sometimes this sense of perspective is lost, and in such moments we might speak of attitudes to sport becoming unhealthily obsessive. I insert the word "unhealthily" here to indicate that there may be more to be said about whether an "obsession" with sport could be healthy. However, while people will doubtless draw the line in a different places, most would draw a line somewhere.

In my survey I found substantial evidence that sports players and spectators will arrange their lives around their sporting interests to a considerable extent. There is clear evidence that sport exercises a cohering function in the lives of many participants which finds an analogue in the way religious faith functions for some people (sometimes, of course and intriguingly, the same people). This notwithstanding however, there was also evidence that even this was a relative rather than absolute organizing principle. When stories were told like the woman telling her sister that she would be her bridesmaid only if the wedding took place on a Saturday afternoon when the team she supported was playing away from home, one senses a chuckle in the narration, a knowing recognition of the extremity of the sentiment expressed. Insofar as the position *is* absolute, that even if after all avenues have been explored the wedding has to clash with a home fixture and the sister indeed refuses to attend, then we may ask those questions about proportionality, and also wonder about the extent to which any judgments made are absolute or contextual.

While losing feels awful because players invest physical and emotional energy in their games, most keep coming back for more. Ultimately, the vast majority are not winners—everyone cannot be a champion. And the "coming back for more" phenomenon is testimony both to the irrepressibility of the human spirit, to the hope that drives so much of our activity, but also to this sense of perspective about what is considered truly important.

The second qualification is that winning means different things for different players and spectators. Not everyone can be the champion, and sports players appear to combine competitiveness with realism in different proportions. In my survey I found that teams are forgiven for losing when they have performed well and a number of players have similar attitudes. Winning is the aim always ("I enjoy the contest and performing well and if it all ends up in the team winning in the right way by playing some good football and overcoming the challenges as well then it doesn't get much better than that for me") but often there is great satisfaction in playing well. A cricketer reports that "I can still derive pleasure from losing if I achieve well on a personal level." An athlete, in what might be thought a more individualistic sport, almost redefines winning in terms of beating her own previous personal best performances. This identification of the importance of performance is significant.

It is arguable that the very best players are necessarily the most competitive, the least willing to accept anything but the highest performance from themselves and one that surpasses their opponents'. But the great majority of players appear to be determined to actualize their best personal performance or perhaps the best performance of their team. Even if they cannot be the best when compared to all others, they want to be the best that they can be. Some sports, such as track and field and marathon-running, lend themselves to this kind of approach easily through the use of measurements that allow more objective comparisons between performances on separate occasions. Sports such as baseball and cricket are statistically rich and allow similar comparisons, while the gathering and use of statistics in football and rugby increasingly allows analogous evaluations to be made. This objectification of performance is especially prominent at elite level, but recreational sports players also want to gain a sense of having been performing at their best level and to go on improving. This works at both macro and micro levels. A cricketer might want to beat his previous highest score as a batsmen or his previous best bowling figures for a match. Or he might want to time that perfect cover drive or square cut while batting, or bowl the unplayably perfect leg-spinner.

These two qualifications are just that: they qualify rather than contradict the general statement that sports players play to win. Taken together they also point us towards our discussion of transcendence: the hope that keeps players coming back to try again, and the determination to be the best one can; these are crucial elements in sporting endeavor.

They both speak of the playing to win that is central to sport, but also qualify it in important ways.

In discussions of sport and religion the term "transcendence" has been frequently associated with the experience of sports players. More often than not, the connection has been to those moments of flow experience that we have already discussed. Flow, it will be recalled, is defined by Csikszentmihalyi as "the state in which people are so involved in an activity that nothing else seems to matter; the experience itself is so enjoyable that people will do it even at great costs, for the sheer sake of doing it."[12] In it, players enter a state in which they feel in control and yet also begin to feel themselves become one with their activity. They "become so involved in what they are doing that the activity becomes spontaneous, almost automatic; they stop being aware of themselves as separate from the actions that they are performing."[13] As well as our discussion while considering play, we returned to flow experiences when considering religious experience. There, it will be recalled, we noted that such moments of flow are often described in mystical terms. Roger Bannister's experience of running gave some credence to this, and Bannister's experience of his sport is not unique.

Michael Murphy and Rhea White have gathered together a very large number of descriptions of such experiences drawing on a bibliography of more than 1500 sources. Their descriptions of what they call "transcendent experiences in sport" operate with a definition that is broader than that which Csikszentmihalyi would strictly call flow experiences. They refer to "moments of illumination, out-of-body experiences, altered perceptions of time and space, exceptional feats of strength and endurance, states of ecstasy."[14] They speak of moments of "surpassing joy" or "serenity," about moments of "unearthly beauty," and of "self-surpassing abilities."[15] Such experiences are most common in sports that "require a prolonged sacrifice of safety or comfort" such as climbing, long-distance running and perilous sailing, but "low-risk games" can also be fruitful. "There are times when the safest games are as fierce and as trying as the ascent of a dangerous mountain."[16] While experienced athletes who have

---

12. Csikszentmihalyi, *Flow*, 4.
13. Csikszentmihalyi, *Flow*, 53.
14. Murphy and White, *In the Zone*, 1.
15. Murphy and White, *In the Zone*, 1.
16. Murphy and White, *In the Zone*, 3.

spent a long time honing their skills might be the prime subjects of such experiences, less expert and more occasional athletes can have them too.[17] Commenting on these reports in general the authors remark that they "show us that sport has enormous power to sweep us beyond our ordinary sense of self, to evoke capacities that have generally been regarded as mystical, occult or religious."[18]

While many of their accounts are vivid and compelling some will be put off by Murphy and White's regular use of such terms as "occult," "psychic," and similar.[19] While they claim that there are similarities between the experiences they report and religious experiences they do not want to push further than that. They are not claiming that such sports experiences *are* religious experiences. Given the reservations we noted in chapter 5 about the way in which sports experiences are described in terms of mysticism this is pertinent. We noted there that experiences that might be described as nature mysticism should not necessarily be thought to be non-religious or even non-theistic, but also that an understanding of religious experience that was basically episodic and focused exclusively on such high points was likely to be unsatisfactory. The experiences described by Murphy and White may or may not be religious in nature: some may be better explained in other ways. However, a number of them do sound rather like the kinds of experience that may be considered moments of transcendence, and that is the generic way in which the subtitle of their book does indeed describe them. Likewise, when Nick Watson speaks of transcendence he does sometimes speak more generally of "self-actualisation, character development" and some form of insight,[20] but for the most part it is the mystical encounter that is in his mind.

However, the term transcendence as I will use it will signify more than this type of isolated experience. It may include the moments of flow, the moments that some will describe as mystical; but it also includes other kinds of experience much less mystical. By experiences of transcendence I am not simply referring to those moments described by Murphy and White, but also more mundane moments of striving and reaching "beyond" the present and its achievements, and also more elongated practices and dispositions that are oriented to this end. Rather like my account of

17. Murphy and White, *In the Zone*, 3.
18. Murphy and White, *In the Zone*, 4.
19. See Higgs and Braswell, *Unholy Alliance*, 180.
20. Watson, "Nature," 110.

religious experience in general, the transcendence of which I am speaking is less a matter of high points and individual episodes (though there may be both of these) but is a broader more inclusive category.

There is certainly wide recognition in the literature for extraordinary high points of sporting experience, the "transcendent experience" in Murphy and White's sense, but (often implicitly) there is also a recognition of the wider sense of transcendence of which I am speaking. In their (non-theological) account Gorn and Goldstein speak of the high points of elite sport, mentioning Mohammed Ali, or a great Super Bowl or World Series. "What they all have in common is the feeling of transcendence, the sense of limitless possibility that sports can give us. Arousing deep longing for beauty, for awe, for shared community, such moments give us glimpses of a better world and nourish our hopes for much that is noble in humankind."[21] Craig Forney's speculative account of American football speaks of it as conveying America's sense of the transcendence of truth, with players looking beyond the ordinary to something or someone beyond.[22]

Michael Novak is a frequent reference point in discussion of theology and sport. He argues that "sports flow outward into action from the deep natural impulse that is radically religious: an impulse of freedom, respectful ritual limits, a zest for symbolic meaning, and *a longing for perfection*."[23] Within the drama of sport and its sense of theatre and liturgy (which applies even to some extent at recreational level), by the rigors of preparation, "by a sense of respect for the mysteries of one's own body and soul, and for powers not in one's control; by a sense of awe for the place and time of competition; by a sense of fate; by a sense of participation in the rhythms and tides of nature itself"[24] this deep natural impulse is expressed. This longing for perfection is closely related to the sense of transcendence in sports that I have in mind. Players may not actually aim for perfection in any *absolute* sense for there will be an implicit contextualizing of what this means for each person and situation, but there is a feeling after the better and their best, both for the perfect moment (the touchdown) and for the sustained performance (throughout a game or season). Novak contends that the rituals of sport serve, even

21. Gorn and Goldstein, *Brief History*, 253.
22. Forney, *Holy Trinity*, 107–10.
23. Novak, *Joy*, 19. Italics mine.
24. Novak, *Joy*, 19.

in our day, a deep human hunger that can only be called religious and "provide an experience of at least a pagan sense of godliness. Among the godward signs in contemporary life, sports may be the single most powerful manifestation."[25] Novak is clear that participation in sports is not of itself enough to make someone "a believer in 'God,' under whatever concept, image, experience, or drive to which one attaches the name. Rather, sports drive one in some dark and generic sense 'godward.' "[26]

This drive of which Novak speaks is fundamental to the understanding of transcendence that I am proposing. It is not disconnected from the high points and moments of flow, though it may be that experiences of flow may be attained independently of such a drive. I am speaking as much here of the hunger as about its sating, to switch metaphors. As Duina puts it,[27] in pursuit of victory there is a sense of deficiency, of something lacking. There is *desire*. This desire cannot be fulfilled. Even when we achieve our goal we find that we are not satisfied: there is another prize that lies beyond. A personal best is only made in order to be surpassed. This suggests, says Duina, that the pursuit of a victory or prize has less to do with the actual contest in which we are currently engaged than with a certain kind of trajectory. It seems to be important that we reach after *something*, that we are stretching ourselves, not standing still.

According to Abraham Maslow this drive for transcendence is an identifiable human *need*. Maslow's work, first published seventy years ago,[28] on a hierarchy of needs has aroused considerable debate among scholars and practitioners. The theory in its original form identified five needs that are arranged (often diagrammatically as a pyramid) in ascending order. Until the first, most basic need is met other needs are not attended to. The initial level included physiological needs such as food and sleep; the second level of safety needs included shelter and personal security; social needs included relationships and affection; esteem needs included a sense of achievement and a good sense of one's own self; self-actualization needs included reaching potential, seeking growth and peak experiences. Maslow's biographical methodology (the theory owed a great deal to work on a number of historic figures) came under criticism, as did his insistence on a strict hierarchy to these needs

25. Novak, *Joy*, 20.
26. Novak, *Joy*, 20.
27. Duina, *Winning*, 167–68.
28. Maslow, "Theory."

that required "lower" needs to be met before "higher" ones might be. Observation suggests that this is not always the case. Both the order and articulation of the needs might also be thought to be ethnocentric: we are socialized in this matter as in every aspect of our experience and one might expect that what or how something is felt as a "need" will vary somewhat from place to place and time to time.

In response to criticism and as his own thinking developed, Maslow refined his hierarchy though he did not dispense with its general principles. The most obvious adjustment was in the elaborations of the five stages that effectively introduced three further stages into the sequence that might be thought to unpack what was implicit in the original scheme. It was in his final, posthumous, publication that Maslow suggested that some of those who achieve self-actualization may go on to a further level of need that he called "self-transcendence." Maslow's work is often presented to suggest that the need for transcendence is an altruistic one: having met one's own needs for self-actualization there follows a need to assist others to do the same, and this in turn leads the self to a state beyond normal human consciousness. However, Maslow himself has a very broad conception of transcendence. In fact, he enumerates thirty-five different modes of transcendence.[29] One of these is the transcendence of the ego and the overcoming of selfishness,[30] but many of the first modes of transcendence he lists suggest an ideal of autonomy and independence mixed with a certain kind of Stoic indifference to circumstances. Maslow goes on to detail other types of transcendence that might be addressed at this highest stage. He speaks of surpassing one's sense of what one thought one could do, or have previously done: "to be able to run faster than one used to, or to be a better dancer or pianist, or a better carpenter, or whatever," he remarks.[31] But the next mode of transcendence he describes involves becoming divine or godlike, going beyond the "merely human." Of course, what he describes is actually a rarely actualized dimension of human nature, a potentiality latent within it. Further modes may involve maintaining peak experiences or what it is that they have opened up to us,[32] or a transcendence of space whereby one is so absorbed that one forgets where one is, or has a mystical sense of

29. Maslow, *Farther Reaches*, 259–69.
30. Maslow, *Farther Reaches*, 261.
31. Maslow, *Farther Reaches*, 264.
32. Maslow, *Farther Reaches*, 265.

oneness with others not present,[33] or even of unity with the cosmos.[34] He also speaks of transcending one's own human limits and imperfections.[35] Some of Maslow's modes of transcendence have something in common with the mystic moments "in the zone" so popular among writers on sport and religion, others seem more mundane; some are episodic, others apparently more dispositional. In arguing that there is some kind of need for an experience of transcendence Maslow echoes the notion that we are, in some way, born to compete, and that pursuit of victory demonstrates a sense of deficiency, or, more positively, a *desire*.

In standard theological discourse the term transcendence has two general uses. The more common one refers to the transcendence of God, but even used in this way the term remains slippery. It may convey God's ontological distinctiveness, God's otherness from the world rooted in the Creator/creature distinction, or God's precedence over the world that flows from God as creative source. It may point us towards a moral distinction, to the holiness of God as against the taintedness of fallen creation; or be used with still further connotations.[36] Transcendence predicated of God generally communicates otherness and distance. This transcendence is usually balanced by an account of God's immanence. God is both distant and near, separate from us and seeking us out. Theologically an adequate account of God needs to find a place for both God's transcendence and immanence, and to show how the two concepts require one another.

The second and increasingly common use of "transcendence" is in theological discourse describing human experience. It has, for instance, become a key concept in discussions of spirituality, both of Christian and more secular kinds.[37] This may owe something to Maslow's thought, but also to accounts of the human condition shaped by existentialist and other modern philosophy. John Macquarrie speaks about the peculiarly human experience of self-reflection which shows that uniquely among creatures human persons are open to their existence and aware of what

---

33. Maslow, *Farther Reaches*, 265.

34. Maslow, *Farther Reaches*, 266–67.

35. Maslow, *Farther Reaches*, 267–68.

36. See, e.g., Macquarrie, *Principles*, 120, Tillich, *Systematic*, I, 263, and Brunner, *God*, 175ff.

37. See, for instance: Haase et al., "Simultaneous Concept"; Coward and Reed, "Self-Transcendence"; Robinson, "Spiritual Journey."

they are and what they might be.[38] Whereas other created objects have their natures given to them, there is something about human nature which includes potentiality, possibilities within which persons must "responsibly discriminate." He goes on, "because selfhood is not a ready-made 'nature,' or collection of properties, but a potentiality that has to be responsibly actualized, man can either attain to authentic selfhood or miss it, and so fall below the kind of being that can properly be called 'existence' in the fullest sense."[39]

It is this dynamic character of human being that Macquarrie describes as transcendence, saying that it is our "very nature to be always transcending or passing beyond any given stage of [our] condition."[40] This transcendence is a going out beyond our (current) selves to be/come a newer, more authentic self, "existing" in a richer way and actualizing the genuine possibilities that are before us. While some such possibilities may be generic human potentials, others will be culture- and context-dependent: my possibilities may not be the same as yours, and my current possibilities will not be the same as those that were before me a few decades ago.[41] We recall that Berger spoke of the way that human beings live always in and by hope and express this hope in what he called "projects." As human persons go out from themselves and transcend their presently actualized selves, sometimes their transcendence expresses itself in artifacts—and we might even say that they become immanent in these artifacts: a painter in a great masterpiece on canvas, a composer or performer in the concerto they produce, and perhaps a sports person in their display during a game as the commentators speak of individuals or a members of a team "expressing themselves" in their play.

In his *In Search of Deity* Macquarrie connects God's transcendence and immanence by using the analogy of an artist:

> The artist fully transcends his work, which he conceives in his imagination and then gives to it an embodied form, whether it be a painting or a poem or a piece of music. Once it has this form, the art-work has a measure of independence. Yet the artist is now immanent in his work. He has put something of himself

38. Macquarrie, *Principles*, 60–61.
39. Macquarrie, *Principles*, 61.
40. Macquarrie, *Principles*, 62.
41. There are similarities here to the process notion of God's initial aim offered to all actual entities. See, e.g., Griffin, *Theodicy*, 280–81.

into it and, though it is external to him, it can also be considered like an extension of his personal being.[42]

Whereas Macquarrie deploys this analogy to illustrate a balancing of divine transcendence and immanence, reflection upon it may lead us to associate divine transcendence and human transcendence. The act of transcendence of the (human) artist in his or her creativity is here an analogue for divine transcendence and divine creativity. As such, it also suggests that our "need" to transcend ourselves, to seek authentic existence, is itself a mirror of God's own self-transcending creativity in creation. We may speak of God's immanence in the divine "project" of creation that is also an expression of God's transcendence.

It will be recalled from earlier discussion that Irenaeus proposed that humankind was not created perfect and complete and fell, but was created immature and with the potentiality to actualize themselves. Humanity, we noted, is made open to God and also open to its own growth and flourishing. This Irenaean interpretation of the creation of humanity in the *imago Dei* suggests that human persons are created with the potentiality of maturity and fullness: human persons grow into this potential or may fall back from it. This potential may also be understood as a growing towards God; in becoming authentically human, persons made in God's image also live towards God and may enjoy communion with God—a process that ancient writers called deification. As Macquarrie puts it (referencing Heidegger), the human person "is something that reaches beyond itself."[43] This suggests, as we have been outlining here, that there is in humankind a continual reaching beyond itself towards God *and* its own true self. These are not two separate movements but the same one understood from different perspectives. This view is rooted in the Christian doctrine of creation: humanity is not created in a static, mature, and perfect *imago Dei*, but as a dynamic creature of potential, reaching beyond itself to God.

The experience of sport, and in particular of the competitive element in sport, variously understood, essentially includes a determination to be better, to be the best one can be. We recall the Olympic motto considered earlier: *Citius, Altius, Fortius*. Whatever else may be said about this motto

---

42. Macquarrie, *Deity*, 177. He goes on to note, following William Temple, that for all its usefulness this analogy fails to express adequately "the intimacy of God's indwelling of the world."

43. Macquarrie, *Humanity*, 32.

(see chapters 1 and 2), its drive for "faster, higher, stronger" captures something of the desire ingrained in sporting activity, a desire for (self-) transcendence. John Paul II, himself something of a mountaineer, spoke of the mountains as a challenge, provoking "the human person, the young and not only the young, to make an effort to surpass himself."[44] This is as true for the climber competing against nature and against herself, as it is for the individual golfer attempting to beat par and other players; as true for the NFL quarterback seeking the great Super Bowl prize, as for the jogger trying to defy the effects of his sedentary lifestyle; as true when the Little League player tries to do well by timing a shot, curving a pass, or finding the sweet spot, as for the swimmer shaving microseconds off the turn in order to beat their best time and win championships at High School, the Olympics, or just manage the feat without swallowing a liter of water. In each case s/he is seeking an elusive and transient moment of perfection. The golfer working on her swing, the soccer player dribbling in between cones on the training ground, the Olympian sprinters, jumpers and lifters—all these are pushing themselves to the very limit, trying to go beyond themselves to a new realization of a beautiful and effective moment. To do this with a group appears, for some at least, to intensify the experience.[45] When players really compete and try to be the best that they can be, determined to win if they can, they are engaged in a kind of quest for perfection. Despite the commentator's hyperbole and sometimes the urging of fans or coaches or peers, it is a quest that is bound to fail—or at least to be realized only fleetingly and provisionally. When an athlete sets a new personal best all they have done is established another target to beat. The best performance always lies in front of the athlete. English test cricketer James Anderson is widely considered one of the best fast bowlers in the world. Asked to describe his best ever ball he answers, "I've not bowled it yet."[46] It appears that in truly competitive sport continuous reaching after improvement "disturbs" players who are always lured on by this ideal of perfection.

This movement towards self-transcendence seems to be an essential element of all serious sport: players train for it, spectators wait for it and celebrate it. Humanity in the *imago Dei* is a dynamic creature of potential, reaching beyond itself to God, and sport exemplifies this human

44. Feeney, *Catholic Ideal*, 143.
45. See Cohen et al., "Rowers' High."
46. William Leith, "Best Bowler in the World. Probably."

characteristic in a distinctive way. This human restlessness, this striving for better, is ultimately a striving after God. We recall Augustine's famous statement from the beginning of his *Confessions*, "because you made us for yourself, and our hearts find no peace until they rest in you."[47]

For Jean-Paul Sartre, an atheist existentialist, the unsettling desire that leads to the human person's attempts at self-transcendence ensnares us in what amounts to a futile attempt to be God. This is the human attempt to overcome the absurdity of our predicament, as the finite and contingent person attempts to ground itself in necessity and self-subsistence. Sartre thinks of this futile reaching as an attempt at transcendence and goes so far as to claim that "man fundamentally is the desire to be God."[48] The reaching out is an *over*reaching, futile and absurd, not simply because human beings cannot be God—for Sartre the notion of God is itself absurd and self-contradictory—but because human life cannot be grounded in anything other than the human person's decision to create their own meaning, to create a self-programmed authenticity. While Sartre's position will not, in the final analysis, commend itself to Christian theologians, we may recall Tillich's admission that it is humanity's very potentiality that opens men and women up to *hubris*. "Hubris is the self-elevation of man into the sphere of the divine. Man is capable of such self-elevation because of his greatness."[49] Tillich recalls the Greek tragedies in which men and women fall victim to awful fates not so much in their weakness as in their flawed strengths. In the terms of Macquarrie's account of human existence, it is because of humankind's unique ability to reflect upon its own existence, to realize as yet unfulfilled potential, and in its distinctiveness from the rest of creation, that we find the possibility of sin as well as of flourishing, for inauthentic as well as authentic existence.

But the Sartrean negative perspective need not represent a final judgment on the matter. Gabriel Marcel, writing more or less simultaneously with Sartre in the middle of the twentieth century, offers an analysis of the human condition that is both similar and yet decisively alternative. Where Sartre sees absurdity and despair in the human need for and attempts at transcendence, Marcel saw hope. He spoke at times of his "metaphysic of hope." This metaphysic is not a comprehensive

47. Augustine, *Confessions*, 1/1, 21.

48. Sartre, *Being*, 566.

49. Tillich, *Systematic, II*, 57.

explanation of reality, but suggests intuitions of fundamental mystery over which we have no power and which we cannot possess. Hope is such a mystery, as also are freedom, love, and even evil.[50] He understands the human need for transcendence to be a fundamental fact of human life, though he is cautious about extending its meaning too broadly. He prefers to contrast transcendence with immanence, and thereby preserve what he calls its "vertical" element.[51]

When speaking of human transcendence, Marcel argues, "there must exist a possibility of having an experience of *the* transcendent as such."[52] Marcel appears to have believed that the reaching outward and upward is always a reaching out *to* God. We might paraphrase Marcel as saying that experience of transcendence tends towards experience of the Transcendent. This is to suggest that, just as our experience of self-transcendence mirrors the divine act of creativity by which God becomes immanent in the world, so in turn our acts of self-transcendence are always directed not simply at actualizing our truer and newer self but are also directed to the Transcendent source of our act of self-transcendence. Our self-transcendence is, in its way, an openness to and a seeking for God who created humankind with this capacity to go beyond itself, to reach for God. This is the drive, the longing for perfection of which Novak speaks.

Karl Rahner's account of humanity's openness toward God is marked by a similar sense of this restless desire, which Rahner roots in human consciousness. That consciousness, marked by questioning and enquiry, always points beyond itself, and human persons transcend themselves in the act of reflection that is distinctively human. This drive to self-transcendence evident in human consciousness reaches out to the mysterious transcendent ground of our being. Rahner argues that this sense of transcendence and the Transcendent leaks, as it were, into all of human life.

> Man can try to evade the mysterious infinity which opens up before him in his questions. Out of fear of the mysterious he can take flight to the familiar and the everyday. But the infinity which he experiences himself exposed to also permeates his everyday activities. Basically he is always still on the way. Every

50. See Macquarrie, *Twentieth-Century*, 360.
51. Marcel, *Mystery I*, 49.
52. Marcel, *Mystery I*, 57. Italics his.

goal that he can point to in knowledge and in action is always relativized, is always a provisional step. Every answer is always just the beginning of a new question. Man experiences himself as infinite possibility because in practice and in theory he necessarily places every sought-after result in question. He always situates it in a broader horizon which looms before him in its vastness . . . Man is not the unquestioning and unquestioned infinity of reality. He is the question which rises up before him, empty, but really and inescapably, and which can never be settled and never adequately answered by him.[53]

Rahner describes this restless desire as a quest to answer the question that our very existence poses to us. But only God can answer this question, the answer always lies beyond our grasp. Human transcendence, says Rahner, strictly speaking, has God alone as its reference point. It "knows only *God* and nothing else." Moreover, in its reaching out to God it is also a "being known by God himself."[54]

This latter point is an important element in the understanding of transcendence. We are not simply speaking here of a human attempt to "be God" (Sartre), or be *like* God (Niebuhr), or displace God from the true center of our existence (Tillich). This would locate the notion we are considering within an understanding of sin, whereas we are seeking to give an account of it that is much closer to—indeed, perhaps part of—an understanding of salvation. Tillich and Macquarrie helped us to see the thin line between the two, and how one tips into the other. Without the acknowledgement that in this human disposition of "reaching" outwards and upwards which we are describing in terms of transcendence *God also reaches towards us* we would be left with another rather strident iteration of liberal notions of natural theology. In fact, Rahner does not just claim that God *also* reaches towards human beings who are reaching out towards the final mystery of God in a kind of answering movement; he asserts that human self-transcendence is itself only possible *because* of God's self-offering to created beings. Our very striving and reaching is only possible at all because of God's striving and reaching for us. Our openness to the mysterious ground of our existence cannot be separated from and is enabled by God's own openness to us in gracious self-giving.

53. Karl Rahner, *Foundations*, 34. Cp Rahner, *Practice*, 46-50.

54. Karl Rahner, *Foundations*, 58, italics his. Christologically, we might note, Jesus Christ is the model in which humanity "reaches its highest . . . perfection, the realization of the highest possibility of man's being" (*Investigations*, I, 183).

The movements of what we might call grace and nature are always bound up together, so that God's offer of God's self to us is prior to all human freedom and self-understanding.[55]

The human act of transcendence that is rooted in divine transcendence is not simply a striving for God but a God-given means by which we reach out to God and may be met by an answering reaching for us. "*May* be met": like Marcel's mystery, this "divine reaching" cannot be controlled by us, but is divine gift, grace. While our existence poses the question that drives us always to go beyond, to transcend ourselves, we hear Karl Rahner say that only God can answer this question, we will always fall short of an answer that is in any sense definitive.

A key difference between theologies of sport and play can now be brought into clearer focus. Sport is *agon*, its element of competition involves a striving, whether against an opponent, or oneself, or perhaps natural forces or elements. This embodied *agon* requires a major investment of mind and body and always involves an effort at transcendence. Sport is always a reaching outward and upward and in this movement outward and upward the sportsman or -woman finally reaches outward or upward to God, who enables the human "reaching" and who may in turn graciously "reach down" to them. This (sporting) human transcendence has God as its reference point: it "knows only *God* and nothing else" as Rahner puts it. We have already noticed in an earlier chapter that in participation in creative play the player might be said to participate in the play of God. This helps us to make sense of the notion that the reaching out to God is also a "being known by God himself." The reaching out to God holds within it the possibility that God will reveal Godself to us: that the reaching out will be met, as it were, by a reaching back. It must be stressed again that this is no magical moment that can be manufactured through technique or practice or repetition. Just as flow experiences remain outside the control of their subjects, so this sense of participation and encounter is comprehended only as grace. As we heard Küng reflecting on listening to Mozart:

> One need not perceive them, but one can—there is no compulsion here. If I allow myself to be open, then precisely in this event of music that speaks without words I can be touched by an inexpressible, unspeakable mystery. In this overwhelming, liberating experience of music, which brings such bliss, I can

55. Rahner, *Foundations*, 27.

myself trace, feel and experience the presence of a deepest depth or highest height. Pure silence, silent joy, happiness. To describe such experience and revelation of transcendence religious language still needs the word God.[56]

Irenaeus, whose account of creation we have found helpful, believed that the "glory of God is a human person fully alive."[57] In the invigoration of sporting experience there is indeed a sense of "aliveness" that will be known by many sports participants. Sometimes, the anticipation of this experience will itself be enlivening as the player wonders whether the next game will be the one in which new heights are scaled, or contemplates the prospect of *this week* getting it right, getting it better. There may be a chemical reaction here as the endorphins do their work, but the sensation of timing the ball just so and on the sweet spot of club or bat, or of hitting that perfect rhythm while running around the park, and so on, can make even the very amateur athlete feel alive in vibrant ways. To feel alive in these ways in the special time and place created by our play can indeed feel like being fully alive. It is a function of transcendence in sport, and characterizes sport rather than play. To this precise question, to the possibility of encountering God and (as it were) *which* God, we will return.

Vicarious Sport

The term "vicarious religion" is associated with Grace Davie. Her important work on the sociology of religion beginning in Britain but broadening to include first the European context and then a more global perspective has already been referred to in this book. One of Davie's early conceptual distinctions was between "believing" and "belonging," intending thus to direct attention to a significant proportion of the population who do not belong to any organized religion but who still maintain some religious belief. This was Davie's proposal to account for the marked contrast between the larger number who reported religious belief and the much smaller number who appeared in the statistics of church membership and attendance. More recently she has proposed a new conceptual tool to explore and explain this disparity, vicarious religion, which she defines as "the notion of religion performed by an active minority but on behalf of

56. Küng, *Mozart*, 34.

57. Irenaeus, *Against Heresies*, 4.20.7.

a much larger number, who (implicitly at least) not only understand, but, quite clearly, approve of what the minority is doing."[58] This "on behalf of" can encompass the performing of ritual, the act of believing itself and the upholding of moral codes, as well as the offering of space for public debate.

The concept of vicarious religion as such, fruitful and interesting though it is, is not my major interest here. Throughout this book we have been considering sport as an activity that is both played and watched. We have noticed how spectators have been present at primordial sporting events since men and women first played what might approximate to sport. In the last two chapters our focus has been mostly on those who play, and it is time now to refocus on those who watch. We customarily refer to those who watch sport, generally at elite level, as spectators. I want to suggest that this is an inadequate description of them, and that it would be more fruitful to think of their relationship to sport as a vicarious one.

I have already drawn on the work of theologians reflecting on music at a number of points and at this point it may be useful to refer briefly again to music. Whereas spectator sport might be said to involve players and spectators, music could be said to involve a composer, performers, and an audience. The element of creativity is most obvious in the case of composer and performer, though in different ways. However, Küng and Barth give ample testimony to the effect that music has on those who neither compose nor perform but simply listen. We might, perhaps, speak of a sense in which performers perform on behalf of the audience. Members of the audience, rather like a sporting crowd, will follow the performance with greater or lesser degrees of general musical knowledge and knowledge of the particular piece being performed, and this will affect their appreciation of it in different ways. At its best the musical performance will draw them into the special time of musical performance to which we alluded earlier, and will engage them with the piece in ways that can be intense and absorbing. They may tap their feet, conduct with their pencil, and to the annoyance of those around them in the concert hall even hum along at times. Their engagement with the music will be more than just a passive listening.

This comparison is worth making for a number of reasons, and one of these is to question whether listening to music might be considered

58. Davie, "Vicarious," 22–23.

to be rather more worthwhile, engaging, and even more spiritual than watching a football match. I suspect that it often is so regarded. Of course, music has had very obvious links to organized religion and much of the canon of Western classical music has been composed to serve explicitly religious purposes. But might there also be a hidden assumption that some kinds of cultural practices are superior to others in their propensity for deeper human experience, and could there be a kind of cultural elitism also lurking beneath such assumptions? There is at least an interesting comparison to be made between the vicarious experience of music through listening and the vicarious experience of sport that spectating offers.

As indicated earlier, there was considerable congruence between the responses of players and spectators to the survey questions I posed. Spectators were the larger group by some way among the almost five hundred respondents and, if anything, exhibited an even "stronger" set of responses to the questions even when the gist of the answers was similar. These stronger responses were more marked among, though not confined to, those who watch sports in the stadium as opposed to only on television (or listening on radio). The greater degree of commitment and investment required to attend games live appears to require or create a more intense relationship with the sport for most people—though some remained deeply committed even if they could seldom or never attend live. Attendance at live sport also creates bonds between spectators. This may happen among groups who watch in homes or bars too, but the larger numbers in the stadium together with the more intense nature of the experience seems to add something new. Even if the individual knows only a few members of the large crowd (or perhaps none at all) they can develop solidarity with the whole and begin to shape their identity in relation to them. The repeated nature of this assembling together for regular fans will, I suspect, make a clear difference from the musical audience referred to earlier that will have a less obvious ongoing corporate existence.

The responses to which I will refer in this section may seem similar to those already referenced. However, they come (with exceptions identified) from spectators rather than players. Their similarity might appear to border on the repetitious but is evidence of the congruence of responses among spectators and participants.

I summarized the reasons for playing sport into five categories: fitness and health; relief of general stress; social motives; enjoyment of competition; and just simply enjoyment. I then also suggested some less conscious reasons for playing: sociocultural explanations such as developmental needs and those relating to the establishing and maintaining of identity and consumption. Finally we reflected upon the possibility of religious motivations, and considered whether the experience of sport might be thought of as religious experience.

Describing those who watch sport merely as "spectators" would give the impression that large crowds of people watch others seeking these experiences and making meaning through sport. (We will come in due course to the question of whether professional sports players play for reasons that are anything like the reasons given by recreational sports players.) This seems a rather unexciting possibility. I suppose that it might at first sight appear similar to the audience in concert halls or theatres. It is not my task to examine *those* experiences now, though I suspect that when examined carefully it may also be suggested that "watching" is an unsatisfactory way of describing the role of the audiences of music and drama.

According to Michael Novak, attempts to explain sports in ways that demystify them, perhaps because of suspected corruption or in reaction to perceived obsessions about them, "falsify the deep springs of sport." As an ardent fan himself, he declares that "they do not explain to me the substance of my own love of sports." He continues:

> Fans are not mere spectators. If they wanted no more than to pass the time, to find diversion, there are cheaper and less internally exhausting ways. Believers in sport do not go to sports to be entertained; to plays and dramas, maybe, but not to sports. Sports are far more serious than the dramatic arts, much closer to primal symbols, metaphors, and acts, much more ancient and more frightening. Sports are mysteries of youth and ageing, perfect action and decay, fortune and misfortune, strategy and contingency.[59]

This sense of exhaustion will be well known to spectators of tense sports matches. In a way that perhaps makes the contrast too stark, Novak argues that while watching prime-time TV may distract or amuse him, watching sport on TV is fundamentally different in nature. In the latter

59. Novak, *Joy*, 24.

an outcome is uncertain but matters greatly, with the emotion of the match (and the result) lingering afterwards. Whereas TV entertainment can leave its viewers passive, those who watch sports in a stadium or on their sofa tend not to be passive but actively engaged.

Novak's exaggerated comparison makes his point. Of course, compelling TV drama can also engage viewers, and its "result" can also linger emotionally. "Entertainment" may not be the correct word for such experiences either, with its connotations of distraction and frivolity. And some who watch sport may well also do so for the entertainment value, not caring very much who wins.[60] But the sports fan who Novak seeks to explain, the fan like himself, has a different and much more engaged relationship to the action. Novak has a throwaway line: "wives can tell, rather quickly, whether their husbands' teams have won or lost."[61] This is innocently true in the sense that the emotional effects of defeat linger for spectators, and partners who are tuned into one another detect changes of this sort like barometers indicating a change in the weather. There is also a much more sinister aspect to it however. Domestic violence in Glasgow doubles when Rangers play Celtic in one of their regular derby matches,[62] and authorities in New Zealand consider that a similar spike sometimes accompanies All Black rugby defeats.[63] These appalling reports give macabre credence to the argument that watching sport is rather more (or, perhaps, less in these instances) than entertainment.

The responses from my survey certainly included responses about entertainment. Generally they were mixed in with other reported motives for spectating and may be said, for the more ardent fans, to be the equivalent of the players who said that they played for enjoyment. Indeed, enjoyment is another frequently occurring response. Just as people play sport for fun, so others watch it for fun. But how can we unpack this reported enjoyment?

60. For example, various studies have explored the question of different *types* of football fan. The German scholar Wilhelm Heitmeyer, in his study of fan violence around football games, suggested that there are three types of German football fan: the consumer-oriented fan picks games primarily on the basis of a desire to be entertained; the football-oriented fan attends in order to see their team win; the adventure-oriented fan seeks excitement in the game, or around it. All three groups have mixed socioeconomic composition, and the latter two may be drawn into violence. SIRC, "Football Violence," 54, 68.

61. Novak, *Joy*, 26.

62. Jack, "So Much;" Dickson et al., "Domestic Violence."

63. *New Zealand Herald*, "Women suffer."

As with players, spectators reported watching sport in order to relieve stress. Some speak of being bored or irascible in the off-season. One football fan speaks of the adrenaline rush in a way reminiscent of playing. A number speak of being able to express themselves differently from normal in the context of watching sport. In a sports context some behavior is socially acceptable that elsewhere might not be. One remarks that he took a friend who observed that "he'd never seen me like this before." An American fan observes that "it is fun, exciting, a release. There are few situations in which it is socially acceptable to jump and cheer and yell, and watching sport is one of those situations." Here we come close to the catharsis question once more. As previously mentioned, the notion that sport has a cathartic effect is seriously questioned by research. In fact, there is evidence that when spectators watch aggressive sports their own aggression levels may rise rather than fall in the immediate aftermath of a game.[64] While there is some evidence that players are less aggressive after the game, research into spectators appears to point the other way. Environmental factors can exacerbate this: noise, temperature, crowding, and observing violence. "Increases in player hostility seemingly cause spectators to become more aggressive themselves" whether watched "live" or on TV. "It is pure fiction that spectators watching combatant sports on television or from the stands are miraculously drained of their aggressive impulses."[65]

Nevertheless, it does seem, and is accepted by scholars, that in our routinized modern industrial life the opportunities for risk and exhilaration have diminished, while occasions for strong excitement have become rarer. The shouting, screaming, and gesturing of the sports fan offers an alternative repertoire of behavior to more restrained roles such as parent or employee. Allen Guttmann suggests that studies of spectators may, as it were, take the temperature too quickly after games. In the immediate aftermath, with adrenaline still flowing, it may well be that aggression levels appear to be raised. Perhaps, he says, aggression needs to be measured not just before kick-off and after the final whistle, as studies have tended to, but in a way that frames the whole sport experience—the build-up to the match and the socializing following on from the event—perhaps a period spanning a whole weekend rather than a few hours. Then we might find evidence that there is some safety-valve effect

64. Wann et al., *Sports Fans*, 52–53.
65. Wann et al., *Sports Fans*, 114–15.

in sports spectating, some stabilizing catharsis.[66] It is, as is acknowledged even by the skeptics, both an intuitively attractive notion and a feeling widely reported by sports fans themselves. This relief of stress, if indeed we may speak of it for spectators, seems also to be as close as spectating can come to offering a fitness and health motivation for involvement.

Duina is again helpful and links this question to another, broader one. He notes that Geertz believed that the condition and purpose of human existence is the imposition of meaning. With modern lives often seeming dull, or routine, sporting events come to bear more meaning than otherwise they might.[67] Their uncertainty, coupled with their safety, allows us to play with meanings in sports because we feel secure in doing so. "Competitive events may have had a privileged position in the history of our society precisely because they are at once places to release in a safe and regulated manner drives and instincts that are otherwise repressed in civilized communities *and* because, as our society becomes ever more automated and mechanical, we increasingly see those events as ideal forums for the production of meaning (especially if these meanings are somehow related to darker and subconscious forces within us)."[68]

The social motivation for spectating is very clear indeed. A few extracts from my survey responses demonstrate this (all of the following from rugby league supporters):

> I will never give up watching rugby league, it is in my family and I love the sport. I love taking friends to the games that have never seen it before and introducing them to the game I love.

> Couldn't give it up—been part of my social life and family life for 50 years.

> Watching my team is a "great conversation starter, brings me and my two teenage boys together."

> Now slightly disabled I miss it so much when I can't make it. Friendship, excitement, camaraderie, atmosphere would be missed.

And so on, with similar answers from other sports. "All my social life revolves around it. Couldn't give it up if I tried." People make and

---

66. Guttmann, *Spectators*, 154–58.

67. See Ellis, "Meanings," 178–82, for some further reflection on sport as a meaning-making activity.

68. Duina, *Winning*, 155–56, italics his.

maintain friendships through spectating, and also express family traditions through it. The generational continuity seems especially significant. Asked why they support a particular team many respond that it is the family team, that their father or grandfather supported them, though the respondent may have never lived in the town where the team is based. "It is important to me because I have been a Saints supporter all my life. My granddad signed me up as part of the original Saints supporters club the same day I was born!"

Close to this generational connection is another kind of local identity response. Duina observes that competitors can come to represent collectivities, larger communities. Three-quarters of Americans report that they are proud when their nation does well in international sport. Tiger Woods' initial successes in golf carried social and ethnic significance.[69] In my survey a rugby union fan reports that

> My team is Bristol Rugby and I buy three season tickets and new shirts every year. I'm proud to live in the city and the club is part of that identity.

> Another fan says: "I have always supported the same team . . . it's local and it gives me a sense of belonging."

> Yes, I think it's important to support your home town team . . . I feel that the team embodies the town. We are proud of our team's recent success and that's why I feel everyone should get behind them.

> I live over an hour away [so supporting my home town team] also represents a significant link to my roots.

> Supporting my team is "identity, it is part of who I am."

> I support my local town team because I think the team represents the town and therefore represents me.

One fan says: "It is a way of defining you as a person because you are attached to a country or community."

I have quoted from these responses more extensively in part to indicate the volume of responses along these lines, and in part to illustrate the depth and passion involved. What becomes clear from reading such responses is the extent to which sports spectating, perhaps even more than playing, appears to constitute the identity of these respondents.

69. Duina, *Winning*, 149–50.

"Rugby is as much a part of me as skin and bones," says one. The social motivations reported in survey responses here morph into the less conscious motivations to do with identity and meaning. Except that here, these motivations often appear more conscious.

The enjoyment of competition is also widely reported among spectator respondents. Interestingly, it is often American respondents who articulate this most clearly ("Sports have a high entertainment value. It would be difficult to give up watching them, I would miss watching the competition") but it is present throughout the responses. One way in which it is present is in the importance ascribed to winning. One or two respondents rebuked me for asking a "stupid question" about how important winning was. A football fan comes straight from the Vince Lombardi school in saying, "Winning is everything. Losing isn't an option." Fans report on the importance of winning in a final, or against local rivals. One brilliantly succinct St Helen's rugby league fan says "Win = brilliant, happy; lose = not quite as good. Against Wigan or in a final, then gutted."

But here we also see further evidence of a sense of proportion that may surprise some. Most spectating responses were gained from posting my survey onto fans forum websites. These sites are visited by fairly committed supporters. However, even for this group a significant majority who responded to the question about winning maintained that it was very important but not the only thing that mattered. A good quality game was important, a strong performance from one's team, a good effort that did not "let the side down"—or indeed the town, when such identifications are strong.

How do you feel when winning? "When they win I am pleased, if they get beat by a better team then fair enough as long as the players have been committed" is a typical response. Another says that "Winning is important but so is knowing how to lose; you can't know the pleasure of one without knowing the pain of the other." One might observe about the responses overall that winning is not *quite* everything.

This sense of proportion was mirrored in the question that asked whether they could easily give up their sport attachment. "I'd be sad to give it up but would do so if there was a serious enough reason." Giving it up would be "like missing a limb." Some recognize that changing family circumstances might require a different form of attachment—to switch from stadium to sofa, for instance. One fan speaks for many in saying "I could not easily give it up, but [it is] not a life or death choice,

I would miss the chance to see friends and visit other places." It seems that sports fans report that they could not give up their sport—except when they had to. Which means that they would prefer not to give it up, prefer very strongly indeed, but they recognize that sometimes other calls upon them might take precedence. Nearly all, in admitting this, also note in some way the loss they would feel if such a sacrifice were required, and given the motivations we have discerned already it is easy to see that these sacrifices would be real and could have negative effects on other spheres of their lives.

So far I have mapped the reported responses from spectators in my survey onto those of players and found that they are broadly similar. People tend to play and spectate for similar reasons. We have also seen that the sociocultural explanations for playing sport find resonances in spectating. Is there any evidence for what we considered in the previous chapter as "religious" motivations?

Perhaps the first thing to notice is that there is evidence among players and spectators of some superstitious practices. For spectators, this is linked to a desire to affect the outcome of a game just as much as for players. One suspects that, pressed hard, this may prove quite a soft set of practices, and sometimes represent a sense of whacky fun rather than hard-held conviction. Nevertheless, "I like to have lucky things to make it feel like I have an influence," says one fan.

No question directly addressed this in my survey: it was felt dangerous to put questions that might appear loaded or leading. The survey gave no explicit signal of the religious or theological interests in an attempt to illicit unprompted indications, if any, of such factors. It did ask about aesthetics in sport, and here there was a strong body of evidence in the responses of players and spectators appreciating the complexity, the simplicity, the choreography, the color, the spectacle, and so on. The more technically sophisticated took particular pleasure in seeing well-executed difficult moves, with some knowledge necessary to appreciate just how impressive a feat they were witnessing. Increasingly prominent on UK TV is the use of super slow-motion camera work that produces images that often underline the grace, skill, and power of moves and players. There was wide appreciation for this aspect of watching sport.

Beyond that we might look to the testimony about the ultimacy of sports, this important part of people's lives that would be so difficult to give up. The fact that, when push comes to shove, most agreed that they could give up their sports (that they were *pen*ultimate rather than ultimate) qualifies this without enabling us to disregard it. There is again something paradoxical here that we noted earlier: sport is very important while also being trivial. For many sports fans and players it will routinely seem vital and ultimate, but is cast into a new light by some new development, tragedy or other change in circumstance.

In the previous chapter I described religious experience as falling into five categories: the mystical, the charismatic, the regenerative, the communal, and the nurturing. The responses to my survey demonstrate something of all five. The most obvious are the communal and nurturing, with a great deal of reporting of important social experience and the sense of belonging that regular support brings. But there are also reports from those who find their sports spectating renewing and re-creational. Whether by allowing the expression of otherwise taboo feelings or behavior, or through the sense of purpose and focus that their sports involvement brings, I believe that we can read the experience of sports fans as regenerative. There is behavior that might be described as charismatic in the grandstands. Ecstatic moments when spectators appear seized by some outside agency, or when they express themselves without inhibition. I grant, though, that this does seem to stretch things rather. The mystical moment however would not seem so strange to those who become so engaged in the games they watch that other concerns fade. Moments of high ecstasy are reported. Spectators are passive here to the extent that they feed off the action on the field rather than directly cause things to happen, and such moments pass—necessarily, because a final whistle or hooter will sound. Sports players often gain an intuitive understanding of their sport that is not easily distilled into a discursive reason,[70] and there is something of this too among fans. Again, comparisons with music are possible.

The congruence among responses and motivations, linked to the intensity of the experience of the spectator and the inadequacy of descriptions of spectating as entertainment, leads me to suggest that vicarious sport is a more adequate description of what is going on here than the term spectating indicates. When we speak of a spectator we habitually think of one who stands apart, detached from what he is watching. This is

70. There are, for instance, many articles—more and less scholarly—which seek to explain how David Beckham could curve the free kick towards goal to such impressive effect. He possessed, most argue, an intuitive knowledge of physics gained through playing rather than in a lab or from a text book.

not what appears to be going on here. The sports spectator is involved. A fan makes this distinction clearly: "I am not just a spectator—I am a supporter. I turn up every week not just to watch the team, but to support, cheer, and encourage them." Rather than just observing what happens the supporters believe that they can influence what happens. Their raucous and partisan support during the game suggests an involvement that goes beyond commenting on proceedings. Club management and players repeatedly testify to the help given to performance by fans. Their celebration afterwards, or indeed their gloomy match dissections, indicate a continuing involvement in match-day action.[71] The representational aspect of team sport adds to this. One American fan expresses this sense of close identification neatly: "I feel elated when my team wins as if I had played myself. I throw tantrums when my team loses . . . it is not a pretty sight." Fans do continue to feel that their team represents them even though this has been muddied somewhat in the USA by moveable franchises and elsewhere at elite level by the mobility of the top players following market forces. There seems to be a strong case for saying that those on the field of play are playing *on behalf of* those who are in the stands. Things might be a little more complicated than that. In Davie's use of "vicarious religion" the majority on behalf of whom the minority practice, believe, and so on, are absent from religious observance and practice. In "vicarious sport" some of the supporters may be absent, but a great number of them are very obviously not and there is a symbiotic relationship between players and supporters that the term vicarious alone may not sufficiently convey. However, it does go some way to help us explain both how and why supporters come to identify with the players they watch, how the performance of the players can have such a vivid effect upon them, and how they are emotionally engaged and affected. The modern fan wearing "replica" kit or uniform looks like the players with whom he or she identifies, appears to be a team member with them, speaks of "us" and "we" when referring to the team, and during the game their bodies move in apparent synchronicity: "we draw back our arm as the quarterback passes, we flinch when the pass-receiver is clotheslined,"[72] and so on.

The key question that emerges now is whether the kind of transcendent experience that we explored earlier in relation to players might

71. A similar point is made more negatively by Hamilton, "Spectacle," 183.
72. Guttmann, *Spectators*, 181.

also be communicated to spectators. Can spectators participate in the transcendent activity of the players whom they watch? Or, indeed, can players catalyze such transcendent experience for spectators, experience that may or may not exactly mirror their own (the players') experience? What the survey shows is once more a parallel sense of that desire among spectators which we discussed with regard to players. Despite all the qualifications we have noted, winning and wanting to win are important; they are part (and the clearest part) of the drive that keeps spectators going back for more even after defeats and disappointments. Hope springs eternal in the grandstands. This English football fan expresses a sense of restless desire even when coated with realism: "When [my team] win— [my reaction] ranges from happiness to ecstasy; [when it] loses—from disappointment (again) to really feeling low. In the case of England, I saw them win the World Cup in 1966 and in recent years have come to realize I may never see them win again in my lifetime. Of course, I can't quite come to admit that to myself so for every competition, the juices get ramped up again! (I love it.)" This distinguishes the spectator from the supporter too. The person who really is just a spectator may be happy to be entertained, and lacks this need, this desire, this hope that characterizes the supporter or fan. The spectator sits back and is diverted; the supporter lives in hope, always reaching out through players and team to a new actualization that is beyond the immediate present. The spectator lives in ease, or in escaping from mundane cares; the supporter lives in restless longing. This driving desire also makes the sporting experience a vicarious one for one of my typical respondents: "Winning is important . . . The experience of watching is completely transformed by supporting one of the teams involved, I start to live every kick." As Guttmann puts it, "The process of identification is a complex one . . . Vicariously, we can maul a staggered boxer or shudder to receive a knockout punch. We are what we watch."[73]

It was easy enough in speaking about players to detect what Novak calls the hunger for perfection in sports, a quality which he says adheres closely to the core of being human. I have suggested that this coheres well with an understanding of human nature that owes something to an Irenaean reading of the creation narrative and also to the account of human existence offered by more modern theologians and philosophers.

73. Guttmann, *Spectators*, 180f. Guttmann's discussion of identification with sports stars and teams has many valuable insights: 170–85.

Novak observes that it is the experience of this drive that leads human beings of every age to resort to religious language. This powerful drive, says Novak, pulses through us beyond our power to control or quell, *"driving us beyond our present selves."* [74] This restless drive and desire is so deep in our natures, he suggests, that we may say that "it *is* the human spirit." It can be distorted but, well-targeted, "it soars like an arrow toward the proper beauty of humanity." He goes on, "Sports nourish this drive as well as any other institution in our society . . . Sports are, in a word, a form of godliness."[75] The experience of the supporter of sports is a vicarious manifestation of this restless desire. Unable directly to transcend our givenness, to be the best, to execute the perfect shot, we invest ourselves in those who will do it on our behalf. This may be denigrated as second-hand sport, as a shedding of personal responsibility, or an inability to live authentically instead relying on the living of others. Or it may be seen more positively as an expression of corporate identification, as the extending of our potential, no less appropriate than the transcending pleasure of listening to Mozart's music when we can neither compose nor perform as well ourselves.

While the evil that is a distortion of the good manifests itself for players in various kinds of cheating, in an obsessive attitude to sport, for supporters there are equivalent distortions. The violence of crowds will certainly be one of them, a plague that has beset European football in particular but from which other sports are not immune. Sports crowds have probably always tended toward the rowdy, a reflection of the high emotion that can be generated in the heat of competition. It must also be said the causes of football hooliganism remain under debate, and not all theories relate it to what happens on the field. It is possible that for some intent on violence sport is the pretext rather than the reason for the mayhem. But sports supporters can exhibit the distorting effects of human sin in other ways: in inappropriate attitudes to alcohol, in racism or sexism, and through obsessive behavior of various kinds. Sports reflect society, they do not exist in a bubble. The question is then: is there anything in the nature of sport that exacerbates the problems that we can identify? Is sport a contributory factor to human sin, or merely an extension of the human stage upon which there is already ample opportunity for it? To these and other questions we turn next.

74. Novak, *Joy*, 27. Italics mine.
75. Novak, *Joy*, 27.

Sin and Salvation in Sport?

Sin has been mentioned a number of times, and we must briefly make some general observations on the subject before moving on to ask about salvation in sport. Tertullian and Augustine both saw the Roman Games as causes of frenzy that deranged their spectators, and urged their contemporaries to avoid them. Tertullian, we recall, also had harsh words for participants who pursued violence against an opponent in order to preserve themselves. Not all sports are violent, and by the standards of ancient games we have established that our modern sports are civilized affairs. But is there something inherent in sport that might lead us into temptation?

We have considered at some length the issue of competition. In brief, I suggested that competition is not peculiar to sport, and a very great deal of contemporary life is competitive, some in an organized or institutional way. In these spheres too men and women try to gain unfair advantages, abuse opponents and sometimes themselves, bend rules, and so on. Sport might be construed, with the Marxist, as capitalism in training shoes; as a distraction, or an institutionalizing in recreation of the winner-takes-all attitudes that govern socioeconomic life. Few commentators in sport would want to see it in this way, though the Marxist critique should always keep us alert to a "bread-and-circuses" use of sports that stages massive and spectacular events in order to draw us into collusion with those whose interests are served in the *status quo*. As I write, the people of Brazil have been complaining in the streets about the costs of staging the Olympics and the FIFA World Cup. The Marxist-type question is worth asking sometimes even if it fails to give an adequate and complete account of what is going on in sport.

However, in general I believe that we can affirm that the *drive to transcendence* which sport allows human persons to express is, notwithstanding the distortions occasioned by competition in sport as with competition in other spheres, an important and wholesome human reality. A reality not vitiated by its distortion any more than the "goods" of love and sex are vitiated by possessiveness, manipulation, and pornography, for instance. It may be however that sport, with its ability to dramatize this drive in such vivid ways that in turn kindle high emotions and strong feelings, is vulnerable to some of the distortions of human good in particular ways. We have said that we have pointed to what we might call the particular traction that human sin has on this given sphere of activity, but while we do that we also bear in mind that other spheres of activity might also be said to have their own peculiar point of traction. The Puritans believed that "sport" could be an occasion for idleness, drunkenness, gambling, and a disproportionate importance given to it alongside other claims on our time. They were correct in all particulars. Sport *can* be an occasion for these things, though it need not be. The more measured response to these dangers has been to see them in the light of the many benefits that sport can bring rather than discount sports altogether for fear of contamination.

Much of the discussion of sin in sport is focused on competition and what it does or does not do to participants and supporters. Understandings of sin are often individualistic and couched in terms of personal morality. This is a partial account of the problems. In chapter 2 we considered a number of different aspects of sport's social reality. Each of them raised concerns for those who want to reflect on sport from a Christian theological perspective. They each suggest complex accounts of sin that indicate a more social perspective.

The influence of business on sport is huge and pervasive, whether in the millions of pounds which buy and pay players via sponsors, or the investment in sporting goods for ordinary punters to consume. "Follow the money" is always good advice to those who want to understand why and for whose benefit things happen—and not just in sport. The sin that money brings into sport is not simply personal greed—whether that of the multimillion-pound athlete, or of the fan who must own all the most expensive gear. Any attempt to come to terms with the influence of business on sport (and perhaps sport on business) must grapple with a more complex and less individualistic account of sin in which structures, institutions, and social pressures have to be accounted for.

But the influence of business on sport is not new: the ancient Greeks knew it well, and the first elite English cricketers did too—it has been omnipresent. If nothing else, a history of sport ought to help us see that there is little new under the sun. We saw also that the impact of business on sport has not always been negative. Technological advances have often been powered by business interests and these have often enhanced the quality of play, the spectator experience, and safety for all. The contemporary mass media are both a product of these business concerns and also offer an opportunity to shine a critical light upon them. The freedom of the press is as important in maintaining the integrity of sport as in other spheres. The question to be raised about business or the media in sport is not, "should there be any?" but "how does the sporting community manage the influence of commercial interests for the benefit of players and supporters while also minimizing negative impact on the game experience?"

Questions like this can only be answered properly sport by sport but they clearly provide an opportunity for a Christian voice to speak into ongoing concerns. Most elite football clubs in England, for instance, now have chaplaincies. When the work of these is described it is often presented in terms of personal evangelism and pastoral support to players and staff. These are important tasks and will naturally figure in an appropriate ministry. The challenge is to broaden the concern of chaplains away from this rather individualistic and individual-oriented approach and address bigger structural issues: to be the voice that articulates the concern of the ordinary supporter about the way that sponsors are calling tunes, or commercial motives alone dictating kick-off times or merchandising and refreshments, and which alerts clubs to their responsibilities to the local communities, for instance. This will be an uncomfortable place to be, as prophetic locations usually are, not least because these chaplaincies are usually present more by grace than by right. To ask awkward questions might be a quick way to the exit, but a Christian concern for sport does not stop at instrumentalizing the game for the purposes of evangelism. If sport is to be evaluated positively as an activity in which a divinely bestowed capacity for play is expressed and in which opportunities for personal transcendence present themselves, then it deserves to be seen as more than just a vehicle for the Christian message to individuals however important that is.

In earlier chapters of this book I suggested that seeing everything through the lens of sinful, competitive pride was neither helpful nor accurate. We turned to Tillich as an example of a more fully rounded conception of sin and we saw in feminist critiques that sometimes sin was better understood as a *lack* of pride, a lowered sense of self or possibility than in the notion of hubristic self-assertion so often taken to be normative. There is something similar in Moltmann's observation early in *Theology of Hope*, recalling the central place within the sporting dynamic of the restless drive, the yearning for perfection, the hope of victory.

> If faith thus depends on hope for its life, then the sin of unbelief is manifestly grounded in hopelessness . . . it is usually said that sin in its original form is man's wanting to be as God. But that is only the one side of sin. The other side of such pride is hopelessness, resignation, inertia and melancholy . . . Temptation thus consists not so much in the titanic desire to be as God, but in weakness, timidity, weariness, not wanting to be what God requires of us.[76]

Sin in sport may be a failure to hope, to express the restless desire for authenticity that Novak suggested was at the root of our very humanness.

We also noted the usefulness and importance of the idea of original sin in relation to sport. Every part of human life is affected by sin, and this sin is not simply the totality of individual wills. Somehow the whole is greater than the parts. As a result we are enmeshed within a tissue of sin that reaches into sport and distorts it, as the good always tends to be distorted.

One other issue needs to be mentioned. According to some, *professional* sportsmen and -women are particularly under suspicion: because they are paid to play they become especially vulnerable to a disproportionate desire to win, and more likely to use foul means to achieve their end. Moreover, they are not "playing" any more for playing's sake, instead they are "playing" for their mortgage or rent, or for that luxury villa or car.

Whether professional sports players are more likely to cheat is, I think, open to question. Again we might need to differentiate an answer from sport to sport. Elite footballers might be playing for higher stakes but they are also playing in a much more public space with a far greater likelihood of being found out than players in the local park. Their wider experience in the game will certainly expose them to a wide range of illegal strategies, but as readers of Michael Green's series of books know recreational players have always been adept at developing winning ways that may or may not be technically legal.[77] Professional rugby players may try to do things on the blind side of the referee, and footballers will often take a handful of shirt as they try to tackle, but all of this can be seen easily in my local park as well as in a large stadium. Cycling, and track and field, because of the apparent prevalence of performance-enhancing drug use may be different, and it may show the increased premium given

76. Moltmann, *Hope*, 22.

77. E.g., Green, *Coarse Sport*. His other titles explore individual sports.

to individual endurance or speed as opposed to team sports where the pressures are different.

However, the idea that professionals are not really "playing" because they get paid is simply ridiculous. The fact that Mozart was paid for all his work, and indeed that he wrote quite specifically to pay his bills and clear his debts, does not stop his work being regarded as masterful nor did it prevent Barth seeing in it a truly playful spirit. Bernard Suits' vision of work was that any activity that was enjoyed for its own sake could be regarded as play and that in Utopia (perhaps now we might call it Playtopia?) everyone would be occupied in activities that were enjoyed for their own sake. This could include stamping out a widget, molding clay into a vase, writing a sonata, changing a washer, and writing a theological paper, as well as playing tiddlywinks or baseball. The language has changed subtly here. Rather than speaking of play as being an *end* in itself (autotelic) we are speaking of play being something that is *enjoyable* for its own sake. Borrowing the Greek word for joy and delight, *chara*, we might therefore describe play as *autocharatic* rather than *autotelic*. We play because we enjoy it for its own sake.

In fact, the autotelic nature of play does seem to me to be open to question, or at least to qualification. Once we have described the way that play creates its own world of time and space there is a sense that the lusory goals will necessarily be goals within that newly created world and will not refer to things that are beyond it. But this has to be qualified. We noted that play has a developmental function, and we noted that human beings might be considered *homo ludens*, natural players in effect. But if play has a developmental function whatever lusory goals are present wholly internal to the game there is also some other goal (albeit rather more vague) beyond it. If human beings are natural players then we play to express our nature, we play to be human. This too seems to represent some qualification on the autotelic nature of play. Play in sport also serves various goals. When we heard players and spectators gives reasons for their playing, the majority who responded in terms of enjoyment were getting close to saying that they played it *for its own sake*. But these same people also played for fitness, or for social bonding, thus playing sport for a non-lusory purpose. Players who play to earn a living add a new non-lusory reason for playing, but they are not unique. We all do things for multiple reasons. Generally, as well as all the other reasons, we play sport because it is fun, because it is autocharatic. There will be days when the professional does not enjoy their sport—though the same can be said of the recreational player too. However, one quite often hears the pro say that she is "enjoying her game" and that this motivates them for further sacrificial training, or to stave off retirement for a while.

Some of the most challenging issues for sport arise in the areas of gender and ethnicity. Because of the ingrained connections between modern sports and masculinity, and because commercial and media interests have traditionally been controlled by men, sport has often been problematic for women. They have been marginalized in its shaping and development, belittled or ignored in their participation, seen as supporters of men rather than agents in their own right. There are one or two signs in the UK that things may be changing. The Football Association has re-established the elite women's football league (though not without controversy) and the 2013 Women's European Championships have received more TV and newspaper coverage than any comparable competition before. Women's cricket and rugby have a rising profile at international level too. In tennis, and track and field, female athletes often receive coverage similar to men.

There are also emerging stories of how women succeed in breaking the gender stereotypes that constrain and limit them, and go on to forge new identities that allow women to contemplate new possibilities. I have referred to student work on sailing already. Another vivid example is found in Dianne Chisholm's response to the article by Marion Young that we considered in chapter 2. Young had analyzed the throwing action of girls and found that women experienced their bodies as "other" and acted out in their comportment the restrictions of patriarchy. Writing more than thirty years after Young, Chisholm has a double objection to her: first that she has implicitly idealized masculine motility as the human norm, and second that she has assumed that the older feminine experience of embodiment that she described as "throwing like a girl" remains a continuing paradigm for women's experience.[78] Instead Chisholm offers a reflection on the story of Lynn Hill. Hill is a leading climber whose ascent to high regard in the climbing community parallels many of her impressive ascents up giddy cliffs and mountains. Hill shows that "climbing like a girl" can mean not a constricted activity that is a poor shadow of its ideal male expression, but a kind of movement with its own integrity and possibilities, some of which surpass those experienced by the best men in

78. Chisholm, "Climbing," 11.

climbing. She has simultaneously redefined what good climbing is, giving it a feminine form, and also shown that Young's gloomy assumption that women will always throw (or climb) like girls is moribund. Women can climb in their own way, and in a way that is not inferior to the way men climb. Hill's story "presents a paradigm case study of woman's ability to move freely in the world and in rapport with nature."[79]

What interests me in this narrative is not simply the possibility of the creation of new feminine norms that enable women to break out of the space into which patriarchy had confined them, but that it is precisely through a sporting activity that this has become possible. In a way which parallels our earlier discussion of how winning appears to affirm life more comprehensively than anything as limited and parochial as the game which has actually been won, so Chisholm suggests here that new possibilities for self-understanding and relationships are possible through these sporting acts of transcendence: that in successful climbing some more profound and pervasive ascent has taken place. Hill's cliff ascent is an apt metaphor and paradigm for the transcendence to new possibilities which might be discovered in other sporting spheres. The task for women's football, for instance, may not be to show itself as a slightly slower, slightly less pulverizing version of the men's game, but to find a way of inhabiting the game that is distinctively feminine and that showcases and nurtures qualities that may be distinctive to it. Chisholm's account gives us further reason to hope that, while we can easily enough find causes for concern in sport, and even as our forebears believed occasions for sin, we might also find possibilities of something more positive and salvific.

We begin to move here then from sin towards salvation. In our discussion of Muscular Christianity in chapter 1 we noted the view that the movement, especially in its developed form, in effect offered a secularized soteriology. As the YMCA embraced sport with increasing zeal, their attitude changed in a fundamental way, Erdozain suggests. Instead of using sport as a means to an end (the end of conversion or deepening piety), a sporting sprat to catch a spiritual mackerel, sport began to serve another end (the end of fitness and general well-being). The "salvation" on offer at the gym thus became secularized.

There are a number of observations that might be made about this. First, I have already noted the tendency among modern sports

79. Chisholm, "Climbing," 35.

chaplaincies and ministries to construe their engagement with sports clubs and players in an instrumental way: the rationale for involvement is often evangelism or individual pastoral care, and even the latter can be for the sake of "seeking an opening for the gospel." What the YMCA lost, it might be said, has been recovered in the many sports ministries and chaplaincies that have developed since.[80] While many Evangelicals would doubtless argue that this is the most urgent call on resources, it seems to the present writer that as an understanding of salvation it is as partial and unsatisfactory as one that would explain everything in the secularized terms of fitness and well-being. Salvation is bigger than this, and God's desire to save is not simply about what Mohammed Ali famously called "pie in the sky when you die."[81] A doctrine of salvation based on the life, death, and resurrection of Jesus will be richer than this. We might recall, for instance, that the New Testament Greek word *sozo*, usually translated "I save," has a very rich range of meanings. As well as "save" it can mean "make safe from danger, heal, deliver from evil," and more. Jesus' own ministry is marked by teaching and actions that convey forgiveness and acceptance,[82] by healing acts[83] and powerful demonstrations of God's deliverance from evil.[84] His teaching celebrates the value of those on the margins,[85] and calls men and women to live in a world where extra miles are traveled and other cheeks are offered.[86] He speaks to, parties with,[87] and touches those who sensible ordinary people would avoid.[88] When Zacchaeus responds to Jesus at the meal table and puts right his own grievous wrongs, Jesus declares that "*today* salvation has come to this house."[89] Whatever salvation is, it is a far richer reality than something that is reduced to one's individual spiritual (usually disembodied and post-mortem) welfare, however important a part of it that may be.

80. There is an excellent account of the development of these ministries focusing especially on the USA and upon their relationship to Muscular Christianity in Ladd and Mathisen, *Muscular Christianity*.

81. Bingham and Wallace, *Muhammad Ali*, 63.

82. Luke 6:37.

83. Matt 12:13.

84. Mark 1:25.

85. Luke 10:36; 14:21.

86. Matt 5: 39, 41.

87. Mark 2:15.

88. Mark 1:41

89. Luke 19: 9.

Second, we have already discussed the notion of sport as autotelic, and I suggested that there were reasons to qualify this requirement, perhaps indeed to qualify the autotelic nature of all play. We rarely do anything for one reason, even when the thing we are doing may constitute its own reason. We are complicated creatures. The motivations for playing sport observed in empirical data-gathering and through more general reflection are layered and many. However, while we need to take care about insisting that sport be considered an end in itself as if no other considerations or motives might have a place, we can (as I have argued above) properly affirm that sport can be enjoyed for its own sake even when it also serves some other purpose. Rather than autotelic I suggested we describe it as autocharatic. Sport enjoyed for its own sake may also have felicitous side effects, as it were. Some of these may be therapeutic. The Greek word from which we derive "therapeutic" occurs more than forty times in the New Testament, it is a companion for *sozo*, meaning "to heal." Some of the healing and other positive impacts of sport flow from simply enjoying it. How one calculates the contribution this makes to human flourishing I am not sure, but human flourishing should certainly be considered part of the richness of any notion of salvation. Perhaps the very ability to play sport, relatively free of inhibition and outside control from state authorities or other constraints, is itself a sign of that proto-flourishing.

Third, and perhaps by now clear enough, we should be cautious about assuming that a concern for and celebration of the fitness and welfare benefits of sport (which figured prominently in the declared motives of players in my survey) itself alone constitutes a secularizing of soteriology. Paul's implicit command to the Corinthians, that they must treat their bodies as temples of the Holy Spirit,[90] was often deployed in the Muscular Christianity movement as part of a rationale to prioritize bodily health as a proper spiritual goal. However one bases such an argument there would surely be little opposition now to the suggestion that Christians, and all men and women, should look after their bodies and treat them with respect as gifts from God. Even putting it like this suggests that we are separate from our bodies, a misleading idea based on Greek philosophy rather than Scripture. We are psychosomatic unities, in a complex but real sense we *are* our bodies. This is one reason why orthodox Christianity has insisted on speaking of the resurrection of the body

90. 1 Cor 6:19–20.

rather than the immortality of the soul: only the former notion conveys the sense that the whole person (that is, an embodied person) is born to new life with God for eternity. It is this agreed need to treat our bodies with respect that can form the basis for challenging some of the abuses in sport that we have discussed. Steroid use for shot-putters and repeated painkilling injections to enable those in contact sports to keep playing through injury do not constitute respect for our bodies. However, a concern for fitness and health does have a proper part in a fully rounded doctrine of salvation. Where Erdozain is correct is insofar as this concern for fitness and health *displaces* other parts of this fully rounded doctrine. We may suggest that when salvation has become *only* a matter of fitness and health (or, for that matter, *only* a matter of eternal destiny), then a reductionist soteriology is operating; but the presence of such elements at all within a soteriology should be welcomed rather than discarded.

There is not the time or space here to develop and defend an adequate and fully rounded doctrine of salvation. However, we have already encountered some clues as to what it might look like. We considered earlier that sin might require a somewhat contextual definition, contrasting masculine and feminine accounts, for instance. Thus we need to be ready to conclude that salvation will not always look the same. The healing, making safe from danger, and so on, will look different where the diseases and dangers are different, and we might expect a wide range of "saving" realities to present themselves for our reflection.

Sport is widely deployed by publicly funded agencies, charities and NGOs in a variety of social projects. Sport can thus be used to establish or bolster self-esteem and confidence, to foster strategies of social inclusion, and to create safe places for vulnerable groups. Tess Kay's research on the "uses" of sport in such regards is informative. The focus of her research into Muslim women who enter sports programs designed to promote access to higher education is on the way the young women negotiate skillfully between the expectations and desires of their families and the Islamic tradition on the one hand, and the expectations and desires common in the host culture (in this case, the UK) on the other. However, in giving us a detailed account of how and to what extent the access-through-sports program is successful in its aims Kay also shows not only how future programs might be organized to be more successful but also how the experience of participation in sport could also play a real (if sometimes modest) part in enabling human flourishing. As one young participant in the program recognizes, apart from the enjoyment of participation it also brings such bonuses as "communicating with each other, learning to respect one another, helping one another, building your self-confidence and esteem."[91]

Is self-esteem really part of what we mean by salvation? Is the person who gains a clearer sense of a true identity thus being saved? I have already made a case for a richer and multi-dimensional conception of salvation marked in part by human flourishing. Part of what that entails includes an ability to grasp the possibilities for one's own life, as well as open up possibilities for others, and indeed to see the possibilities that may be looked for in conjunction with others. In involves realizing our (God-given) gifts and using our (God-given) playfulness to become creatures more fully conformed to God's purposes. These will include purposes that can be both individually and socially defined, but fuller participation in the realizing of potential is to some extent dependent on a more confident sense of self, of worth and acceptance, in short of ourselves as God's creation. The account of human existence that we considered earlier gave a prominent place to concepts such as creativity, potential, authenticity, together with the related concept of transcendence, and it fits well with some of the possibilities of sport. Quite apart from the possibility of transcendence, sport offers opportunities for aspects of human flourishing (and, as conceded, for distortion and human stunting) in particular ways.

If we take healing as a core metaphor at the heart of salvation we may observe that, in between the states of being truly sick and truly healthy, there are many intermediate states of becoming sick or regaining health. I am thinking here, in soteriological terms, of a distinction something like the one Tillich makes in speaking of the relationship of men and women to the New Being, as he characterizes salvation. First salvation can be seen as participation in the New Being, and this constitutes the process of regeneration. This is, in the terms I have just used, the regaining of health. Tillich goes on to specify two further stages: salvation as acceptance of the New Being, or justification; and salvation as transformation by New Being, or sanctification.[92] He describes these three stages as conversion—justification—sanctification, but it is also possible to see in the first stage, that of participation in the New Being, a less than fully conscious ap-

91. Kay, "Daughters of Islam," 348.
92. Tillich, *Systematic, II,* 203–7.

prehension of (re-gained) health. I am not going to speculate here about what might constitute "enough health" or "sufficient salvation," let alone ask for what end such sufficiency is required. Rather I want to suggest that when we use a God-given playfulness and experience benefits that are self-evidently good and that serve human flourishing in an experience that may be described itself as a reaching out for the Transcendent as we strain at self-transcendence, it seems to me difficult not to say that this is some kind of experience of healing and wholeness. It may be such an experience in only the tiniest measure, as nothing compared with matters of greater moment in other spheres: it is not my argument to claim either exclusivity or superiority for the sporting moment.

Two points arise obviously here. First, if there is anything like salvation going on here it is clearly a salvation that will often, perhaps mostly, occur outside the church. Salvation in sport is a reminder of God at work in the world beyond (though including) the church. There must surely be analogues in other spheres of human activity, including the arts, politics, and development work. Who would not say that the provision of safe water in a village plagued by waterborne disease is not a case of "today salvation has come to this house"? That is a dramatic instance, but believing in God's Holy Spirit at work in the world wherever men and women begin to "regain health" may remind us also that God's salvation is often known by broken-but-mending human persons in fragments. Any fragment of salvation known through sport (recognizing again that it is not "full salvation") is an embodied salvation. Too often the salvation offered within the church is seriously disembodied. When churches and mission agencies took to sport as a means to an end from the mid-nineteenth century onwards perhaps they recognized the need to correct a balance. There may be discussion about the proper importance to accord this sportingly embodied salvation in a total soteriological picture, but I suggest that it needs to be discussed rather than ignored or dismissed.

Second, can we say that *God* saves through sport? I may have alarmed some readers not least by the suggestion that our striving for excellence, our straining to win, our seeking the Transcendent through moments of transcendence is a means to lay hold of some kind of experience of salvation. Put like that it seems more like our efforts to save ourselves than it does God's salvation breaking into our lives and doing for us what we cannot do for ourselves. In these theological matters grace is paramount. God saves us, we do not save ourselves. This can only be made sense of when we make some other assumptions about God at work in the world. God is not merely at work in the church, but is immanent in the world and at work everywhere for human wholeness, overcoming sin and leading men and women into greater fullness of life. But a more specific point can be made. God the player has created us *homo ludens*, restless creatures seeking to grow and mature, and seeking after God. Insofar as the move to transcendence in sport might be a seeking after God and might be met by an answering movement by God then we might feel more confident in speaking of salvation in sport. The key thing here is that, in the working of God's Spirit, and in our participation in the life of the playful God in our own sporting play, we may affirm that God saves in sport, it is not we who save ourselves. Sporting journalists often use religious language in covering sports events. Salvation features in many a headline, and talk of moments of redemption is not uncommon. Perhaps, somewhere beyond the clichéd hyperbole there is some theological truth in all this after all.

Conclusion

"The Theology Behind All Cultural Expressions"

S PORTS FIXTURES REACH THEIR final moments leaving fans in a variety of moods. Some will feel elated, others despondent; some games will still be in the balance with success still uncertain, in others the result (one way or the other) will have been clear for some time. I must let my readers map their own experience onto these familiar emotions in arriving at this point in the book. In concluding I will consider briefly aspects of the argument in this book. What is offered here is not properly a summary because many important parts of the argument will not be mentioned, but it will allow us to call to mind several moves and connections within the whole. Like the highlights package so familiar to many TV sports fans it aims to pick out certain features from the game, give a flavor of it, and so permit a little punditry from commentators. This will lead then into a consideration of some loose ends—topics that have been given insufficient attention—and then finally into some observations about the type of theological argument that has been offered.

Highlights

Historically we identified three themes or phases that indicate the attitude of the church towards, and the relationship of religious practice to, sports. In our first phase sports were seen as part of the ritual apparatus which were a means of regulating the relationship of humanity, or specifically a tribe or group, with a god or gods. In my narrative we were able most clearly to identify these kinds of practices with early pre-Christian rituals, and with religious practices which developed in parallel to Christianity among South and North American peoples. But the phases are not hermetically sealed and the presence of something like football in a French medieval Easter liturgy is a reminder that, though not in a widespread way, there have been times in the history of the church also when sport has been a medium through which the divine–human relationship has been conducted. Later developments flowing out of Muscular Christianity hint at other ways in which individuals, and perhaps communities (certainly, non-ecclesial communities such as schools), made use of sport in order to explore and express their relationship with God in some sense. The apostle Paul probably knew of the games from his visits to Corinth, and the suggestion that he disapproved of them seems hard to sustain. Indeed, he used them illustratively to speak about living the Christian life before God. However, the early Christian period, as evidenced in Tertullian and Augustine in particular in our study, did see strident opposition to the Roman Games with their gratuitous violence and association with paganism and immorality.

In the second phase, sports and their associated activities are often considered negatively. It is this sense of "guilt by association" that often figures too in Puritan critiques of sport. Much of the intervening period, while we may struggle to describe the kinds of games and pastimes in which people engaged as sports in a way continuous with the modern meaning of that term, had seen a process of accommodation with the church often found as (an admittedly tetchy and changeable) landlord for these primitive sporting activities. The Puritans were, like the Fathers, concerned about violence but also about the activities that tended to be associated with sport—or in the case of idleness, the *lack* of activity. There were issues of stewardship, though some scholars suggest that economic motives were sometimes passed off as theological ones. Despite the strident voices of Tertullian and the Puritans, the fact that these voices were repeatedly raised is probably an indication that this second phase may be best described as one of both accommodation and opposition to sport.

The nineteenth-century realization that a church in decline was failing to make contact with large sections of the population led some church leaders to question the austere forms of Christianity that frowned upon any extra-ecclesial activity apart from work which was found engaging and enjoyable. The third phase had begun, in which sport came to be no longer merely tolerated by some while disparaged by others, but was now positively seen as an ally in mission that opened up new possibilities of human flourishing. Just as church leaders began to grasp these new possibilities in the elite schools to begin with, sport was being reimagined as a more civilized and regulated activity which—rather than being perceived as a route to dissolution—was now understood as potentially character-building. Some of the thinkers of the age used theological arguments such as those regarding the body as God's temple, though it is also possible to argue that these theological or spiritual concerns may have elided with others concerning such things as masculinity in an industrializing world in which some thought the church feminized its members. As suggested above, sport could now be conceptualized as a legitimately spiritual matter and a sphere in which one's faith and one's relationship with God could be deepened.

While the Fathers' concerns about the Roman Games seem rather remote from most of our sanitized modern sport, the Puritan critique, I suggested, still needs to be taken seriously. Sport can produce excess, and lead to disproportionate and disordered patterns of behavior. It can be accompanied by ancillary behaviors that might be thought to erode rather than build up traditional Christian virtues. These reservations took on a more contemporary feel when we considered the place of sport in the present day. While these three phases can be crudely identified with historical developments, and are to an extent sequential, in fact they all also remain contemporary. Even after the Victorian settlement on sport, when we have moved to a much more positive evaluation of it, we need to be alert to its distortions and dangers. The roles of commercial interests and the media, its function as a site of consumerism, and the tangles of gender, ethnicity, and politics, each indicated reasons for caution. However, it is also clear that sport reflects the society that creates it, and few if any sporting sins are more egregious than those that might be noticed in most other social spheres.

Just as the developments of the nineteenth century offered a way to see sport as wholesome and even spiritual, so also the coincidence of declining interest in organized religion and the rise of what we could at last begin to think of as modern sport suggested that it was worth asking whether sport might actually be fulfilling some of the same functions for our Western contemporaries as organized religion did for many in previous generations. There are good grounds for thinking that this is the case, and many of the characteristics of modern sport in elite and popular forms can be mapped onto analyses of the nature of religion and religious practice. The fit is not exact, but is close enough for us to believe that there is some substance in this thesis.

For some the suggestion that sport might be understood in these ways may seem far-fetched, but by rooting such reflection in an understanding of sporting play and deep in humanity's basic instincts as *homo ludens*, and by discerning this further back in the very nature of the creative love of God, *Deus ludens*, we might begin to see how the religious dimensions of sport may have something more than an entirely accidental basis. Tracing this through Old Testament texts and religious practices gave further pointers, and Peter Berger's case that understood play itself as a pointer to a reality that transcended the everyday added further momentum. Just as the notion of play might help us to understand the creative activity of God we also came to see it as a useful way of conceptualizing the "end" of creation that I described as a "playful end."

The argument of the last two chapters has given a central place to the factors that distinguish sport from other kinds of play—the *agon* or contest, and the desire to win. While this sometimes has regrettable consequences, the desire to win in itself betokens a deeper human desire. It is a reaching outward and upward, a reaching beyond our current capabilities and compass; it is, ultimately, an attempt at transcendence that seeks the Transcendent. In terms of historic attitudes to sport, there is here something of the positive evaluation which characterized both our first and third phases. This Transcendent, God, is the source of our desire and striving, for humanity is made in the *imago Dei*. Indeed, it is made possible by God reaching "down" to humanity in gracious love. The desire to win in sport, at the heart of sport's peculiar form of play, may not be the only form in which this transcendent/Transcendent encounter takes place but given what we know about play, and about the way in which sport itself appears to take on (quasi-) religious characteristics, there is little surprising here. God too is a winner as well as a player, our winning and the desire to win is some kind of presentiment or anticipation of God's victory: through sport, a locus of salvation in its way, we may participate in this victory of God over sin, chaos, and death.

Some Loose Ends

Before I make some concluding observations about the type of argument I have made I must pause to notice some of the topics I have not, or not properly, engaged. Among the major areas upon which I would have valued the opportunity for further reflection I mention three here.

The first is the notion of *place*. In considering sport in relation to characterizations of religion we noticed that religion often has special places, locations considered sacred and marked off from ordinary space. There is a clear parallel here to the way in which sporting play creates its own time during a game, a new time that—we noted—has a complex relationship to ordinary chronologies. The creation of special places might be thought to be even more obvious. The venue of the ancient Olympics was itself a shrine to the gods, and elements of religious ritual made the Meso–American courts a religious as well as a sporting location. Even in Rome the spectacle of their games created venues that stood out from their environment. In more modern sports, venues take on storied meaning for groups of players and supporters that are not adequately explained simply in terms of describing them as "home" sporting grounds. The locations are invested with greater significance than this. St Andrews for golf, Wembley Stadium for football, the Millennium Stadium for rugby, Lord's for cricket, Wimbledon for tennis, are some striking examples of sporting places with national and international resonances within the UK. Each country will have its own list of such special sporting places, but it would be wrong to assume that only such high profile venues gather about them the hint of the sacred. More local venues also take on the nature of "hallowed turf," and sports fans have frequently sought physical souvenirs (or relics) from stadia as some indication of this.

Reading FC, the club based in the town of Reading about thirty-five miles west of London, currently play in the second tier of English professional football. Though for most of their history they have played in the lower leagues they finally progressed to the highest division for the first time in 2006. The club's story has a "rags to riches" feel, and its new stadium (1998) is a fine example of its type, set on the edge of town with good communications and parking. Much of the club's history belongs to other places—there have been five previous stadia, most notably its Elm Park ground. But the new Madejski Stadium appears to bear much of the sentiment and significance attached to the previous homes. One might compare its opening to the commissioning or blessing of a new place of worship. The regular "congregation" will have a similar litany of grumbles as they adjust to the unfamiliar as any group of churchgoers. In the corner of this modest club's car park is a Garden of Remembrance. Its explanatory plaque reports that it has been "dedicated in memory of those who faithfully supported Reading FC in adversity and prosperity. *May they rest in peace.*"[1] According to the club's website, the garden offers a "pleasant environment for people to sit in quiet reflection, as well as a place for those associated with the club to have their ashes scattered." Those who wish to arrange the latter are urged to contact the club chaplain, whose contact details are given.

Reading FC's Garden of Remembrance, or something like it, will be repeated in countless sporting clubs across the world. The presence of such locations does not make the stadia in which they are located sacred: something else has already done that in the estimate of many of the club's supporters. Their presence does, however, underline the specialness of place in the sporting drama, and offers another example of the ways in which straightforwardly religious practices (such as the scattering of ashes, or sitting in quiet contemplation) and sporting practices that appear to have religious dimensions to them have become intertwined and are associated in important ways with place. As with many religious holy sites, the "sacredness" of sporting venues appears to be connected with great players, with generations of supporters, with memorable moments in the narrative of the clubs and teams. It is the people of the club, and what has been done by them and for them in that venue, that have sanctified the place. More could be done to explore these themes, and give them a surer foundation in appropriate empirical work.

Mention of a football club's chaplain leads me to identify a second topic that I have only brushed against and where further work would be useful: *sports ministries and chaplaincies.* The interaction of Christian ministry with sporting activities and societies has a long history. Since the nineteenth-century rapprochement that owed so much to the Muscular Christianity movement, churches and quasi-ecclesial agencies have been heavily involved with sports. Internationally, the YMCA had a major impact in shaping initial involvement into the twentieth century on both sides of the Atlantic. Ladd and Mathisen[2] chart this involvement

1. "Garden of Remembrance."
2. *Muscular Christianity.*

in relation to the major American organizations. There may have been something of a hiatus, certainly in the UK, after the churches that founded many sports clubs withdrew from them, handing them over to "secular" leadership. However, in recent years the UK has seen a rapid growth in the number of professional clubs that have appointed chaplains (as in the case of Reading FC), and organizations like Baseball Chapel[3] appoint "chapel leaders" to professional baseball clubs in the USA. Assorted sports ministries work with athletes, and churches and para-church groups run mission initiatives that use sports activity as a means of outreach.

What most of these groups have in common is a clear use of sports contacts (and often celebrity) for evangelical purposes. Sport is, in effect, instrumentalized for the gospel; it is a vehicle for some larger purpose. The mission statements of a number of Christian agencies working in sports can give this impression, though in practice pastoral support is also frequently part of the package offered by organizations and chaplains. The question that hovers around such pastoral support is often whether it too is "merely" instrumental, that is, whether this care is offered not for its own sake but as an act of witness to serve an overarching evangelistic aim.

This study has highlighted the way in which sport is embedded within and reflects the society in which it is played. While occasionally allowing sport to challenge social mores and destructive social forces, this relationship can and does also reinforce and legitimate them. It is uncomfortably true, for instance, that too often sport has merely reflected the social and cultural milieu in which its games are played without challenging the implicit racism or sexism that is present there. This is despite its usefulness for evangelistic purposes; indeed, its very usefulness in these ways may occasionally marginalize such concerns. An authentic Christian engagement with sport is unlikely to rest at simply using it for its own ends but will engage with it prophetically. Given that sports ministries and chaplains are often present in sports clubs as guests, they must sometimes work hard to ensure that their role does not appear to parallel that of the court prophet in Old Testament times who often ended up colluding with authority or simply speaking the words that authority wanted—or could bear—to hear. Such comparisons may be too dramatic, but similar questions can be put to many chaplaincies in other spheres

3. See Baseball Chapel website: http://www.baseballchapel.org. For a critical discussion of the work of Baseball Chapel see Krattenmaker, *Onward*, 87–106.

such as the military or healthcare, and the point must be taken seriously. How do those engaged in sports ministry avoid a crudely instrumental attitude to sport that turns a blind eye to its problematic aspects and so fails to engage authentically with sport in a rounded Christian way? It will be complained with some justification that such a depiction of these ministries is a crude caricature, and a full and rounded examination of sports ministries requires proper qualitative research. Such research would, I am sure, show a much more nuanced and holistic picture.

The question of soteriology that was flagged in the previous chapter appears to offer the opportunity for sports ministries to engage with sport from an holistic perspective seeing sport as of worth in itself and not just for its instrumental value. Sport can be a significant contributory factor in the human flourishing that is part of the larger context in which Christian understandings of salvation must be set. The experience of transcendence in sport that has been a key element in this book's argument must also figure in some way here, with sports ministers having an opportunity to reflect with players and spectators about the meaning of this "gift," as well as other aspects of the religio-sporting experience.

The third topic to which I would like to have given more attention is that of sport as a virtue-forming activity.[4] This connects naturally with a focus on the experience of playing sport and what it does to those who participate directly or vicariously. The Muscular Christians believed that sport formed the Christian man (and it usually was a man), and the respondents to my survey reported similar convictions. There was some ambivalence about whether sport expressed attitudes formed elsewhere or inculcated those characteristics, or both, but a connection between dispositions and character on the one hand and the sport one watched or played on the other is widespread among sporting participants. My argument from play sought to root our experience of playing in general in both human nature and culture and also the divine nature: *homo ludens* made in the image of *Deus ludens*. The drive to win (understood broadly) is a powerful instance of the experience of transcendence. Further, all our reaching to become what we might be, a God-given impulse, is met by the God who reaches out to us so that something very like "religious experience" appears to open up through sport, making possible an encounter with *Deus Victor*. As was argued in chapter 4, if participation in sport can

---

4. There have been some insightful discussions of this: see, e.g., Hoffman, *Good Game*, 193–218, Higgs, *Stadium*, 189–207, and Baker, *Playing*, 253–60.

be seen as a participation in God's playful creativity and therefore even a participation in God's self, then it should not surprise us that sport can be a positive good in society and in the lives of its individuals for it would appear that the "goods" of sport are not coincidental but inhere within them. If playing is potentially a participation in God how could it avoid forming the person or community?

What is needed to explore this more fully is further empirical work with sports players and watchers that works from a clearly theological point of interest. Such an enquiry would doubtless expose a complicated mutuality between factors which are shaped through and brought to sporting experience, and which would reinforce our understandings of sport as embedded in other social practices and attitudes. The emerging picture would be unlikely to be neat and straightforward. However, this important hypothesis, this widely held intuition that sport forms its participants in positive ways needs to be examined and tested theologically. Tess Kay shows what can be done through a more sociological lens; we now need to draw on such work but supplement it from a practical theological perspective. While this book has occasionally suggested the usefulness (or even imminence) of such enquiries it has not been possible to begin to do proper justice to the issues that such a fuller investigation of the topic would raise.

Concluding Observations on a Practical Theology of Sport

It remains now only to offer some brief observations about the kind of argument that I have pursued in this book, especially in its later chapters.

> If a person who had been deeply moved by the mosaics of Ravenna, the ceiling paintings of the Sistine Chapel, or the portraits of the older Rembrandt, were asked whether his experience had been religious or cultural, he would find the question difficult to answer. It might be correct to say that the subject is cultural in form and religious in substance. It is cultural because it is not attached to a specific ritual act; but it is religious because it touches on the question of the Absolute and the limits of human existence. This is as true of music, poetry, philosophy and science as it is of painting.[5]

5. Tillich, *Boundaries*, 331.

And, we might add, sport.

In various ways in this book we have considered arguments or analyses that appear to require us to distinguish between the religious or sacred and secular realms. Our historical narrative noticed the move from an ancient sporting ritual with its roots clearly in religious practice to a more secular pastime or distraction. By the time of the Puritans "sports" appeared to have been placed very clearly in a set of activities that could be regarded as secular, though they would not have used the term. Only in the nineteenth century does an explicitly religious motivation for sports—and now we really are beginning to speak of sports in the modern sense—re-emerge. The theological arguments I have put forward, in different ways, undercut this distinction between the sacred and the secular. The notion that sport itself has a (quasi-) religious character relativizes the distinction. The notion that through play, and through sporting transcendence, we may in some way commune with God and in reaching out to God be met by the God who reaches out to us—indeed, equips us first with our reaching-out-ness, so to speak—further weakens any attempt to distinguish religious and secular.

Tillich's reference to great works of art reflects his analysis of culture, in particular that religion and culture are not different spheres occupying, as it were, separate spaces within the human landscape—a sacred space and a secular space. In fact, insofar as religious activity and reflection *is* confined to a special and separated realm, Tillich believes that this is a sign of the fallenness of humankind: the separation is a symptom of our estrangement from our true selves.[6] For Tillich, religion was "the state of being grasped by an ultimate concern" and "this state cannot be restricted to a special realm."[7] Its unconditional character suggests that it relates to every aspect of life such that "in all preliminary concerns, ultimate concern is present, consecrating them."[8] The religious dimension of ordinary experience Tillich described through the metaphor of depth. The religious moment is (potentially) the dimension of depth in all experience. This depth directs our attention to "that which is ultimate, infinite, unconditional in man's spiritual life."[9] The ultimate concerns of humanity can manifest themselves particularly in what Tillich calls the "creative

6. Tillich, *Culture*, 42.

7. Tillich, *Culture*, 41.

8. Tillich, *Culture*, 41.

9. Tillich, *Culture*, 7.

functions of the human spirit . . . in the moral sphere as the unconditional seriousness of the moral demand . . . in the realm of knowledge as the passion of longing for ultimate reality . . . in the aesthetic function of the human spirit as the infinite desire to express ultimate meaning."[10]

One way of expressing part of my argument might be to paraphrase it in Tillichian terms and suggest that play in general, and its form in sport in particular, is a cultural location at which this dimension of depth opens up to us. Sport, as we noted, often feels like a matter of ultimate concern, just as play in creating its own world feels all-consuming and entire. On closer examination, however, we discovered that when we step back from sport for a moment we gain a sense of perspective that qualifies this in important ways. We see it then as a penultimate matter—though one that is peculiarly open to convey ultimate concern because of its immersive nature, and because of what we called the playful participation in God, and the reaching out for that which is beyond. This resonates with Tillich's understanding of works of art as of penultimate concern. Only God is our final concern.

It is because of these convictions that Tillich can attempt a theology of culture, defined as "the attempt to analyze the theology behind all cultural expressions, to discover the ultimate concern in the ground of a philosophy, a political system, an artistic style, a set of ethical or social principles."[11] The argument in this book attempts to offer a practical theology of sport: it takes sport seriously as a "cultural expression" and seeks the theology (in Tillich's terms) "behind" it, attempts to discover the ultimate concern in what Tillich calls its "ground," and it does so through using all the traditional sources of Christian theology correlated with empirical data from sports participants, and informed by historical and more social scientific perspectives.

The term "correlation" is also an important one for Tillich's thought, and is at the heart of his theological method. This method makes "an analysis of the human situation out of which the existential questions arise, and it demonstrates that the symbols used in the Christian message are the answer to these questions."[12] To begin, as Tillich suggests he is beginning, with an analysis of human culture, will seem to many to place the theological cart before the horse. He seeks to avoid, among other

10. Tillich, *Culture*, 8.
11. Tillich, *Systematic, I*, 45.
12. Tillich, *Systematic, I*, 70.

things, what he thinks of as a supranaturalistic approach that understands revelation propositionally such that it appears to "have fallen into the human situation like strange bodies from a strange world"[13] with no mediation between the revealer and the receiver of the revelation. However, we might question whether this really is where Tillich begins: his impetus for the existential analysis of human life is drawn from faith. He enters this process, after all, as a theologian, coming at the questions, so to speak, from the community of faith. Despite appearances he is in fact starting with theology, or at least, as a theologian. It might similarly be observed that those who claim always to "begin with the Bible" are insufficiently aware of what they take to the Bible from their culture as they set out on their hermeneutical journey. The question of theological starting points is more complex than usually allowed, and the origin of the spiral movement of practical theology is difficult to designate as on one side or other of a dualism such as between sacred and profane, or revelation and culture. Not only is it difficult to discern where we are actually located at any one point in the spiral, but also the sharp separation between these poles is perhaps not entirely helpful.

In any case, as Paul Fiddes remarks, Tillich believed "that human beings only ask questions about ultimate meaning because they are already seized and held by the 'spiritual presence.' At its roots, thought Tillich, culture is linked to the depths of Being, so that God is in our asking of questions about meaning as much as in the answers."[14] This notion of God-in-our questions recalls our discussion of Rahner in chapter 6, where we noted that our capacity, our need for transcendence is itself God-given: that the God who meets us in our reaching-out not only reaches out to us in the encounter but has enabled and prompted it. God is in the realization of the dimension of depth itself. Both the question and the answer originate in God, and the "Christian message provides the answers to the questions implied in human existence . . . [and the answers] are 'spoken' *to* human existence from beyond it."[15] In every mo-

---

13. Tillich, *Systematic, I*, 70.

14. Fiddes, *Seeing*, 25, or as Tillich himself makes a related point: "God answers man's questions, and under the impact of God's answers man asks them." Tillich, *Systematic, I*, 69.

15. Tillich, *Systematic, I*, 72. Italics his. The content of the Christian message is derived from the "revelatory events on which Christianity is based," and the theologian knows that his answer will always be informed by "the *logos* of being, manifest in Jesus as the Christ." *Systematic, I*, 71–72.

ment when the dimension of depth opens up, in every divine–human encounter, a word is spoken into the human situation from beyond it "answering" the divinely originated question which arises within the human situation; this process opens up the opportunity to understand what we might call religious experience as a possibility in every sphere of human culture.

Like Tillich, we began our investigation in human culture, attempting to describe and understand the complex and many layered phenomenon of modern sport, though as I have just argued, the investigation was always looking through the lens of the Christian community. This process raised questions about the experience of playing sport (and about the vicarious playing of sport) and for answers to these questions we turned to what Tillich calls the Christian message—though because "culture is linked to the depths of Being," God was in our questions as much as our answers. As these answers took shape we "returned to culture" through the survey data gathered seeking a dialogue between the word " 'spoken' *to* human existence from beyond it" and the experience of sportsmen and -women. At certain points issues of praxis have been noted, and a practical theology of sport will not only seek to describe, analyze, and explain but also to consider the relationship of implicit and explicit theological positions with the practices which embody, sustain, and contradict them as well as those practices for which a practical theological understanding of sport might lead us to work.

We noted in chapter 6 Novak's contention that sport's rituals serve a deep human hunger and that they "provide an experience of at least a pagan sense of godliness." Novak goes on: "Among the godward signs in contemporary life, sports may be the single most powerful manifestation."[16] He also conceded that sports would not turn a player into "a believer in 'God,' under whatever concept, image, experience, or drive to which one attaches the name. Rather, sports drive one in some dark and generic sense 'godward.' "[17] The dimension of depth may be experienced without it being recognized for what it is; we may encounter the Transcendent God in our God-given moments of transcendence but not always be able to name God in so doing. As Novak recognizes, the God encountered in sport appears to be an Unknown God.

16. Novak, *Joy*, 20.
17. Novak, *Joy*, 20.

If we turn from culture back to the Christian message once more, Acts 17:22–34 seems a natural place at which to alight. The context is quite different. It is not the Athenians at play that Paul sees from the Areopagus, but the Athenians surrounded by the accoutrements of their pagan devotions. Commentators differ in the extent to which they think that Paul is merely flattering his listeners[18] or attempting to engage in serious dialogue with them.[19] Paul would have known for sure that many of the aspects of pagan worship celebrated in ancient Athens would have been found abhorrent by most Christians and Jews, but here he seems unwilling to allow this knowledge to override the possibility that these pagan Athenians may have been communing with the living God incognito. "Their religious yearning, even though a bit of a scandal to a monotheistic Jew, is the inarticulate and uninformed yearning of the pagan for the God whom only the Scriptures can disclose."[20] In engaging with the dimensions of depth opened up through sporting experience, participants show a yearning that may seem not unlike that which Paul recognized in Acts 17. Many sportsmen and -women may also be attending the shrine of the Unknown God.

The Paul of Acts 17 tells his audience that their searching for God is itself a gift from God (17:27), and that this God is not far from us, indeed, quoting a pagan poet, "in him we live and move and have our being" (17:28). We recall Karl Rahner's argument that, not only is God the only reference point of all human transcendence, but that that striving for transcendence is rooted in the human openness to mystery, and is itself God-given. Our striving and reaching for the Unknown God is only possible at all because God has made us to strive and reach for God, and also reached out for and to us. Our openness to the mystery of human existence, what Novak might call our "godwardness," cannot be separated from and is enabled by God's own openness to us in gracious self-giving: grace and nature are bound together in an unbreakable cord. We are perhaps not so far here from Barth's assertion in his tirade against natural theology, that "the Holy Ghost . . . does not stand in need of any point of contact but that which he himself creates,"[21] for it is God's prevenient gracious activity alone that makes possible any kind of truly religious

18. Willimon, *Acts*, 142.
19. Gaventa, *Acts*, 250.
20. Willimon, *Acts*, 143.
21. Brunner and Barth, *Natural*, 125.

experience. Sport may be the product of human culture, and we may feel more or less comfortable about describing it as divine gift, but it appears to be a peculiarly "deep" (in Tillich's sense) activity through which the God-given capacity for transcendence may find expression.

To argue along these lines is to go further than C. S. Lewis might have gone, but perhaps not so very much further. Lewis' essay on Christianity and culture compares the values encountered in great literature with the values of the Christian faith. He calls such values "sub-Christian," but the term does not have the very negative connotation that it may at first suggest. They certainly are less than Christian values as Lewis understands them, but they also represent the "immediately sub-Christian,"[22] that is, the highest level that can be attained without attaining to the values of the Christian faith. He describes them as an "antepast" of true spiritual value, resembling them as the moon resembles the sun. He goes on: "But though 'like is not the same', it is better than unlike. Imitation may pass into initiation. For some it is a good beginning. For others it is not; culture is not everyone's road into Jerusalem, and for some it is a road out."[23]

Lewis' metaphor of the antepast is an archaic one—perhaps in our time of cosmopolitan cuisine *antipasto*, starter, or *hors d'oeuvre* would serve better to indicate the first stage of a meal—but it appears to fit well with the Areopagus speech, and the recognition of a starter's culinary potential resonates with much that has been argued in earlier chapters here. At the least, it might lead us to say, the kind of experiences in sport which can be described as a reaching-out to the God who enables our reaching-out and in turn reaches back to us, are a preparation, an *hors d'oeuvre*, an anticipation, of the larger and more wholesome, more nourishing and complete experiences in which women and men may name the one who in gracious and open love encounters them in Jesus Christ.[24] Moreover, Lewis is correct to point out that not everyone will "travel to Jerusalem" through an experience of culture—or, we must add, of sport. For some, as Lewis suggests, it may lead in another direction altogether. It is worth noting this timely and realistic reminder: some of the more problematic

22. Lewis, "Culture," 39.

23. Lewis, "Culture," 40. For a little more on "though 'like is not the same', it is better than unlike," see Lewis, *Last Battle*, 152–54.

24. Robert Johnston argues that even when "our human reach toward the transcendent can be met by God's outstretched arm breaking into" our experience this is at best a preliminary experience, something short of the whole, and only given final content and meaning through God's definitive revelation in Christ. Johnston, *Play*, 74–75.

aspects of sport may form its participants in undesirable ways, and a distorted competitiveness is as likely to lead away from as toward God.

But Lewis does say that "imitation may pass into initiation" and I have had good meals where the starter has been the best course: it can do more than whet the appetite and from a skillful chef be almost a feast in itself. And there are moments when Lewis himself seems to be willing to go further.[25] So when all this is said, and the completeness of a salvation in which Jesus is named as Lord is noted and celebrated, we are left with the question whether it is possible to have a real and positive encounter with God and for such an encounter not to be *in some way* salvific. If our playing is a participation in God, and the desire to transcend our current capabilities can lead us to the very face of God, can this leave us (as it were) exactly where we were before we began? I am certainly not intending to suggest that a complete experience of salvation might be found through sport alone, but at every point we have had to fall back on grace, and my argument has tried to suggest that grace may be known even when it cannot be named. Salvation is a process which encompasses human flourishing in many forms in time and eternity and which has its origin in God's loving grace. It is a journey, rather than a one-off event, and sport can be an element in that process of God's saving activity even when it is not a moment of conscious faith in God, and it can be an instance of the prevenient work of divine grace in the human heart which is a part of salvation itself.

25. See Lewis, *Last Battle*: "the creatures came rushing on . . . But the others looked in the face of Aslan and loved him, though some of these were very frightened at the same time . . . There were some queer specimens among them," 140; and Aslan is reported as saying to a devoted follower of Tash, "unless thy desire had been for me thou wouldst not have sought so long and so truly. For all find what they truly seek," 149.

Bibliography

Alighieri, Dante. *Divine Comedy: Paradise*, 3:27.1–5. Translated by Allen Mandelbaum. Online: *The World of Dante*, http://www.worldofdante.org/comedy/dante/paradise.xml/3.27.

Allred, David. "The Platonic Foundation of The Great Divorce." *Into the Wardrobe: A C. S. Lewis Web Site*. Online: http://cslewis.drzeus.net/papers/platonic.html.

Amos, Clare. *The Book of Genesis*. Peterborough: Epworth, 2004.

Aquinas, Thomas. *Summa Theologiae*, vol. 44: 2a2æ 155–70. Translated by Thomas Gilby O.P. London: Eyre & Spottiswoode, 1972.

Astley, Jeff. *Ordinary Theology: Looking, Listening and Learning in Theology*. Aldershot: Ashgate, 2002.

Augustine, *Confessions*. Translated by R. S. Pine-Coffin. London: Penguin, 1961.

Aulén, Gustaf. *Christus Victor*. Translated by A. G. Hebert. London: SPCK, 1931.

Australian Bureau of Statistics. "Participation in Sport and Physical Recreation, Australia, 2011–12." Online: http://www.abs.gov.au/AUSSTATS/abs@.nsf/Details Page/4177.02011-12?OpenDocument.

Bailey, Edward. *Implicit Religion: An Introduction*. London: Middlesex University Press, 1998.

Bain-Selbo, Eric. *Game Day and God: Football, Faith, and Politics in the American South*. Macon, GA: Mercer University Press, 2009.

Baker, William J. *Sports in the Western World*. Revised ed. Urbana: University of Illinois, 1988.

Bannister, Roger. *The First Four Minutes*. 2nd ed. Stroud: Sutton, 2004.

Baptist Union of Great Britain. *Baptist Hand-book* 1879. London: BUGB, 1879.

BARB. "Viewing Data, Top 10s." Online: http://www.barb.co.uk/viewing/weekly-top-10?_s=5&period[]=201304060128.

Barrett, C. K. *The First Epistle to the Corinthians*. 2nd edition [1st edition 1968]. London: A. & C. Black, 1971.

Barth, Karl. *Church Dogmatics II/1*. Translated by T. H. L. Parker, W. B. Johnston, Harold Knight, and J. L. M. Hare. Edinburgh: T. & T. Clark, 1957.

———. *Church Dogmatics III/1*. Translated by J. W. Edwards, O. Bussey, and Harold Knight. Edinburgh: T. & T. Clark, 1958.

———. *The Epistle to the Romans*. 6th ed. London: Oxford University Press, 1933.

———. *Wolfgang Amadeus Mozart*. Grand Rapids, MI: Eerdmans, 1986.

Bascombe, Chris. "Liverpool Eager to Secure a Lucrative New Shirt Deal with Standard Chartered." *Daily Telegraph*, November 13, 2012. Online: http://www.telegraph

.co.uk/sport/football/teams/liverpool/9676379/Liverpool-eager-to-secure-a-lucrative-new-shirt-deal-with-Standard-Chartered.html.

Baseball Chapel. Online: http://www.baseballchapel.org.

Baudrillard, Jean. *The Consumer Society*. London: Sage, 1998.

Bauman, Zygmunt. *Work, Consumerism, and the New Poor*. Buckingham: Open University, 1998.

Baxter, Richard. *A Christian Directory: or, A summ of practical theology and cases of conscience. Directing Christians, how to use their Knowledge and Faith; How to improve all Helps and Means, and to Perform all Duties; How to Overcome Temptations, and to escape or mortifie every Sin*. 2nd ed. London: Nevil Simmons, 1678.

BBC. "The History of the Show." Online: http://news.bbc.co.uk/sport1/hi/question_of_sport/qs_history/default.stm.

BBC. "London 2012 Olympics Deliver Record Viewing Figures for BBC." Online: http://www.bbc.co.uk/mediacentre/latestnews/2012/olympic-viewing-figs.html.

BBC Governance Unit. "Governors' Genre Review: Religious Output on BBC One, January 2005." Online: http://news.bbc.co.uk/1/shared/bsp/hi/pdfs/09_05_05_religious_output.pdf .

BBC Motorsport. "Sponsorship Guide." Online: http://news.bbc.co.uk/sport1/hi/motorsport/formula_one/sponsorship_guide/default.stm.

BBC Press Office. "David Taviner Appointed Series Editor of Songs of Praise." Online: http://www.bbc.co.uk/pressoffice/pressreleases/stories/2009/08_august/05/songs.shtml.

BBC TV. *The Man Behind the Racquet*. Produced by Peter Small. BBC TV. Revised version, first broadcast July 8, 2013.

Beckford, Martin. "ITV Will Broadcast just One Hour of Religious Programming This Year." *Daily Telegraph*, June 23, 2010. Online: http://www.telegraph.co.uk/news/religion/7846218/ITV-will-broadcast-just-one-hour-of-religious-programming-this-year.html.

Bede. *Ecclesiastical History of the English Nation*. Oxford: Blackwell, 1949.

Begbie, Jeremy. *Theology, Music and Time*. Cambridge: Cambridge University Press, 2000.

Bellah, Robert. "Civil Religion in America." In *American Civil Religion*, edited by Russell E. Richey and Donald G. Jones, 21–44.

Benson, Andrew. "Formula 1 Teams Showing Signs of Money Problems." BBC Sport. Online: http://www.bbc.co.uk/sport/0/formula1/21469518.

Berger, Peter L. *A Rumour of Angels*. Harmondsworth: Pelican, 1971.

———. *The Social Reality of Religion*. Harmondsworth: Penguin, 1973.

Berger, Peter, Grace Davie, and Eefie Fokas. *Religious America, Secular Europe? A Theme and Variations*. Farnham: Ashgate, 2008.

Bergkamp, Denis. "You Climb One Mountain and See a Higher One." *The Observer*, Saturday September 21, 2013. Online: http://www.theguardian.com/football/2013/sep/21/dennis-bergkamp-arsenal-love-game.

Bianchi, Eugene. "Pigskin Piety." *Christianity and Crisis: A Christian Journal of Opinion*, 32/2 (1972) 31–34.

Bingham, Howard L., and Max Wallace. *Muhammad Ali's Greatest Fight: Cassius Clay vs the United States of America*. Plymouth: Evans, 2013.

Birley, Derek. *A Social History of English Cricket*. London: Aurum, 1999.

Billy Elliott. Directed by Stephen Daldry. Working Title, 2000.

Blowers, Paul L. "On the 'Play' of Divine Providence in Gregory Nazianzen and Maxiumus the Confessor." In *Re-Reading Gregory of Nazianzus: Essays on History, Theology, and Culture*, edited by Christopher A. Beeley, 199–217. Baltimore, MD: Catholic University of America, 2012.

Bornkamm, Günther. *Jesus of Nazareth.* London: Hodder & Stoughton, 1973.

Brailsford, Dennis. *British Sport: A Social History.* Cambridge: Lutterworth, 1992.

———. *Sport and Society: Elizabeth to Anne.* London: Routledge & Kegan Paul, 1969.

Bretherton, Luke T. *Christianity and Contemporary Politics.* Oxford: Wiley-Blackwell, 2010.

Brierley, Peter. *UK Church Statistics, 2005–2015.* Tonbridge: ADBC Publishers, 2011.

British Youth for Christ. "Kick London" project. Online: http://www.yfc.co.uk/local-centres/london/kick-london/.

Brohm, Jean-Marie. *Sport: A Prison of Measured Time.* Translated by Ian Fraser. London: Ink Links, 1978.

Brown, Callum G. *The Death of Christian Britain: Understanding Secularisation.* London: Routledge, 2001.

Brown, Colin. "Campbell Interrupted Blair as He Spoke of His Faith: 'We Don't Do God.'" *Daily Telegraph*, May 4, 2003. Online: http://www.telegraph.co.uk/news/uknews/1429109/Campbell-interrupted-Blair-as-he-spoke-of-his-faith-We-dont-do-God.html.

Bruce, F. F. *I & II Corinthians.* London: Marshall, Morgan & Scott, 1971.

Bruce, Steve. *God is Dead: Secularization in the West.* Oxford: Blackwell, 2002.

———. *Religion in Modern Britain.* Oxford: Oxford University Press, 1995.

———. *Religion in the Modern World: From Cathedrals to Cults.* Oxford: Oxford University Press, 1996.

Brueggemann, Walter. *Genesis.* Atlanta: John Knox, 1982.

———. *Reverberations of Faith: A Theological Handbook of Old Testament Themes.* Louisville: Westminster John Knox, 2002.

Brunner, Emil. *The Christian Doctrine of God. Dogmatics Volume 1.* Translated by Olive Wyon. Philadelphia: Westminster, 1974.

Brunner, Emil, and Karl Barth. *Natural Theology. Comprising "Nature and Grace" by Emil Brunner and the Reply "No!" by Karl Barth.* Translated Peter Fraenkel. London: Bles, 1946.

Byrne, James M. "The Category 'Religion' Reconsidered." *The Way*, 1998 Supplement, 102–12.

Callis, Ron Dassett, and Steve Rowland. *The First 125 years of the Ranelagh Harriers, 1881–2006.* Revised ed. Cranleigh, Surrey: Ranelagh Harriers, 2006.

Callois, Roger. *Man, Play and Games.* Translated by Meyer Barash. Urbana: University of Illinois, 2001.

Cameron, Andrew J. B. "Augustine on Lust." In *Still Deadly: Ancient Cures for the Seven Sins*, edited by Brian S. Rosner and Andrew J. B. Cameron, 33–49. Sydney: Aquila, 2007.

Carl-Diem-Institut. *The Olympic Idea: Pierre de Coubertin, Discourses and Essays.* Stuttgart: Sportverlag, 1966.

Carmody, Denise L. *Feminist Theology.* Oxford: Blackwell, 1995.

Carrington, Ben. "Sport, Masculinity and Black Cultural Resistance." *Journal of Sport and Social Issues*, 22/3 (August 1998), 275–98.

Carrington, Ben, and Ian McDonald. "The Politics of 'Race' and Sports Policy." In *Sport and Society: A Student Introduction,* edited by Barrie Houlihan, 125–42. London: Sage, 2001.

Cashmore, Ernest. *Black Sportsmen.* London: Routledge & Kegan Paul, 1982.

Census of Religious Worship in England and Wales, 1851. Online: http://archive.org/details/censusgreatbritoomanngoog.

Chariots of Fire. Directed by Hugh Hudson. Twentieth Century Fox, 1981.

Cherwell League. Online: http://www.cherwellcricketleague.com.

Chaves, Mark, and Laura Stephens. "Church Attendance in the United States." In *Handbook of the Sociology of Religion,* edited by Michelle Dillon, 85–95. Cambridge: Cambridge University Press, 2003.

Chisholm, Dianne. "Climbing like a Girl." *Hypatia* 23/1 (2008), 9–40.

Christenson, Marcus, and Paul Kelso. "Soccer Chief's Plan to Boost Women's Game? Hotpants." *The Guardian,* January 16, 2004. Online: http://www.guardian.co.uk/uk/2004/jan/16/football.gender.

Clement. *First Epistle.* Online: http://www.earlychristianwritings.com/text/1clement-lightfoot.html.

Coakley, Jay. *Sports in Society: Issues and Controversies.* 5th ed. St Louis: Mosby, 1995.

———. *Sports in Society: Issues and Controversies.* 8th ed. New York: McGraw Hill, 2004.

Cohen, Emma E. A., Robin Ejsmond-Frey, Nicola Knight, and R. I. M. Dunbar. "Rowers' High: Behavioural Synchrony is Correlated with Elevated Pain Thresholds." *Biology Letters* 6/1 (2010), 106–8.

Collins, Raymond F. *First Corinthians.* Collegeville MN: Liturgical, 1999.

Conn, David, "Hillsborough Service Sees Truth Lift Spirits amid Remembrance of the 96." *The Guardian,* April 16, 2013. Online: http://www.guardian.co.uk/football/blog/2013/apr/16/hillsborough-service-truth-lifts-spirits-96.

———. "Premier League finances: The Full Club-by-Club Breakdown and Verdict." *The Guardian,* April 18, 2013. Online: http://www.guardian.co.uk/football/2013/apr/18/premier-league-finances-club-by-club.

Conner, Megan. "John Eliot Gardiner: This Much I Know." *The Observer Magazine,* March 31, 2013. Online: http://www.guardian.co.uk/lifeandstyle/2013/mar/30/john-eliot-gardener-conductor.

Cooper, Rob. "Record TV Audience for Murray Triumph as 17.3m Britons are Glued to Their Sets on One of the Hottest Days of the Year." *Daily Mail,* July 8, 2013. Online: http://www.dailymail.co.uk/news/article-2358149/Andy-Murray-wins-Wimbledon-Record-TV-audience-17-3m-Britons-glued-sets.html.

Costello, Mike. "East German Athletes were 'Chemical Field Tests.' " BBC Sport Athletics. Online: http://www.bbc.co.uk/sport/0/athletics/22269445.

Coubertin, Pierre de. "Opening Address to the Conference of Arts, Letters and Sports." In *The Olympic Idea: Pierre de Coubertin, Discourses and Essays,* edited by the Carl-Diem-Institut, 16–18.

———. "The Philosophic Foundations of Modern Olympism." In *The Olympic Idea: Pierre de Coubertin, Discourses and Essays,* edited by the Carl-Diem-Institut, 130–34.

Covil, Eric C. "Radio and its Impact on the Sports World." *American Sportscasters Online.* No pages or date. Online: http://www.americansportscastersonline.com/radiohistory.html.

Coward, Doris D., and Pamela G. Reed. "Self-Transcendence: A Resource for Healing at the End of Life." *Issues in Mental Health Nursing* 17/3 (1996), 275–88.

Cox, Harvey. *The Feast of Fools. A Theological Essay on Festivity and Fantasy.* Harvard University Press: Cambridge, MA, 1969.

Csikszentmihalyi, Mihaly. *Flow: The Classic Work on How to Achieve Happiness.* London: Random House, 2002.

Cuming, G. J., and Derek Baker. *Popular Belief and Practice, Studies in Church History,* 8. Cambridge: Cambridge University Press, 1972.

Dalglish, Kenny. *Dalglish: An Autobiography.* London: Hodder & Stoughton, 1996.

Daniels, Bruce. *Puritans at Play: Leisure and Recreation in Colonial New England.* London: Macmillan, 1995.

Davie, Grace. *Europe: The Exceptional Case.* London: Darton, Longman & Todd, 2002.

———. *Religion in Britain since 1945: Believing without Belonging.* Oxford: Blackwell, 1994.

———. *The Sociology of Religion.* London: Sage, 2007.

———. "Vicarious Religion: A Methodological Challenge." In *Everyday Religion: Observing Modern Religious Lives,* edited by Nancy T. Ammerman. Oxford: Oxford University Press, 2007.

Dawn, Marva. *A Royal Waste of Time: The Splendor of Worshipping God and Being Church for the World.* Grand Rapids, MI: Eerdmans, 1999.

Deans, Jason. "TV Ratings: 18 Million Tune in for German Whitewash." *The Guardian,* July 12, 2010. Online: http://www.guardian.co.uk/media/2010/jul/12/world-cup-final-tv-ratings.

———. "World Cup Final: BBC Scores in TV Ratings Battle." *The Guardian,* July 12, 2010. Online at http://www.guardian.co.uk/media/2010/jul/12/world-cup-final-tv-ratings.

Deardorff II, Donald, and Julie D. Deardorff. "Escaping the Gender Trap: Sport and the Equality of Christ." In *The Image of God in the Human Body: Essays on Christianity and Sports,* edited by Donald Deardorff II and John White, 195–216. Lewiston NY: Edward Mellen, 2008.

Dewar, Alison Mackenzie. "Incorporation of Resistance? Towards an Analysis of Women's Responses to Sexual Oppression in Sport." *International Review for the Sociology of Sport* 26/1 (March 1991) 15–23.

———. "Sexual Oppression in Sport: Past, Present, and Future Alternatives." In *Sport in Social Development: Traditions, Transitions and Transformations,* edited by Alan G. Ingham and John W. Loy, 147–66. Champaign IL: Human Kinetics, 1993.

Dickson, Alex, Colin Jennings, and Gary Koop. "Domestic Violence and Football in Glasgow: Are Reference Points Relevant?" Online: http://personal.strath.ac.uk/gary.koop/dickson_jennings_koop.pdf.

Dillon, Michelle. *Handbook of the Sociology of Religion.* Cambridge: Cambridge University Press, 2003.

Donnelly, Peter. "Sport and Social Theory." In *Sport and Society: A Student Introduction,* edited by Barrie Houlihan, 11–27. London: Sage, 2001.

Donovan, Peter. *Interpreting Religious Experience.* London: Sheldon, 1979.

Doward, Jamie. "Running in This London Marathon is a Way of Dealing with My Mum's Death." *The Guardian,* April 22, 2012. Online: http://www.guardian.co.uk/sport/2012/apr/22/london-marathon-running-micah-true.

Drees, Ludwig. *Olympia: Gods, Artists and Athletes.* London: Pall Mall, 1968.

Duina, Francesco. *Winning: Reflections on an American Obsession*. Princeton: Princeton University Press, 2011.

Dunning, Eric, and Kenneth Sheard. *Barbarians, Gentlemen and Players: A Sociological Study of the Development of Rugby Football*. 2nd ed. London: Routledge, 2005.

Dunning, Eric, Patrick Murphy, and John Williams. *The Roots of Football Hooliganism: An Historical and Sociological Study*. Routledge & Kegan Paul, 1988.

East Midlands Football. Online: http://www.emfootball.co.uk/attend.html.

Edge, Alan. *Faith of our Fathers: Football as a Religion*. Edinburgh: Mainstream, 1999.

Ellis, Robert. "Play up! Play up! And Play the Game! Cricket and Our Place in the World." In *Wisdom, Science and the Scriptures. Essays in Honour of Ernest Lucas*, edited by Stephen Finamore and John Weaver, 243–61. Oxford and Bristol: Regent's Park College and Bristol Baptist College, 2012.

———. "The Meanings of Sport: An Empirical Study into the Significance Attached to Sporting Participation and Spectating in the UK and US." *Practical Theology* 5.2 (April 2012), 169–88.

Elmer Gantry. Directed by Richard Brooks. United Artists, 1960. Screenplay online: http://www.script-o-rama.com/movie_scripts/e/elmer-gantry-script-transcript-lancaster.html.

Elyot, Sir Thomas. *The Boke Named the Governour*. New York: Garland, 1992.

Erdozain, Dominic. *The Problem of Pleasure: Sport, Recreation and the Crisis of Victorian Religion*. Woodbridge Suffolk: Boydell, 2010.

———. "Revival as Cultural Spotlight: The Strange Case of Rugby Football and the Welsh Revival of 1904–5." In *Revival and Resurgence in Christian History*, edited by Kate Cooper and Jeremy Gregory, 275–85. Woodbridge: Boydell, 2008.

ESPN. "Adidas to Sponsor MLS through 2018." Online: http://espn.go.com/sports/soccer/news/_/id/5511821/adidas-mls-sign-8-year-sponsorship-contract.

ESPNCricInfo: "Ashes Climax Watched by a Fraction of 2005 Audience." Online: http://www.espncricinfo.com/engvaus2009/content/story/422272.html.

ESPN FC. "English Premier League Stats: Team Attendance – 2009–10." Online: http://espnfc.com/stats/attendance?league=eng.1&year=2009&cc=5739.

Fairchild, Mary. "Christian Athlete Profile—Trevor Marsicano's Faith." *Christianity*. Online: http://christianity.about.com/od/christiancelebrities/qt/trevormarsicano.htm.

Farmer, H. H. *The World and God. A Study of Prayer, Providence and Miracle in Christian Experience*. Revised ed. London: Nisbet, 1936.

Feeney, Robert. *The Catholic Ideal: Exercise and Sports*. Fort Collins, CO: Aquinas, 2005.

Fiddes, Paul S. *Participating in God*. London: Darton, Longman & Todd, 2000.

———. *The Promised End*. Oxford: Blackwell, 2000.

———. *Seeing the World and Knowing God: Hebrew Wisdom and Christian Doctrine in a Late-Modern Context*. The Bampton Lectures, 2005. Oxford University Press: Oxford: 2013.

FIFA. "Fair Play Code." Online: http://images.supersport.com/PSL2008_FIFAFair.pdf.

———. "My Game is Fair Play." Online: http://www.fifa.com/aboutfifa/social responsibility/fairplay/index.html.

Finamore, Stephen, and John Weaver. *Wisdom, Science and the Scriptures. Essays in Honour of Ernest Lucas*. Oxford and Bristol: Regent's Park College and Bristol Baptist College, 2012.

Finke, Roger, and Rodney Stark. *The Churching of America, 1776–1990: Winners and Losers in Our Religious Economy.* New Brunswick, NJ: Rutgers University Press, 1992.

Fleming, Scott, and Alan Tomlinson. "Racism and Xenophobia in English Football." In *The Sports Studies Reader,* edited by Alan Tomlinson, 304–8.

Football Economy.Com. Online: http://www.footballeconomy.com/stats/stats_att_01. htm and http://www.footballeconomy.com/stats/stats_tv_01.htm.

Formula One.Com. "Exclusive Interview with ING's Isabelle Conner." November 16, 2007. Online: http://www.formula1.com/news/interviews/2007/11/7103.html.

Forney, Craig A. *The Holy Trinity of American Sports: Civil Religion in Football, Baseball and Basketball.* Macon, GA: Mercer, 2007.

Foster, Lynn V. *Handbook to Life in the Ancient Maya World.* New York: Oxford University Press, 2005.

Fox, Michael V. "Ideas of Wisdom in Proverbs 1–9." *Journal of Biblical Literature,* 116/4 (1997), 613–33.

———. *Proverbs 1–9. A New Translation with Introduction and Commentary.* The Anchor Bible. New York: Doubleday, 2000.

Fredericks, Daniel C., and Daniel J. Estes. *Ecclesiastes and the Song of Songs.* Apollos Old Testament Commentary. Nottingham: Apollos, 2012.

"Garden of Remembrance." Online: http://www.readingfc.co.uk/news/article/garden-of-remembrance-040113-579073.aspx.

Gaventa, Beverly Roberts. *Acts.* Nashville: Abingdon, 2003.

Geddes, Ellen. "Gendered Identities: How Does Participation in Sport Affect the Construction and Performance of Gendered Identifies among Young Girls." BA diss., University of Oxford, 2012.

Ghazi bin Muhammad, Prince. *The Sacred Origin of Sports and Culture.* Louisville KY: Fons Vitae, 1998.

Gill, N. S. "Chapters of 'Portrait of a Priestess: Women and Ritual in Ancient Greece.'" Online: http://ancienthistory.about.com/od/greeksociety/tp/Priestess.htm.

Gill, Robin. *The "Empty Church" Revisited.* Aldershot: Ashgate, 2003.

Gloucester Cathedral. "The Gloucester Golfer." Online: http://www.gloucestercathedral.org.uk/index.php?page=the-gloucester-golfer.

Goldblatt, David. *The Ball is Round: A Global History of Football.* London: Viking, 2006.

Golden, Mark. *Sport and Society in Ancient Greece.* Cambridge: Cambridge University Press, 1998.

Gorn, Elliot J., and Warren Goldstein. *A Brief History of American Sports.* Urbana, IL: University of Illinois, 2004.

Green, Michael. *The Art of Coarse Sport.* London: Arrow, 1970.

Griffin, David Ray. *God, Power, and Evil: A Process Theodicy.* Philadelphia: Westminster, 1976.

The Guardian. "Luis Suárez Banned for Eight Matches for Racial Abuse of Patrice Evra." December 20, 2011. Online: http://www.guardian.co.uk/football/2011/dec/20/luis-suarez-patrice-evra-racism.

Guardini, Romano. *The Spirit of the Liturgy.* Translated by Ada Lane. London: Sheed & Ward, 1935. Online: http://fdlc.org/Liturgy_Resources/Guardini/Chapter5.htm.

Gurney, Dorothy Frances. "God's Garden." In *God's Garden and Other Verses,* 9. London: Burns, Oates & Washbourne, 1934.

Guttman, Allen. *A Whole New Ball Game: An Interpretation of American Sports.* Chapel Hill: University of North Carolina Press, 1988.

———. *From Ritual to Record: The Nature of Modern Sports.* 2nd ed. New York: Columbia University Press, 2004.

———. *Sports Spectators.* New York: Columbia University Press, 1986.

Haase, J. E., T. Britt, D. D. Coward, N. K. Leidy, and P. E. Penn. "Simultaneous Concept Analysis of Spiritual Perspective, Hope, Acceptance and Self-Transcendence." *Journal of Nursing Scholarship,* 24 (1992), 141–47.

Hackney and Leyton Football League. Online: http://www.hackneyandleytonfootball league.co.uk/#/the-league/4523387331.

Hadaway, C. Kirk, and Penny Long Marler. "Did You Really Go to Church This Week? Behind the Poll Data." *The Christian Century* 115/15 (May 6, 1998) 472–75.

Hadaway, C. Kirk, Penny Long Marler, and Mark Chaves. "What the Polls Don't Show: A Closer Look at U.S. Church Attendance." *American Sociological Review* 58/6 (December 1993) 741–52.

Hamilton, Malcolm. *The Sociology of Religion.* 2nd ed. London: Routledge, 1995.

Hamilton, Mark. "An Augustinian Critique of our Relationship to Sport." In *Theology, Ethics and Transcendence in Sports,* edited by Jim Parry et al., 25–34.

———. "Sport as Spectacle and the Perversion of Play." In *The Image of God in the Human Body: Essays on Christianity and Sports,* edited by Donald Deardorff II and John White, 173–93. Lewiston NY: Edward Mellen, 2008.

Hamilton, Tyler, and Daniel Coyle. *The Secret Race: Inside the Hidden World of the Tour de France: Doping, Cover-ups, and Winning at All Costs.* London: Bantam, 2012.

Hancock's Half Hour. Episode: "Sunday Afternoon at Home." BBC. First broadcast in April 1958.

Hansard. Sunday Sports Bill. House of Commons Debate. February 17, 1989, *vol. 147 cc619-56. Online:* http://hansard.millbanksystems.com/commons/1989/feb/17/sunday-sports-bill#S6CV0147P0_19890217_HOC_104.

———. Sunday Sports Bill. *House of Lords Debate. November 5, 1987, vol. 489 cc1132-73.* Online: http://hansard.millbanksystems.com/lords/1987/nov/05/sunday-sports-bill-hl#S5LV0489P0_19871105_HOL_161.

Harris, H. A. *Sport in Greece and Rome.* London: Thames & Hudson, 1972.

Harrison, Victoria S. *Religion and Modern Thought.* London: SCM, 2007.

Hasler, Peter. "Public Interest in Sport is on the Decline." Ipsos MORI. Online at http://www.ipsos-mori.com/researchpublications/researcharchive/929/Public-Interest-In-Sport-Is-On-The-Decline.aspx.

Hays, Richard B. *First Corinthians.* Louisville: John Knox, 1997.

Hayward, Ben. "Vilanova Illness Rocks Barcelona and Puts Soccer and Rivalry in Perspective." *Goal.* Online: http://www.goal.com/en-us/news/88/spain/2012/12/19/3614223/vilanova-illness-rocks-barcelona-and-puts-soccer-and-rivalry.

Heathcott, Brent L. "Jesus is the Quarterback on the Gridiron of Life." *Catholic Review,* Archdiocese of Baltimore. Online: http://catholicreview.org/blogs/musings-of-a-deacon-father/2012/09/18/jesus-is-the-quarterback-on-the-gridiron-of-life.

Henderson, Suzanne Watts. "Taking Liberties with the Text: The Colossians Household Code as Hermeneutical Paradigm." *Interpretation* 60 (2006), 420–432.

Herbert, George. *A Priest to the Temple, or, The Country Parson, His Character, and Rule of Holy Life.* London: T. Garthwait, 1652.

Hibbert, Christopher. *The English: A Social History, 1066–1945.* London: Guild Publishing, 1987.

Hick, John. *Evil and the God of Love*. London: Macmillan, 1966.

Higgs, Robert J. *God in the Stadium: Sports and Religion in America*. Lexington: University of Kentucky, 1995.

Higgs, Robert J., and Michael C. Braswell. *An Unholy Alliance: The Sacred and Modern Sports*. Macon, GA: Mercer University, 2004.

Hill, Christopher. *Society and Puritanism in Pre-Revolutionary England*. London: Secker & Warburg, 1964.

Hillsborough Independent Panel. "Disclosed Material and Report." Online: http://hillsborough.independent.gov.uk/.

Hoffman, Shirl James. *Good Game: Christianity and the Culture of Sports*. Waco: Baylor University Press, 2010.

Home Counties Premier League. http://www.hcpl.com/.

hooks, bell. *Outlaw Culture: Resisting Representations*. London: Routledge, 1994.

Hooper, Walter. *C. S. Lewis: Christian Reflections*. Glasgow: Fount, 1981.

Horne, John, Alan Tomlinson, and Gary Whannel. *Understanding Sport: An Introduction to the Sociological and Cultural Analysis of Sport*. London: E. & F. N. Spon, 1999.

Houlihan, Barrie. *Sport and Society: A Student Introduction*. London: Sage, 2001.

Hughes, Thomas. *The Manliness of Christ*. Cambridge, MA: Riverside, 1880.

———. *Tom Brown at Oxford*. Macmillan: London, 1861.

———. *Tom Brown's Schooldays*. Macmillan: Cambridge, 1857.

Huizinga, Johan. *Homo Ludens: A Study of the Play Element in Culture*. Boston, MA: Beacon, 1955.

Humphrey, Lawrence. *The Nobles or of Nobilitye*. London: Thomas Marsh, 1563.

Ignatius, *Epistle to the Romans*. Online: http://www.earlychristianwritings.com/text/ignatius-romans-lightfoot.html.

Ingham, Alan G., and John W. Loy. *Sport in Social Development: Traditions, Transitions and Transformations*. Champaign IL: Human Kinetics, 1993.

International Olympic Committee (IOC). "Ancient Olympic Games." Online: http://www.olympic.org/ancient-olympic-games.

———. "Commission for Culture and Olympic Education." Online: http://www.olympic.org/culture-and-olympic-education-commission.

———. "Factsheet: Women in the Olympic Movement—Update March 2013." Online: http://www.olympic.org/Documents/Reference_documents_Factsheets/Women_in_Olympic_Movement.pdf.

———. "Olympic Charter: as from 9 September 2013." Online: http://www.olympic.org/Documents/olympic_charter_en.pdf.

Irenaeus, *Against Heresies*. Online: http://www.newadvent.org/fathers/0103.htm.

It's a Knockout. Online: http://www.its-a-knockout.tv/.

Jack, Ian. "So Much in Glasgow has Changed, but Violence against Women Persists." *The Guardian*, Saturday, March 17, 2011. Online: http://www.guardian.co.uk/commentisfree/2011/mar/12/celtic-rangers-glasgow-domestic-violence.

Jacob, Jon. "First University Boat Race Radio Commentary Anniversary." Online: http://www.bbc.co.uk/blogs/aboutthebbc/posts/first-university-boat-race-rad.

James I. *The Kings Majesties Declaration to His Subjects Concerning Lawfull Sports to be Used*. London: Bonham Norton, 1618.

James, C. L. R. *Beyond a Boundary*. London: Serpent's Tail, 1994 (first published 1963).

James, David. "Glazers Brothers' Latest Move Angers Manchester United Fans further with New York Stock Exchange Plans." *Anchor Fan*. Online: http://www.anchorfan.

com/image/big-controversy-over-the-glazers-manchester-united-new-york-stock-exchange-plans-58356.html.

James, William. *The Varieties of Religious Experience: A Study in Human Nature*. The Gifford Lectures 1901–2. London: Longmans, Green & Co., 1929.

Jenkins, David. "The Liberation of 'God.'" An extended introduction to *Theology and Joy* by Jürgen Moltmann, 1–25. Translated by Reinhard Ulrich. London: SCM, 1973.

Johnson, Luke Timothy. *The First and Second Letters to Timothy*. New York: Doubleday, 2001.

————. *The Writings of the New Testament: An Interpretation*. 3rd ed. London: SCM, 2010.

Johnston, Robert K. *The Christian at Play*. Grand Rapids, MI: Eerdmans, 1983.

Kaufman, Jason, and Orlando Patterson. "Cross-National Cultural Diffusion: The Global Spread of Cricket." *American Sociological Review* 70 (February 2005) 82–100.

Kay, Tess. "Daughters of Islam: Family Influences on Muslim Young Women's Participation in Sport." *International Review for the Sociology of Sport* 41/3 (2006) 357–73.

———— "Developing Through Sport: Evidencing Sport Impacts on Young People." *Sport in Society* 12/9 (2009) 1177–91.

———— "Sport and Gender." In *Sport and Society: A Student Introduction*, edited by Barrie Houlihan, 89–104. London: Sage, 2001.

Kay, Tess, and Stephen Bradbury. "Youth Sport Volunteering: Developing Social Capital?" *Sport, Education and Society* 14/1 (2009) 121–40.

Keble, John. "There is a Book, Who Runs May Read." In *The Sacred Poets of the Nineteenth Century*, edited by Alfred H. Miles. London: Routledge, 1907.

Keener, Craig. *Paul, Women and Wives: Marriage and Women's Ministry in the Letters of Paul*. Peabody, MA: Hendrickson, 1992.

Kick London. Online: http://www.yfc.co.uk/local-centres/london/kick-london/.

Kipling, Rudyard. "If." In *The Oxford Book of Children's Verse*, edited by Iona Opie and Peter Opie, 324. Oxford: Oxford University Press, 1973.

Kirsch, George B. *The Creation of American Team Sports: Baseball and Cricket, 1838–72*. Urbana: University of Illinois Press, 1989.

Köhne, Eckart. "Bread and Circuses: The Politics of Entertainment." In *Gladiators and Caesars: The Power of Spectacle in Ancient Rome*, edited by Eckart Köhne and Cornelia Ewigleben, English version edited by Ralph Jackson, 8–30. London: British Museum Press, 2000.

Köhne, Eckart, and Cornelia Ewigleben. *Gladiators and Caesars: The Power of Spectacle in Ancient Rome*, English version edited by Ralph Jackson. London: British Museum Press, 2000.

Kruschwitz, Robert B. "Sports in the Christian Life." *Baylor Sports Study Guide* 5. Center for Christian Ethics, Baylor University, 2008. Online: http://www.baylor.edu/content/services/document.php/75240.pdf.

Küng, Hans. *Mozart: Traces of Transcendence*. Translated by John Bowden. London: SCM, 1992.

Kuper, Simon, and Stefan Szymanski. *Why England Lose: And Other Curious Football Phenomena Explained*. London: HarperSport, 2010.

Ladd, Tony, and James A. Mathisen. *Muscular Christianity: Evangelical Protestants and the Development of American Sport*. Grand Rapids, MI: Baker, 1999.

Lash, Nicholas. *Easter in Ordinary: Reflections on Human Experience and the Knowledge of God*. London: SCM, 1988.

Leeuw, Gerardus van der. *Sacred and Profane Beauty: The Holy in Art*. London: Weidenfeld & Nicolson 1963.

Leith, William. "The Best Bowler in the World. Probably." *The Times Magazine*, August 24, 2013, 22–27.

Lewis, C. S. "Christianity and Culture." In *C. S. Lewis: Christian Reflections*, edited by Walter Hooper, 27–55. Glasgow: Fount, 1981.

———. *The Last Battle*. Hardmondsworth: Puffin, 1964.

———. *Mere Christianity*. London: Fontana, 1955.

Littlejohn, Richard. "Three Lions? More Like the Cowardly Lion from the Wizard of Oz." *Daily Mail*, June 29, 2010. Online: http://www.dailymail.co.uk/debate/article-1290137/WORLD-CUP-2010-Three-Lions-More-like-cowardly-lion-Wizard-Oz.html#ixzz2fARdjGoo.

Little League. "I Won't Cheat." Online: http://www.littleleague.org/learn/programs/iwontcheat.htm.

London 24. "Hodgson Puts English Football 'Crisis' in Perspective after Holocaust Museum Visit." Online: http://www.london24.com/sport/hodgson_puts_english_football_crisis_in_perspective_after_holocaust_museum_visit_1_2232611.

Longman III, Tremper. *Song of Songs*. The New International Commentary of the Old Testament. Grand Rapids, MI: Eerdmans, 2001.

Lowe, Sid. "Xenophobia—a Subject the Spanish Would Rather Avoid." *The Guardian*, February 10, 2009. Online: http://www.guardian.co.uk/football/2009/feb/10/spain-england-racism-friendly-sid-lowe.

Lupson, Peter. *Thank God for Football!* London: SPCK, 2006.

Luther, Martin. *Commentary on the Epistle to the Galatians* (1535). Translated by Theodore Graebner. Grand Rapids, MI: Zondervan, 1949. Online: http://www.iclnet.org/pub/resources/text/wittenberg/luther/gal/web/gal-inx.html#cts.

Lynch, Gordon. *Understanding Theology and Popular Culture*. Oxford: Blackwell, 2005.

Macquarrie, John. *In Search of Deity*. The Gifford Lectures 1983–4. London: SCM, 1984.

———. *In Search of Humanity*. London: SCM, 1982.

———. *Principles of Christian Theology*. 2nd ed. New York: Scribner, 1977.

———. *Twentieth-Century Religious Thought: The Frontiers of Philosophy and Theology, 1900–1970*. 2nd edition. London: SCM, 1971.

———. *Two Worlds are Ours: An Introduction to Christian Mysticism*. Minneapolis, MN: Fortress, 2005.

Maguire, Jennifer Smith. "Body Lessons: Fitness Publishing and the Cultural Production of the Fitness Consumer." *International Review for the Sociology of Sport* 37/3–4 (December 2002) 449–64.

Majendie, Matt. "Drug Cheats are Pushing the Boundaries in Athletics." *The Independent*, May 5, 2013. Online: http://www.independent.co.uk/sport/general/athletics/drug-cheats-are-pushing-the-boundaries-in-athletics-8604176.html.

Mandell, Richard D. *Sport: A Cultural History*. New York: Columbia University Press, 1984.

Mann, Horace. *Religious Worship in England and Wales: Abridged from the Official Report of the Census of Great Britain, 1851, addressed to George Graham Esq., Registrar-General.* London: Routledge, 1854.

Maraniss, David. *When Pride Still Mattered: A Life of Vince Lombardi.* New York: Simon & Schuster, 1999.

Marcel, Gabriel. *The Mystery of Being. Volume I: Reflection and Mystery.* The Gifford Lectures 1949–50. Chicago: Gateway, 1960.

Markovits, Andrei S., and Steven L. Hellerman. *Offside: Soccer and American Exceptionalism.* Princeton: Princeton University Press, 2001.

Maslow, Abraham. "A Theory of Human Motivation." *Psychological Review.* 50 (1943) 370–96.

———. *The Farther Reaches of Human Nature.* New York: Penguin, 1976.

McDougall, Joy Ann. "Sin—No More. A Feminist Revisioning of a Christian Theology of Sin." *Anglican Theological Review* 88/2 (Spring 2006) 215–35.

McRobbie, Angela. *Postmodernism and Popular Culture.* London: Routledge, 1994.

Measuring Worth. Online at http://www.measuringworth.com/index.html.

Mendelsohn, Ezra, ed. *Jews and the Sporting Life.* Studies in Contemporary Jewry, Volume XXIII. New York: OUP, 2008.

Mendelson, Michael. "Saint Augustine." In *The Stanford Encyclopedia of Philosophy* (Winter 2012 edition), edited by Edward N. Zalta. Online: http://plato.stanford.edu/archives/win2012/entries/augustine/.

Mews, Stuart. "Puritanicalism, Sport, and Race: A Symbolic Crusade of 1911." In *Popular Belief and Practice, Studies in Church History 8,* edited by G. J. Cuming and Derek Baker, 303–31. Cambridge: Cambridge University Press, 1972.

Midgley, Neil. "BBC TV Executives View Religion as a Rather Tiresome Obligation." *Daily Telegraph,* May 25, 2010. Online: http://www.telegraph.co.uk/news/7764467/BBC-TV-executives-view-religion-as-a-rather-tiresome-obligation.html.

Miller, Vincent J. *Consuming Religion: Christian Faith and Practice in a Consumer Culture.* London: Continuum, 2004.

Miller, Mary, and Karl Taube. *The Gods and Symbols of Ancient Mexico and the Maya: An Illustrated Dictionary of Mesoamerican Religion.* London: Thames & Hudson, 1993.

Mirror. "An Absolute Triumph." July 28, 2012. Online: http://www.mirror.co.uk/news/uk-news/london-2012-olympic-games-opening-1179820.

Mirror Football, "The Wit and Wisdom of Bill Shankly." Online: http://www.mirrorfootball.co.uk/opinion/blogs/mirror-football-blog/Liverpool-legend-Bill-Shankly-Football-more-important-than-life-and-death-plus-his-other-great-quotes-article570339.html.

Moltmann, Jürgen. *The Coming of God: Christian Eschatology.* Translated by Margaret Kohl. London: SCM, 1996.

———. *The Crucified God.* Translated by R. A. Wilson and John Bowden. London: SCM, 1974.

———. *God in Creation: An Ecological Doctrine of Creation.* The Gifford Lectures 1984–5. Translated by Margaret Kohl. London: SCM, 1985.

———. *Theology and Joy.* Translated by Reinhard Ulrich. London: SCM, 1973.

———. *Theology of Hope: On the Ground and Implications of a Christian Eschatology.* Translated by James W. Leitch from the 5th German edition, 1965. London: SCM, 1967.

Moneyball. Directed by Bennett Miller. Columbia Pictures, 2011.

Mort, Frank. "The Politics of Consumption." In *New Times: The Changing Face of Politics in the 1990s*, edited by S. Hall and M. Jacques, 160–73. London: Lawrence & Wishart, 1989.

Mosey, Roger. "MOTD Viewing Figures Up." BBC, posted May 13, 2008. Online: http://www.bbc.co.uk/blogs/sporteditors/2008/05/so_its_been_a_great.html.

Mulcaster, Richard. *Positions Concerning the Training Up of Children*. Toronto: University of Toronto Press, 1994.

Murphy, Michael, and Rhea A. White. *In the Zone: Transcendent Experience in Sports*. Revised ed. New York: Penguin, 1995.

Murphy-O'Connor, Jerome. *St Paul's Corinth: Texts and Archaeology*. 3rd ed. Collegeville, MN: Liturgical, 2002.

Newbolt, Henry. "Vitaï Lampada." In *Selected Poems of Henry Newbolt*, 87. London: Thomas Nelson, 1940.

Newton, John. "How Sweet the Name of Jesus Sounds." In *Olney Hymns: In Three Parts*, edited by John Newton and William Cowper, 73. London: Thomas Nelson, 1855.

New York Times. "Adidas Bets on Beijing Olympics." January 13, 2006. Online: http://www.nytimes.com/2006/01/30/business/worldbusiness/30iht-adidas.html.

New Zealand Herald. "Women Suffer Rugby Backlash." Online: http://www.nzherald.co.nz/nz/news/article.cfm?c_id=1&objectid=10468736.

NHS. "Benefits of Exercise." Online: http://www.nhs.uk/Livewell/fitness/Pages/whybeactive.aspx.

Niebuhr, Reinhold. *The Nature and Destiny of Man. Vol 1*. New York: Scribners, 1941.

Novak, Michael. *The Joy of Sports*. Revised ed. Lanham, MD: Madison, 1994.

Novatian, *The Trinity, The Spectacle, Jewish Foods, In Praise of Purity, Letters*. Translated by Russell J. DeSimone, OSA. Washington DC: Catholic University of America, 1974.

Office for National Statistics. "Religion 2001 Census." Online: http://data.gov.uk/dataset/religion_2001_census.

———. "Religion in England and Wales 2011." Online at http://www.ons.gov.uk/ons/rel/census/2011-census/key-statistics-for-local-authorities-in-england-and-wales/rpt-religion.html.

———. *Social Trends 39*. London: Palgrave Macmillan, 2009.

———. *Sport and Leisure: Results from the Sport and Leisure Module of the 2002 General Household Survey*. London: HMSO, 2004.

Opie, Iona, and Peter Opie. *The Oxford Book of Children's Verse*. Oxford: Oxford University Press, 1973.

Overman, Steven J. *The Influence of the Protestant Ethic on Sport and Recreation*. Ashgate: Aldershot, 1997.

Oxfordshire County Council. "About Oxfordshire." Online: http://www.oxfordshire.gov.uk/cms/public-site/about-oxfordshire.

Oxfordshire Cricket Association. Online: http://www.oxfordshirecricketassociation.org.uk/clubs/clubs.asp.

Oxfordshire Cricket Board. Online: http://www.oxoncb.com/members/Clubs.

Pannenberg, Wolfhart. *Systematic Theology, Volume II*. Translated by Geoffrey W. Bromiley. Edinburgh: T. & T. Clark, 1994.

Parry, Jim. "The *religio athletae*, Olympism and Peace." In *Sport and Spirituality: An Introduction*, edited by Jim Parry et al., 201–14. New York: Routledge, 2011.

Parry, Jim, Mark Nesti, and Nick Watson, eds. *Theology, Ethics and Transcendence in Sports*. New York: Routledge, 2011.

Parry, Jim, Simon Robinson, Nick J. Watson, and Mark Nesti, eds. *Sport and Spirituality: An Introduction*. New York: Routledge, 2007.

Peacock, Mabel. "The Hood-Game at Haxey, Lincolnshire." *Folk-Lore: A Quarterly Review of Myth, Tradition, Institution and Custom*. 7/4 (December 1896) 330–50.

Peacocke, A. R. *Creation and the World of Science*. The Bampton Lectures 1978. Oxford: Clarendon, 1979.

Pearson, Terry P. "The Composition and Development of Phillip Stubbes's 'Anatomie of Abuses.'" *Modern Language Review* 56/3 (July 1961) 321–32.

Percival, Jenny. "Minister Orders Water Companies to Review Huge 'Rainwater Tax' Bills." *The Guardian*, February 11, 2009. Online: http://www.guardian.co.uk/politics/2009/feb/11/water-bills-rainwater-tax.

Percy, Martyn. *Engaging with Contemporary Culture*. Aldershot: Ashgate, 2005.

Pfitzner, Victor. *Paul and the Agon Motif: Traditional Athletic Imagery in the Pauline Literature*. Leiden: Brill, 1967.

Philip, Robert. "Busst Counts His Blessings and Looks Ahead." *Daily Telegraph*, January 19, 2005. Online: http://www.telegraph.co.uk/sport/2353993/Busst-counts-his-blessings-and-looks-ahead.html.

Polley, Martin. *Moving the Goalposts: A History of Sport and Society since 1945*. London: Routledge, 1998.

Postman, Neil. *Amusing Ourselves to Death: Public Discourse in the Age of Show Business*. London: Methuen, 1987.

Price, Joseph L. "An American Apotheosis: Sport as Popular Religion." In *From Season to Season: Sports as American Religion*, 215–32. Macon, GA: Mercer, 2001.

———. "The Final Four as Final Judgment." In *From Season to Season: Sports as American Religion*, 171–81. Macon, GA: Mercer, 2001.

Price, Nelson. "Jesus the Competitor." *The Christian Athlete*, February 1976.

Putney, Clifford. *Muscular Christianity: Manhood and Sports in Protestant America, 1880–1920*. Cambridge, MA: Harvard University Press, 2001.

Rahner, Hugo. *Man at Play, or Did You Ever Practice Eutrapelia?* London: Burns & Oates, 1965.

Rahner, Karl. *Foundations of Christian Faith*. New York: Crossroad, 2010.

———. *The Practice of Faith*. London: SCM, 1985.

———. *Theological Investigations*, vol. I. London: Darton, Longman & Todd, 1961.

Rees, Timothy. "God is Love: Let Heaven Adore Him." In *Sermons and Hymns by Timothy Rees*, 110. London: Mowbray, 1946.

Reuters. "London 2012 Opening Ceremony Draws 900 Million Viewers." Online: http://uk.reuters.com/article/2012/08/07/uk-oly-ratings-day-idUKBRE8760V820120807.

Richards, Huw. *A Game for Hooligans: The History of Rugby Union*. Edinburgh: Mainstream, 2006.

Richey, Russell E., and Donald G. Jones, eds. *American Civil Religion*. New York: Harper & Row, 1975.

Rippon, Anton. *Gas Masks for Goal Posts: Football in Britain During the Second World War*. Stroud: Sutton, 2007.

Robert Dover's Cotswold Olimpicks. "About the Games." Online: http://www.olimpickgames.co.uk/contentok.php?id=853

Robinson, Leigh. "The Business of Sport." In *Sport and Society: A Student Introduction*, edited by Barrie Houlihan, 165–83. London: Sage, 2001.

Robinson, Simon. "The Spiritual Journey." In *Sport and Spirituality: An Introduction*, edited by Jim Parry et al., 38–58. New York: Routledge, 2007.

Rojas, John-Paul Ford. "BBC Hails 'Stunning' Viewing Figures As 17.1 Million Watch Mo Farah Clinch Olympic 10,000m Gold." *Daily Telegraph*, August 5, 2012. Online: http://www.telegraph.co.uk/sport/olympics/news/9453409/BBC-hails-stunning-viewing-figures-as-17.1-million-watch-Mo-Farah-clinch-Olympic-10000m-gold.html.

Saadi, Sommer. "World Cup TV: Many Viewers, No Profits." *Bloomberg Businessweek*. Online: http://www.businessweek.com/technology/content/jul2010/tc20100714_994644.htm.

Santayana, George. *Reason in Religion: III, The Life of Reason*. New York: Dover, 1982.

Santo, Charles A., and Gerard C. S. Mildner. "Political Economy and the Olympic Games." *HumanKinetics.com*. Online: http://www.humankinetics.com/excerpts/excerpts/political-economy-and-the-olympic-games.

Sartre, Jean Paul. *Being and Nothingness: An Essay on Phenomenological Ontology*. Translated by Hazel E. Barnes. London: Routledge, 2005.

Saturday Review of Politics, Literature, Science and Art. Anonymous review of *Two Years Ago*, by Charles Kingsley. February 21, 1857, 176–77.

Sax, William S. *The Gods at Play: Lila in South Asia*. New York: Oxford University Press, 1995.

Sayre, Joe. "He Flies on One Wing." *Sports Illustrated*, December 26, 1955.

Schele, Linda, and Mary Ellen Miller. *The Blood of Kings: Dynasty and Ritual in Maya Art*. London: Sotheby's, 1986.

Scottish Government. "Scotland's People Annual Report: Results from 2011 Scottish Household Survey." Online: http://www.scotland.gov.uk/Publications/2012/08/5277/13.

Seymour, Harold. *Baseball: The People's Game*. New York: Oxford University Press, 1990.

Sharp, James. *The Bewitching of Anne Gunter: A Horrible and True Story of Football, Witchcraft, Murder, and the King of England*. London: Profile, 2000.

Sing, Susan Saint. "The Energy of Play." In *Theology, Ethics and Transcendence in Sports*, edited by Jim Parry et al., 201–10. New York: Routledge, 2011.

The Skateboard Bible. Nashville, TN: Thomas Nelson, 2012.

SIRC, "Football Violence in Europe: A Report to the Amsterdam Group." Social Issues Research Centre, 1996. Online: http://www.sirc.org/publik/football_violence.pdf.

Sky News HD. "Players and Fans Pray for Bolton's Muamba." Online: http://news.sky.com/story/3985/players-and-fans-pray-for-boltons-muamba.

Smart, Ninian. *The Religious Experience*. 5th ed. Upper Saddle River, NJ: Prentice-Hall, 1996.

———. *The World's Religions*. 2nd ed. Cambridge: Cambridge University Press, 1998.

Smit, Barbara. *Pitch Invasion: Adidas, Puma, and the Making of Modern Sport*. London: Allen Lane, 2006.

Smith, Adam. "The Goal Rush." *Time*, May 7, 2007.

South Jasper Place Minor Baseball Association. "Fair Play Codes." Online: http://sjpbaseball.ca/page.php?page_id=13578.

Spalding, Albert G. *America's National Game: Historic Facts Concerning the Beginning, Evolution, Development and Popularity of Base Ball, with Personal Reminiscences of Its Vicissitudes, Its Victories and Its Votaries*. New York: American Sports Publishing Company, 1911.

The Sports Bible. Nashville, TN: Broadman & Holman, 2012.

Sports Business News. "The 2008 Beijing Summer Olympics—Credit Deserved—NBC's Amazing Olympics." Online: http://sportsbiznews.blogspot.com/2008/08/2008-beijing-summer-olympics-credit.html.

Sports Good News Bible. New York: American Bible Society, 2012.

Stark, Rodney, and Laurence R. Iannaccone. "A Supply-Side Reinterpretation of the 'Secularization' of Europe." *Journal for the Scientific Study of Religion* 33/3 (September 1994) 230–52.

Stead, David. "Sport and the Media." In *Sport and Society: A Student Introduction*, edited by Barrie Houlihan, 184–200. London: Sage, 2001.

Steenberg, M. C. *Irenaeus on Creation: The Cosmic Christ and the Saga of Redemption*. Leiden: Brill, 2008.

Stelling, Jeff. "Jeff Stelling's Stats." *Sky Sports Magazine*, June/July 2011, 12.

St Pancras Amateur Boxing Club. Online: http://stpancrasabc.webs.com/.

Strutt, Joseph. *The Sports and Pastimes of the People of England*. London: J. White, 1801.

Stubbes, Phillip. *The Anatomie of Abuses*. Facsimile of the Bodleian Library manuscript. No page numbers. Amsterdam: Da Capo Press, 1972.

Suits, Bernard. *The Grasshopper: Games, Life and Utopia*. Revised ed. Peterborough, ON: Broad View, 2005.

Sumney, Jerry L. *Colossians: A Commentary*. Louisville, KY: Westminster John Knox, 2008.

Szymanski, Stefan, and Andrew Zimbalist. *National Pastime: How Americans Play Baseball and the Rest of the World Plays Soccer*. Washington: Brookings, 2006.

Tertullian. *On Spectacles*. Online at http://www.earlychristianwritings.com/text/tertullian03.html.

Theophilus of Antioch, *To Autolycus*. Online: http://www.earlychristianwritings.com/theophilus.html.

Tillich, Paul. *The Boundaries of Our Being. A Collection of His Sermons with His Autobiographical Sketch*. London: Collins Fontana, 1973.

———. *Systematic Theology*. Vols I, II and III combined. Welwyn: Nisbet, 1968.

———. *Theology of Culture*. Oxford University Press: London, 1975.

Tocqueville, Alexis de. *Democracy in America, Volume 2*. Cambridge: Sever & Francis, 1862.

Total Football, "Trevor Francis Puts Football in Perspective again." Online: http://www.totalfootballmag.com/other-news/other-football-news/trevor-francis-puts-football-in-perspective-again/.

Twitchell, James B. *Lead Us into Temptation: The Triumph of American Materialism*. New York: Columbia University Press, 1999.

UCLA Magazine. "Rah-rah Boo-hiss." Summer 2004. Online: http://magazine.ucla.edu/year2004/summer04_09_03.html.

Upal, Sunni. "West Ham Tie up Three-Year Sponsorship Deal with Alpari FX." *Daily Mail*, February 5, 2013. Online: http://www.dailymail.co.uk/sport/football/article-2273984/West-Ham-confirm-year-sponsorship-deal-Alpari.html.

Veblen, Thorsten. *The Theory of the Leisure Class: An Economic Study of Institutions.* London: Macmillan, 1912.

Vinton, Nathaniel. "Floyd Landis, Jonathan Vaughters, Travis Tygart and Lance Armstrong Whistleblowers Host Yale Panel on Fight to Expose Cycling's Doping Culture." *New York Daily News,* February 28, 2013. Online: http://www.nydailynews.com/sports/i-team/armstrong-whistleblowers-recall-anti-doping-crusade-article-1.1276605#ixzz2ZKqvDbez.

Waltke, Bruce K. *The Book of Proverbs. Chapters 1–15.* The New International Commentary on the Old Testament. Grand Rapids, MI: Eerdmans, 2004.

Wann, Daniel L., Merrill J. Melnick, Gordon W. Russell, and Dale G. Pease. *Sports Fans: The Psychology and Social Impact of Spectators.* New York: Routledge, 2001.

Ward, Pete. "Colonising the Adult Church: Our Part in the Spread of Consumerism and Commercialisation." *Youth Specialities.Com.* Online: http://www.youthspecialties.com/articles/colonising-the-adult-church-our-part-in-the-spread-of-consumerism-and-comme/.

Warner, Gary. *Competition.* Elgin, IL: David C. Cook, 1979.

Watson, Nick J. "Nature and Transcendence: The Mystical and Sublime in Extreme Sports." In *Sport and Spirituality: An Introduction,* edited by Jim Parry et al., 95–115. New York: Routledge, 2007.

Watson, Nick J., and John White. " 'Winning at All Costs' in Modern Sport: Reflections on Pride and Humility in the Writings of C. S. Lewis." In *Sport and Spirituality: An Introduction,* edited by Jim Parry et al., 61–79. New York: Routledge, 2007.

Weir, Stuart J. "Competition as Relationship: Sport as Mutual Quest towards Excellence." In *The Image of God in the Human Body: Essays on Christianity and Sports,* edited by Donald Deardorff II and John White, 101–21. Lewiston NY: Edward Mellen, 2008.

———. *What the Book Says about Sport.* Oxford: Bible Reading Fellowship, 2000.

Westermann, Claus. *Genesis 1–11.* Translated by John J. Scullion SJ. London: SPCK, 1984.

Whitehead, Alfred North. *Religion in the Making.* New York: Meridian, 1960. (First published 1926).

The White House. "Introduction to Outer Space: An Explanatory Statement Prepared by the President's Science Advisory Committee." Federation of American Scientists. Online: http://www.fas.org/spp/guide/usa/intro1958.html.

Williams, David J. *Paul's Metaphors: Their Context and Character.* Peabody, MA: Hendrickson, 1999.

Williams, Rowan. "Keeping Time." In *Open to Judgement: Sermons and Addresses.* London: Darton, Longman & Todd, 1994, 247–50.

Willimon, Willam H. *Acts.* Louisville: John Knox, 1998.

Witherington III, Ben. *The Letters to Philemon, the Colossians, and the Ephesians: A Socio-Rhetorical Commentary on the Captivity Epistles.* Grand Rapids, MI: Eerdmans, 2007.

Wordsworth, William. "Lines Composed a Few Miles above Tintern Abbey." In *Lyrical Ballads, with a Few Other Poems,* edited by William Wordsworth and Samuel Taylor Coleridge, 201–10. London: Noel Douglas, 1926 (replica of the 1798 edition).

————. "Ode. Intimations of Immortality from Recollections of Early Childhood." In *Poems in Two Volumes, 1807,* edited by Helen Darbishire, 2nd edition, 321–32. Oxford: Clarendon, 1952

Wu, Xifeng, et al. "Minimum Amount of Physical Activity for Reduced Mortality and Extended Life Expectancy: A Prospective Cohort Study." *Lancet* 378 / 9798 (October 2011) 1244–53.

Young, Iris Marion. "Throwing like a Girl: A Phenomenology of Feminine Body Comportment, Motility, and Spatiality." In *On Female Body Experience: Throwing Like a Girl and Other Essays.* 27–45. Oxford: Oxford University Press, 2005.

YouTube. "Calcio Storico Fiorentino." Online: http://www.youtube.com/watch?v=WsRqSNSjy3E and http://www.youtube.com/watch?v=vivRVyg_cks&mode=related&search=.

————. "David Busst Horrific Injury." Online: http://www.youtube.com/watch?v=byOKCMQpxKo.

————. "Haxey Hood 2012." Online: http://www.youtube.com/watch?v=7Su4XASv-Bo.

Name and Subject Index

Scripture Index

∼

NEW TESTAMENT

Lightning Source UK Ltd.
Milton Keynes UK
UKOW04f1444071014

239740UK00003B/9/P